A HISTORY OF THE COUNCILS OF THE CHURCH: VOLUME 1

A HISTORY OF THE CHRISTIAN COUNCILS, FROM THE ORIGINAL DOCUMENTS.

BY
CHARLES JOSEPH HEFELE
BISHOP OF ROTTENBURG,
FORMERLY PROFESSOR OF THEOLOGY IN
THE UNIVERSITY OF TÜBINGEN

A HISTORY OF THE COUNCILS OF THE CHURCH: VOLUME 1

A HISTORY OF THE CHRISTIAN COUNCILS, FROM THE ORIGINAL DOCUMENTS.

BY
CHARLES JOSEPH HEFELE
BISHOP OF ROTTENBURG,
FORMERLY PROFESSOR OF THEOLOGY IN
THE UNIVERSITY OF TÜBINGEN

TRANSLATED FROM THE GERMAN,
AND EDITED BY
WILLIAM R. CLARK, M.A., OXON.
PREBENDARY OF WELLS AND VICAR OF
TAUNTON.

Edited and Re-typeset by Paul A. Böer, Sr.

VERITATIS SPLENDOR PUBLICATIONS

et cognoscetis veritatem et veritas liberabit vos (Jn 8:32)

MMXIV

AD MAJOREM DEI GLORIAM

CONTENTS

A HISTORY OF THE
COUNCILS OF THE CHURCH:
VOLUMES 1 TO 5

CHARLES JOSEPH HEFELE D. D.

A HISTORY OF THE CHRISTIAN COUNCILS, FROM
THE ORIGINAL DOCUMENTS.

BY Charles Joseph Hefele, D. D., BISHOP OF
ROTTENBURG, FORMERLY PROFESSOR OF
THEOLOGY IN THE UNIVERSITY OF TÜBINGEN

Translated from the German, and Edited by WILLIAM R.
CLARK, M. A. OXON., PREBENDARY OF WELLS
AND VICAR OF TAUNTON.

EDINBURGH: T. & T. CLARK, 38, GEORGE STREET.
V1: MDCCCLXXI. V2: 1876. V3: 1883. V4: 1895. V5:
1896.

A HISTORY OF THE COUNCILS OF THE CHURCH: VOLUME 1 A. D. 325.

PREFACE

"NO portion of Church History has been so much neglected in recent times as the History of the Councils. With the exception of a few monographs on particular synods, nothing of importance has appeared on this subject in our days. It is high time that this state of things should be altered, and altered not by a mere adaptation of old materials, but by a treatment of the subject suited to the wants of the present day. This has become less difficult, inasmuch as new documents have been brought to light, and we live in an age when many errors have been abandoned, many prejudices have been put on one side, great progress has been made in critical studies, and a deeper insight into the development of the Christian Church has undoubtedly been gained.

"I have been employed for a good many years in the composition of a History of the Councils of the Church, which should be of a comprehensive character, and founded upon original documents. I may affirm that I have spared no pains to secure accuracy, and have done my best to consult all the literature which bears upon the subject."

The hopes which Dr. Hefele thus expressed in his preface to the first volume of his History have been abundantly fulfilled. He has not only supplied an acknowledged want in his own country in a manner which leaves little to desire, but he has brought within the reach of all German scholars an amount of information in connection with the ancient councils which is to be found only in part even in those large collections of Hardouin and Mansi, which are seldom to be met with in private libraries. It is to be hoped that the interest manifested in that portion of his work which is translated in this volume may induce the publishers to carry it forward at least to the close of the fourth Œcumenical Council.

The Translator was at first in doubt as to the best form in which to present this History to the English public,—whether in the form of a paraphrase, in which case it must have been almost an original work, or as a simple translation. Various considerations induced him to adopt the latter course. There was little difficulty in doing so, as Dr. Hefele's German style, unlike that of many of his Protestant fellow-countrymen, is generally lucid and intelligible. The Editor, when he first undertook the work of preparing the History for English readers, intended to add a number of notes from writers who regard the subject from a different point of view. This he afterwards found to be unnecessary, and the additional notes are accordingly very few. Dr. Hefele is so fair in the statement of facts, that every reader may very easily draw his conclusions for himself.

All possible care has been taken to make the references and quotations correct. It is almost certain, however, that slight mistakes may still be found in these pages; and the Editor will gratefully receive any corrections which may be forwarded to him, and make use of them should a second edition of the work be called for.

W. R. C.

Charles Joseph Hefele, D.D.

INTRODUCTION

SEC. 1. Origin and Authority of Councils

THE two synonymous expressions, concilium and σύνοδος, signify primarily any kind of assembly, even a secular one; but in the more restricted sense of a Church assembly, i.e. of a regularly convoked meeting of the rulers of the Church for the discussion and decision of ecclesiastical business, the word concilium is found for the first time in Tertullian, and σύνοδος in the Apostolical Canons; while the Apostolical Constitutions designate even the ordinary meetings of Christians for divine service by the name of σύνοδος.

That the origin of councils is derived from the Apostolic Synod held at Jerusalem about the year 52, is undoubted; but theologians are not agreed as to whether they were instituted by divine or by human authority. The true answer to this question is as follows: They are an apostolical institution; but the apostles, when they instituted them, acted under the commission which they received from Christ, otherwise they could not have published the decisions of their synod with the words, "It seemed good to the Holy Ghost and to us." They must have been convinced that the Lord of the Church had promised and had granted His Spirit to the assemblies of the Church.

Later synods have acted and spoken in the same conviction, that the Holy Ghost governed the assemblies of the Church; and Cyprian in his time wrote, in the name of the Council over which he presided, A.D. 252, to Pope Cornelius: "It seemed good to us, under the guidance of the Holy Spirit" (Placuit nobis, Sancto Spiritu suggerente). To the same effect the Synod of Arles, A.D. 314, expressed itself: "It seemed good, therefore, in the presence of the Holy Spirit and His angels" (Placuit ergo, præsente Spiritu Sancto et angelis ejus: Hardouin, Collect. Concil. t. i. p. 262). And it was this conviction, which was so universal, that led the Emperor Constantine the Great to call the decree of the Synod of Arles a heavenly judgment (cæleste judicium); and he added, that the judgment of the priests ought to be so received as though the Lord Himself sat and judged (sacerdotum judicium ita debet haberi, ac si ipse DOMINUS residens judicet). Twenty years later he again publicly expressed the same belief, at the close of the first œcumenical council at Nicæa, in these words: "What seemed good to the three hundred holy bishops (that is, the members of the Nicene Synod) is no otherwise to be thought of than as the judgment of the only Son of God" (Quod trecentis sanctis episcopis visum est, non est aliud putandum, quam solius Filii Dei sententia). In perfect agreement with this are the testimonies of all the ancient Fathers, Greek as well as Latin, of Athanasius as of Augustine and Gregory the Great, the latter of whom goes so far as to compare the authority of the first four general councils with the importance of the four holy Gospels.

The earliest synods known to us were held about the middle of the second Christian century in Asia Minor: they were occasioned by the rise of Montanism. It is, however, not improbable that such assemblies were held earlier in the Greek Church, perhaps on account of the Gnostics, inasmuch as the Greeks from the earliest times had more inclination, and also greater need, for synods, than those of the Western Church.

SEC. 2. Different kinds of Synods

It has been customary, in dealing with ecclesiastical statistics, to divide the councils into four classes; but they may be more accurately divided into eight, since there have actually been ecclesiastical assemblies of the kinds described under the following numbers,—two, five, seven, and eight. Foremost of all stand,—

1. The Universal or Œcumenical Councils, at which the bishops and other privileged persons from all the ecclesiastical provinces of the world are summoned to be present under the presidency of the Pope or his legates, and are bound to attend, unless in case of reasonable hindrance; and whose decisions are then received by the whole Church, and have the force of law for all the faithful. Hence it is clear that a council may possibly be intended to be œcumenical, and be summoned as such, and yet not receive the rank of an œcumenical synod,—as when its progress is stopped, or when it does not accomplish its object, or becomes divided, and the like; and for such reasons does not receive the approval of the whole Church, and particularly of the Pope. So it was with the so-called Latrocinium or Robber-Synod at Ephesus, A.D. 449. The bishops of all provinces were summoned, and the papal legates were present; but violence was used which prevented free discussion, so that error prevailed: and this Synod, instead of being recorded with honour, is marked with a brand on the page of history.

2. The second rank is given to General Councils or Synods of the Latin or Greek Church, at which were present the bishops and other privileged persons either of the whole

Latin or of the whole Greek Church, and thus only the representatives of one-half of the whole Church. Thus, in the first instance, the Synod held at Constantinople, A.D. 381, was only a Greek or Eastern general council, at which were present all the four Patriarchs of the East,—those of Constantinople, of Alexandria, of Antioch, and of Jerusalem, with many other metropolitans and bishops. As, however, this Synod was afterwards received by the West, it acquired the rank of an œcumenical council.

3. When the bishops of only one patriarchate or primacy (i.e. of a diocese, in the ancient sense of the word), or of only one kingdom or nation, assembled under the presidency of the patriarch, or primate, or first metropolitan, then we have respectively a national, or patriarchal, or primatial council, which frequently received the name of universal or plenary (universale or plenarium). The bishops of the Latin Church in Africa, for instance, metropolitans and suffragans, often assembled in synods of this kind under the Primate of Carthage; and in the same way the archbishops and bishops of all Spain under their primate, the Archbishop of Toledo. In still earlier times, the metropolitans and bishops of Syria assembled under the Archbishop of Antioch, their supreme metropolitan, afterwards called by the name of Patriarch.

4. A Provincial Synod is considerably smaller, and is formed by the metropolitan of an ecclesiastical province, with his suffragan bishops and other privileged persons.

5. Intermediate between the third and fourth classes are those synods, which are not uncommon in the history of the Church, in which the bishops of several contiguous

ecclesiastical provinces united for the discussion of subjects of common interest. They may be called the Councils of several United Provinces; and they rank lower than the national or primatial synod in this respect, that it is not the complete provinces of a nation or of a primacy which are represented in them.

6. By Diocesan Synods we understand those ecclesiastical assemblies which the bishop holds with his clergy, and over which he presides either personally or by his vicar-general.

7. Councils of a peculiar and even abnormal character, and known as σύνοδοι ἐνδημοῦσαι (Synods of Residents), were often held at Constantinople, when the Patriarch not unfrequently assembled around him bishops who happened to be staying (ἐνδημοῦντες) at Constantinople on private or other business, from provinces and patriarchates the most widely separated, for the discussion of important subjects, particularly for the decision of contests between the bishops themselves. We shall have occasion to adduce more on this subject when we come to discuss the ninth and twenty-eighth canons of Chalcedon.

8. Last of all, there appear in history not a few Mixed Councils (concilia mixta); assemblies in which the ecclesiastical and civil rulers of a kingdom meet together in order to take counsel on the affairs of Church and State. We come across them particularly in the beginning of the middle ages,—not unfrequently in France, in Germany, in England, in Spain, and in Italy. Of this character are the fourth to the seventh Synods of Toledo, many synods held under Pepin, under Charles the Great [Charlemagne] and his successors, among others the Synod of Mainz, A.D.

852, and that held in the year 876 in the Palatium apud Ticinum, at which the election of Charles the Fat was approved by the bishops and princes of Italy. We shall further on meet with several English mixed councils, at which even abbesses were present. All such assemblies were naturally summoned by the King, who presided and brought forward the points which had to be discussed. The discussion was either carried on in common, or the clergy and the nobility separated, and formed different chambers,—a chamber of nobles, and a chamber of bishops,—the latter discussing only ecclesiastical questions. The decisions were often promulgated in the form of royal decrees.

Six grounds for the convocation of great councils, particularly œcumenical councils, are generally enumerated:

1. When a dangerous heresy or schism has arisen.

2. When two Popes oppose each other, and it is doubtful which is the true one.

3. When the question is, whether to decide upon some great and universal undertaking against the enemies of the Christian name.

4. When the Pope is suspected of heresy or of other serious faults.

5. When the cardinals have been unable or unwilling to undertake the election of a Pope.

6. When it is a question of the reformation of the Church, in its head and members.

Besides these, there may be many other kinds of reasons
for the convocation of smaller synods; but all must have
reference to the one supreme aim of all councils—"the
promotion of the well-being of the Church through the
mutual consultation of its pastors." In the ancient Church
there were very many synods assembled, in order to resolve
the contests of the bishops with one another, and to
examine the charges brought against some of their number.

SEC. 3. By whom are Synods convoked?

If it is asked who convokes councils, there can be no
controversy with regard to the greatest number of the eight
kinds just specified. It is undoubted, that the ecclesiastical
head of the diocese, the bishop, has to summon the
diocesan synod; the ecclesiastical head of the province, the
metropolitan, the provincial synod; the ecclesiastical head
of a nation, a patriarchate, etc., the patriarch or primate,
either at his own instance or at the wish of another, as of
the sovereign, calls a national or primatial synod. It is
equally clear, that when several provinces meet in a
combined synod, the right of convocation belongs to the
most distinguished among the metropolitans who meet. At
the σύνοδος ἐνδημοῦσα, it was, of course, naturally
exercised by the Bishop of Constantinople. Consequently,
and from the very nature of the case, the summons to an
œcumenical council must go forth from the œcumenical
head of the Church, the Pope; except in the case, which is
hardly an exception, in which, instead of the Pope, the
temporal protector of the Church, the Emperor, with the
previous or subsequent approval and consent of the Pope,
summons a council of this kind. The case is similar with the
other synods, particularly national synods. In the case of

these, too, the temporal protector of the Church has
occasionally issued the summons instead of the
ecclesiastical ruler; and this not merely in ancient times in
the Græco-Roman Church, but also later in the German
and Roman States. Thus, e.g., Constantine the Great
convoked the Synod of Arles in 314, and Theodosius the
Great the Synod of Constantinople (already mentioned) in
381, in concert with the four Eastern patriarchs; Childebert,
king of the Franks, a national synod at Orleans in the year
549; and Charles the Great, in the year 794, the great Synod
of Frankfurt. Even the Arian sovereign, Theodoric the
Great, at the beginning of the sixth century, gave orders for
the discontinuance of several orthodox synods at Rome.
Further examples are noted by Hardouin.

Among those councils which were called by the emperors,
the latter undertook many kinds of expenses, particularly
the expense of travelling incurred by the numerous bishops,
for whom they ordered houses and carriages to be put at
their disposal at the public expense. This was done by
Constantine the Great at the calling of the Synods of Arles
and Nicæa. They also provided for the entertainment of the
bishops during the sitting of those assemblies. At the later
councils—those of Florence and Trent, for example—
many of the expenses were borne by the Popes, the
Christian princes, and the cities in which the synods were
held.

Bellarmin endeavoured to prove, that it was formally
recognised in the ancient Church that the calling of synods
belonged to the hierarchical chiefs, and the summoning of
œcumenical councils in particular to the Pope; but several
of the passages which he adduces in proof are from the

Pseudo-Isidore, and therefore destitute of all importance, while others rest upon an incorrect explanation of the words referred to. Thus, Bellarmin appeals above all to the legates of Leo I., who at the fourth Œcumenical Council— that of Chalcedon in 451—had demanded the deposition of the Patriarch Dioscurus of Alexandria, because he had ventured to call an œcumenical council without permission from Rome. Their words are: σύνοδον ἐτόλμησε ποιῆσαι ἐπιτροπῆς δίχα τοῦ ἀποστολικοῦ θρόνου. In their obvious meaning, these words bear the sense indicated, and they are generally so explained. As, however, Pope Leo the Great had, by sending his legates, recognised and confirmed the summoning of the Latrocinium, or Robber-Synod—for it is to this that the reference is made—we are under the necessity of understanding that Dioscurus was accused at Chalcedon of thrusting the papal legates into the background, and taking the direction and presidency of the Council into his own hands. This is the way in which it is understood by the Ballerini and by Arendt. At the same time, it must not be overlooked that the general nature of the expression of which the papal legates made choice at Chalcedon, certainly involves the other side of the papal claim, and implies not only the right to preside over synods, but to convoke them.

Bellarmin appeals further to the seventh Œcumenical Council, which in its sixth session rejected the iconoclastic Synod of 754, and refused to recognise it as œcumenical, for this very reason, that the summons for its assembling did not go forth from the Pope. What the Synod does in fact say, however, is, that "this Synod had not the Roman Pope as its co-operator" (οὐκ ἔσχε συνεργὸν τὸν τῶν

Ῥωμαίων πάπαν). There is nothing said in particular of the Pope's taking part or not in the summoning of the Synod.

On the other hand, it is perfectly certain that, according to Socrates, Julius I., even in his time, about the year 341, expressed the opinion that it was an ecclesiastical canon, μὴ δεῖν παρὰ γνώμην τοῦ ἐπισκόπου Ῥώμης κανονίζειν τὰς ἐκκλησίας; and there can be no doubt, if these words are impartially considered, that they mean that it was "not lawful to pass canons of universal obligation at synods without the consent of the Bishop of Rome." The question which is here to be decided, however, is this: Who, as a matter of fact, called or co-operated in calling the œcumenical synods? And the answer is: The first eight œcumenical synods were convoked by the Emperors, all later ones by the Popes; but even in the case of the early synods, there, is a certain participation of the Pope in convoking them, which in individual cases is more or less clearly seen.

1. The fact that the summons to the first Œcumenical Synod proceeded from the Emperor Constantine the Great, cannot be disputed. As, however, none of the letters have come down to us, we cannot tell whether they referred to any consultation with the Pope. On the other hand, it is undeniable that the sixth Œcumenical Synod in 680 expressly asserted that the Synod of Nicæa was summoned by the, Emperor and Pope Sylvester (Κωνσταντῖνος ὁ ἀεισεβέστατος καὶ Σιλβεστρος ὁ ἀοίδιμος τὴν ἐν Νικαίᾳ μεγάλην τε καὶ περίβλεπτον συνέλεγον σύνοδον). The same is stated in the ancient Liber Pontificalis attributed to Pope Damasus; and if this authority be considered of slight value,

the importance of the former must be admitted. Had the sixth Œcumenical Council been held in the West, or at Rome itself, its testimony might perhaps seem partial; but as it took place at Constantinople, and at a time when the bishops of that place had already appeared as rivals of the Bishop of Rome, and moreover the Greeks formed by far the greater number present at the Synod, their testimony for Rome must be regarded as of great importance. Hence even Rufinus, in his continuation of the Ecclesiastical History of Eusebius, says that the Emperor summoned the Synod of Nicæa at the suggestion of the priests (ex sententia sacerdotum); and certainly, if several bishops were consulted on the subject, among them must have been the chief of them all, the Bishop of Rome.

2. With regard to the second Œcumenical Synod, it is commonly asserted, that the bishops who composed it themselves declared that they were assembled at Constantinople in accordance with a letter of Pope Damasus to the Emperor Theodosius the Great. But the document which has been relied upon as authority, refers not to the Synod of the year 381, the second œcumenical, but, as we shall show further on in the history of this Council, to the Synod of the year 382, which actually did meet in accordance with the wish of Pope Damasus and the Western Synod at Aquileia, but was not œcumenical. It is without effect, moreover, that Baronius appeals to the sixth Œcumenical Council to prove that Pope Damasus had a part in the calling of the second Œcumenical Synod. For what the Council says is this: "When Macedonius spread abroad a false doctrine respecting the Holy Spirit, Theodosius and Damasus immediately opposed him, and

Gregory of Nazianzus and Nectarius (his successor in the See of Constantinople) assembled a synod in this royal city." This passage is obviously too vague and indefinite to afford grounds for concluding that Pope Damasus co-operated in the summoning of the Synod. Nay more, the words, "Gregory of Nazianzus and Nectarius assembled a synod," rather exclude than include the co-operation of Damasus. Besides, it should not be forgotten that the Synod in question, held A.D. 381, as we have already remarked, was not originally regarded as œcumenical, and obtained this rank at a later period on its being received by the West. It was summoned as a general council of the Greek or Eastern Church; and if the Pope had no share in convoking it, no inference can be drawn from this fact unfavourable to his claim to summon œcumenical synods.

3. The third Œcumenical Council at Ephesus, in the year 431, was summoned, as the Acts prove, by the Emperor Theodosius, in union with his Western colleague Valentinian III. It is clear, however, that the Pope Celestine I. concurred, from his letter to Theodosius, dated May 15, 431, in which he says that he cannot personally be present at the Synod, but will send his representatives. Still more distinct is his letter to the Council itself, dated May 8, 431, in which he sets before the assembled bishops their duty to protect the orthodox faith, expresses his expectation that they will agree to the sentence which he has already pronounced upon Nestorius, and adds that he has sent his legates, in order that they may give effect to this sentence at Ephesus. The members of the Synod themselves saw and acknowledged that there was here not merely an assent to the convocation of the Synod, but also directions for their

guidance, inasmuch as they declare, in their most solemn act, the sentence of condemnation against Nestorius: "Compelled by the canons and by the letter of our most holy father and fellow-servant Celestine, Bishop of Rome, we have come to this sad sentence of condemnation upon Nestorius." They expressed the same when they said that "the letter of the Apostolic See (to Cyril, which he had communicated to the Synod of Ephesus) had already set forth the sentence and rule to be followed (ψῆφον καὶ τύπον) in the case of Nestorius; and they, the assembled bishops, had, in accordance with this judgment, followed up this rule." It is herein clearly acknowledged that the Pope had not simply, like other bishops, so to speak, passively agreed to the convocation of the Synod by the Emperor, but had actively prescribed to the Synod rules for their guidance; and had thus, not in the literal sense, but in a sense higher and more real, called them to their work.

4. The manner in which the fourth Œcumenical Synod at Chalcedon, A.D. 451, met together, we learn from several letters of Pope Leo I., and of the Emperors Theodosius II. and Marcian. Immediately after the end of the unhappy Robber-Synod, Pope Leo requested the Emperor Theodosius II. (October 13, 449) to bring together a greater council, assembled from all parts of the world, which might best meet in Italy. He repeated this request at Christmas in the same year, and besought the Emperor of the West also, Valentinian III., together with his wife and mother, to support his request at the Byzantine Court. Leo renewed his petition on the 16th of July 450, but at the same time expressed the opinion that the Council would not be necessary, if the bishops without it would subscribe an

orthodox confession of faith. About this time Theodosius
II. died, and was succeeded by his sister S. Pulcheria and
her husband Marcian. Both of them intimated immediately
to the Pope their disposition to call the Synod which had
been desired, and Marcian in particular asked the Pope to
write and inform him whether he would attend personally
or by legates, so that the necessary invitations might be
issued to the Eastern bishops. But Pope Leo now wished at
least for a postponement of the Council. He went even so
far as to say that it was no longer necessary; a change in his
views which has often been made a ground of reproach to
him, but which will be thoroughly discussed and justified at
the proper place in this History of the Councils. We will
only point out, at present, that what Leo had mentioned in
his 69th letter, during the lifetime of Theodosius II., as a
reason for dispensing with the Council, had actually taken
place under Marcian and Pulcheria, inasmuch as nearly all
the bishops who had taken part in the Robber-Synod had
repented of their error, and in conjunction with their
orthodox colleagues had signed the epistola dogmatica of
Leo to Flavian, which was, in the highest sense, an
orthodox confession of faith. Moreover, the incursions of
the Huns in the West had made it then impossible for the
Latin bishops to leave their homes in any great number,
and to travel to the distant Chalcedon; whilst Leo naturally
wished, in the interest of orthodoxy, that many of the
Latins should be present at the Synod. Other motives
contributed to the same desire; among these the fear, which
the result proved to be well grounded, that the Synod might
be used for the purpose of altering the hierarchical position
of the Bishop of Constantinople. As, however, the
Emperor Marcian had already convoked the Synod, the

Pope gave his consent to its assembling, appointed legates, and wrote to the Synod describing their duties and business. And thus he could say with justice, in his later epistle, addressed to the bishops assembled at Chalcedon, that the Council was assembled "by the command of the Christian princes, and with the consent of the Apostolic See" (ex præcepto Christianorum principum et ex consensu apostolicæ sedis); as, on the other hand, the Emperor at an earlier period wrote to the Pope, "The Synod is to be held te auctore." The Pope's share in convoking the Council of Chalcedon was, moreover, so universally acknowledged, that, soon after, the Bishop of Mæsia said, in a letter to the Byzantine Emperor Leo: "Many bishops are assembled at Chalcedon by the order of Leo the Roman Pontiff, who is truly the head of the bishops" (per jussionem Leonis Romani Pontificis, qui vere caput episcoporum).

5. There can be no doubt that the fifth Œcumenical Synod in the year 553, like the first four, was convoked by the Emperor (Justinian I.); but it is also certain that it was not without consultation with the Pope. Vigilius says himself that he had agreed with the Emperor Justinian, in the presence of the Archbishop Mennas of Constantinople and other ecclesiastical and civil rulers, that a great synod should be held, and that the controversy over the three chapters should rest until this synod should decide it. Vigilius expressed his desire for such a synod in a second letter ad universam ecclesiam, whilst he strongly disapproved of the Emperor's intention of putting an end to the controversy by an imperial edict, and was for that reason obliged to take to flight. When they had become reconciled, Vigilius again expressed his desire for the

holding of a synod which should decide the controversy; and the deputies of the fifth Council afterwards declared that he had promised to be present at the Synod. What is certain is, that Vigilius had desired the postponement of the opening, in order to wait for the arrival of several Latin bishops; and in consequence, notwithstanding repeated and most respectful invitations, he took no part in the sessions of the Synod. The breach was widened when, on the 14th of May 553, the Pope published his Constitutum, declaring that he could not agree with the anathematizing of Theodore of Mopsuestia and Theodoret. At the suggestion of the Emperor, the Synod at its seventh session, May 26, 553, decided that the name of Vigilius should be struck out of the diptychs, which was done, so that the Pope and the Council were now in open antagonism. In his decree to Eutychius of Constantinople, however, dated December 8, 553, and in his second Constitutum of February 23, 554, Vigilius approved of the decrees of the fifth Synod, and pronounced the bishops who had put them forth—that is, the members of the Synod—to be his brethren and his fellow-priests.

6. The case of the sixth Œcumenical Synod, A.D. 680, is quite the same as that of the third. The Emperor Constantine Pogonatus convoked it, and requested the Pope to send legates to it. Pope Agatho, however, not only did this, which involves an assent to the imperial convocation of the Synod; but he sent to the Emperor, and thus also to the Council, a complete exposition of the orthodox faith, and thus prescribed to it a rule and directions for its proceedings; and the Synod acknowledged this, as the Synod of Ephesus had done, inasmuch as they

say, in their letter to Agatho, "Through that letter from thee we have overcome the heresy … and have eradicated the guilty by the sentence previously brought concerning them through your sacred letter" (ex sententia per sacras vestras literas de iis prius lata).

7. The seventh Œcumenical Synod—the second of Nicæa, in the year 787—was suggested to the Empress Irene by the Patriarch Tarasius of Constantinople, who endeavoured to restore the reverence for images and union with Rome. The Empress and her son, the Emperor Constantine, approved of this; but before the imperial letters of convocation were issued, they sent an ambassador to Pope Hadrian I. with a letter, in which they requested him to be present at the projected Œcumenical Synod, either personally or at least by his representatives. In the October of the following year, Hadrian I. sent an answer to the Emperor and Empress, as well as to the Patriarch, and promised to send his legates to the intended Synod, which he afterwards did, and thereby practically declared his consent to its convocation. Nay more, in his letter to Charles the Great, he goes so far as to say, "And thus they held that Synod according to our appointment" (et sic synodum istam secundum nostram ordtinationem); and thereby ascribes to himself a still closer participation in the holding of this Synod.

8. The last synod which was convoked by an emperor was the eighth œcumenical, which was held at Constantinople in the year 869. The Emperor Basil the Macedonian had dethroned his former colleague Michael III., or The Drunken, and deposed his creature, the schismatical Photius, from the patriarchal chair, replacing the unlawfully

deposed Ignatius, and thereby restoring the union of the Greek and Latin Churches. As, however, Photius still had followers, the Emperor considered it necessary to arrange the ecclesiastical relations by means of a new œcumenical council, and for that purpose sent an embassy to Pope Nicolas I., requesting him to send his representatives to the intended Council. In the meantime Nicolas died; but his successor, Hadrian II., not only received the imperial message, but sent the legates, as it had been wished, to the Council, and thereby gave his consent to the convocation of this Œcumenical Synod.

All the subsequent œcumenical synods were held in the West, and summoned directly by the Popes, from the first of Lateran, the ninth Œcumenical Synod, to the holy Synod of Trent, while smaller synods were still convoked by Kings and Emperors; and Pope Leo X. declared in the most decided way, at the eleventh session of the fifth Lateran Synod, with a polemical reference to the so-called propositions of Constance, that the Pope had the right to convoke, to transfer, and to dissolve œcumenical synods.

SEC. 4. Members of Councils

In considering the further question, who has a right to be a member of a synod, it is necessary first to distinguish between the diocesan and other synods. For whilst in the latter either the only members or at least the chief members are bishops, the diocesan synod, with the exception of the president, is made up of the other clergy; and whilst the privileged members of the other synods have a votum decisivum, a vote in determining the decrees of the synod, those of the diocesan synod have only a votum consultativum, a right to be present and speak, but not to vote on the decrees. Here the bishop alone decides, the others are only his counsellors, and the decision is pronounced in his name. The members of the diocesan synod are divided into three classes.

1. Those whom the bishop is bound to summon, and who are bound to appear. To this class belong deans, archpresbyters, vicarii foranei, the vicar-general, the parochial clergy by deputies; and, according to more recent law and custom, the canons of cathedral churches, the provost and canons of collegiate churches, and the abbates sæculares.

2. Those whom the bishop may, but need not summon, but who are bound to come when he summons them; for example, the prebendaries of cathedrals who are not canons.

3. Lastly, those who in general are not bound to appear, as the clerici simplices. But if the synod has for its special purpose to introduce an improvement in the morals of the clergy, or to impart to them the decisions of a provincial synod, these must also appear when they are summoned.

With respect to the members of other kinds of synods, ancient Church history gives us the following results:—

1. The earliest synods were those held in Asia Minor about the middle of the second century, on the occasion of Montanism. Eusebius does not say who were present at them; but the libellus synodicus informs us that one of these synods was held at Hierapolis by Bishop Apollinaris

with twenty-six other bishops, and a second at Anchialus by Bishop Sotas and twelve other bishops.

2. The next synods in order were those which were held respecting the celebration of Easter, in the second half of the second century. With reference to these, Polycrates of Ephesus tells us that Pope Victor had requested him to convoke in a synod the bishops who were subordinate to him, that he did so, and that many bishops had assembled with him in synod. In the chapters of Eusebius in which these two classes of councils are spoken of, only bishops are mentioned as members of the Synod. And, in the same way, the libellus synodicus gives the number of bishops present at each council of this time, without referring to any other members.

3. The letters of convocation for an œcumenical synod were directed to the metropolitans, and to some of the more eminent bishops; and the metropolitans were charged to give notice to their suffragans. So it was, e.g., at the convocation of the third Œcumenical Synod, for which an invitation was sent to Augustine, who was already dead. The invitation to appear at the synod was sometimes addressed to the bishops collectively, and sometimes it was simply required that the metropolitans should personally appear, and bring merely the most able of their suffragans with them. The latter was the case, e.g., in the summoning of the third and fourth Councils; to Nicæa, on the contrary, the bishops seem to have been invited without distinction. Sometimes those bishops who did not attend, or who arrived too late, were threatened with penalties, as well by the Emperors, e.g. by Theodosius II., as by earlier and later ecclesiastical canons.

4. The chorepriscopi (χωρεπίσκοποι), or bishops of country places, seem to have been considered in ancient times as quite on a par with the other bishops, as far as their position in synods was concerned. We meet with them at the Councils of Neocæsarea in the year 314, of Nicæa in 325, of Ephesus in 431. On the other hand, among the 600 bishops of the fourth Œcumenical Council at Chalcedon in 451, there is no chorepiscopus present, for by this time the office had been abolished; but in the middle ages we again meet with chorepiscopi of a new kind at Western councils, particularly at those of the French Church, at Langres in 830, at Mainz in 847, at Pontion in 876, at Lyons in 886, at Douzy in 871. Bishops without a diocese have a certain resemblance to these; and such we meet with at synods, as in the year 585 at Mâcon in France. It is disputed whether those who are merely titular bishops have a right to vote at a council; and it has generally been decided in this way, that there is no obligation to summon such, but when they are summoned they have a right to vote.

5. Towards the middle of the third century we find a departure from this ancient practice of having only bishops as members of synods, first in Africa, when Cyprian assembled, at those synods which he held with reference to the restoration of the lapsed, besides the bishops of his province and his clergy, confessores et laicos stantes, i.e. those laymen who lay under no ecclesiastical penance. So there were present at the Synod held by S. Cyprian on the subject of baptism by heretics, on the 1st of September (probably A.D. 256), besides eighty-seven bishops, very many priests and deacons, and maxima pars plebis. And the Roman clergy, in their letter to Cyprian on the subject,

request that the bishops will take counsel in synods, in common with the priests, deacons, and laicis stantibus. It must not be overlooked, however, that Cyprian makes a difference between the membership of the bishops and of others. We learn from his thirteenth letter, that the bishops come together with the clergy, and the laity are only present (præpositi cum clero convenientes, præsente etiam stantium plebe); from his sixty-sixth letter, that the priests, etc, were the assessors of the bishops (compresbyteri, qui nobis assidebant). In other places Cyprian speaks only of the bishops as members of the synod, and from other passages it comes out that the bishops had at these synods taken the advice and opinion of the laity as well as the clergy. It is never, however, in the least degree indicated that either the clergy or the laity had a votum decisivum; but the contrary is evident, namely, that in the Synod of Cyprian referred to, which was held September 1, 256, only bishops were voters.

6. Eusebius relates that a great number of bishops of Asia assembled in synod at Antioch in the year 264 or 265, on the subject of Paul of Samosata, and he adds that their priests and deacons came with them. In the following chapter Eusebius gives an account of the Synod at Antioch in 269, and makes special reference to the priest of Antioch, Malchion, who was present at the Synod, and by his logical ability compelled Paul of Samosata, who wanted to conceal his false doctrine, to explain himself clearly. In addition to this, Eusebius gives in the thirtieth chapter the circular letter which this Synod, after pronouncing the deposition of Paul, addressed to the rest of the Church. And this letter is sent forth not in, the name of the bishops

only, but of the other clergy who were present as well; and among these Malchion is named in the superscription, whilst the names of many of the bishops—and according to Athanasius there were seventy present—are wanting. We see, then, that priests and deacons were members of several synods; but we cannot determine from the original documents how far their rights extended, and whether they had more than a mere consultative voice in the acts of the synod. As far as analogy can guide us, it would appear they had no more.

7. In the two Arabian Synods which were held on the subject of Beryllus and the Hypnopsychites, Origen held a place similar to that which had been occupied by Malchion. The bishops summoned him to the Synod, so as to render his learning and ability serviceable to the Church; but it was the bishops themselves who held the Synod.

8. In many synods of the following centuries, besides the bishops, priests and deacons were present. So it was at Elvira, at Arles, at Carthage in 397, at Toledo in 400, etc. The bishops and priests had seats, but the deacons had to stand. The decrees of the ancient synods were for the most part signed only by the bishops. It was so at the Councils of Ancyra, of Neocæsarea—although in this case the subscriptions are somewhat doubtful; at the first and second Œcumenical Councils, those of Nicæa and Constantinople; at the Councils of Antioch in 341, of Sardica, etc. Sometimes also the priests and deacons subscribed the decrees, and then either immediately after the name of their own bishop, as at Arles, or else after the names of all the bishops. It was, however, not so common for the priests and deacons to join in the subscription, and

it did not occur in the fourth or fifth century: for we find that, even in the case of synods at which we know that priests and deacons were present, only bishops subscribed; as at Nicæa, at Carthage in 397, 389, 401, at Toledo in 400, and at the Œcumenical Councils of Ephesus. and Chalcedon.1 At a later period we meet again, at some synods, with signatures of priests and deacons, as at Lyons in 830.1 The difference between the rights of the priests and those of the bishops is made clear by the signatures of the Council of Constantinople under Flavian in 448. The deposition of Eutyches which was there pronounced was subscribed by the bishops with the formula, ὁρίσας ὑπέγραψα, definiens subscripsi, and afterwards by twenty-three archimandrites, or superiors of convents, merely with the word ὑπέγραψα without ὁρίσας.1 At the Robber-Synod of Ephesus, on the contrary, along with other anomalies, we find the Archimandrite Barsumas of Syria signing, as a fully privileged member of the Synod, with the word ὁρίσας, and that because the Emperor Theodosius II. had summoned him expressly.

9. It is easily understood, and it is shown by the ancient acts of councils, that priests and deacons, when they were the representatives of their bishops, had a right to give, like them, a votum decisivum, and subscribed the acts of the synod with the formula ὁρίσας. And this is expressed at a much later period by the Synods of Rouen in 1581, and of Bordeaux in 1583,—by the latter with the limitation that only priests should be sent as the representatives of the bishops.

10. Other clergymen, deacons in particular, were employed at synods, as secretaries, notaries, and the like—at Ephesus

and Chalcedon, for instance; and they had often no insignificant influence, particularly their head, the primicerius notariorum, although they had no vote. Some of these notaries were official, and were the servants of the synod; but besides these, each bishop could bring his own notary or secretary with him, and employ him to make notes and minutes of the sessions: for it was only at the Robber-Synod that the violent Dioscurus allowed no other notaries than his own, and those of some of his friends. From the nature of the case, there is nothing to prevent even laymen from being employed in such work; and we are informed distinctly by Æneas Sylvius that he performed such duties, as a layman, at the Synod of. Basle. It is, moreover, not at all improbable that the secretarii divini consistorii, who were present at some of the ancient synods—at Chalcedon, for instance—were secretaries of the Imperial Council, and consequently laymen.

11. Besides the bishops, other ecclesiastics have always been brought in at councils, œcumenical as well as inferior, for the purpose of consultation, particularly doctors of theology and of canon law, as well as deputies of chapters and superiors of monasteries; and bishops were even requested to bring such assistants and counsellors with them to the synod. So it was at the Spanish Council at Tarragona in 516. But, at the same time, the fundamental principle is undoubted, that the vote for the decision of a question belonged to the bishops, as to those whom the Holy Ghost has appointed to rule the Church of God, and to all others only a consultative voice; and this was distinctly recognised by the Synods of Rouen in 1581, and Bordeaux in 1583 and 1684, partly in the most general way,

in part specifically with reference to the deputies of chapters, titular and commendatory abbots. There has been a doubt with respect to abbots, whether they held a place similar to that of the bishops or not; and a different practice seems to have prevailed at different places and times. We have already seen that in the ancient Church the archimandrites had no vote, even when they were priests. On the other hand, a Synod at London, under the famous Dunstan Archbishop of Canterbury, A.D. 1075, declares: "Besides the bishops and abbots, no one must address the Synod without the permission of the archbishop." The abbots are here plainly assigned a place of equality with the bishops as members of the Synod; and they subscribed the acts of this Synod like the bishops. In the same way the abbots subscribed at other synods, e.g. at Pontion in France, A.D. 876, at the Council held in the Palatium Ticinum, at Cavaillon, and elsewhere; but, on the other hand, at many other councils of the same time, as well as at those of an earlier and later period, the bishops alone, or their representatives, signed the decrees. So it was at Epaon in 517, at Lyons in 517, at Ilerda and Valencia in Spain in 524, at Arles in 524, at Carthage in 525, at Orange in 529, at Toledo in 531, at Orleans in 533; so also at Cavaillon in 875, at Beauvais in 875, at Ravenna in 877, at Tribur in 895. The archdeacons seem to have been regarded very much in the same way as the abbots, inasmuch as they appeared at synods not merely as the representatives of their bishops; but sometimes they signed the acts of the council, even when their bishop was personally present. So it was at the Synod of London already mentioned. At the end of the middle ages it was the common view that abbots and cardinal priests and cardinal deacons as well had a votum decisivum at the synods,—a fact which is expressly stated, as far as regards the abbots, by the historian of the Synod of Basle, Augustinus Patricius, a Piccolomini of the fifteenth century. He adds, that only the Council of Basle allowed the anomaly, and conceded to other ecclesiastics the right of voting. But we must remark that, according to the statement of the famous Cardinal D'Ailly, even so early as at the Synod at Pisa in 1409, the doctors of divinity and of canon law had a votum decisivum; and that the Council of Constance extended this right, by adopting the division of the Council into nations. These were, however, anomalies; and after this stormy period had passed by, the ancient ecclesiastical order was restored, that only bishops, cardinals, and abbots should have the votum decisivum. A place of equality with the abbots was naturally assigned to the generals of those widespread orders, which had a central authority. This was done at the Council of Trent. With regard to the abbots, a distinction was made between those who possessed real jurisdiction, and those who were only titular or commendatory. To these last there was conceded no more than the votum consultativum; e.g. in the Synod at Rouen in 1581, and Bordeaux in 1583. The former went so far as to refuse to acknowledge any such right as belonging to the abbots; and a later synod at Bordeaux, in the year 1624, plainly declared that it was an error (erronea opinio) to affirm that any others besides bishops had a decisive voice in a provincial synod (præter episcopos quosdam alios habere vocem decisivam in concilio provinciali). In practice, however, abbots were still admitted, only with the distinction that the bishops were members of the synod "by divine right" (jure divino), and

the abbots only "by ecclesiastical appointment"
(institutione ecclesiastica).

12. We have already seen, that in the time of Cyprian, both
in Africa and in Italy, laymen were allowed to be present at
synods. This custom was continued to later times. Thus,
e.g., the Spanish Synod at Tarragona, in 516, ordained that
the bishops should bring to the Synod with them, besides
the clergy, their faithful sons of the laity. Viventiolus
Archbishop of Lyons, in the letter by which he summoned
a synod at Epaon in 517, says: "Laicos permittimus
interesse, ut quæ a solis pontificibus ordinanda sunt et
populus possit agnoscere." [We permit the laity to be
present, that the people may know those things which are
ordained by the priests alone.] Moreover, the laity had the
power of bringing forward their complaints with reference
to the conduct of the clergy, inasmuch as they had a right
to ask for priests of good character. The fourth Synod of
Toledo, in 633, says expressly, that laymen also should be
invited to the synods. So, in fact, we meet with
distinguished laymen at the eighth Synod of Toledo in 653,
and at the second of Orange in 529. In English synods we
find even abbesses were present. Thus the Abbess Hilda
was at the Collatio Pharensis, or Synod of Whitby, in 664,
where the question of Easter and of the tonsure, and other
questions, were discussed; and the Abbess Ælfleda, the
successor of Hilda, at the somewhat later Synod on the
Nith in Northumberland. This presence of abbesses of the
royal family is, however, exceptional, even when these
assemblies were nothing else than concilia mixta, as
Salmon, l.c., explains them to be. That, however,
distinguished and well-instructed laymen should be

introduced without delay into provincial synods, was expressly decided by the Congregatio interpret, concil. by a decree of April 22, 1598; and the Cæremoniale episcoporum refers to the same, when it speaks of the seats which were to be prepared at provincial synods for the laity who were present. Pignatelli recommends the bishops to be prudent in issuing such invitations to the laity; but we still find in 1736 a great many laymen of distinction present at the great Maronite Council which was held by Simon Assemani as papal legate. At many synods the laity present signed the acts; but at others, and these by far the most numerous, they did not sign. At the Maronite Council just mentioned, and at the second of Orange, they did sign. It is clear from the passage already adduced, referring to the Synod of Epaon, that these laymen were admitted only as witnesses and advisers, or as complainants. It is remarkable that the laity who were present at Orange signed with the very same formula as the bishops,—namely, consentiens subscripsi; whilst in other cases the bishops made use of the words definiens subscripsi; and the priests, deacons, and laymen simply used the word subscripsi. As was natural, the position of the laity at the concilia mixta was different: from the very character of these, it followed that temporal princes appeared as fully qualified members, side by side with the prelates of the Church.

13. Among the laity whom we find at synods, the Emperors and Kings are prominent. After the Roman Emperors embraced Christianity, they, either personally or by their representatives and commissaries, attended the great synods, and particularly those which were œcumenical. Thus, Constantine the Great was personally present at the

first Œcumenical Council; Theodosius II. sent his
representatives to the third, and the Emperor Marcian sent
his to the fourth; and besides, at a later period, he was
personally present, with his wife Pulcheria, at the sixth
session of this Council of Chalcedon. So the Emperor
Constantine Pogonatus attended at the sixth Œcumenical
Council; at the seventh, on the other hand, Irene and her
son Constantine Porphyrogenitus were present only by
deputies; whilst at the eighth the Emperor Basil the
Macedonian took part, sometimes personally and
sometimes by representatives. Only in the case of the
second and fifth Œcumenical Synods we find neither the
Emperors nor their representatives present; but the
Emperors (Theodosius the Great and Justinian) were at the
time present in the city of Constantinople, where those
councils were held, and in constant communication with
the Synod.

It was, as we perceive, simply at the œcumenical synods
that the Emperors were present. To this fact Pope Nicholas
I. expressly appeals in his letter to the Emperor Michael,
A.D. 865, and infers from it that all other synods ought to
be held without the presence of the Emperor or his
representatives. In agreement with this Pope, a few years
later the eighth Œcumenical Council declared, that it was
false to maintain that no synod should be held without the
presence of the Emperor; that, on the contrary, the
Emperors had been present only at the œcumenical
councils; and, moreover, that it was not proper for
temporal princes to be present at provincial synods, etc.,
for the condemnation of the clergy. They might have
added, that so early as the fourth century the bishops

complained loudly when Constantine the Great sent an imperial commissioner to the Synod of Tyre in 335.

In the West, on the contrary, the Kings were present even at national synods. Thus, Sisenand, the Spanish King of the West Goths, was present at the fourth Council of Toledo in the year 633, and King Chintilan at the fifth of Toledo in 638; Charles the Great at the Council of Frankfurt in 794, and two Anglo-Saxon Kings at the Collatio Pharensis, already mentioned, in 664. We find royal commissaries at the eighth and ninth Synods of Toledo in 653 and 655. In later times the opinion gradually gained ground, that princes had a right to be present, either personally or by representatives, only at the œcumenical councils. Thus we find King Philip le Bel of France at the fifteenth Œcumenical Synod at Vienne in 1311, the Emperor Sigismund at the Council of Constance, and the representatives (oratores) of several princes at the last Œcumenical Synod at Trent. Pius IV. and Pius V. forbid the presence of a royal commissary at the Provincial Synod of Toledo; but the prohibition came too late. When, however, a second Provincial Synod was held at Toledo in 1582, in the presence of a royal commissary, Rome, i.e. the Congregatio Concilii, delayed the confirmation of the decrees until the name of the commissary was erased from the acts of the Synod. The Archbishop of Toledo, Cardinal Quiroga, maintained that such commissaries had been present at the ancient Spanish synods; but Rome held fast by the principle, that except in œcumenical synods, ubi agitur de fide, reformatione, et pace (which treated of faith, reformation, and peace), no commissaries of princes had a right to be present. At the later œcumenical synods, this presence of princes or of their representatives beyond all doubt had no other significance than to ensure protection to the synods, to increase their authority, and to bring before them the special wishes of the different states and countries. The celebrated Cardinal D'Ailly long ago expressed this judgment clearly; and, as a matter of fact, there was never conceded to a prince or his orator the right to vote, unless he was also a bishop. In reference to the most ancient œcumenical synods, it has even been maintained that the Emperors were their presidents; and this leads us to the further question of the presidency of the synods.

SEC. 5. The Presidency of Councils

As the presidency of a diocesan synod belongs to the bishop, of a provincial synod to the metropolitan, of a national to the primate or patriarch, so, in the nature of the case, the presidency of an œcumenical council belongs to the supreme ruler of the whole Church—to the Pope; and this is so clear, that the most violent partisans of the episcopal system, who assign to the Pope only a primacy of honour (primatus honoris), yet do not in the least impugn his right to preside at œcumenical synods. The Pope may, however, exercise this presidency in person, or he may be represented, as has frequently been the case, by his legates. Against this papal right of presidency at œcumenical synods the Reformers brought forward the objection, that the history of the Church showed clearly that the Emperors had presided at some of the first eight councils. There was, indeed, no difficulty in bringing forward proof in support of their assertion, since Pope Stephen V. himself writes that the Emperor Constantine presided at the first Council of

Nicæa, and the ancient acts of the synods frequently refer to a presidency of the Emperor or his representatives. But all such objections, however dangerous they may at first seem to be to our position, lose their power when we come to consider more closely the state of things in connection with the ancient councils, and are willing to discuss the matter impartially.

Let us begin with the eighth Œcumenical Synod, as the last of those which here come into question—that is to say, the last of the Oriental Synods—and from this ascend back to the first

1. Pope Hadrian II. sent his legates to the eighth Œcumenical Synod, on the express written condition, addressed to the Emperor Basil, that they should preside. The legates, Donatus Bishop of Ostia, Stephen Bishop of Nepesina, and Marinus a deacon of Rome, read this letter before the Synod, without the slightest objection being brought forward. On the contrary, their names were always placed first in the minutes; the duration of the sessions was decided by them; and they gave permission for addresses, for the reading of the acts of the Synod, and for the introduction of other members of the Synod; and appointed the questions for discussion. In short, they appear in the first five sessions without dispute as the presidents of the Synod. At the sixth and following sessions the Emperor Basil was present, with his sons Constantine and Leo; and he obtained the presidency, as the acts relate. But these acts clearly distinguish the Emperor and his sons from the Synod; for, after naming them, they add, "the holy and œcumenical Synod agreeing" (conveniente sancta ac universali synodo). Thus we perceive that the Emperor and

his sons are not reckoned among the members of the Synod, whilst the papal legates are constantly placed first among the members. It is the legates, too, who in these later sessions decide the subjects which shall be brought forward: they also are the first who sign the acts of the Synod, and that expressly as presidents (præsidentes); whilst the Emperor gave a clear proof that he did not regard himself as the real president, by wishing to sign them after all the bishops. The papal legates, on the other hand, entreated him to place his own and his sons' names at the top; but he decidedly refused this, and at last consented to sign after the representatives of the Pope and the Oriental bishops, and before the other bishops. In perfect agreement with this, Pope Hadrian II., in his letter to the Emperor, commended him for having been present at this Synod, not as judge (judex), but as witness and protector (conscius et obsecundator). Still less than the Emperors themselves had the imperial commissaries who were present at synods a right of presidency, since their names were placed, in all minutes of the sessions, immediately after the representatives of the patriarchs, but before the other bishops, and they did not subscribe the acts at all. On the other hand, it may be said that the patriarchs of the East—Ignatius of Constantinople, and the representatives of the others—in some measure participated in the presidency, since they are always named along with the Roman legates, and are carefully distinguished from the other metropolitans and bishops. They form, together with the Roman legates, so to speak, the board of direction, deciding in common with them the order of the business, regulating with them the rule of admission to the synod. They subscribe, like the legates, before the Emperor, and are named in the minutes and in the separate sessions before the imperial commissaries. But, all this being granted, the papal legates still take undeniably the first place, inasmuch as they are always the first named, and first subscribe the acts of the Synod, and, what is particularly to be observed, at the last subscription make use of the formula, "presiding over this holy and œcumenical synod" (huic sanctæ et universali synodo præsidens); whilst Ignatius of Constantinople and the representatives of the other patriarchs claim no presidency, but subscribe simply with the words, "As receiving this holy and œcumenical synod, and agreeing with all things which it has decided, and which are written here, and as defining them, I subscribe" (sanctam hanc et universalem synodum suscipiens, et omnibus quæ ab ea judicata et scripta sunt concordans, et definiens subscripsi). Moreover, as we find a remarkable difference between them and the papal legates, so there is also, on the other side, a considerable difference between their signature and that of the other bishops. The latter, like the Emperor, have simply used the words, suscipiens subscripsi, without the addition of definiens, by which the votum decisivum was usually indicated.

2. At all the sessions of the seventh Œcumenical Synod, the papal legates, the Archpresbyter Peter and the Abbot Peter, came first; after them Tarasius Archbishop of Constantinople, and the representatives of the other patriarchs; next to them the other bishops; and, last of all, the imperial commissaries. The decrees were signed in the same order, only that the imperial commissaries took no part in the subscription. The Empress Irene and her son were present at the eighth and last session of the Council as

honorary presidents, and signed the decrees of the first seven sessions, which had been already signed by the bishops. According to a Latin translation of the acts of this Synod, it was only the papal legates, the Bishop of Constantinople, and the representatives of the other Eastern patriarchs, who on this occasion made use of the word definiens in subscribing the decrees, just as at the eighth Council; but the Greek version of the acts has the word ὁρίσας in connection with the signature of the other bishops. Besides, we must not omit to state that, notwithstanding the presidency of the papal legates, Tarasius Archbishop of Constantinople had the real management of the business at this Synod.

3. At the sixth Œcumenical Synod the Emperor Constantine Pogonatus was present in person, together with several high officials of the state. The minutes of the sessions name him as president, and give the names of his officials immediately after his own. They next proceed to the enumeration of the proper members of the Synod, with the formula, "the holy and œcumenical Synod being assembled" (συνελθούσης δὲ καὶ τῆς ἁγίας καὶ οἰκουμενικῆς συνόδου),—thereby distinguishing, as in the case already mentioned, the Emperor and his officials from the Synod proper; and name as its first members the papal legates, the priests Theodore and George, and the deacon John. So these legates are the first to subscribe the acts of the Council; and the Emperor signed at the end, after all the bishops, and, as is expressly stated, to give more authority to the decrees of the Synods, and to confirm them with the formula, "We have read and consented" (legimus et consensimus). He thus made a distinction between himself

and the Synod proper; whilst it cannot, however, be denied that the Emperor and his plenipotentiaries often conducted the business of the Synod.

4. At the fifth Œcumenical Council, as has been already pointed out, neither the Emperor (Justinian) nor yet the Pope or his legate was present. It was Eutychius, the Archbishop of Constantinople, who presided.

5. The fourth Œcumenical Council is of more importance for the question now before us. So early as on the 24th of June 451, Pope Leo the Great wrote to the Emperor Marcian that he had named Paschasinus Bishop of Lilybæum as his legate (prædictum fratrem et coepiscopum meum vice mea synodo convenit præsidere). This legate, Paschasinus, in the name of himself and his colleagues (for Leo associated with him two other legates—the Bishop Lucentius and the Priest Boniface), at the third session of Chalcedon, issued the announcement that Pope Leo had commanded them, insignificant as they were, to preside in his place over this holy synod (nostram parvitatem huic sancto concilio pro se præsidere præcepit); and soon after, Pope Leo wrote to the bishops of Gaul, speaking of his legates, in the following terms: "My brothers who presided in my stead over the Eastern Synod" (Fratres mei, qui vice mea orientali synodo præsederunt). Pope Vigilius afterwards asserted the same, when, in a circular letter addressed to the whole Church, he says, "over which our predecessor of holy memory, Pope Leo, presided by his legates and vicars" (cui sanctæ recordationis decessor noster papa Leo per legatos suos vicariosque præsedit). Of still greater importance is it that the Council of Chalcedon itself, in its synodal letter to Pope Leo, expressly says, ὧν (i.e. the

assembled bishops) σὺ μὲν ὡς κεφαλὴ μελῶν ἡγεμόνευες ἐν
τοῖς τὴν σὴν τάξιν ἐπέχουσι; that is to say, "Thou, by thy
representatives, hast taken the lead among the members of
the Synod, as the head among the members of the body"
These testimonies—especially the last—are of so much
weight, that they would seem to leave no room for doubt.
And yet, on the other hand, it is a matter of fact that
imperial commissaries had the place of honour at the Synod
of Chalcedon, in the midst, before the rails of the altar; they
are the first named in the minutes; they took the votes,
arranged the order of the business, closed the sessions, and
thus discharged those functions which belong to the
president of an assembly. In the sixth session the Emperor
Marcian was himself present, proposed the questions, and
conducted the business. In these acts the Emperor and his
commissaries also appear as the presidents, and the papal
legates only as first among the voters. How, then, can we
reconcile the contradiction which apparently exists between
these facts and the statements already made? and how
could the Council of Chalcedon say that, by sending his
legates, the Pope had taken the lead among the members of
the Synod? The solution of the difficulty is to be found in
the same synodical letter written by the Pope to the Synod.
It reads thus: "Faithful Emperors have used the presidency
for the better preservation of order" (βασιλεῖς δὲ πιστοὶ
πρὸς εὐκοσμίαν ἐξῆρχον). In fact, this presidency which was
granted to the imperial commissaries referred only to the
outward working—to the material conducting of the
business of the synod. They were not connected with the
internal work, and left the decisions of the synods without
interference, gave no vote in the determination of questions
concerning the faith, and repeatedly distinguished between

themselves and the council. The acts of Chalcedon also show the same distinction. After having mentioned the imperial commissaries, they add these words, "the holy Synod assembled," etc. We may add also, that neither the Emperor nor his commissaries signed the acts of the Council of Chalcedon: it was the Pope's legate who always signed first, and repeatedly added to his name, even when the Emperor was present, the title of synodo præsidens

We are thus gradually able to explain the double relations existing between the papal legates and the imperial commissaries, quite analogous to that expressed in the words of Constantine the Great: "And I am a bishop. You are bishops for the interior business of the Church" (τῶν εἴσω τῆς ἐκκλησίας); "I am the bishop chosen by God to conduct the exterior business of the Church" (ἐγὼ δὲ τῶν ἐκτὸς ὑπὸ Θεοῦ καθεσταμένος). The official conduct of business, so to speak, the direction τῶν ἔξω as well as the seat of honour, was reserved for the imperial commissaries. The Pope's legates, although only having the first place among the voters, had the presidency, κατὰ τὰ εἴσω, of the synod, that is, of the assembly of the bishops in specie; and when the imperial commissaries were absent, as was the case during the third session, they had also the direction of the business.

6. The Emperor Theodosius II. nominated the Comes Candidian as his representative at the third Œcumenical Council, held at Ephesus in 431. In a letter addressed to the assembled fathers, the Emperor himself clearly determined the situation of Candidian towards the Council. He says: "I have sent Candidian to your Synod as Comes sacrorum

domesticorum; but he is to take no part in discussions on doctrine, since it is not allowable to any one, unless enrolled among the most holy bishops, to intermeddle in ecclesiastical discussions" (ἀθέμιτον γὰρ, τὸν μὴ τοῦ καταλόγου τῶν ἁγιωτάτων ἐπισκόπων τυγχάνοντα τοῖς ἐκκλησιαστικοῖς σκέμμασιν ... ἐπιμίγνυσθαι).

The Emperor then positively indicates what were to be the duties of Candidian: namely, that he was to send away the laity and the monks, if they repaired in too great numbers to Ephesus; he was to provide for the tranquillity of the city and the safety of the Synod; he was to take care that differences of opinion that might arise between the members of the Synod should not degenerate into passionate controversies, but that each might express his opinion without fear or hindrance, in order that, whether after quiet or noisy discussions upon each point, the bishops might arrive at a unanimous decision. Finally, he was to prevent any one from leaving the Synod without cause, and also to see that no other theological discussion should be entered into than that which had occasioned the assembling of the Synod, or that no private business should be brought up or discussed.

Pope Celestine I. on his side had appointed the two bishops Arcadius and Projectus, together with the priest Philippus, as his legates, and had instructed them to act according to the advice of Cyril, and to maintain the prerogatives of the Apostolic See. The Pope had before nominated Cyril as his representative in the Nestorian matter, and in his letter of 10th of August 430 he invested him with full apostolic power. It is known that from the beginning Candidian showed himself very partial to the friends of Nestorius, and tried to postpone the opening of the Council. When, however, Cyril held the first sitting on the 24th June 431, the Count was not present, and so his name does not appear in the minutes. On the contrary, at the head of the list of the bishops present is found the name of Cyril, with this significant observation, "that he took the place of Celestine, the most holy Archbishop of Rome." Cyril also directed the order of the business, either in person, as when he explained the chief object of the deliberations, or else through Peter, one of his priests, whom he made primicerius notariorum. Cyril was also the first to sign the acts of the first session, and the sentence of deposition pronounced against Nestorius.

In consequence of this deposition, Count Candidian became the open opponent of the Synod, and the protector of the party of Antioch, who held an unlawful council of their own under John of Antioch. Cyril notwithstanding fixed the 10th July 431 for the second session, and he presided; and the minutes mention him again as the representative of Rome. The other papal legates, who had not arrived in time for the first, were present at this second session; and they shared the presidency with Cyril, who continued to be called in the accounts the representative of the Pope. Cyril was the first to sign; after him came the legate Arcadius; then Juvenal of Jerusalem; next, the second legate Projectus; then came Flavian bishop of Philippi; and after him the third legate, the priest Philip. All the ancient documents are unanimous in affirming that Cyril presided over the Council in the name of Pope Celestine. Evagrius says the same; so Pope Vigilius in the profession of faith which he signed; and Mansuetus Bishop of Milan, in his letter to the Emperor Constantine Pogonatus.1 In other documents Pope Celestine and Cyril are indiscriminately called presidents of the third Œcumenical Council; the acts of the fourth1 assert this several times, as well as the Emperor Marcian,1 and in the fifth century the Armenian bishops in their letter to the Emperor Leo.1

7. When we pass on to the second Œcumenical Council, it is perfectly well known and allowed that it was not presided over either by the Pope Damasus or his legate; for, as has been already said, this Council was not at first considered œcumenical, but only a general council of the Eastern Church. The first sessions were presided over by Meletius Archbishop of Antioch, who was the chief of all the bishops present, as the Archbishop of Alexandria had not arrived at the beginning. After the death of Meletius, which happened soon after the opening of the Council, it was not the Archbishop of Alexandria, but the Archbishop of Constantinople, Gregory of Nazianzus, who was the president, and after his resignation his successor Nectarius. This took place through the decision of the Council, which in its third session had assigned to the Bishop of new Rome—that is, Constantinople—the precedency immediately after the Bishop of old Rome.

8. The solution of the question respecting the presidency of the first Œcumenical Council is not without difficulty; and the greatest acumen has been displayed, and the most venturesome conjectures have been made, in order to prove that in the first Council, at any rate, the Pope was not the president. They have endeavoured to prove that the presidency belonged to the Emperor, who in a solemn discourse opened the series of the principal sessions, and

took part in them, seated in the place of honour. But
Eusebius, who was an eye-witness of the Council, and pays
the greatest possible respect to the Emperor, says most
explicitly: "After that (meaning after the opening discourse
by the Emperor) the Emperor made way for the presidents
of the Synod" (παρεδίδου τὸν λόγον τοῖς τῆς συνόδου
προέδροις). These words prove that Constantine was
simply the honorary president, as the Emperor Marcian was
subsequently in the sixth session of the Council of
Chalcedon; and, as a matter of course, he left to the
ecclesiastical presidents the conducting of the theological
discussions. In addition to the testimony of the eye-witness
Eusebius, we have to the same effect the following
documents:—(a.) The acts of the Council of Nicæa, as far
as they exist, contain the signatures of the bishops, but not
that of the Emperor. And if that is true which the Emperor
Basil the Macedonian said at the eighth Œcumenical
Council, that "Constantine the Great had signed at Nicæa
after all the bishops," this proves conclusively that
Constantine did not consider himself as the president
proper of the Council. (b.) Besides, the Emperor was not
present in person at the commencement of the Synod. It
must, however, have had its presidents before the Emperor
arrived; and a short sentence in Eusebius alludes to these
presidents: παρεδίδου ... τοῖς προέδροις; that is, "He left
the management of the continuation with those who had
before presided." (c.) When several complaints of the
bishops against each other were presented to him, the
Emperor had them all burnt, and declared that it was not
becoming for him to give judgment upon priests. (d.) We
will finally recall these words of the Emperor already
quoted, that he was the bishop of the outward

circumstances of the Church; words which entirely agree with the position in the Council of Nicæa which we have assigned to him.

Who was, then, really the president of the Synod? Some have tried to solve the question by considering as president that bishop who was seated first at the right hand of the Emperor, and saluted him with a discourse when he entered the Synod. But here arise two observations: first, from the Greek word προέδροις it would appear that there were several presidents; and besides, it is not positively known who addressed the discourse to the Emperor. According to the title of the eleventh chapter of the third book of the Life of Constantine by Eusebius, and according to Sozomen, it was Eusebius of Cæsarea, the historian, himself; but as he was not a bishop of any apostolic or patriarchal see, he could not possibly have had the office of president. We cannot say either with the Magdeburg Centuriators, that Eusebius was president because he was seated first on the right side; for the president sat in the middle, and not at one side; and those patriarchs who were present at the Council (we use this term although it had not begun to be employed at this period), or their representatives, were probably seated together in the middle, by the side of the Emperor, whilst Eusebius was only the first of the metropolitans seated on the right side. It is different with Eustathius Archbishop of Antioch, who, according to Theodoret, pronounced the speech in question which was addressed to the Emperor. He was one of the great patriarchs; and one of his successors, John Archbishop of Antioch, in a letter to Proclus, calls him the "first of the Nicene Fathers." The Chronicle of Nicephorus expresses itself in the same way about him. He cannot, however, be considered as the only president of the Council of Nicæa; for we must regard the expression of Eusebius, which is in the plural (τοῖς προέδροις); and, besides, it must not be forgotten that the Patriarch of Alexandria ranked higher than the Patriarch of Antioch. To which, thirdly, it must be added, that the Nicene Council itself, in its letter to the Church of Alexandria, says: "Your bishop will give you fuller explanation of the synodical decrees; for he has been a leader (κύριος) and participator (κοινωνός) in all that has been done." These words seem to give a reason for the theory of Schröckh and others, that Alexander and Eustathius were both presidents, and that they are intended by Eusebius when he speaks of the πρόεδροι. But apart from the fact that the word κύριος is here used only as an expression of politeness, and designates perhaps merely a very influential member of the Synod, and not the president, there is this against the theory of Schröckh, which is expressly asserted by Gelasius of Cyzicus, who wrote a history of the Council of Nicæa in the fifth century: "And Hosius was the representative of the Bishop of Rome; and he was present at the Council of Nicæa, with the two Roman priests Vitus and Vincentius." The importance of this testimony has been recognised by all; therefore every means has been tried to undermine it Gelasius, it is said, writes these words in the middle of a long passage which he borrowed from Eusebius; and he represents the matter as if he had taken these words also from the same historian. Now they are not to be found in Eusebius; therefore they have no historical value. But it must be remarked, that Gelasius does not copy servilely from Eusebius; but in different places he gives details which are not in that author, and which he had learned from other sources. Thus, after the passage concerning Hosius, he inserts some additional information about the Bishop of Byzantium. A little further on in the same chapter, he changes the number of two hundred and fifty bishops, given by Eusebius, into "three hundred and more," and that without giving the least indication that he is repeating literally the words of Eusebius. We are therefore brought to believe that Gelasius has acted in the same way as to Hosius in this passage, by introducing the information derived from another source into the passage taken from Eusebius, and not at all from having misunderstood Eusebius.

When Baronius and several other Catholic ecclesiastical historians assign to the papal legate Hosius the honour of the presidency, they are supported by several authorities for this opinion besides Gelasius. Thus, S. Athanasius, in his Apologia de fuga, thus expresses himself about Hosius: ποίας γὰρ οὐ καθηγήσατο; that is to say, "Of what synod was he not president?" Theodoret speaks just in the same way: Ποίας γὰρ οὐχ ἡγήσατο συνόδου. Socrates, in giving the list of the principal members of the Council of Nicæa, writes it in the following order: "Hosius, Bishop of Cordova; Vitus and Vincentius, priests of Rome; Alexander, Bishop of Alexandria; Eustathius, Bishop of Antioch; Macarius, Bishop of Jerusalem." We see that he follows the order of rank: he would therefore never have placed the Spanish bishop, Hosius, before the great patriarchs of the East, if he had not been the representative of the Pope.

An examination of the signatures of the Council of Nicæa leads us again to the same conclusion. It is true that there are many variations to be found in these signatures, if several manuscripts are consulted, and that these manuscripts are often faulty and defective, as Tillemont has conclusively shown; but in spite of these defects, it is a very significant fact, that in every copy, without one exception, Hosius and the two Roman priests sign the first, and after them Alexander Patriarch of Alexandria signs. On this subject the two lists of signatures given by Mansi may be consulted, as well as the two others given by Gelasius: in these latter Hosius expressly signs in the name of the Church of Rome, of the Churches of Italy, of Spain, and of the West; the two Roman priests appear only as his attendants. In Mansi's two lists, it is true, nothing indicates that Hosius acted in the Pope's name, whilst we are informed that the two Roman priests did so. But this is not so surprising as it might at first sight appear, for these Roman priests had no right to sign for themselves: it was therefore necessary for them to say in whose name they did so; whilst it was not necessary for Hosius, who as a bishop had a right of his own.

Schröckh says that Hosius had his distinguished position on account of his great influence with the Emperor; but this reasoning is very feeble. The bishops did not sign according as they were more or less in favour with Constantine. If such order had been followed, Eusebius of Cæsarea would have been among the first. It is highly important to remark the order in which the signatures of the Council were given. The study of the lists proves that they followed the order of provinces: the metropolitan signed first, and after him the suffragans; the metropolitan of another province followed, and then his suffragan bishops, etc. The enumeration of the provinces themselves was in no particular order: thus the province of Alexandria came first, then the Thebäid and Libya, then Palestine and Phœnicia; not till after that the province of Antioch, etc. At the head of each group of signatures was always written the name of the ecclesiastical province to which they belonged; and this is omitted only in the case of Hosius and the two Roman priests. They signed first, and without naming a diocese. It will perhaps be objected, that as the Synod was chiefly composed of Greek bishops, they allowed the Westerns to sign first out of consideration for them; but this supposition is inadmissible, for at the end of the lists of the signatures of the Council are found the names of the representatives of two ecclesiastical provinces of the Latin Church. Since Gaul and Africa are placed at the end, they would certainly have been united to the province of Spain, if Hosius had represented that province only, and had not attended in a higher capacity. Together with the two Roman priests, he represented no particular church, but was the president of the whole Synod: therefore the name of no province was added to his signature,—a fresh proof that we must recognise in him and his two colleagues the πρόεδροι spoken of by Eusebius. The analogy of the other œcumenical councils also brings us to the same conclusion; particularly that of the Council of Ephesus, in which Cyril of Alexandria, an otherwise distinguished bishop, who held the office of papal legate, like Hosius at Nicæa, signed first, before all the other legates who came from Italy.

It would be superfluous, in the consideration of the question which is now occupying us, to speak of the œcumenical councils held subsequently to these eight first, since no one doubts that these more recent councils were presided over either by the Pope or his legates. We will therefore conclude the discussion of this point with the remark, that if in some national councils the Emperor or Kings were presidents, it was either an honorary presidency only, or else they were mixed councils assembled for State business as well as for that of the Church.

The Robber-Synod of Ephesus, which was held in 449, departed from the rule of all the œcumenical councils in the matter of the presidency; and it is well to mention this Synod, because at first it was regarded as an œcumenical council. We have before said that the presidency of it was refused to the Pope's legates; and by order of the Emperor Theodosius II., who had been deceived, it was bestowed upon Dioscurus of Alexandria. But the sensation produced by this unusual measure, and the reasons given at Chalcedon by the papal legates for declaring this Synod of Ephesus to be invalid, indisputably prove that we may here apply the well-known axiom, exceptio firmat regulam.

SEC. 6. Confirmation of the Decrees of the Councils

The decrees of the ancient œcumenical councils were confirmed by the Emperors and by the Popes; those of the later councils by the Popes alone. On the subject of the confirmation of the Emperors we have the following facts:—

1. Constantine the Great solemnly confirmed the Nicene Creed immediately after it had been drawn up by the Council, and he threatened such as would not subscribe it with exile. At the conclusion of the Synod he raised all the decrees of the assembly to the position of laws of the

empire; declared them to be divinely inspired; and in several edicts still partially extant, he required that they should be most faithfully observed by all his subjects.

2. The second Œcumenical Council expressly asked for the confirmation of the Emperor Theodosius the Great, and he responded to the wishes of the assembly by an edict dated the 30th July 381.

3. The case of the third Œcumenical Council, which was held at Ephesus, was peculiar. The Emperor Theodosius II. had first been on the heretical side, but he was brought to acknowledge by degrees that the orthodox part of the bishops assembled at Ephesus formed the true Synod. However, he did not in a general way give his confirmation to the decrees of the Council, because he would not approve of the deposition and exclusion pronounced by the Council against the bishops of the party of Antioch. Subsequently, however, when Cyril and John of Antioch were reconciled, and when the party of Antioch itself had acknowledged the Council of Ephesus, the Emperor sanctioned this reconciliation by a special decree, threatened all who should disturb the peace; and by exiling Nestorius, and by commanding all the Nestorian writings to be burnt, he confirmed the principal decision given by the Council of Ephesus.

4. The Emperor Marcian consented to the doctrinal decrees of the fourth Œcumenical Council, held at Chalcedon, by publishing four edicts on the 7th February, 13th March, 6th and 28th July 452.

5. The close relations existing between the fifth Œcumenical Council and the Emperor Justinian are well

known. This Council merely carried out and sanctioned what the Emperor had before thought necessary and decided; and it bowed so obsequiously to his wishes, that Pope Vigilius would have nothing to do with it. The Emperor Justinian sanctioned the decrees pronounced by the Council, by sending an official to the seventh session, and he afterwards used every endeavour to obtain the approbation of Pope Vigilius for this Council.

6. The Emperor Constantine Pogonatus confirmed the decrees of the sixth Council, first by signing them (ultimo loco, as we have seen); but he sanctioned them also by a very long edict which Hardouin has preserved.

7. In the last session of the seventh Œcumenical Council, the Empress Irene, with her son, signed the decrees made in the preceding sessions, and thus gave them the imperial sanction. It is not known whether she afterwards promulgated an especial decree to the same effect.

8. The Emperor Basil the Macedonian and his sons signed the acts of the eighth Œcumenical Council. His signature followed that of the patriarchs, and preceded that of the other bishops. In 870 he also published an especial edict, making known his approval of the decrees of the Council.

The papal confirmation of all these eight first œcumenical councils is not so clear and distinct:

1. The signatures of the Pope's legates, Hosius, Vitus, and Vincentius, subscribed to the acts of the Council before the other bishops, must be regarded as a sanction from the See of Rome to the decrees of Nicæa. Five documents, dating from the fifth century, mention, besides, a solemn approval

of the acts of the Council of Nicæa, given by Pope Sylvester and a Roman synod of 275 bishops. It is granted that these documents are not authentic, as we shall show in the history of the Council of Nicæa; but we nevertheless consider it very probable that the Council of Nicæa was recognised and approved by an especial act of Pope Sylvester, and not merely by the signature of his legates, for the following reasons:—

It is undeniable, as we shall presently see, that

α. The fourth Œcumenical Council looked upon the papal confirmation as absolutely necessary for ensuring the validity of the decrees of the Council; and there is no good ground for maintaining that this was a new principle, and one which was not known and recognised at the time of the Nicene Council.

β. Again, in 485, a synod, composed of above forty bishops from different parts of Italy, was quite unanimous in asserting, in opposition to the Greeks, that the three hundred and eighteen bishops of Nicæa had their decisions confirmed by the authority of the holy Roman Church (confirmationem rerum atque auctoritatem sanctæ Romanæ Ecclesiæ detulerunt).

γ. Pope Julius I. in the same way declared, a few years after the close of the Council of Nicæa, that ecclesiastical decrees (the decisions of synods) ought not to be published without the consent of the Bishop of Rome, and that this is a rule and a law of the Church.

δ. Dionysius the Less also maintained that the decisions of the Council of Nicæa were sent to Rome for approval; and it is not improbable that it was the general opinion upon this point which contributed to produce those spurious documents which we possess.

2. When the Pope and the Western bishops heard the decrees of the Council of Constantinople, held in 381, subsesequently accepted as the second Œcumenical Council, they expressed in an Italian synod their disapproval of some of the steps taken, although they had not then received the acts of the Council. Soon after they had received the acts, Pope Damasus gave his sanction to the Council. This is the account given by Photius. This approval, however, must have related only to the Creed of Constantinople; for the canons of this Council were rejected by Pope Leo the Great, and subsequently, towards the year 600, still more explicitly by Pope Gregory the Great. That the Creed of Constantinople had, however, the approbation of the Apostolic See, is shown by the fact that, in the fourth General Council held at Chalcedon, the papal legates did not raise the least opposition when this creed was quoted as an authority, whilst they protested most strongly when the canons of Constantinople were appealed to. It was, in fact, on account of the creed having been approved of by the Holy See, that afterwards, in the sixth century, Popes Vigilius, Pelagius II., and Gregory the Great, formally declared that this Council was œcumenical, although Gregory at the same time refused to acknowledge the canons it had promulgated.

3. The third Œcumenical Council was held in the time of Pope Celestine, and its decisions were signed by his legates, S. Cyril, Bishops Arcadius and Projectus, and the Priest Philip. Besides this sanction, in the following year

Celestine's successor, Pope Sixtus III., sanctioned this Council of Ephesus in a more solemn manner, in several circular and private letters, some of which have reached us.

4. The decisions of the fourth Œcumenical Council, held at Chalcedon, were not only signed by the papal legates present at the Council, except the canons, and thus obtained a first sanction from the Apostolic See; but the Council, at the conclusion of its sessions, sent all the acts of the Synod to the Pope, in order to obtain assent, approval, and confirmation for them, as is expressly set forth in the letter written by the Synod to the Pope with these acts. We there read: πᾶσαν ὑμῖν τῶν πεπραγμένων τὴν δύναμιν ἐγνωρίσαμιν εἰς σύστασιν ἡμετέραν καὶ τῶν παρ' ἡμῶν πεπραγμένων βεβαιωσιν τε καὶ συγκατάθεσιν (We acknowledge the whole force of the things which have been done, and the confirmation of all that we have accomplished, to be dependent upon your approval). The Emperor Marcian, like the Council, requested the Pope to sanction the decrees made at Constantinople in a special epistle, which he said would then be read in all the churches, that every one might know that the Pope approved of the Synod. Finally, the Archbishop of Constantinople, Anatolius, expressed himself in a similar way to the Pope. He says: "The whole force and confirmation of the acts has been reserved for the authority of your Holiness" (Gestorum vis omnis et confirmatio auctoritati Vestræ Beatitudinis fuerit reservata). However, Pope Leo confirmed only those articles of the Council of Chalcedon which concerned the faith: he expressly rejected the twenty-eighth canon, which granted inadmissible rights to the Bishop of Constantinople, without taking into

account the sixth canon of Nicæa. Leo pronounced the same judgment in several letters addressed either to the Emperor or to the Empress Pulcheria; and he charged his nuncio at Constantinople, Julian Bishop of Cos, to announce to the Emperor that the sanction of the Holy See to the Council of Chalcedon should be sent to all the bishops of the empire.

5. We have already seen that it was after a protracted refusal that Pope Vigilius finally sanctioned the decrees of the fifth Œcumenical Council. We have still two documents which refer to this question,—a decree sent to S. Eutychius Bishop of Constantinople, and the constitutum of February 23, 554.

6. The decisions of the sixth Œcumenical Council were signed and accepted not only by the Pope's legates; but, like the Council of Chalcedon, this Synod also desired a special sanction from the Pope, and asked for it in a letter written by the Synod to the Pope, whom they name Caput Ecclesiæ, and his see prima sedes Ecclesiæ œcumenicæ. The successor of Pope Agatho, Leo II., gave this sanction in letters addressed to the Emperor and to the bishops of Spain, which still exist. It is true that Baronius has endeavoured to prove these letters to be spurious, because they also mention the anathema pronounced against Pope Honorius; but their authenticity cannot be doubted on good grounds, and it has been successfully maintained by others, particularly by Pagi, Dupin, Dom Ceillier, Bower, and Natalis Alexander.

7. As the Pope had co-operated in the convocation of the seventh Œcumenical Council, which was presided over by

his legates, so it was expressly sanctioned by Hadrian I., as he says himself in a letter to Charles the Great. His words are: Et ideo ipsam suscepimus synodum. However, the Pope would not immediately send his sanction of the Council to the Emperor of Constantinople, who had asked it of him, because the Emperor did not accede to two demands of the See of Rome with respect to the jurisdiction of the Patriarchal See, and the restitution of the property of the Church. Subsequently Pope Hadrian confirmed the sanction which he gave to the second Council of Nicæa, by having its acts translated into Latin, sending them to the Western bishops, and defending them against the attacks of the French bishops in the "Caroline Books."

8. Finally, the eighth Œcumenical Council had not merely that kind of sanction which is involved in the signatures of the Pope's legates at the end of its acts: it desired a more solemn and express approbation, and Hadrian II. yielded to this desire; and in his letter addressed to the Emperor, he sanctioned the dogmatic part of the decisions of the Synod, but noted his dissatisfaction with respect to other points. The fact that the Pope confirmed this Council is, moreover, made clear by his subsequently having a Latin translation of its acts made by the learned abbot and librarian Anastasius, and by the fact that Anastasius without hesitation calls it an Œcumenical Council in the preface addressed to the Pope at the commencement of his translation.

It would be superfluous to show that the Popes always confirmed the œcumenical councils of later times; for it is universally known that the influence of the Popes in all later Western councils has been greater, and that of the Emperor less, than in the first eight councils. Popes have often presided in person over these more recent councils, and then they could give their approbation orally. So it was in the ninth, the tenth, and the eleventh Œcumenical Councils: it was also the case in all the subsequent ones, except those of Basle and Trent; but the latter asked for and obtained an express confirmation from the Pope. Even in the middle ages several distinguished canonists demonstrated with much perspicuity that this papal approbation was necessary for the validity of œcumenical councils; and we shall see the reason for this statement: for the discussion of the celebrated question, "Is the Pope superior or inferior to an œcumenical council?" necessarily leads us to study more closely the relations which obtain between the Pope and the œcumenical council.

SEC. 7. Relation of the Pope to the Œcumenical Council

As every one knows, the Councils of Constance and Basle asserted the superiority of the œcumenical council to the Holy See; and the French theologians placed this proposition among the quatuor propositiones Cleri Gallicani—the so-called Gallican Liberties. Other theologians have affirmed the contrary, saying that the Pope is superior to an œcumenical council: for example, Roncaglia, in his learned reply to Natalis Alexander's dissertation; also, before Roncaglia, the pros and cons had been disputed at great length and with much animation. The Ultramontanes especially relied upon the fact that, at the fifth Council of Lateran, Pope Leo declared, without the least opposition in the Synod, that the authority of the Pope extended super omnia concilia. The Gallicans could only reply to this as follows: (a.) The Pope, it is true, had a document read in the Council which contained this sentence, and it passed without opposition; but the Council did not give any formal decision: it did not make a solemn decree of this proposition, (b.) The Pope only used this sentence argumentando, and not definiendo, in order to use it as a proof, but without giving it as a general proposition; and (c.) it is not certain that the fifth Lateran Council should be considered œcumenical. Many maintain that Pope Martin V. sanctioned the decree of the Council of Constance establishing the superiority of the œcumenical council to the Pope, and Eugene IV. also sanctioned a similar decree from the Council of Basle. In point of fact, however, these two Popes sanctioned only a part of the decrees of the Councils of Basle and Constance. As for those of Basle, Eugene only sanctioned those which treated of three points, viz. the extinction of heresy, the pacification of Christendom, and the general reform of the Church in its head and in its members. When, therefore, Martin V. declared at the last session of the Council of Constance, that he approved and ratified all that had been decreed by the present holy Œcumenical Council of Constance in materiis fidei conciliariter (that is, by the whole Council, and not merely by individual nations), this approval had immediate reference only to the special matter of Falkenberg (see vol. vii. p. 368 of Hefele's Conciliengeschichte): he said nothing at all on the decrees respecting the superiority of an œcumenical council to the Pope; and if this Pope, in the bull of the 22d February 1418, required of every one the recognition of the Council of Constance as being œcumenical, and that all which it had decreed in favorem fidei et salutem animarum must be received and believed (vol. vii. p. 347), he evidently avoided giving it a complete and universal confirmation. His words, which we have quoted above, have a decidedly restrictive character. He indicated by them that he excluded some of the decrees of the Council from his approbation (evidently those referring to the superiority of the Council); but for the sake of peace, he did not choose to express himself more clearly. His successor, Eugenius IV., declared himself with greater distinctness in 1446, when he accepted the whole Council of Constance, and all its decrees, absque tamen præjudicio juris, dignitatis, et præeminentiæ sedis apostolicæ. There can be no question that by this he intended to exclude from his approbation the decrees of Constance respecting the superiority of an œcumenical synod to the Pope. Finally, it must not be forgotten that, on the 4th September 1439, Pope Eugene IV. and the Synod of Florence, in an especial constitution, Moses, solemnly rejected the proposition that the council is superior to the Pope,—a proposition which had just been renewed in the thirty-third session of the Council of Basle, and had been there made a dogma.

In confining themselves to this question, Is the Pope superior or inferior to a general council? the Gallicans and the Ultramontanes did not understand that they were keeping on the surface of a very deep question, that of the position of the Holy See in the economy of the Catholic Church. A much clearer and deeper insight into the question has more recently been shown; and the real question may be summed up in the following propositions:—An œcumenical council represents the whole Church: there must therefore be the same relation between the Pope and the council as exists between the

Pope and the Church. Now, is the Pope above or below the Church? Neither the one nor the other. The Pope is in the Church; he necessarily belongs to it; he is its head and its centre. The Church, like the human body, is an organized whole; and just as the head is not superior or inferior to the body, but forms a part of it, and is the principal part of it, so the Pope, who is the head of the Church, is not superior or inferior to it: he is therefore neither above nor below the general council. The human organism is no longer a true body, but a lifeless trunk, when the head is cut off; so an assembly of bishops is no longer an œcumenical council when it is separated from the Pope. It is therefore a false statement of the question, to ask whether the Pope is above or below the general council. On the other side, we may rightly ask, Has an œcumenical council the right to depose the Pope? According to the Synods of Constance and Basle and the Gallicans, the Pope may be deposed for two principal reasons: (1) ob mores; (2) ob fidem, that is to say, ob hæresim. But, in reality, heresy alone can constitute a reason for deposition; for an heretical Pope has ceased to be a member of the Church: he therefore can be its president no longer. But a Pope who is guilty of ob mores, a sinful Pope, still belongs to the visible Church: he must be considered as the sinful and unrighteous head of a constitutional kingdom, who must be made as harmless as possible, but not deposed. If the question arises of several pretenders to the pontifical throne, and it is impossible to distinguish which is in the right, Bellarmin says that in this case it is the part of the council to examine the claims of the pretenders, and to depose those who cannot justify their claims. This is what was done by the Council of Constance. In proceeding to this deposition, however, the

Council has not the authority of an œcumenical council: it cannot have that authority until the legitimate Pope enters into relation with it, and confirms it. The question is evidently only of the deposition of a pretender, who has not sufficient claim, and not that of a Pope legitimately elected. The Council of Constance would not have had any right to depose even John xxiii. if (a) the validity of this Pope's election had not been doubtful, (b) and if he had not been suspected of heresy. Besides, he abdicated, thus ratifying the deposition which had been pronounced.

We see from these considerations, of what value the sanction of the Pope is to the decrees of a council. Until the Pope has sanctioned these decrees, the assembly of bishops which formed them cannot pretend to the authority belonging to an œcumenical council, however great a number of bishops may compose it; for there cannot be an œcumenical council without union with the Pope.

SEC. 8. Infallibility of Œcumenical Councils

This sanction of the Pope is also necessary for ensuring infallibility to the decisions of the council. According to Catholic doctrine, this prerogative can be claimed only for the decisions of œcumenical councils, and only for their decisions in rebus fidei et morum, not for purely disciplinary decrees. This doctrine of the Catholic Church upon the infallibility of œcumenical councils in matters of faith and morality, proceeds from the conviction, drawn from Holy Scripture, that the Holy Spirit guides the Church of God (consequently also the Church assembled in an œcumenical council), and that He keeps it from all error; that Jesus Christ will be with His own until the end of the world; that the gates of hell (therefore the powers of error) will never prevail against the Church. The apostles evinced their conviction that the Holy Spirit is present in general councils, when they published their decrees with this formula, Visum est Spiritui sancto et nobis (it seemed good to the Holy Ghost and to us), at the Synod held at Jerusalem. The Church, sharing this conviction of the apostles, has always taught that the councils are infallible in rebus fidei et morum, and has considered all those who did not believe in this infallibility to be heretics, and separate from the Church. Constantine the Great called the decrees of the Synod of Nicæa a divine commandment (θείαν ἐντολήν). Athanasius, in his letter to the bishops of Africa, exclaimed: "What God hath spoken through the Council of Nicæa endureth for ever." S. Ambrose is so thoroughly convinced of the infallibility of the general council, that he writes: "Sequor tractatum Nicæni concilii a quo me nec mors nec gladius poterit separare" (I follow the guidance of the Nicene Council, from which neither death nor sword will be able to separate me). Pope Leo the Great, speaking of his explanation respecting the two natures in Jesus Christ, says expressly that it has already been corroborated by the "consensu irretractabili" of the Council of Chalcedon; and in another letter, "non posse inter catholicos reputari, qui resistunt Nicæno vel Chalcedonensi concilio" (that they cannot be counted among Catholics who resist the Council of Nicæa or Chalcedon). Pope Leo again says in this same letter, that the decrees of Chalcedon were given "instruente Spiritu sancto," and that they are rather divine than human decrees.

Bellarmin and other theologians quote a great number of other texts, drawn from the works of the Fathers, which prove that this belief in the infallibility of œcumenical councils has always been part of the Church's creed. We select from them this of Gregory the Great: "I venerate the four first œcumenical councils equally with the four Gospels" (sicut quatuor Evangelia). Bellarmin as well as Steph. Wiest have refuted every objection which can be brought against the infallibility of œcumenical councils.

The same infallibility must be accorded to councils which are not œcumenical, when their decrees have received the sanction of the Pope, and been accepted by the whole Church. The only formal difference, then, existing between these councils and those which are œcumenical is this, that all the bishops of the Church were not invited to take part in them.

SEC. 9. Appeal from the Pope to an Œcumenical Council

The question, whether one can appeal from the decision of a Pope to that of an œcumenical council, is highly important, and has often been ventilated. Pope Celestine I., as early as the fifth century, declared that such an appeal was inadmissible. It is true that, in the first centuries, questions were often considered by the councils which had before been decided by the Pope; but, as Peter de Marca has shown, that was not an appeal properly so called. He also shows that the Emperor Frederick II. was the first who formally appealed from the decision of a Pope to that of a general council. Pope Martin V., and subsequently Pope Pius II., were led again to prohibit these appeals, because they recurred too often, and especially on account of the exorbitant demands of the Council of Constance. Julius II. and Paul V. renewed these prohibitions in the sixteenth century. In 1717 a great sensation was caused by the appeal of many Jansenists to a general council against the Bull Unigenitus of Pope Clement XI. But in his brief Pastoralis officii the Pope threatened with excommunication every one who promoted the appeal, and did not sign the Bull Unigenitus; and also compelled the abandonment of the appeal, and the dispersion of the appealing party. Even the Protestant historian Mosheim wrote against this appeal, and plainly showed the contradiction there was between it and the Catholic principle of the unity of the Church; and indeed it must be confessed, that to appeal from the Pope to a council, an authority usually very difficult to constitute and to consult, is simply to cloak ecclesiastical insubordination by a mere formality.

SEC. 10. Number of the Œcumenical Councils

Bellarmin reckons eighteen œcumenical councils as universally acknowledged; but on the subject of the fifth Lateran Council, he says that it was doubted by many: "Au fuerit vere generale; ideo usque ad hanc diem quæstio superest, etiam inter catholicos." Some historians have also raised doubts as to the œcumenical character of the Council held at Vienne in 1311. There are therefore only the following sixteen councils which are recognised without any opposition as œcumenical:—

1. That of Nicæa in 325.

2. The first of Constantinople in 381.

3. That of Ephesus in 431.

4. That of Chalcedon in 451.

5. The second of Constantinople in 553.

6. The third of Constantinople in 680.

7. The second of Nicæa in 787.

8. The fourth of Constantinople in 869.

9. The first Lateran in 1123.

10. The second Lateran in 1139.

11. The third Lateran in 1179.

12. The fourth Lateran in 1215.

13. The first of Lyons in 1245.

14. The second of Lyons in 1274.

15. That of Florence in 1439.

16. That of Trent, from 1545 to 1563.

The œcumenical character of the following synods is contested:—

1. That of Sardica, about 343–344.

2. That in Trullo, or the Quinisext, in 692.

3. That of Vienne in 1311.

4. That of Pisa in 1409.

5. That of Constance, from 1414 to 1418.

6. That of Basle, from 1431 to 1439.

7. The fifth Lateran, from 1512 to 1517.

We have elsewhere considered whether the Synod of Sardica can lay claim to the title of œcumenical, and we will again take up the question at the proper time. We may here recapitulate, in five short propositions, the result of our researches:—

a. The history of the Council of Sardica itself furnishes no reason for considering it to be œcumenical.

b. No ecclesiastical authority has declared it to be so.

c. We are not therefore obliged to consider it to be œcumenical; but we must also add,

d. That it was very early, and has been in all ages, highly esteemed by the orthodox Church.

e. Besides, it is of small importance to discuss its œcumenical character, for it gave no decree in rebus fidei, and therefore issued no decisions with the stamp of infallibility. As for disciplinary decrees, whatever council promulgates them, they are subject to modification in the course of time: they are not irreformable, as are the dogmatic decrees of œcumenical councils.

The Trullan Council, also called the Quinisext, is considered to be œcumenical by the Greeks only. The Latins could not possibly have accepted several of its decrees, which are drawn up in distinct opposition to the Roman Church: for instance, the thirteenth canon, directed against the celibacy observed in the West; the thirty-sixth canon, on the equal rank of the Bishops of Constantinople and of Rome; and the fifty-fifth canon, which forbids the Saturday's fast.

The Council of Vienne is generally considered to be the fifteenth Œcumenical Council, and Bellarmin also accedes to this. The Jesuit Damberger, in his Synchronical History of the Middle Ages, expresses a different opinion. "Many historians," he says, "especially French historians, consider this Council to be one of the most famous, the most venerable, and the most important which has been held, and regard it as the fifteenth Œcumenical. The enemies of the Church will gladly accept such an opinion. It is true that Pope Clement v. wished to call an œcumenical council, and of this the Bull of Convocation speaks; but Boniface VIII. had also the same desire, and yet no one would give such a name to the assembly which he opened at Rome on the 13th October 1302. It is also true that, after the bishops of all countries have been summoned, the title and weight of an œcumenical council cannot be refused to a synod under the pretext that many bishops did not respond to the invitation; but the name demands at least that the assembly should be occupied with the common and universal concerns of the Church—that they should come to decisions which should then be promulgated for the obedience of the faithful. Now," says Damberger, "nothing of all this took place at the Council of Vienne." We reply, that this last statement is a mistake. The Council promulgated a whole series of decrees, which in great measure relate to the whole Church, and not merely to one province only—for example, those concerning the Templars; and these decrees were certainly published.

Moreover, the fifth Lateran Council, which we admit to be œcumenical, spoke of that of Vienne, in its eighth session, as a generale. A different judgment must be given respecting the Council of Pisa, held in 1409. It was naturally from the beginning considered to be without weight or authority by the partisans of the two Popes whom it deposed, viz. Gregory XII. and Benedict XIII. The Carthusian Boniface Ferrer, brother to S. Vincent Ferrer, and legate of Benedict XIII. at this Synod, called it an heretical and diabolical assembly. But its character as œcumenical has also been questioned by those who took no part for either of the two antipopes—by Cardinal de Bar, and a little subsequently by S. Antonine Archbishop of Florence. We might add to these many friends of reform, like Nicholas of Clémonge and Theodoric of Brie, who were dissatisfied with it. Gerson, on the contrary, who about this time wrote his book De Auferibilitate Papæ, defended the decrees of the Council of Pisa. Almost all the Gallicans have tried, as he did, to give an œcumenical character to this Council, because it was the first to make use of the doctrine of the superiority of a general council to the Pope. But in order that a council should be œcumenical, it must be recognised as such by the whole of Christendom. Now, more than half the bishops of Christendom (episcopatus dispersus), as well as whole nations, have protested against its decisions, and would not receive them. For this reason, neither ecclesiastical authority nor the most trustworthy theologians have ever numbered it among the œcumenical councils. It must also be said that some Ultramontanes have had too little regard for this Council, in saying that the election made by it of Pope Alexander V.

was valueless, and that Gregory XII. was still the legitimate Pope until his voluntary abdication in 1415.

The Gallicans were very anxious to prove the Council of Constance to be œcumenical. It is true that it was assembled in a regular manner; but, according to the principles we have explained above, it necessarily lost its œcumenical character as long as it was separated from the head of the Church. The sessions, however, which were held after the election of Pope Martin V., and with his consent and approbation—that is, sessions 42 to 45—must be considered as those of an œcumenical council. The same consideration must be given to the decrees of the earlier sessions, which concern the faith (res fidei), and were given conciliariter as they were approved by Pope Martin V. There was no special enumeration of them given by the Pope; but he evidently intended those condemning the heresies of Huss and Wickliffe. Natalis Alexander endeavours to show that this sanction also comprehended the fourth and fifth sessions, and their decrees establishing the superiority of councils over the Pope. But Roncaglia has refuted his opinion, and maintained the right view of the matter, which we have already asserted. As for those who entirely refuse an œcumenical character to the Council of Constance in all its parts, it suffices for their refutation to recall, besides the approbation of Martin V., what Pope Eugene IV. wrote on the 22d July 1446 to his legates in Germany: "Ad imitationem ss. PP. et prædecessorum nostrorum, sicut illi generalia concilia venerari consueverunt, sic generalia concilia Constantiense et Basileense ab ejus initio usque ad translationem per nos factam, absque tamen præjudicio juris, dignitatis et præeminentiæ S. Sedis apostolicæ ... cum omni reverentia et devotione suscipimus, complectimur et veneramur" [In imitation of the most holy Popes our predecessors, as they have been wont to venerate general councils, so do we receive with all reverence and devotion, embrace and venerate the General Councils of Constance and Basle, yet without prejudice to the right dignity and pre-eminence of the Holy Apostolic See]. The moderate Gallicans maintain that the Council of Basle was œcumenical until its translation to Ferrara, and that it then lost this character; for it would be impossible to consider as œcumenical the conciliabulum which remained behind at Basle, and was continued later at Lausanne under the antipope Felix V. Edmund Richer and the advanced Gallicans, on the contrary, consider the whole of the Council of Basle to be œcumenical, from its stormy beginning to its inglorious end. Other theologians, on the contrary, refuse this character to the Council of Basle in all its sessions. This is the opinion of Bellarmin, Roncaglia, and L. Holstenius. According to Gieseler, Bellarmin has given the title of œcumenical to the Council of Basle in another passage of his celebrated Disputationes. This is not so. Bellarmin says that the Council of Basle was legitimate at its opening, that is to say, so long as the papal legate and a great number of bishops were present; but subsequently, when it deposed the Pope, it was only a conciliabulum schismaticum, seditiosum, et nullius prorsus auctoritatis. It was by Bellarmin's advice that the acts of the Council of Basle were not included in the collection of œcumenical councils made at Rome in 1609.

Those who are absolutely opposed to the Council of Basle, and refuse the œcumenical character to all its sessions, give the following reasons:—

a. There was only a very small number of bishops (7–8) at the first sessions of this Synod, and therefore one cannot possibly consider it to be an œcumenical council.

b. Before its second session, this Council, promising no good results, was dissolved by Pope Eugene IV.

c. From this second session, according to the undeniable testimony of history, the assembly was ruled by passion; its members were embittered against each other; business was not carried on with becoming calmness, but in the midst of complete anarchy; the bishops' secretaries spoke and shouted in the sessions, as Æneas Sylvius and others testify.

d. Eugene IV. did certainly at a later period, after the fifteenth session, confirm all that had been done in the preceding; but this confirmation was extorted from him when he was ill, and by the threat that, if he did not consent to give it, he should lose the adherence of the princes and cardinals, and be deposed from the papal chair.

e. This confirmation has no value, even supposing that the Pope gave it in full consciousness, and with entire freedom; for it was only signed by him on condition that the members of the Council of Basle should repeal all the decrees which they had given against the authority of the Pope, which they never did.

f. The Pope simply allowed the Council to continue its sessions, and he withdrew his bull of dissolution again; but these concessions imply no sanction of what the Council had done in its preceding sessions, and the Pope took care to declare this himself.

It appears to us to be going too far to refuse an œcumenical character to the whole Council of Basle. The truth, according to our view, lies between this opinion and that of the moderate Gallicans in this way:

a. The Council of Basle was a true one from the first session to the twenty-fifth inclusive, that is, until its translation from Basle to Ferrara.

b. In these twenty-five sessions we must accept as valid only such decrees as treat, 1st, Of the extinction of heresy; 2d, Of the pacification of Christendom; 3d, Of the reformation of the Church in its head and in its members;—and always on condition that these decrees are not prejudicial to the papal power, and are approved by the Pope.

Our authority for the establishment of these two propositions is Pope Eugene IV. himself, who, in a bull read during the sixteenth session of the Council of Basle, sanctions those decrees of the preceding sessions which treat of these three points. In the letter already mentioned, which he wrote on the 22d July 1446 to his legates in Germany, he says: "As my predecessors have venerated the ancient councils (evidently meaning œcumenical councils), so do I receive cum omni reverentia et devotione, etc., the General Councils of Constance and Basle, and this latter ab ejus initio usque ad translationem per nos factam, absque tamen præjudicio juris, dignitatis et præ-eminentiæ, S. Sedis apostolicæ ac potestatis sibi et in eadem canonice sedentibus concessæ."

But it is asked whether this acceptance be admissible, whether ecclesiastical authority had not already broken the staff over the whole Council of Basle. A passage in a bull published by Pope Leo X., in the eleventh session of the fifth Œcumenical Lateran Council, has been made use of for the support of this objection. It is as follows: "Cum ea omnia post translationem ejusdem Basileensis Concilii.... a Basileensi conciliabulo seu potius conventicula quæ præsertim post hujusmodi translationem concilium amplius appellari non merebatur, facta exstiterint ac propterea nullum robur habuerint." In this passage Pope Leo X. condemns what was resolved during the latter sessions of the Council of Basle, and which was taken into the pragmatic sanction of Bourges in 1438; and on this occasion he speaks of the Council of Basle in a very unfavourable manner. But apart from the fact that we might allege against this passage, which asserts the superiority of the Pope over a general council, what the Gallicans have already adduced against it, we will observe: (a.) Even in this passage Pope Leo distinguishes between the Council of Basle, the assembly held before the translation, and the conciliabulum which began after the translation. (b.) It is true that he does not speak favourably of the Council itself, and the word præsertim seems to imply blame; but the Pope's language can be easily explained, if we reflect that he has in view the decrees which diminish the power of the Pope,—decrees which were afterwards inserted in the pragmatic sanction. He might therefore speak unfavourably of these decisions of the Council of Basle, as Pope Eugene IV. did, without rejecting the whole Synod of Basle.

It must also be understood in what sense Father Ulrich Mayr of Kaisersheim was condemned by Pope Clement XIV., viz. for maintaining that the twenty-five first sessions of the Council of Basle had the character and weight of sessions of an œcumenical council. The opinion of Mayr is very different from ours: we do not accept all the decrees of the twenty-five first sessions, but only those which can be accepted under the conditions enumerated above.

Some theologians, particularly Gallicans, since the time of Louis XIV., will not recognise the fifth Lateran Council as œcumenical, on account of the small number of its members; but the true reason for their hostility against this Council is that, in union with the Crown of France, it abolished the pragmatic sanction of Bourges, which asserted the liberties of the Gallican Church, and concluded. another concordat These attacks cannot, however, be taken into consideration: for the great majority of Catholic theologians consider this Council to be œcumenical; and even France, at an earlier period, recognised it as such. Here, then, we offer a corrected table of the œcumenical councils:—

1. That of Nicæa in 325.

2. The first of Constantinople in 381.

3. That of Ephesus in 431.

4. That of Chalcedon in 451.

5. The second of Constantinople in 553.

6. The third of Constantinople in 680.

7. The second of Nicæa in 787.

8. The fourth of Constantinople in 869.

9. The first of Lateran in 1123.

10. The second of Lateran in 1139.

11. The third of Lateran in 1179.

12. The fourth of Lateran in 1215.

13. The first of Lyons in 1245.

14. The second of Lyons in 1274.

15. That of Vienne in 1311.

16. The Council of Constance, from 1414 to 1418; that is to say: (a.) The latter sessions presided over by Martin V. (sessions 41–45 inclusive); (b.) In the former sessions all the decrees sanctioned by Pope Martin V., that is, those concerning the faith, and which were given conciliariter.

17. The Council of Basle, from the year 1431; that is to say: (a.) The twenty-five first sessions, until the translation of the Council to Ferrara by Eugene IV.; (b.) In these twenty-five sessions the decrees concerning the extinction of heresy, the pacification of Christendom, and the general reformation of the Church in its head and in its members, and which, besides, do not strike at the authority of the apostolic chair; in a word, those decrees which were afterwards sanctioned by Pope Eugene IV.

17b. The assemblies held at Ferrara and at Florence (1438–42) cannot be considered as forming a separate œcumenical council. They were merely the continuation of the Council of Basle, which was transferred to Ferrara by Eugene IV. on the 8th January 1438, and from thence to Florence in January 1439.

18. The fifth of Lateran, 1512–17.

19. The Council of Trent, 1545–63.

SEC. 11. Customs observed in Œcumenical Councils with respect to Signatures, Precedence, Manner of Voting, etc.

In some countries—for instance, in Africa—the bishops held rank in the councils according to the period of their consecration; in other parts they ranked according to the episcopal see which they filled. The priests and deacons representing their absent bishop occupied the place belonging to that bishop in those councils which were held in the East; but in the West this custom was not generally followed. In the Spanish councils the priests always signed after the bishops. The Council of Arles (A.D. 314), in the signatures to which we cannot remark any order, decided that if a bishop brought several clerics with him (even in minor orders), they should give their signatures immediately after their bishop, and before the bishop who followed. The order of the signatures evidently indicates also the order of precedence. This Council of Arles gives an exception to this rule, for the Pope's legates—the two priests Claudian and Vitus—signed only after several bishops; whilst in all the other councils, and even in the Eastern, the legates always signed before all the other bishops and the patriarchs, even though they were but simple priests.

In the thirteenth century Pope Clement IV. ordained that, in order to distinguish the bishops from the exempt abbots in the synods, the latter should only have mitres bordered with gold, without pearls, without precious stones, or gold plates. The abbots who were not "exempt" were only to have white mitres, without borders.

The members of the councils ordinarily were seated in the form of a circle, in the centre of which was placed the book of the Holy Scriptures. There were added also sometimes the collections of the ecclesiastical canons, and the relics of the saints. Behind each bishop was generally seated the priest who accompanied him; the deacon used to sit lower, on one side, or before the bishop.

With respect to the ceremonies at the opening of the ancient Spanish councils, we have an order of the fourth Council of Toledo, which met in 633 (can. 4), which prescribed as follows: "Before sunset on the day appointed (May 18), all those who are in the church must come out; and all the doors must be shut, except the one by which the bishops enter, and at this door all the ostiarii (porters) will station themselves. The bishops will then come and take their places, according to the times of their ordination. When they have taken their places, the elected priests, and after them the deacons, will come in their turn to take their places. The priests sit behind the bishops; the deacons are in front; and all are seated in the form of a circle. Last of all, those laity are introduced whom the council by their election have judged worthy of the favour. The notaries who are necessary are also introduced.

"All keep silence. When the archdeacon says, 'Let us pray' (orate), all prostrate themselves upon the ground. After several moments, one of the oldest bishops rises and recites a prayer in a loud voice, during which all the rest remain on their knees. The prayer having been recited, all answer 'AMEN;' and they rise when the archdeacon says, 'Stand up' (crigite vos). While all keep silent, a deacon, clad in a white alb, brings into the midst the Book of the Canons, and reads the rules for the holding of councils. When this is ended, the metropolitan gives an address, and calls on those present to bring forward their complaints. If a priest, a deacon, or a layman has any complaint to make, he makes it known to the archdeacon of the metropolitan church; and the latter, in his turn, will bring it to the knowledge of the council. No bishop is to withdraw without the rest, and no one is to pronounce the council dissolved before all the business is ended." The Synod concluded with a ceremony similar to that of the opening; the metropolitan then proclaimed the time of celebrating Easter, and that of the meeting of the next synod, and some bishops were chosen to assist the metropolitan at Christmas and Easter.

Before the Council of Constance, they voted by numbers in all the councils; but at that Council, to neutralize the advantage the Italian prelates derived from their large number, the votes were given by nations. Five nations— Italy, France, Germany, England, and Spain—each had right to one vote; and within the nation they of course voted by numbers. Another arrangement was introduced into the Council. They divided, without distinctions of nationality, all who were present at the Synod into four great commissions—of the Faith, of the Peace, of the Reform of the Church, and of general business. Each commission had its own president, and they combined the commissions three times a week. When a commission had made a decree, it was communicated to the other three; and if it was approved by three commissions at the least, it was announced as a decree of the Synod by the president of the Council in a general session.

In the councils which followed that of Basle this manner of voting was abandoned; and when, at the commencement of the Council of Trent, the Pope's legates asked if they would vote by nations or by heads, the latter was the method which was recommended, as being the most conformable to the traditions of the Church. This is at least what Sarpi and Pallavicini relate. Sarpi adds, that several Fathers of the Council of Trent would have demanded to vote by nations; but this statement is refuted by Pallavicini, who proves that no one made that demand, and that the question asked by the legates was simply a prudential measure. The Council of Trent introduced a practice which was a departure from ancient custom. In the ancient councils the discussions upon the decrees to be promulgated took place during the sessions themselves; and the acts of these councils contain discussions of great length. In the Council of Trent, on the contrary, each matter was first carefully discussed in particular commissions; and when all was ready, and in fact decided upon, they presented the decree to the general session for confirmation. The acts of the Council of Trent, for this reason, contain no discussions, but only decrees, etc.

The decisions of the synods were regularly published in the name of the synod itself; but sometimes, when the Pope presided, the decrees were published in the form of papal decrees, with the addition of the formula: "with the approbation of the sacred œcumenical council" (sacra universali synodo approbante). This took place at the third, the fourth, and the fifth Lateran Councils, and in part also at the Council of Constance.

SEC. 12. Histories of the Councils

James Merlin, canon and chief penitentiary of the metropolitan church of Paris, was the first who had a collection of the acts of the councils published. This edition, naturally very incomplete, appeared at Paris in 1523, in one folio volume, in two parts. A second impression was published at Köln in 1530, enriched by two documents, the golden bull of Charles IV., and the bull of Pius II. in which he forbade an appeal from the Pope to an œcumenical council. The third edition, in octavo, published at Paris in 1536, had no additions. Like all the collections of the councils which have been made after it, with the exception of the Roman edition of 1609, the edition of Merlin contained, with the acts of the œcumenical councils, those of several provincial synods, as well as many papal decretals. It may be mentioned that this alone had the collection of the false Isidorian Decretals printed in a continuous form, whilst in the more recent collections they are distributed in chronological order, assigning to each council or each Pope the part attributed to him by the pseudo-Isidore.

In 1538 there appeared at Köln a second collection of the acts of the councils (two volumes folio), fuller than that of Merlin. It was published by the Belgian Franciscan, Peter Crabbe, who, to make it more complete, had searched in no less than five hundred libraries. The second edition, enlarged, dated 1551, is in three folio volumes. Lawrence Servius, the celebrated convert and Carthusian, published at Köln another and somewhat more complete collection of the councils in 1657, in four folio volumes; and the printer, Dominic Nicolini, put forth at Venice, in 1585, with the assistance of the Dominican Dominic Bollanus, a new impression, in five volumes folio.

Professor Severin Binius, canon of Köln, surpassed his predecessors by publishing another collection of the councils, in four volumes folio, in 1606. The text of the councils was enriched by historical and critical notes, taken for the most part from Baronius. The second editions, which were published in 1618 and 1636, are still better than the first. The latter was published at Paris by Charles Morel, in nine volumes, as the Roman collection of the acts of the councils could here be made use of. This Roman collection contained only the acts of the œcumenical councils. It consisted of four folio volumes, and was compiled between 1608 and 1612 under the authority of Pope Paul V. This work gave for the first time the original Greek text of many of the synodal acts, copied from the manuscripts of the Vatican and other MSS. The learned Jesuit Sirmond was the principal author of this collection; he wrote the interesting introduction which was prefixed to the whole work. At the beginning of the acts of each council there is a succinct but by no means worthless history of that council in Latin, which has been inserted into several other more modern collections,—in particular, into that of Mansi. We have already said that, by the advice of Bellarmin, the acts of the Synod of Basle were not admitted into this collection.

This Roman edition has served as a basis for all subsequent editions: these have added the acts of the national and provincial synods, besides the most important edicts and decrees of the Popes, all of them avoiding several faults and several singularities of the Roman editors. In these more recent editions the text has often also been improved by the study of various MSS., and has been enriched by many fragments and original documents which were wanting in the Roman edition.

The first collection which was made after the Roman collection is the Collectio Regia, which appeared at Paris in 1644 at the royal printing press, in thirty-seven folio volumes.

The printing and all the material part is magnificent, but the same praise cannot be awarded to the editing; for even those faults of the Roman edition which had been pointed out by Father Sirmond still remained uncorrected. In spite of the great number of its volumes, the royal edition is nearly one-fourth less complete than that of the Jesuit Philip Labbe (Labbeus) of Bourges. Labbe died in 1667, whilst he was labouring on the ninth and tenth volumes of his collection; but Father Gabriel Cossart, a member of the same order, continued his work, which appeared at Paris in 1674. Stephen Baluze wished to add to this edition a supplement which would contain four volumes in folio, but only one volume has seen the light. Almost all the French savans quote from this edition of Labbe's with Baluze's supplement, making use of all these works, and consulting, besides, a very large number of MSS. John Hardouin, a Jesuit, gave a new Conciliorum Collectio regia maxima ad P. Labbei et P. Gabrielis Cossarti ... labores haud modica accessione facta, etc. Hardouin had been in 1685 entrusted with this work by the French clergy, on the condition that he submitted it for examination to Dr. Vitasse, professor of the Sorbonne, and to Le Merre, an advocate of the Parliament. Hardouin submitted only for a short time to this condition, and gained the protection of Louis XIV., who accepted the dedication of the work, and allowed it to be printed at the royal press. These different circumstances gave to the work a kind of official character, which contributed not a little to render it suspected by the Jansenists and Gallicans, as Hardouin in his dedication to Louis XIV. showed himself a very warm partisan of the Bull Unigenitus, and the bull itself was inserted in the last volume; besides which, the Index rerum betrayed an opposition to Gallican principles. He took care to point out especially (see, e.g., the art. on the authority of councils) the decisions of the Popes or of the councils which were opposed to the principles and maxims of the Gallican divines. Louis XIV. died at the moment when the printing of the work was almost finished; and as the Duke of Orleans, who then became regent, favoured the Jansenists, and showed himself hostile to the Bull Unigenitus, advantage was taken to complain to the Parliament of the publication of Hardouin's work. Parliament ordered Elias Dupin, Chas. Vitasse, Denys Léger, and Philip Anquetil to draw up a report on the subject; in consequence of which the sale of the work was prohibited, as being opposed to the principles of the State, and to those of the Gallican Church (1716). They destroyed all the copies they could seize, but happily some had already been sent from France. Later on, the Parliament was obliged to yield to the wishes loudly expressed in various quarters for the publication of the work. They authorized it, but on the condition that the Jesuits should add a volume of corrections, thinking they would by these means weaken the Ultramontanism of Hardouin. This volume appeared in 1722, printed at the royal press, under the title, Addition ordonnée par arrêt du Parlement, pour être jointe à la Collection des Conciles, etc. In the following year the Jesuits obtained the free publication of Hardouin's edition, without its being accompanied by the additional volume; and they gained their point so well, that that volume was even suppressed. Since then the Jansenists have republished it at Utrecht in 1730 and 1751, with this title, Avis des censeurs nommés par le Parlement de Paris pour examiner, etc.

Since Hardouin's edition has been widely circulated, it has become the favourite text-book of learned men among Catholics as well as Protestants. It is this which Benedict XIV. always quotes in his work, De synodo Diæcesana. It is composed of a rich collection of conciliar acts and other important documents, and extends as far as 1714, thus going much further than Mansi's celebrated edition. It is recommended on account of its very beautiful and correct although small type, and especially for the five very complete tables which it contains.

These tables contain: (1) a chronological table of all the Popes; (2) a table of all the councils; (3) an index episcoporum, et aliorum qui conciliis interfuerunt; (4) an index geographicus episcopatuum; (5) lastly, a very complete index rerum et verborum memorabilium. On account of these advantages, we have also used and quoted Hardouin's collection in our History of the Councils, along with the more complete work of Mansi. Salmon has analysed the details of Hardouin's collection, and has given a long list of its faults. As doctor of the Sorbonne, Salmon was not able to judge favourably of Hardouin's collection, to which he would rather have preferred that of Labbe and Cossart. He has, however, acknowledged the improvements and additions which distinguish Hardouin's work.

The collections which follow have been made since the publication of Salmon's work. The first is that of Nicholas Coleti, which appeared at Venice under the title, Sacrosancta concilia ad regiam editionem exacta. The Dominican Mansi, who became Archbishop of Lucca, his native town, compiled a supplement to Coleti's work. Several years afterwards, Mansi undertook a new collection of the acts of the councils, which should be more complete than all those which had hitherto appeared. He kept his word; and at the commencement of 1759, thirty-one volumes in folio of this edition appeared at Florence, with the title, Sacrorum conciliorum nova et amplissima collectio, in qua præter ea quæ Phil. Labbæus et Gabr. Cossartus et novissime Nicolaus Coleti in luccm edidere, ea omnia insuper suis in locis optime disposita exhibentur, quæ Jo. Dom. Mansi Lucensis, congregationis Matris Dei, evulgavit. Editio Novissima, ab eodem Patre Mansi, potissimum favorem etiam et opem præstante Em. Cardinali Dominico Passioneo, S. Sedis apostolicæ bibliothecario, aliisque item eruditissimis viris manus auxiliatrices ferentibus, curata, novorum conciliorum, novorumque documentorumque additionibus locupletata, ad MSS. codices Vaticanos Lucenes aliosque recensita et perfecta. Accedunt etiam notæ et dissertationes quam plurimæ; quæ in cæteris editionibus desidcrantur. This edition was not completed, and the thirty-first volume reached only to the fifteenth century. It had consequently no indices, and its type, although larger and more modern than that of Hardouin's edition, is yet very inferior to the latter in accuracy. The order of the subjects in the latter volumes is sometimes not sufficiently methodical, and is at variance with the chronology.

By the side of these general collections there are other works, which contain only the acts of the councils held in particular countries. To these belong—

1. The Concilia Germaniæ, by Schannat and Harzheim, in eleven volumes folio (Cöln 1749–1790); Binterim, Pragmatische Geschichte der deutschen National- Provincial- und vorzüglichsten Diöcesan-concilien (Mainz 1835–1848), in seven volumes octavo, which reached as far as the end of the fifteenth century. We may, besides, consult, for the history of the German councils: (a) Lünig, Entwurf der in Deutschland von Anfang des Christenthums gehaltenen General- Provincial- und Partikularconcilien, in his Spicilegium des deutschen Reichsarchivs, P. i. p. 822; (b) Pfaff, Delineatio collectionis novæ conciliorum Germaniæ, reprinted in Fabricius, Biblioth. Græca, ed. Harless, t. xii p. 310 sqq.; (c) Joh. And. Schmid, Diss. de historiâ conciliorum Moguntinensium, Helmst. 1713; (d) De conciliis Moguntinis, in the work of Georg Christian Johannes, Scriptor. Mogunt. vol. iii. p. 281

sqq. Cf. Walch, Hist. der Kirchenvers. S. 53, and Salmon, l.c. p. 382 sqq.

2. Concilia antiqua Galliæ, by Father Sirmond (Paris 1629), in three volumes folio, and one volume folio,—a supplement added by his cousin De La Lande in 1666. Concilia novissima Galliæ a tempore concilii Tridentini celebrata, ed. Ludov. Odespun de la Mechinière, a priest of Tours (Paris 1646), one volume folio. Shortly before the Revolution, the Benedictines of the congregation of S. Maur undertook a complete collection of the councils of France; but one folio volume alone appeared (Paris 1789), with the title, Conciliorum Galliæ tam editorum quam ineditorum Collectio, temporum ordine digesta ab anno Christi 177 ad an. 1563, cum epistolis pontificum, principum constitutionibus et aliis ecclesiasticæ rei Gallicanæ monumentis. Opera et studio monachorum congregationis S. Mauri, t. i. ab anno 177 ad annum 591. Paris, sumptibus Petri Didot. In folio.

3. Garcias Loaisa was the first to publish a collection of the Spanish councils, at Madrid 1593, in one volume folio. That of Cardinal Joseph Saenz de Aguirre is much more complete: Collectio maxima Conciliorum omnium Hispaniæ et novi orbis (Rome 1693), in four volumes folio. More recent is the Collectio canonum Ecclesiæ Hispanæ ex probatissimis et pervetustis Codicibus nunc primum in lucem edita a publica Matritensi bibliotheca (per FRANC. ANT. GONZALEZ, publ. Matr. bibl. præfectum), Matriti, ex typographia regia, 1808. In folio.

4. England and Ireland had two collections. The older is that of Henry Spelman: Concilia, decreta, leges,

constitutiones in re Ecclesiarum orbis Britannici, London, t. i. 1639, t. ii. 1664; the third volume, although announced, never appeared. That of David Wilkins followed, which is better and more complete: Concilia Magna Britanniæ et Htberniœ, ed. DAV. WILKINS (London 1734), in four volumes folio.

5. Sacra concilia Ecclesiæ Romano-catholicæ in regno Unqariæ, a collection due to Father Charles Peterfy (Vienna 1742), in two volumes folio.

6. There does not exist a general collection of the Italian councils, but the councils of certain periods or of certain provinces have been in part collected. There is, e.g., a collection of the synods held at Milan, by S. Charles Borromeo (in his complete works); a Synodicon Beneventanensis Ecclesiæ, by Vinc. Mar. Orsini (Pope Benedict XIII.), Beneventum 1695, folio.

Among the numerous works on the history of the councils, the most useful to consult are:

1. John Cabassutius' Notitia Ecclesiastica historiarum conciliorum et canonum, Lyons 1680, folio. Very often reprinted.

2. Hermant, Histoire des Conciles, Rouen 1730, four volumes 8vo.

3. Labbe, Synopsis Historica Conciliorum, in vol. i. of his Collection of Councils.

4. Edm. Richer, Historia conciliorum generalium (Paris 1680), three volumes 4to. Reprinted in 8vo at Cöln.

5. Charles Ludovic Richard, Analysis conciliorum generalium et particularium. Translated from French into Latin by Dalmasus. Four volumes 8vo, Augsburg 1778.

6. Christ Wilh. Franz Walch, Entwurf einer vollständigen Historie der Kirchenversammlungen, Leipzig 1759.

7. Fabricius, Bibliotheca Græca, edit. Harless, t. xii. p. 422 sqq., in which is contained an alphabetical table of all the councils, and an estimate of the value of the principal collections.

8. Alletz, Concilien-Lexikon, translated from French into German by Father Maurus Disch, a Benedictine and professor at Augsburg, 1843.

9. Dictionnaire universel et complet des Conciles, tant généraux que particuliers, etc., rédigé par M. l'Abbé P——, prêtre du Diocèse de Paris, published by the Abbé Migne (Paris 1846), two volumes 4to.

In the great works on ecclesiastical history—for example, in the Nouvelle Bibliothèque des auteurs Ecclesiastiques, by El. Dupin, and the Historia Literaria of Cave, and particularly in the excellent Histoire des auteurs sacrés, by Remi Ceillier—we find matters relating to the history of the councils. Salmon, l.c. p. 387 sqq., and Walch in his Historie der Kirchenversammlungen, pp. 48–67, have pointed out a large number of works on the history of the councils. There are also very valuable dissertations on the same subject in.

1. Christian Lupus' Synodorum generalium ac provincialium decreta et canones, scholiis, notis ac historica

actorum dissertatione illustrata, Louv. 1665, Bruxelles 1673, five volumes 4to.

2. Lud. Thomassin, Dissertationum in Concilia generalia et particularia, t. i. Paris 1667; reprinted in Rocaberti, Bibl. pontificia, t. xv.

3. Van Espen, Tractatus Historicus, exhibens scholia in omnes canones conciliorum, etc., in his complete works.

4. Barth. Caranza has written a very complete and useful abstract of the acts of the councils in his Summa Conciliorum, which has often been re-edited.

5. George Daniel Fuchs, deacon of Stuttgart, has, in his Bibliothek der Kirchenversammlungen (four volumes, Leipsic 1780–1784), given German translations and abstracts of the acts of the councils in the fourth and fifth centuries.

6. Francis Salmon, Doctor and Librarian of the Sorbonne, has published an Introduction to the Study of the Councils, in his Traité de l'Etude des Conciles et de leurs collections, Paris 1724, in 4to, which has often been reprinted.

BOOK I
ANTE-NICENE COUNCILS

CHAPTER I
COUNCILS OF THE FIRST TWO CENTURIES

THE first Christian Council, the type and model of all the others, was held at Jerusalem by the apostles between the years 50 and 52 A.D., in order to solve the question of the universal obligation of the ancient law. No other councils were probably held in the first century of the Christian era; or if they were, no trace of them remains in history. On the other hand, we have information of several councils in the second century. The authenticity of this information is not, it is true, equally established for all; and we can acknowledge as having really taken place only those of which Eusebius Pamphili, the father of Christian Church history, speaks, or other early and trustworthy historians. To these belong, first of all:—

SEC. 1. Synods relative to Montanism

Eusebius has given us, in his Church History, a fragment of a work composed by Apollinaris Bishop of Hierapolis in Phrygia, in which the following words occur: "The faithful of Asia, at many times and in many places (πολλάκις καὶ πολλαχῇ τῆς Ἀσίας), came together to consult on the subject of Montanus and his followers; and these new doctrines were examined, and declared strange and impious." This fragment unfortunately gives no other details, and does not point out the towns at which these synods were held; but the Libellus Synodicus of Pappus tells us that Apollinaris, the holy Bishop of Hierapolis in

Asia, and twenty-six of his colleagues in the episcopate, held a provincial council at Hierapolis, and there tried and condemned Montanus and Maximilla the false prophets, and at the same time Theodotus the currier (the celebrated anti-Trinitarian). Further on he adds: "A holy and particular (μεϱιϰή) synod, assembled under the very holy Bishop Sotas of Anchialus (in Thrace, on the Black Sea), and consisting of twelve other bishops, convicted of heresy the currier Theodotus, Montanus, and Maximilla, and condemned them."

The Libellus Synodicus, to which we are indebted for these details, it is true, can lay claim to no very early origin, as it was compiled by a Greek towards the close of the ninth century. But this Greek derived his statements from ancient authentic sources; and what he says of the two synods agrees so perfectly with the statement of Eusebius, that in this passage it is worthy of all confidence. We read in Eusebius' Church History (book v. cc. 16 and 19), that Apollinaris of Hierapolis, and Sotas of Anchialus, contemporaries of Montanus, zealously opposed his errors, and wrote and preached against him. Sotas even wished to exorcise the evil spirit from Priscilla, a companion of Montanus; but these hypocrites, adds Eusebius, did not consent to it.

The strong opposition which these two bishops made to Montanus makes it probable that they gave occasion to several of the numerous synods in which, according to the summaries of Eusebius, the Church rejected Montanism.

The date of these synods is nowhere exactly pointed out. The fragment which is given in Eusebius proves that they

were held shortly after the commencement of the
Montanist agitations; but the date of the rise of Montanism
itself is uncertain. The Chronicle of Eusebius gives 172; S.
Epiphanius 126 in one place, and 156 or 157 in another. He
says, besides, that Maximilla died about A.D. 86. In this
there is perhaps an error of a whole century. Blondel,
relying on these passages, has shown that Montanus and his
heresy arose about 140 or 141; and, more recently,
Schwegler of Tübingen has expressed the same opinion.
Pearson, Dodwell, and Neander, on the contrary, decide for
156 or 157; Tillemont and Walch for 171. As for our own
opinion, we have adopted Blondel's opinion (the year 140),
because the Shepherd of Hermas, which was certainly
anterior to 151, and was written when Pius I. was Pope,
seems already to oppose Montanism. In this case, the
synods with which we are occupied must have taken place
before 150 of the Christian era. The Libellus Synodicus
gives a contrary decision to this, although it attributes to the
same synods the condemnation of the currier Theodotus,
whose apostasy can only be fixed at the time of the
persecution by M. Aurelius (160–180). In reality, Theodotus
was excommunicated at Rome by Pope Victor towards the
close of the second century (192–202). In allowing that
sentence of condemnation had been pronounced against
him before that time in certain synods of Asia Minor and of
Thrace (he was living at Constantinople at the time of his
apostasy), those synods which, according to the Libellus
Synodicus, have also condemned Montanism could not
have been held before M. Aurelius: they must therefore
have been held under that Emperor. The supposition that
Theodotus and Montanus were contemporary would oblige
us to date these councils between A.D. 160 and 180; but to

us it appears doubtful whether these two were contemporaries, and the conclusion that they were so seems to result from a confusion of the facts. In reality, the author of the ancient fragment given us by Eusebius speaks also of a Theodotus who was one of the first followers of Montanus, and shared his fate, i.e. was anathematized in the same synods with Montanus and Maximilla. He depicts him as a well-known man. The author of the Libellus Synodicus having read this passage, and finding that the ancient Synods of Hierapolis and Anchialus had condemned a Theodotus, easily identified the currier Theodotus with the Theodotus whom the author of the fragment declared to be celebrated in his time. If this is so, nothing will hinder our placing the rise of Montanism and the Synods of Hierapolis and Anchialus before A.D. 150.

SEC. 2. Synods concerning the Feast of Easter

The second series of councils in the second century was caused by the controversy regarding the time of celebrating Easter. It is not quite correct to regard the meeting of S. Polycarp of Smyrna, and Anicetus Bishop of Rome, towards the middle of the second century, as a synod properly so called; but it is certain that towards the close of the same century several synods were occasioned by the Easter controversy. Eusebius, in the passage referred to, only shows in a general way that these synods were held in the second half of the second century; but S. Jerome gives a more exact date, he says in his Chronicle, under the year 196: "Pope Victor wrote to the most eminent bishops of all countries, recommending them to call synods in their provinces, and to celebrate in them the feast of Easter on the day chosen by the Church of the West."

Eusebius here agrees with S. Jerome; for he has preserved to us a fragment of a letter written by Polycarp from Ephesus, in which this bishop says that Victor had required him to assemble the bishops who were subordinate to him: that he had done so, but that he and all the bishops present at this synod had pronounced for the practice of the Quartodecimans or of S. John; that these bishops, the number of whom was considerable, had approved of the synodical letter which he had drawn up, and that he had no fear (on account of the threats of Victor), "because we must obey God rather than man." We see from this fragment, that at the moment when the synods convoked at the request of Victor in Palestine pronounced in favour of the Western practice in Palestine, Pontus, Gaul, and Osrhoëne, a great synod of bishops from Asia Minor, held at Ephesus, the see of Polycarp, had formally declared against this practice; and it is precisely from the synodical letter of this council that we have the fragment given above.

Bishop Victor then wished to exclude the bishops of Asia Minor from the communion of the Church; but other bishops turned him from his purpose. S. Irenæus, in particular, addressed a letter to him on this occasion, in the name of the bishops of Gaul, over whom he presided; a letter in which, it is true, he defended the Western custom of celebrating Easter, but in which also he prayed Victor not to excommunicate "a great number of churches, who were only guilty of observing an ancient custom," etc. This fragment has also been preserved to us by Eusebius; and we may consider it as a part of the synodical letter of the bishops of Gaul, since, as Eusebius makes him remark, Irenæus expressly declared "that he wrote in the name of his brethren of Gaul, over whom he presided." It may be asked if the synod here spoken of is the same as that mentioned by Eusebius in another place, and which we mentioned above. If it be the same, it must be admitted that, at the request of Victor, there was at first a synod of the Quartodecimans in Asia Minor, and that it was only later on, when the result was known, that other councils were also assembled, and especially in Gaul. It may be also that S. Irenæus presided over two successive councils in Gaul, and that in the first he declared himself for the Western practice regarding Easter, in the second against the threatening schism. This is the opinion of the latest biographer of S. Irenæus, the Abbé J. M. Prat. The Synodicon (Libellus Synodicus) only speaks of one synod in Gaul, presided over by Irenæus, on the subject of the Easter controversy; and he adds that this synod was composed of Irenæus and of thirteen other bishops.

The Libellus Synodicus also gives information about the other councils of which Eusebius speaks, concerning the question of Easter. Thus:

a. From the writing of the priests of Rome of which we have spoken, and which was signed by Pope Victor, the Libellus Synodicus concludes, as also does Valesius in his translation of the Eccles: Hist. of Eusebius, that there must have been a Roman synod at which, besides Victor, fourteen other bishops were present. This is opposed by Dom Constant in his excellent edition of the Epistolæ Pontif. p. 94, and after him by Mosheim in his book De Rebus Christianorum ante Constant. M. p. 267, who remarks that Eusebius speaks of a letter from the Roman priests and Pope Victor, and not of a synod. But it has often happened, especially in the following centuries, that the decrees of the synods, and in particular of the Roman synods, have only been signed by the president, and have been promulgated by him under the form of an edict emanating from him alone. This is what is expressly said by a Roman synod held by Pope Felix II. in 485.

b. According to the Synodicon, two synods were held in Palestine, on the subject of the Easter controversy: the one at Jerusalem, presided over by Narcissus, and composed of fourteen bishops; and the other at Cæsarea, comprising twelve bishops, and presided over by Theophilus.

c. Fourteen bishops were present at the Asiatic Synod of Pontus, under the presidency of Bishop Palmas, whom the Synodicon calls Plasmas.

d. Eighteen bishops were present at that of Osrhoëne; the Libellus Synodicus does not mention who presided.

e. It speaks also of a synod held in Mesopotamia, on the subject of Easter, which also counted eighteen bishops (it is probably the same synod as that of Osrhoëne).

f. And, lastly, of a synod at Corinth, presided over by Bishop Bacchyllus; whilst Eusebius says expressly that Bacchyllus of Corinth did not publish any synodical letter on the subject of the celebration of Easter, but simply a private letter.

SEC. 3. Doubtful Synods of the Second Century

The anonymous author of the Prædestinatus speaks of three other synods of the second century. According to him,

a. In A.D. 125 a synod was held of all the bishops of Sicily, presided over by Eustathius of Libybæum and Theodorus of Palermo. This synod considered the cause of the Gnostic Heraclionites, and sent its acts to Pope Alexander, that he might decide further in the matter.

b. In 152 the heresy of the Colarbasians, another Gnostic sect, was anathematized by Theodotus Bishop of Pergamum in Mysia, and by seven other bishops assembled in synod.

c. In 160 an Eastern synod rejected the heresy of the Gnostic Cerdo.

The Libellus Synodicus mentions, besides:

a. A synod held at Rome, under Pope Telesphorus (127–139), against the currier Theodotus, the anti-Trinitarian.

b. A second synod at Rome, held under Pope Anicetus, upon the Easter question, at the time when Polycarp Bishop of Smyrna visited the Pope.

c. A third Roman synod under Victor, and which condemned Theodotus, Ebion, and Artemon.

d. A fourth Roman synod, also held under Victor, and which anathematized Sabellius and Noëtus.

e. Finally, a synod of the confessors of Gaul, who declared against Montanus and Maximilla in a letter addressed to the Asiatics.

These eight synods mentioned by the author of Prædestinatus and by the Libellus Synodicus are apparently

Charles Joseph Hefele, D.D.

imaginary: for, on one side, there is not a single ancient and original document which speaks of them; and on the other, the statements of these two unknown authors are either unlikely or contrary to chronology. We will instance, for example, the pretended Roman synod, presided over by Victor, which anathematized Sabellius. In admitting that the usual date, according to which Sabellius would have lived a full half-century later (about 250), may be inexact, as the Philosophoumena recently discovered have proved, yet it is clear from this document that Sabellius had not yet been excluded from the Church under Pope Zephyrinus (202–218), the successor of Victor, and that he was not excommunicated until the time of Pope Calixtus.

It is also impossible that Theodotus the currier should have been condemned by a Roman synod held under Telesphorus, since Theodotus lived towards the close of the second century. It is the same with the pretended Sicilian Council in 125. According to the information afforded to us by the ancients, especially S. Irenæus and Tertullian, Heracleon changed the system of Valentine. He could not then have flourished till after 125. As to Pope Alexander, to whom this synod is said to have rendered an account of its acts in 125, he died a martyr in 119.

It is also by mistake that we have been told of a synod in which Pope Anicetus and Polycarp both took part. The interview of these two bishops has been confounded with a synod: it is the same with the pretended Synod of Gaul, held against Montanus.

The author of the Libellus Synodicus has evidently misunderstood Eusebius, who says on this subject: "The

111

news of what had taken place in Asia on the subject of Montanus (the synod) was known to the Christians of Gaul. The latter were at that time cruelly persecuted by Marcus Aurelius; many of them were in prison. They, however, gave their opinion from their prison on the matter of Montanus, and addressed letters to their brethren of Asia, and to Eleutherus Bishop of Rome." It will be seen that the question here is not of a synod, but of letters written by confessors (the Libellus Synodicus also mentions confessors).

Finally, a ninth council, which is said to have conveyed to the Bishop of Seleucia a patriarchal right over the whole of Assyria, Media, and Persia, is evidently an invention; and the mention of a Patriarchate on this occasion is a patent anachronism, as has been proved by Assemani in his Bibliothèque Orientale.

CHAPTER II
THE SYNODS OF THE THIRD CENTURY

SEC. 4. First Half of the Third Century

THE series of synods of the third century opens with that
of Carthage, to which Agrippinus bishop of that city had
called the bishops of Numidia and of proconsular Africa. S.
Cyprian speaks of this Synod in his seventy-first and
seventy-third letters, saying that all the bishops present
declared baptism administered by heretics to be void; and
he supports his own view on this subject by what had
passed in this ancient Synod of Carthage. This Synod was
probably the most ancient of Latin Africa; for Tertullian,
who recalls the Greek synods as a glory, tells not of one
single council being held in his country. According to
Uhlhorn it was about 205, according to Hesselburg about
212, that the work of Tertullian, de Jejuniis,. was composed;
therefore the Synod in question must have been held either
after 205 or after 212. It has not been possible up to this
time to verify this date more exactly. But the newly-
discovered φιλοσφούμενα, falsely attributed to Origen, and
which were probably written by Hippolytus, have given
more exact dates; and Döllinger, relying upon this
document, has placed the date of this Synod of Carthage
between 218 and 222. The Philosophoumena relate, indeed,
that the custom of re-baptizing—that is to say, of repeating
the baptism of those who had been baptized by heretics—
was introduced under the Bishop of Rome, Callistus (in
some churches in communion with him). One can scarcely
doubt but that this passage referred to Bishop Agrippinus
and his Synod at Carthage; for S. Augustine and S. Vincent
of Lérins say expressly that Agrippinus was the first who

introduced the custom of re-baptism. The Synod of Carthage, then, took place in the time of Pope Callistus I., that is to say, between 218 and 222. This date agrees with the well-known fact that Tertullian was the first of all Christian writers who declared the baptism of heretics invalid; and it may be presumed that his book de Baptismo exerted a certain influence upon the conclusions of the Council of Carthage. It is not contradicted by the forty-sixth (forty-seventh) apostolic canon, which orders bishops, under pain of deposition, to re-baptize those who had been baptized by a heretic; for it is known that these so-called apostolic canons were composed some centuries later.

S. Cyprian speaks, in his sixty-sixth letter, of a synod held long before (jampridem) in Africa, and which had decided that a clergyman could not be chosen by a dying person as a guardian; but nothing shows that he understood by that, the synod presided over by Agrippinus, or a second African council.

The great Origen gave occasion for two synods at Alexandria. About the year 228, being called into Achaia on account of the religious troubles reigning there, Origen passed through Palestine, and was ordained priest at Cæsarea by his friends Alexander Bishop of Jerusalem and Theoctistus Bishop of Cæsarea, although there were two reasons for his non-admission to holy orders: first, that he belonged to another diocese; and secondly, that he had castrated himself. It is not known what decided him or the bishops of Palestine to take this uncanonical step. Demetrius of Alexandria, diocesan bishop of Origen, was very angry with what had been done; and if we regard it from the ecclesiastical point of view, he was right. When

Origen returned to Alexandria, Demetrius told him of his displeasure, and reproached him with his voluntary mutilation. But the principal grievance, without doubt, had reference to several false doctrines held by Origen: for he had then already written his book de Principiis and his Stromata, which contain those errors; and it is not necessary to attribute to the Bishop of Alexandria personal feelings of hatred and jealousy in order to understand that he should have ordered an inquiry into Origen's opinions under the circumstances. Origen hastened to leave Alexandria of his own accord, according to Eusebius; whilst Epiphanius says, erroneously, that Origen fled because, shortly before, he had shown much weakness during a persecution. His bitterest enemies have never cast a reproach of this nature at him. Demetrius, however, assembled a synod of Egyptian bishops and priests of Alexandria in 231, who declared Origen unworthy to teach, and excluded him from the Church of Alexandria. Demetrius again presided over a second synod at Alexandria, without this time calling his priests, and Origen was declared to be deprived of the sacerdotal dignity. An encyclical letter published by Demetrius made these resolutions known in all the provinces.

According to S. Jerome and Rufinus, a Roman assembly, probably called under Pope Pontian, shortly after deliberated upon this judgment; and Origen after that sent to Pope Fabian (236–250) a profession of faith, to explain and retract his errors. Several writers have thought that the word senatus must not be understood in the sense of a synod, and that we are to consider it only as an assembly of the Roman clergy. Döllinger, on the contrary, presumes that Origen had taken part in the discussions of the priest Hippolytus with Pope Callistus and his successors (Origen had learned to know Hippolytus at Rome, and he partly agreed with his opinions), and that for this reason Pontian had held a synod against Origen.

A little before this period, and before the accession of Pope Fabian, a synod was certainly held at Iconium in Asia Minor, which must have been of great authority in the controversy which was soon to begin on the subject of the baptism of heretics. Like the Synod of Carthage, presided over by Agrippinus, that of Iconium declared every baptism conferred by a heretic to be invalid. The best information upon this Council has been furnished us by the letter which Bishop Firmilian of Cæsarea in Cappadocia, who showed himself so active in this controversy, addressed to S. Cyprian. It says: "Some having raised doubts upon the validity of baptism conferred by heretics, we decided long ago, in the Council held at Iconium in Phrygia, with the Bishops of Galatia, Cilicia, and the other neighbouring provinces, that the ancient practice against heretics should be maintained and held firm (not to regard baptism conferred by them)." Towards the end of the letter we read; "Among us, as more than one Church has never been recognised, so also have we never recognised as holy any but the baptism of that Church. Some having had doubts upon the validity of baptism conferred by those who receive new prophets (the Montanists), but who, however, appear to adore the same Father and the same Son as ourselves, we have assembled in great number at Iconium: we have very carefully examined the question (diligentissime tractavimus), and we have decided that all baptism administered outside the Church must be rejected." This letter then speaks of the Council of Iconium as of a fact already old; and it says also, that it was occasioned by the question of the validity of baptism administered by Montanists. Now, as Firmilian wrote this letter about the middle of the third century, it follows that the Council of Iconium, of which he often speaks as of an ancient assembly held long before (jampridem), took place about twenty years before the writing of his letter Dionysius Bishop of Alexandria, about the middle of the third century, also says: "It is not the Africans (Cyprian) who have introduced the custom of re-baptizing heretics: this measure had been taken long before Cyprian (πρὸ πολλοῦ), by other bishops at the Synod of Iconium and of Synnada."

In these two passages of his letter to S. Cyprian, Firmilian gives us a fresh means of fixing the date of the Synod of Iconium, saying formally several times: "We assembled ourselves at Iconium; we have examined the question; we have decreed," etc. It results from this, that he was himself present at this Synod. On the other side, the jampridem and other similar expressions justify us in placing this Synod in the first years of Firmilian's episcopate. Now we know from Eusebius that Firmilian flourished so early as in the time of the Emperor Alexander Severus (222–235) as Bishop of Cæsarea; so that we can, with Valesius and Pagi, place the celebration of the Synod of Iconium in the years 230–235. Baronius, by a very evident error, assigns it to the year 258.

According to all probability, we must refer to the Synod of Iconium a short passage of S. Augustine, in the third chapter of his third book against Cresconius, in which he speaks of a synod composed of fifty Eastern bishops.

Dionysius the Great, Bishop of Alexandria, speaks, we have seen, not only of the Synod of Iconium, but also of a Synod of Synnada, a town also situated in Phrygia. In this Synod, he says, the baptism by heretics was also rejected. We may conclude from his words that the two assemblies took place about the same time. We have no other information on this subject.

We know very little about the concilium Lambesitanum, which, says S. Cyprian, in his fifty-fifth letter to Pope Cornelius, had been held long before in the Lambesitana Colonia (in Numidia) by ninety bishops, and condemned a heretic named Privatus (probably Bishop of Lambese) as guilty of several grave offences." The Roman priests also mention this Privatus in their letter to S. Cyprian; but they do not give any further information concerning him.

A better known council was that which was held about the year 244, at Bostra in Arabia Petræa (now Bosrah and Bosserat), on account of the errors of Beryllus, bishop of this town. It is known that Beryllus belonged to the party of the Monarchians, generally called Patripassianists. This bishop held other erroneous opinions, which were peculiar to himself, and which it is now very difficult to distinguish.

The attempt made by the Arabian bishops to bring back Beryllus from his errors having failed, they called in Origen to their aid, who then lived at Cæsarea in Palestine. Origen came and conversed with Beryllus, first in private, then in presence of the bishops. The document containing the discussion was known to Eusebius and S. Jerome; but it was afterwards lost. Beryllus returned to the orthodox doctrine, and later expressed, it is said, his gratitude to Origen in a private letter.

Another controversy was raised in Arabia about the soul, as to whether it passed away (fell asleep) with the body, to rise (awake) at the resurrection of the body. At the request of one of the great Arabian synods, as Eusebius remarks, Origen had to argue against these Hypnopsychites, and he was as successful as in the affair of Beryllus. The Libellus Synodicus adds that fourteen bishops were present at the Synod, but it does not mention, any more than Eusebius, the place where it was held.

About the same period must also have been held two Asiatic synods, on the subject of the anti-Trinitarian (Patripassian) Noetus; S. Epiphanius is the only one to mention them, and he does so without giving any detail, and without saying where they took place. The assertion of the author of Prædestinatus, that about this time a synod was held in Achaia against the Valesians, who taught voluntary mutilation, is still more doubtful, and very probably false. The very existence of this sect is doubtful.

We are on more solid historical ground when we approach the tolerably numerous synods which were celebrated, chiefly in Africa, about the middle of the third century. The letters of S. Cyprian especially acquaint us with them. He first speaks, in his sixty-sixth letter, of an assembly of his colleagues (the bishops of Africa), and of his fellow-priests (the presbyters of Carthage), and so of a Carthaginian Synod, which had to decide upon a particular case of ecclesiastical discipline. A Christian named Geminius

Victor, of Furni in Africa, had on the approach of death appointed a priest named Geminius Faustinus as guardian to his children. We have seen above, that an ancient synod of Africa, perhaps that held under Agrippinus, had forbidden that a priest should be a guardian, because a clergyman ought not to occupy himself with such temporal business. The Synod of Carthage, held under S. Cyprian, renewed this prohibition, and ordained, in the spirit of that ancient council, that no prayers should be said or sacrifices (oblationes) offered for the deceased Victor, as he had no claim to the prayers of priests who had endeavoured to take a priest from the holy altar. In the letter of which we speak, S. Cyprian gave an account of this decision to the Christians of Furni. The Benedictines of Saint Maur presume that this letter was written before the outbreak of the persecution of Decius, which would place this Synod in the year 249.

SEC. 5. First Synods at Carthage and Rome on account of Novatianism and the "Lapsi" (251)

The schism of Felicissimus and the Novatian controversy soon afterwards occasioned several synods. When, in 248, S. Cyprian was elected Bishop of Carthage, there was a small party of malcontents there, composed of five priests, of whom he speaks himself in his fortieth letter. Soon after the commencement of the persecution of Decius (at the beginning of the year 250) the opposition to Cyprian became more violent, because in the interest of the discipline of the Church he would not always regard the letters of peace which some martyrs without sufficient consideration gave to the lapsi. He was accused of exaggerated severity against the fallen, and his own absence (from February 250 until the month of April or May 251) served to strengthen the party which was formed against him. An accident caused the schism to break out. Cyprian had from his retreat sent two bishops and two priests to Carthage, to distribute help to the faithful poor (many had been ruined by the persecution). The deacon Felicissimus opposed the envoys of Cyprian, perhaps because he considered, the care of the poor as an exclusive right of the deacons, and because he would not tolerate special commissioners from the bishop on such a business. This took place at the end of 250, or at the beginning of 251. Felicissimus had been ordained deacon by the priest Novatus unknown to Cyprian, and without his permission, probably during his retreat Now, besides the fact that such an ordination was contrary to all the canons of the Church, Felicissimus was personally unworthy of any ecclesiastical office, on account of his deceitfulness and his corrupt manners. Cyprian, being warned by his commissioners, excommunicated Felicissimus and some of his partisans on account of their disobedience; but the signal for revolt was given, and Felicissimus soon had with him those five priests who had been the old adversaries of Cyprian, as well as all those who accused the bishop of being too severe with regard to the lapsi, and of despising the letters of the martyrs. These contributed to give to the opposition quite another character. Till then it had only been composed of some disobedient priests; henceforth the party took for a war-cry the severity of the bishop with regard to the lapsi. Thus not only the lapsi, but also some confessors (confessores) who had been hurt by the little regard that Cyprian showed for the libelli pacis, swelled the ranks of the revolt. It is not known whether Novatus was in the number of the five priests who were the first movers of the party. By some it is asserted, by others denied. After, having in vain recalled the rebels to obedience, Cyprian returned to Carthage, a year after the festival of Easter in 251; and he wrote his book de Lapsis as a preparation for the Synod which he assembled soon afterwards, probably during the month of May 251. The Council was composed of a great number of bishops, and of some priests and deacons: he excommunicated Felicissimus and the five priests after having heard them, and at the same time set forth the principles to be followed with regard to the lapsi, after having carefully examined the passages of Scripture treating of this question. All the separate decrees upon this subject were collected into one book, which may be considered as the first penitential book which had appeared in the Church; but unfortunately it is lost. Cyprian makes us acquainted with the principal rules in his fifty-second letter: namely, that all hope must not be taken away from the lapsed, that, in excluding them from the Church, they may not be driven to abandon the faith, and to fall back again into a life of heathenism; that, notwithstanding, a long penance must be imposed upon them, and that they must be punished proportionally to their fault.1 It is evident, continues Cyprian, that one must act differently with those who have gone, so to speak, to meet apostasy, spontaneously taking part in the impious sacrifices, and those who have been, as it were, forced to this odious sacrilege after long struggles and cruel sufferings: so also with those who have carried. with them in their crime their wife, their children, their servants, their friends, making them also share their fall, and those who have only been the victims, who have sacrificed to the gods in order to serve their families and their houses; that there should no less be a difference between the sacrificati and the libellatici, that is to say, between those who had really sacrificed to the gods, and those who, without making a formal act of apostasy, had profited by the weakness of the Roman functionaries, had seduced them, and had made them give them false attestations; that the libellatici must be reconciled immediately, but that the sacrificati must submit to a long penance, and only be reconciled as the moment of their death approached; finally, that as for the bishops and priests, they must also be admitted to penance, but not again permitted to discharge any episcopal or sacerdotal function.

Jovinus and Maximus, two bishops of the party of Felicissimus, who had been reproved before by nine bishops for having sacrificed to the gods, and for having committed abominable sacrilege, appeared before the Synod of Carthage. The Synod renewed the sentence originally given against them; but in spite of this decree, they dared again to present themselves, with several of their partisans, at the Synod of Carthage, held the following year.

Cyprian and the bishops assembled around him decided to send their synodical decisions of 251 to Rome, to Pope Cornelius, to obtain his consent with regard to the measures taken against the lapsi. It was the more necessary to understand each other on the subject of these measures, as the Roman Church had also been troubled by the Novatian schism. Pope Cornelius assembled at Rome in the autumn—probably in the month of October 251—a synod composed of sixty bishops, without counting the priests and deacons. The Synod confirmed the decrees of that of

Carthage, and excommunicated Novatian and his partisans. The two authors who have preserved these facts for us are Cyprian and Eusebius. It must be remarked that several editors of the acts of the councils, and several historians, misunderstanding the original documents, have turned the two Synods of Carthage and Rome (251) into four councils. The Libellus Synodicus also speaks of another council which must have been held the same year at Antioch, again on the subject of the Novatians; but one can hardly rely on the Libellus Synodicus when it is alone in relating a fact.

The Novatian schism could not be extirpated by these synods. The partisans of Felicissimus and of Novatian made great efforts to recover their position. The Novatians of Carthage even succeeded in putting at their head a bishop of their party named Maximus, and they sent many complaints to Rome on the subject of Cyprian's pretended severity, as, on the other side, the persecution which was threatening made fresh measures necessary with regard to the lapsi. Cyprian assembled a fresh council at Carthage on the Ides of May 252, which sixty-six bishops attended. It was probably at this council that two points were discussed which were brought forward by the African Bishop Fidus. Fidus complained at first that Therapius Bishop of Bulla (near Hippo) had received the priest Victor too soon into the communion of the Church, and without having first imposed upon him the penance he deserved. The Synod declared that it was evidently contrary to the former decisions of the councils, but that they would content themselves for this time with blaming Bishop Therapius, without declaring invalid the reconciliation of the priest Victor, which he had effected. In the second place, Fidus enunciated the opinion that infants should be baptized, not in the first days after their birth, but eight days after; to observe, with regard to baptism, the delay formerly prescribed for circumcision. The Synod unanimously condemned this opinion, declaring that they could not thus delay to confer grace on the new-born.

The next principal business of the Synod was that concerning the lapsi; and the fifty-fourth letter of S. Cyprian gives us an account of what passed on this subject. The Synod, he says, on this subject decided that, considering the imminent persecution, they might immediately reconcile all those who showed signs of repentance, in order to prepare them for the battle by means of the holy sacraments: Idoneus esse non potest ad martyrium qui ab Ecclesia non armatur ad prælium. In addressing its synodical letter to Pope Cornelius (it is the fifty-fourth of S. Cyprian's letters), the Council says formally: Placuit nobis, sancto Spiritu suggerente. The heretic Privatus, of the colonia Lambesitana, probably bishop of that town, who, as we have seen, had been condemned, again appeared at the Council; but he was not admitted. Neither would they admit Bishops Jovinus and Maximus, partisans of Felicissimus, and condemned as he was; nor the false Bishop Felix, consecrated by Privatus after he became a heretic, who came with him. They then united themselves with the fallen bishop Repostus Saturnicensis, who had sacrificed during the persecution, and they gave the priest Fortunatus as bishop to the lax party at Carthage. He had been one of S. Cyprian's five original adversaries.

A short time after, a new synod assembled at Carthage on the subject of the Spanish bishops Martial and Basilides. Both had been deposed for serious faults, especially for having denied the faith. Basilides had judged himself to be unworthy of the episcopal dignity, and declared himself satisfied if, after undergoing his penance, he might be received into lay communion. Martial had also confessed his fault; but after some time they both appealed to Rome, and by means of false accounts they succeeded in gaining over Pope Stephen, who demanded that Basilides should be replaced in his bishopric, although Sabinus had been already elected to succeed him. Several Spanish bishops seem to have supported the pretensions of Basilides and Martial, and placed themselves, it appears, on their side; but the Churches of Leon, of Asturia, and of Emerita, wrote on this subject to the African bishops, and sent two deputies to them—Bishops Sabinus and Felix, probably the elected successors of Basilides and Martial Felix Bishop of Saragossa supported them with a private letter. S. Cyprian then assembled a council composed of thirty-seven bishops; and we possess the synodical letter of the assembly, in his sixty-eighth epistle, in which the deposition of Martial and Basilides is confirmed, the election of their successors is declared to be legitimate and regular, the bishops who had spoken in favour of the deposed bishops are censured, and the people are instructed to enter into ecclesiastical communion with their successors.

SEC. 6. Synods relative to the Baptism of Heretics (255–256)

To these synods concerning the lapsi, succeeded three African councils on the subject of baptism by heretics. We have seen that three former councils—that of Carthage, presided over by Agrippinus; two of Asia Minor, that of Iconium, presided over by Firmilian, and that of Synnada, held at the same period—had declared that baptism conferred by heretics was invalid. This principle, and the consequent practice in Asia Minor, would appear to have occasioned, towards the end of the year 253, a conflict between Pope Stephen and the bishops of Asia Minor, Helenus of Tarsus and Firmilian of Cæsarea, sustained by all the bishops of Cilicia, of Cappadocia, and the neighbouring provinces; so that Stephen, according to Dionysius the Great, threatened these bishops with excommunication because they repeated the baptism conferred by heretics. Dionysius the Great mediated with the Pope in favour of the bishops of Asia Minor; and the letter which he wrote prevented their being excluded from the Church. The first sentence of this letter would even allow it to be supposed that peace was completely re-established, and that the bishops of Asia Minor had conformed to the demand of the Pope. However, later on, Firmilian is again found in opposition to Rome.

The Easterns then stirred up the controversy on the baptism of heretics before S. Cyprian; and when Eusebius says, πρῶτος τῶν τότε Κυπριανός, κ.τ.λ., this passage must be thus understood: Cyprian was the most important, and in this sense the first, of those who demanded the re-baptism of heretics.

Let us now turn our attention to Africa, and particularly to S. Cyprian. Some African bishops being of the opinion that those who abandoned heretical sects to enter the Church must not be re-baptized, eighteen bishops of Numidia, who held a different opinion, and rejected baptism by heretics, asked of the Synod of Carthage of 255 if it were necessary to re-baptize those who had been baptized by heretics or schismatics, when they entered the Church. At this Synod, presided over by S. Cyprian, there were twenty-one bishops present: the seventieth epistle of Cyprian is nothing but the answer of the Synod to the eighteen Numidian bishops. It declares "that their opinion about the baptism of heretics is perfectly right; for no one can be baptized out of the Church, seeing there is only one baptism which is in the Church," etc.

Shortly afterwards, Cyprian being again consulted on the same question by Quintus, bishop in Mauritania, who sent him the priest Lucian, sent in answer the synodical letter of the Council which had just separated; and besides, in a private letter joined to this official document, he stated his personal opinion on the validity of the baptism of heretics, and answered some objections.

All the bishops of Africa were probably not satisfied with these decisions; and some time after, about 256, Cyprian saw himself obliged to assemble a second and larger council at Carthage, at which no fewer than seventy-one bishops were present. S. Cyprian relates that they treated of a multitude of questions, but the chief point was the baptism of heretics. The synodical letter of this great assembly, addressed to Pope Stephen, forms S. Cyprian's seventieth letter. The Council also sent to the Pope the letter of the preceding Synod to the eighteen Numidian bishops, as well as the letter of S. Cyprian to Quintus, and reiterated the assertion "that whoso abandoned a sect ought to be re-baptized;" adding, "that it was not sufficient (parum est) to lay hands on such converts ad accipiendum Spiritum sanctum, if they did not also receive the baptism of the Church." The same Synod decided that those priests and deacons who had abandoned the catholic Church for any of the sects, as well as those who had been ordained by the sectarian false bishops, on re-entering the Church, could only be admitted into lay communion (communio laicalis). At the end of their letter, the Synod express the hope that these decisions would obtain Stephen's approval: they knew, besides, they said, that many do not like to renounce an opinion which has once been adopted; and more than one bishop, without breaking with his colleagues, will doubtless be tempted to persevere in the custom which he had embraced. Besides this, it is not the intention of the Synod to do violence to any one, or to prescribe a universal law, seeing that each bishop can cause his will to be paramount in the administration of his Church, and will have to render an account of it to God. "These words," Mattes has remarked, "betray either the desire which the bishops of Africa had to see Stephen produce that agreement by his authority, which did not yet exist, and which was not easy to establish; or else their apprehensions, because they knew that there was a practice at Rome which did not accord with the opinion of Cyprian." This last was, in fact, the case; for Pope Stephen was so little pleased with the decisions of the Council of Carthage, that he did not allow the deputies of the African bishops to appear before him, refused to communicate with them, forbade all the faithful to receive them into their houses, and did not hesitate to call S. Cyprian a false Christian, a false apostle, a deceitful workman (dolosus operarius). This is at least what Firmilian relates. Pope Stephen then pronounced very explicitly, in opposition to the Africans, for the validity of the baptism of heretics, and against the custom of repeating the baptism of those who had already received it from heretics. The letter which he wrote on this occasion to Cyprian has unfortunately been lost, and therefore his complete argument is unknown to us; but Cyprian and Firmilian have preserved some passages of the letter of Stephen in their writings, and it is these short fragments, with the comments of Cyprian and Firmilian, which must serve to make known to us with some certainty the view of Stephen on the baptism of heretics.

It is commonly admitted that S. Cyprian answered this violence of Stephen's by assembling the third Council of Carthage; but it is also possible that this assembly took place before the arrival of the letter from Rome. It was composed of eighty-seven bishops (two were represented by one proxy, Natalis Bishop of Oëa) from proconsular Africa, from Numidia, and from Mauritania, and of a great number of priests and of deacons. A multitude of the laity were also present at the Synod. The acts of this Synod, which still exist, inform us that it opened on the 1st September, but the year is not indicated. It is probable that it was in 256.

First was read the letter of the African Bishop Jubaianus to Cyprian on the baptism of heretics, and the answer of Cyprian; then a second letter from Jubaianus, in which he declared himself now brought to Cyprian's opinion. The Bishop of Carthage then asked each bishop present freely to express his opinion on the baptism of heretics: he declared that no one would be judged or excommunicated for differences of opinion; for, added he, no one in the assembly wished to consider himself as episcopus episcoporum, or thought to oblige his colleagues to yield to him, by inspiring them with a tyrannical fear (perhaps this was an allusion to Pope Stephen). Thereupon the bishops gave their votes in order, Cyprian the last, all declaring that baptism given by heretics was invalid, and that, in order to admit them into the Church, it was necessary to re-baptize those who had been baptized by heretics.

About the same time Cyprian sent the deacon Rogatian with a letter to Firmilian Bishop of Cæsarea, to tell him how the question about the baptism of heretics had been decided in Africa. He communicated to him at the same time, it appears, the acts and documents which treated of this business. Firmilian hastened to express, in a letter still extant, his full assent to Cyrian's principles. This letter of Firmilian's forms No. 75 of the collection of the letters of S. Cyprian: its contents are only, in general, an echo of what S. Cyprian had set forth in defence of his own opinion, and in opposition to Stephen; only in Firmilian is seen a much greater violence and passion against Stephen,—so much so, that Molkenbuhr, Roman Catholic Professor at Paderborn, has thought that a letter so disrespectful towards the Pope could not be genuine.

We are entirely ignorant of what then passed between Cyprian and Stephen, but it is certain that church communion was not interrupted between them. The persecution which soon afterwards broke out against the Christians under the Emperor Valerian, in 257, probably appeased the controversy. Pope Stephen died as a martyr during this persecution, in the month of August 257. His successor Xystus received from Dionysius the Great, who had already acted as mediator in this controversy on the baptism of heretics, three letters in which the author earnestly endeavoured to effect a reconciliation; the Roman priest Philemon also received one from Dionysius. These attempts were crowned with success; for Pontius, Cyprian's deacon and biographer, calls Pope Xystus bonus et pacificus sacerdos, and the name of this Pope was written in the diptychs of Africa. The eighty-second letter of Cyprian also proves that the union between Rome and Carthage was not interrupted, since Cyprian sent a deputation to Rome during the persecution, to obtain information respecting the welfare of the Roman Church, that of Pope Xystus, and in general about the progress of the persecution. Soon after, on the 14th September 258, Cyprian himself fell, in his turn, a victim to the persecution of Valerian.

It remains for us now, in order fully to understand the controversy on the baptism of heretics, to express with greater precision the opinions and assertions of Cyprian and Stephen.

1. We must ask, first of all, which of the two had Christian antiquity on his side.

a. Cyprian says, in his seventy-third letter: "The custom of baptizing heretics who enter the Church is no innovation amongst us: for it is now many years since, under the episcopate of Agrippinus of holy memory, a great number of bishops settled this question in a synod; and since then, up to our days, thousands of heretics have received baptism without difficulty." Cyprian, then, wishing to demonstrate the antiquity of his custom, could not place it earlier than

Agrippinus, that is to say, than the commencement of the third century (about 220 years after Christ); and his own words, especially the "since then" (exinde), show that it was Agrippinus who introduced this custom into Africa.

b. In another passage of the same letter, Cyprian adds: "Those who forbid the baptism of heretics, having been conquered by our reasons (ratione), urge against us the custom of antiquity (qui ratione vincuntur, consuetudinem nobis opponunt)." If Cyprian had been able to deny that the practice of his adversaries was the most ancient, he would have said: "They are wrong if they appeal to antiquity (consuetudo); it is evidently for us." But Cyprian says nothing of the kind: he acknowledges that his adversaries have antiquity on their side, and he only tries to take its force from this fact, by asking, "Is antiquity, then, more precious than truth? (quasi consuetudo major sit veritate);" and by adding, "In spiritual things we must observe what the Holy Spirit has (afterwards) more fully revealed (id in spiritualibus sequendum, quod in melius fuerit a Spiritu sancto revelatum)." He acknowledges, therefore, in his practice a progress brought about by the successive revelations of the Holy Spirit.

c. In a third passage of this letter, S. Cyprian acknowledges, if possible more plainly, that it was not the ancient custom to re-baptize those who had been baptized by heretics. "This objection," he says, "may be made to me: What has become of those who in past times entered the Church from heresy, without having been baptized?" He acknowledges, then, that in the past, in præteritum, converts from heresy were not re-baptized. Cyprian makes answer to this question: "Divine mercy may well come to their aid; but because one has erred once, it is no reason for continuing to err (non tamen, quia aliquando erratum est, ideo semper errandum est)." That is to say, formerly converts were not re-baptized; but it was a mistake, and for the future the Holy Spirit has revealed what is best to be done (in melius a Spiritu sancto revelatum).

d. When Pope Stephen appealed to tradition, Cyprian did not answer by denying the fact: he acknowledges it; but he seeks to diminish the value of it, by calling this tradition a human tradition, and not legitimate (humana traditio, non legitima).

e. Firmilian also maintained that the tradition to which Stephen appealed was purely human, and he added that the Roman Church had also in other points swerved from the practice of the primitive Church—for example, in the celebration of Easter. This example, however, was not well chosen, since the Easter practice of the Roman Church dates back to the prince of the apostles.

f. Firmilian says, in another passage of this same letter, that it was anciently the custom also in the African Churches not to re-baptize the converts: "You Africans," he says, "can answer Stephen, that having found the truth, you have renounced the error of your (previous) custom (vos dicere Afri potestis, cognita veritate errorem vos consuetudinis reliquisse)." Nevertheless, Firmilian thought that it was otherwise in Asia Minor, and that the custom of re-baptizing converts was traced back to a very far-off period; but when he wishes to give the proof of it, he only finds this one: "We do not remember (!) when this practice began amongst us." He appeals, in the last place, to the Synod of

Iconium, which we know was not held until about the year 230.

g. It is worthy of remark, that even in Africa all the bishops did not pronounce in favour of the necessity of a fresh baptism, which would certainly have been the case if the practice of Agrippinus and Cyprian had always prevailed in Africa.

h. A very important testimony in favour of Stephen, and one which proves that the ancient custom was not to re-baptize, is given by the anonymous author of the book de Rebaptismate, a contemporary and probably a colleague of Cyprian. This author says that the practice maintained by Stephen, that of simply laying hands on the converts without re-baptizing them, is consecrated by antiquity and by ecclesiastical tradition (vetustissima consuetudine ac traditione ecclesiastica), consecrated as an ancient, memorable, and solemn observance by all the saints, and all the faithful (prisca et memorabilis cunctorum emeritorum sanctorum et fidelium solemnissima observatio), which has in its favour the authority of all the churches (auctoritas omnium Ecclesiarum), but from which unhappily some have departed, from the mania for innovations.

i. S. Vincent of Lérins agrees with the author we have just quoted, when he says that Agrippinus of Carthage was the first who introduced the custom of re-baptizing, contra divinum canonem, contra universalis Ecclesiæ regulam, contra morem atque instituta majorum; but that Pope Stephen condemned the innovation and re-established the tradition, retenta est antiquitas, explosa novitas.

k. S. Augustine also believes that the custom of not re-baptizing heretics is an apostolical tradition (credo ex apostolica traditione venientem), and that it was Agrippinus who was the first to abolish this very safe custom (saluberrima consuetudo), without succeeding in replacing it by a better custom, as Cyprian thought.

l. But the gravest testimony in this question is that of the Philosophoumena, in which Hippolytus, who wrote about 230, affirms that the custom of re-baptizing was only admitted under Pope Callistus, consequently between 218 and 222.

m. Before arriving at the conclusion to be deduced from all these proofs, it remains for us to examine some considerations which appear to point in an opposite direction.

(a.) In his book de Baptismo, which he wrote when he was still a Cátholic, and before this work in a Greek document, Tertullian shows that he did not believe in the validity of baptism conferred by heretics. But, on considering it attentively, we find that he was not speaking of all baptism by heretics, but only of the baptism of those who had another God and another Christ. Besides, we know that Tertullian is always inclined to rigorism, and he certainly is so on this point; and then, living at Carthage at the commencement of the third century, being consequently a contemporary of Agrippinus, perhaps even being one of his clergy, he naturally inclined to resolve this question as Agrippinus resolved it, and his book de Baptismo perhaps exerted an influence upon the resolutions of the Synod of Carthage. Also Tertullian does not pretend that it was the primitive custom of the Church to re-baptize: his words rather indicate that he thought the contrary. He says, Sed circa hæreticos sane quid custodiendum sit, digne quis retractet; that is to say, "It would be useful if some one would study afresh (or examine more attentively) what ought to be done about heretics, that is to say, in relation to their baptism."

(β.) Dionysius the Great says, in a passage which Eusebius has preserved: "The Africans were not the first to introduce this practice (that of re-baptizing converts): it is more ancient; it was authorized by bishops who lived much earlier, and in populous Churches." However, as he only mentions the Synods of Iconium and of Synnada before the Africans, his expression much earlier can only refer to these assemblies, and he adduces no earlier testimony for the practice of Cyprian.

(γ.) Clement of Alexandria certainly speaks very disdainfully of baptism by heretics, and calls it a foreign water; he does not, however, say that they were in the habit of renewing this baptism.

(δ.) The Apostolical Canons 45 and 46 (or 46 and 47, according to another order) speak of the non-validity of baptism by heretics; but the question is to know what is the date of these two canons: perhaps they are contemporary with the Synods of Iconium and of Synnada, perhaps even more recent.

We are hardly able to doubt, then, that in the ancient Church, those who returned to the orthodox faith, after having been baptized by heretics, were not re-baptized, if they had received baptism in the name of the Trinity, or of JESUS.

2. Let us see now whether Pope Stephen considered as valid baptism conferred by all heretics, without any exception or condition. We know that the Synod of Arles in 314, as well as the Council of Trent, teaches that the baptism of heretics is valid only when it is administered in the name of the Father, of the Son, and of the Holy Ghost. Were the opinions and assertions of Stephen agreeable to this doctrine of the Church?

At first sight Stephen appears to have gone too far, and to have admitted all baptism by heretics, in whatever manner it was conferred. His chief proposition, as we read it in S. Cyprian, is expressed in these terms: Si quis ergo a quacunque hæresi venerit ad nos, nil innovetur nisi quod traditum est, ut manus illi imponatur in pœnitentiam. He seems, then, to declare valid all baptism by heretics, in whatever manner it might have been administered, with or without the formula of the Trinity. Cyprian argues, in a measure, as if he understood Stephen's proposition in this sense. However,

a. From several passages in the letters of S. Cyprian, we see that Pope Stephen did not thus understand it.

(α.) Thus (Epist. 73, p. 130) Cyprian says: "Those who forbid the baptism of heretics lay great stress upon this, that even those who had been baptized by Marcion were not re-baptized, because they had already been baptized in the name of Jesus Christ." Thus Cyprian acknowledges that Stephen, and those who think with him, attribute no value to the baptism of heretics, except it be administered in the name of Jesus Christ.

(β.) Cyprian acknowledges in the same letter (p. 133), that heretics baptize in nomine Christi.

(γ.) Again, in this letter, he twice repeats that his adversaries considered as sufficient baptism administered out of the Church, but administered in nomine Christi.

(δ.) Cyprian, in answering this particular question—if baptism by the Marcionites is valid—acknowledges that they baptize in the name of the Trinity; but he remarks that, under the name of the Father, of the Son, and of the Holy Ghost, they understand something different from what the Church understands. This argument leads us to conclude that the adversaries of S. Cyprian considered baptism by the Marcionites to be valid, because they conferred it in the name of the Trinity.

b. Firmilian also gives testimony on the side of Stephen.

(α.) He relates, indeed, that about twenty-two years before he had baptized a woman in his own country who professed to be a prophetess, but who, in fact, was possessed by an evil spirit. Now, he asks, would Stephen and his partisans approve even of the baptism which she had received, because it had been administered with the formula of the Trinity (maxime cui nec symbolum Trinitatis defuit)?

(β.) In the same letter Firmilian sums up Stephen's opinion in these terms: In multum proficit nomen Christi ad fidem et baptismi sanctificationem, ut quicunque et ubicunque in nomine Christi baptizatus fuerit, consequatur statim gratiam Christi.

c. If, then, Cyprian and Firmilian affirm that Pope Stephen held baptism to be valid only when conferred in the name of Christ, we have no need to have recourse to the testimony either of S. Jerome, or of S. Augustine, or of S. Vincent of Lérins, who also affirm it.

d. The anonymous author of the book de Rebaptismate, who was a contemporary even of S. Cyprian, begins his work with these words: "There has been a dispute as to the manner in which it is right to act towards those who have been baptized by heretics, but still in the name of Jesus Christ: qui in hæresi quidem, sed in nomine Dei nostri Jesu Christi, sinttincti."

e. It may again be asked if Stephen expressly required that the three divine Persons should be named in the administration of baptism, and if he required it as a condition sine qua non, or if he considered baptism as valid when given only in the name of Jesus Christ. S. Cyprian seems to imply that the latter was the sentiment of Pope Stephen, but he does not positively say so anywhere; and if he had said it, nothing could have been legitimately concluded against Pope Stephen, for Cyprian likes to take the words of his adversaries in their worst sense. What we have gathered (α δ and b a) tends to prove that Pope Stephen regarded the formula of the Trinity as necessary. Holy Scripture had introduced the custom of calling by the short phrase, baptism in the name of Christ, all baptism which was conferred in virtue of faith in Jesus Christ, and conformably to His precepts, consequently in the name of the Holy Trinity, as is seen in the Acts of the Apostles and in the Epistle to the Romans. It is not, then, astonishing that Pope Stephen should have used an expression which was perfectly intelligible at that period.

f. In this discussion Pope Stephen seems to believe that all the heretics of his time used the true formula of baptism, consequently the same formula among themselves, and the same as the Church. He declares this opinion clearly in these words, adduced from his letter by Firmilian: Stephanus in sua epistola dixit: hæreticos quoque ipsos in baptismo convenire; and it was on this account, added the Pope, that the heretics did not re-baptize those who passed from one sect to another. To speak thus, was certainly to affirm that all the sects agreed in administering baptism with the formula prescribed by our Lord.

S. Cyprian also attributes to Pope Stephen words which can be explained very well if we study them with reference to those quoted by Firmilian. According to S. Cyprian, Stephen had said: "We must not re-baptize those who have been baptized by heretics, cum ipsi hæretici proprie alterutrum ad se venientes non baptizent;" that is to say, the different sects have not a special baptism of their own (proprie non baptizent): and it is for this reason that heretics do not re-baptize those who pass from one sect to another. Now if the different sects have not special baptism, if they baptize in the same way—conveniunt in baptismo—as Firmilian makes Pope Stephen affirm, they hold necessarily the universal and primitive mode of Christian baptism; consequently they use the formula of the Trinity.

It is difficult to say whether, in admitting this hypothesis, Stephen falls into an historical error: for, on one side, S. Irenæus accuses the Gnostics of having falsified the baptismal formula, and of having used different erroneous formulas; and consequently he contradicts Stephen; and, on the other side, S. Augustine appears to agree with him, saying: Facilius inveniuntur hæretici qui omnino non baptizent quam qui non illis verbis (in nomine Patris, etc.) baptizent.

g. We may be inclined to make an objection against Stephen on the subject of the Montanists. There is no doubt, in fact, that Stephen considered the baptism of these heretics to be valid, while the Church afterwards declared it to be of no value. But Stephen's opinion is not in this contrary to the doctrine of the Church; neither did the Council of Nicæa (can. 19) mention the Montanists among those whose baptism it rejected. It could not do so any more than Stephen; for it was not until long after the time of Stephen and of the Council of Nicæa that a degenerate sect of Montanists fell away into formal anti-Trinitarianism.

3. It remains for us to understand what, according to Stephen's opinion, was to be done with the converts after their reception into the Church. These are Stephen's words on this subject: Si quis ergo a quacumque hæresi venerit ad nos, nil innovetur nisi quod traditum est, ut manus illi imponatur in pœnitentiam. There is a sense which is often given to this passage, as follows: "No innovation shall be made; only what is conformable to tradition shall be observed; hands shall be laid on the convert in sign of penitence." But this interpretation is contrary to grammatical rules. If Stephen had wished to speak in this

sense, he would have said: Nihil innovetur, sed quod traditum est observetur, etc. Hence Mattes translates the words of Stephen thus: "Nothing shall be changed (as regards the convert) but what it is according to tradition to change; that is to say, that hands shall be laid upon him," etc.

Stephen adds, in pœnitentiam, that is, that "it is necessary that a penance should be imposed on the convert." According to the practice of the Church, a heretic who enters into the Church ought first to receive the sacrament of penance, then that of confirmation. One may ask, if Stephen required these two sacraments, or if he only required that of penance? Each of these sacraments comprehended the imposition of hands, as some words of Pope Vigilius clearly indicate; and consequently by the expression, manus illi imponatur, Stephen may understand the administration of the two sacraments. To say that there is only in pœnitentiam in the text, is not a very strong objection; for this text is only a fragment, and Cyprian has transmitted to us elsewhere other texts of Stephen's thus abridged. The manner in which the adversaries of Pope Stephen analysed his opinions shows that this Pope really required, besides penance, the confirmation of the converts. Thus, in his seventy-third letter, Cyprian accuses his adversaries of self-contradiction, saying: "If baptism out of the Church is valid, it is no longer necessary even to lay hands on the converts, ut Spiritum Sanctum consequatur et signetur;" that is to say: You contradict yourselves if you attribute a real value to baptism by heretics; you must also equally admit the validity of confirmation by heretics. Now you require that those who have been confirmed by heretics should be so again. S. Cyprian here forgets the great difference which exists between the value of baptism and of confirmation; but his words prove that Stephen wished that penance and confirmation should be bestowed upon converts.

The same conclusion is to be drawn from certain votes of the bishops assembled at the third Council of Carthage (256). Thus Secundinus Bishop of Carpi said: "The imposition of hands (without the repetition of baptism, as Stephen required) cannot bring down the Holy Spirit upon the converts, because they have not yet even been baptized." Nemesianus Bishop of Thubuni speaks still more clearly: "They (the adversaries) believe that by imposition of hands the Holy Spirit is imparted, whilst regeneration is possible only when one receives the two sacraments (baptism and confirmation) in the Church." These two testimonies prove that Stephen regarded confirmation as well as penance to be necessary for converts.

4. What precedes shows that we must consider as incorrect and unhistorical the widespread opinion, that both Stephen and Cyprian carried things to an extreme, and that the proper mean was adopted by the Church only as the result of their differences.

5. It is the part of Dogmatic Theology, rather than of a History of the Councils, to show why Cyprian was wrong, and why those who had been baptized by heretics should not be re-baptized. Some short explanation on this point will, however, not be out of place here.

S. Cyprian repeated essentially Tertullian's argument, yet without naming it, and thus summed it up: "As there is only one Christ, so there is only one Church: she only is the way of salvation; she only can administer the sacraments; out of her pale no sacrament can be validly administered." He adds: "Baptism forgives sins: now Christ left only to the apostles the power of forgiving sins; then heretics cannot be possessed of it, and consequently it is impossible for them to baptize." Finally, he concludes: "Baptism is a new birth; by it children are born to God in Christ: now the Church only is the bride of Christ; she only can, therefore, be the means of this new birth."

In his controversy against the Donatists (who revived Cyprian's doctrine on this point), S. Augustine demonstrated with great completeness, and his accustomed spiritual power, two hundred and fifty years afterwards, that this line of argument was unsound, and that the strongest grounds existed for the Church's practice defended by Stephen. The demonstration of S. Augustine is as simple as powerful. He brought out these three considerations:—

a. Sinners are separated spiritually from the Church, as heretics are corporally. The former are as really out of the Church as the latter: if heretics could not legally baptize, sinners could not either; and thus the validity of the sacrament would absolutely depend upon the inward state of the minister.

b. We must distinguish between the grace of baptism and the act of baptism: the minister acts, but it is God who gives the grace; and He can give it even by means of an unworthy minister.

c. The heretic is, without any doubt, out of the Church; but the baptism which he confers is not an alien baptism, for it is not his, it is Christ's baptism, the baptism which He confers, and consequently a true baptism, even when conferred out of the Church. In leaving the Church, the heretics have taken many things away with them, especially faith in Jesus Christ and baptism. These fragments of Church truth are the elements, still pure (and not what they have as heretics), which enable them by baptism to give birth to children of God.

After S. Augustine, S. Thomas Aquinas, S. Bonaventura, the editors of the Roman Catechism, and others, have discussed the question anew; and the principal propositions upon which the whole subject turns are the following:—

(α.) He who baptizes is a simple instrument, and Christ can use any instrument whatever, provided that he does what Christ (the Church) wills that he should do. This instrument only performs the act of baptism; the grace of baptism comes from God. Thus any man, even a heathen, can administer baptism, provided that he will do as the Church does; and this latitude with respect to the administrant of baptism is not without reason: it is founded upon this, that baptism is really necessary as a means of salvation.

(β.) Baptism, then, by a heretic will be valid, if it is administered in the name of the Father, and of the Son, and of the Holy Ghost, and with the intention of doing as the Church does (intentio faciendi, quod facit ecclesia).

(γ.) Should he who has thus been baptized, after remaining a long time in heresy, acknowledge his error and his separation from the Church, he ought, in order to be admitted into the Church, to submit to a penance (manus impositio ad pœnitentiam); but it is not necessary to re-baptize him.

(δ.) The sacraments are often compared to channels through which divine grace comes to us. Then, when any one is baptized in a heretical sect, but is baptized according to the rules, the channel of grace is truly applied to him, and there flows to him through this channel not only the remission of sins (remissio peccatorum), but also sanctification and the renewal of the inner man (sanctificatio et renovatio interioris hominis); that is to say, he receives the grace of baptism.

(ε.) It is otherwise with confirmation. From the time of the apostles, they only, and never the deacons, their fellow-workers, had the power of giving confirmation. Now, too, it is only the legitimate successors of the apostles, the bishops, who can administer this sacrament in the Church. If, therefore, any one has been confirmed whilst he was in heresy, he can have been so only by a schismatical or heretical bishop or priest; so that his confirmation must be invalid, and it is necessary that the imposition of hands should be repeated, ut Spiritum sanctum consequatur et signetur.

Doctor Mattes has brought out, with much depth, in the dissertation which we have already frequently quoted, the different reasons for believing that baptism and marriage may be administered by those who are not Christians.

SEC. 7. Synod of Narbonne (255–260)

The councils of Christian Africa have chiefly occupied our attention so far: we are now to direct attention to those of the other countries of the Roman Empire, and first to those of Gaul. It is known that, about the middle of the third century, seven missionary bishops were sent into Gaul by Pope Fabian, and that one of them was S. Paul, first bishop of Narbonne. The acts of his life which have reached us speak of a synod held at Narbonne on his account between 255 and 260. Two deacons, whom the holy bishop had often blamed for their incontinence, wished to revenge themselves on him in a diabolical manner. They secretly put a pair of women's slippers under his bed, and then showed them in proof of the bishop's impurity. Paul found himself obliged to assemble his colleagues in a synod, that they might judge of his innocence or culpability. While the bishops continued the inquiry for three days, an eagle came and placed itself upon the roof of the house where they were assembled. Nothing could drive it away, and during those three days a raven brought it food. On the third day Paul ordered public prayer that God would make known the truth. The deacons were then seized by an evil spirit, and so tormented, that they ended by confessing their perfidy and calumny. They could only be delivered through prayer, and they renewed their confession. Instead of judging Paul, the bishops threw themselves at his feet, and with all the people entreated his intercession with God. The eagle then took flight towards the East.

Such is the account given in the Acts. They are ancient, but full of fables, and, as Remi Ceillier and others have already shown, cannot constitute a serious historical document.

SEC. 8. Synods at Arsinöe and Rome (255–260)

We have, unlike the case last considered, the most thoroughly historical records of the assembly over which Dionysius the Great, Archbishop of Alexandria, presided at Arsinöe, and of which he speaks himself in Eusebius. Nepos, an Egyptian bishop, also a very venerable man, and author of some Christian canticles, had fallen into the error of the Millenarians, and had endeavoured to spread it. Dying some time after, he could not be judged; and his primate, Dionysius the Great, had to content himself with refuting the opinions which he had propagated. He did so in two books, περὶ ἐπαγγελιῶν. Besides this, about 255, Dionysius being near to Arsinöe, where the errors of Nepos had made great progress, assembled the priests (of Nepos) and the teachers of the place, and prevailed upon them to submit their doctrine to a discussion which should take place before all their brethren, who would be present at it. In the debate they relied upon a work by Nepos, which the Millenarians much venerated. Dionysius disputed with them for three days; and both parties, says Dionysius himself, showed much moderation, calmness, and love of truth. The result was, that Coration, chief of the party of Nepos, promised to renounce his error, and the discussion terminated to the satisfaction of all.

Some years later, about 260, the same Dionysius the Great, from his manner of combating Sabellius, gave occasion for the holding of a Roman synod, of which we shall speak more at length in giving the history of the origin of Arianism.

SEC. 9. Three Synods at Antioch on account of Paul of Samosata (264–269)

Three synods at Antioch in Syria occupied themselves with the accusation and deposition of the bishop of that town, the well-known anti-Trinitarian, Paul of Samosata.

Sabellius had wished to strengthen the idea of unity in the doctrine of the Trinity, by suppressing the difference between the persons, and only admitting, instead of the persons, three different modes of action in the one person of God; consequently denying the personal difference between the Father and the Son, and identifying them both. In his doctrinal explanation of the mystery of the Trinity, Paul of Samosata took an opposite course: he separated the one from the other, the Father and the Son, far too much. He set off, as Sabellius did, from a confusion of the divine persons, and regarded the Logos as an impersonal virtue of God in no way distinct from the Father. In JESUS he saw only a man penetrated by the Logos, who, although miraculously born of a virgin, was yet only a man, and not the God-man. His inferior being was ἐκπαρθένου; his superior being, on the contrary, was penetrated by the Logos. The Logos had dwelt in the man Jesus, not in person, but in quality, as virtue or power (οὐκ οὐσιωδῶς ἀλλὰ κατὰ ποιότητα). Moreover, by an abiding penetration, He sanctified him, and rendered him worthy of a divine name. Paul of Samosata further taught, that as the Logos is not a person, so also the Holy Spirit is only a divine virtue, impersonal, belonging to the Father, and distinct from Him only in thought.

Thus, while Paul on one side approached Sabellianism, on the other side he inclined towards the Subordinatians of Alexandria. We will not discuss whether Jewish errors, of which Philastrius accuses him, were mixed with this monarchianism, as this is merely an accessory question. Theodoret says more accurately, that Paul sought, by his anti-Trinitarian doctrines, to please his protectress and sovereign Zenobia, who was a Jewess, and consequently held anti-Trinitarian opinions.

The new error was so much the more dangerous, as the ecclesiastical and political position of its author was of great importance. He filled the highest see in the East. We know also, that in 264 or 265 a great number of bishops assembled at Antioch; particularly Firmilian of Cæsarea in Cappadocia, Gregory Thaumaturgus and his brother Athenodorus, the Archbishop Helenus of Tarsus in Cilicia, Nicomas of Iconium, Hymenæus of Jerusalem, Theotecnus of Cæsarea in Palestine (the friend of Origen), Maximus of Bostra, and many other bishops, priests, and deacons. Dionysius the Great of Alexandria had also been invited to the Synod; but his age and infirmities prevented him from going in person, and he died a short time after. He had wished at least to be able in writing to defend the doctrine of the Church against Paul of Samosata, as he had before defended it against Sabellius. According to Eusebius, he addressed a letter to the church at Antioch, in which he would not even salute the bishop. Without entirely confirming this statement furnished by Eusebius, Theodoret relates that in that letter Dionysius exhorted Paul to do what was right, whilst he encouraged the assembled bishops to redoubled zeal for orthodoxy. From these testimonies we may conclude that Dionysius wrote three letters—one to Paul, another to the bishops in Synod, a third to the church at Antioch; but it is also true that one single letter might easily contain all that Eusebius and Theodoret attribute to Dionysius.

In a great number of sessions and discussions they sought to demonstrate the errors of Paul, and entreated him to return to orthodoxy; but the latter, cleverly dissembling his doctrine, protested that he had never professed such errors, and that he had always followed the apostolic dogmas. After these declarations, the bishops being satisfied, thanked God for this harmony, and separated.

But they found that they were soon obliged to assemble again at Antioch. Firmilian appears to have presided over this fresh assembly, as he had over the first: its exact date is not certainly known. The Synod explicitly condemned the new doctrine introduced by Paul. As, however, Paul promised to renounce and retract his errors (as he had absolutely rejected them as his in the first Synod), Firmilian and the bishops allowed themselves to be deceived a second time.

Paul did not keep his promise, and soon, says Theodoret, the report was spread that he professed his former errors as before. However, the bishops would not cut him off immediately from communion with the Church: they tried again to bring him back to the right way by a letter which they addressed to him; and it was only when this last attempt had failed that they assembled for the third time at Antioch, towards the close of the year 269. Bishop Firmilian died at Tarsus in going to this Synod. According to Athanasius, the number of assembled bishops reached seventy, and eighty according to Hilarius. The deacon Basil, who wrote in the fifth century, raises it even to a hundred and eighty. Firmilian being dead, Helenus presided over the assembly, as we are expressly assured by the Libellus Synodicus. Besides Helenus, Hymenæus of Jerusalem, Theotecnus of Cæsarea in Palestine, Maximus of Bostra, Nicomas of Iconium, and others, were present. Among the priests who were present at the Synod, Malchion was especially remarkable, who, after having taught rhetoric with much success at Antioch, had been ordained priest there on account of the purity of his manners and the ardour of his faith. He was chosen by the bishops assembled at Antioch as the opponent in discussion of Paul of Samosata, on account of his vast knowledge and his skill in logic. The notaries kept an account of all that was said. These documents still existed in the time of Eusebius and of Jerome; but we have only some short fragments preserved by two writers of the sixth century—Leontius of Byzantium and Peter the deacon.

In these disputations Paul of Samosata was convicted of error. The Council deposed him, excommunicated him, and chose in his place Domnus, son of his predecessor Demetrian Bishop of Antioch. Before dissolving itself, the Council sent to Dionysius Bishop of Rome, to Maximus of Alexandria, and to the bishops of all the provinces, an encyclical letter, which we still possess in greater part, in which was an account of the errors and manners of Paul of Samosata, as well as of the deliberations of the Council respecting him. It is there said, "that Paul, who was very poor at first, had acquired great riches by illegal proceedings, by extortions and frauds, professedly promising his protection in lawsuits, and then deceiving those who had paid him. Besides, he was extremely proud and arrogant: he had accepted worldly employments, and preferred to be called ducenarius rather than bishop; he always went out surrounded by a train of servants. He was reproached with having, out of vanity, read and dictated letters while walking; with having, by his pride, caused much evil to be said of Christians; with having had a raised throne made for him in the church; with acting in a theatrical manner—striking his thigh, spurning things with his foot, persecuting and scorning those who during his sermons did not join with the clappers of hands bribed to applaud him; with having spoken disparagingly of the greatest doctors of the Church, and with applause of himself; with having suppressed the Psalms in honour of Christ, under the pretext that they were of recent origin, to substitute for them at the feast of Easter hymns sung by women in his honour; with having caused himself to be praised in the sermons of his partisans, priests and chorepiscopi. The letter further declared that he had denied that the Son of God descended from heaven, but that he personally had allowed himself to be called an angel come from on high; that, besides, he had lived with the subintroducti, and had allowed the same to his clergy. If he could not be reproached with positive immorality, he had at least caused much scandal. Finally, he had fallen into the heresy of Artemon; and the Synod had thought it sufficient to proceed only on this last point. They had therefore excommunicated Paul, and elected Domnus in his place. The Synod prayed all the bishops to exchange the litteras communicatorias with Domnus, whilst Paul, if he wished, could write to Artemon. It is with this ironical observation that the great fragment of the synodical letter preserved by Eusebius terminates. It is thought that in Leontius of

Byzantium are to be found some more fragments of this letter treating of Paul's doctrine. Much more important is an ancient tradition, that the Synod of Antioch must have rejected the expression ὁμοούσιος. This is, at least, what semi-Arians have maintained; whilst S. Athanasius says "that he had not the synodical letter of the Council of Antioch before his eyes, but that the semi-Arians had maintained, in their Synod of Ancyra of 358, that this letter denied that the Son was ὁμοούσιος τῷ πατρί." What the semi-Arians affirmed is also reported by Basil the Great and Hilary of Poitiers. Thus it is impossible to maintain the hypothesis of many learned men, viz. that the semi-Arians had falsified the fact, and that there was nothing true about the rejection of the expression ὁμοούσιος by the Synod of Antioch. The original documents do not, however, show us why this Synod of Antioch rejected the word ὁμοούσιος; and we are thrown upon conjectures for this point.

Athanasius says that Paul argued in this way: If Christ, from being a man, did not become God—that is to say, if He were not a man deified—then He is ὁμοούσιος with the Father; but then three substances (οὐσίαι) must be admitted—one first substance (the Father), and two more recent (the Son and the Spirit); that is to say, that the divine substance is separated into three parts.

In this case Paul must have used the word ὁμοούσιος in that false sense which afterwards many Arians attributed to the orthodox: in his mind ὁμοούσιος must have signified the possessor of a part of the divine substance, which is not the natural sense of the word. Then, as Paul abused this expression, it may be that for this reason the Synod of

Antioch should absolutely forbid the use of the word ὁμοούσιος. Perhaps Paul also maintained that the ὁμοούσιος: answered much better to his doctrine than to that of the orthodox: for he could easily name as ὁμοούσιος with the Father, the divine virtue which came down upon the man Jesus, since according to him this virtue was in no way distinct from the Father; and in this case, again, the Synod would have sufficient ground for rejecting this expression.

These explanations would be without any use if the two creeds which were formerly attributed to this Council of Antioch really proceeded from it. In these creeds the word ὁμοούσιος is not only adopted, but great stress is laid upon it. The two creeds also have expressions evidently imitated from the Nicene Creed,—a fact which shows that they could not have proceeded from the Synod of Antioch. If in 269 such a profession of faith in the mystery of the Holy Trinity had been written at Antioch, the Fathers of Nicæa would have had much easier work to do, or rather Arianism would not have been possible.

We have already said that the synodical letter of the Council of Antioch was addressed to Dionysius Bishop of Rome. The Synod did not know that this Pope died in the month of December 269: thus the letter was given to his successor, Felix I., who wrote immediately to Bishop Maximus and the clergy of Alexandria to define the orthodox faith of the Church with greater clearness against the errors of Paul of Samosata.

Paul continued to live in the episcopal palace, notwithstanding his deposition, being probably supported by Zenobia; and he thus obliged the orthodox to appeal to the Emperor Aurelian after this prince had conquered Zenobia and taken Antioch in 272. The Emperor decided that "he should occupy the episcopal house at Antioch who was in connection with the bishops of Italy and the see of Rome." Paul was then obliged to leave his palace with disgrace, as Eusebius relates.

We have up to this time spoken of three Synods of Antioch, all of them held with reference to Paul of Samosata; but a certain number of historians will admit only two, as we think, wrongly. The synodical letter of the last Council of Antioch says distinctly that Firmilian went twice on this account to Antioch, and that on his third journey to be present at a new synod, consequently at a third, he died. As the synodical letter is the most trustworthy source which can be quoted in this case, we ought to prefer its testimony to Theodoret's account, who mentions only two Synods of Antioch. As for Eusebius, whose authority has been quoted, it is true that he first mentions only one synod, then in the following chapter another Synod of Antioch; but this other he does not call the second—he calls it the last. What he says in the twenty-seventh chapter shows that he united into one only the first and second Synods. "The bishops," he says, "assembled often, and at different periods." But even if Eusebius had spoken of only two synods, his testimony would evidently be of less value than the synodical letter.

It is with these Synods of Antioch that the councils of the third century terminate. The Libellus Synodicus certainly mentions another synod held in Mesopotamia; but it was only a religious conference between Archelaus Bishop of

Carchara (or, more correctly, Caschara) in Mesopotamia, and the heretic Manes. As for the pretended Eastern Synod in the year 300, in which the patriarchs of Rome, of Constantinople (an evident anachronism), of Antioch, and of Alexandria, are said to have granted to the Bishop of Seleucia the dignity of patriarch of the whole of Persia, it is a pure invention.

CHAPTER III
THE SYNODS OF THE FIRST TWENTY YEARS OF THE FOURTH CENTURY

SEC. 10. Pretended Synod of Sinuessa (303)

IF the document which tells us of a Synod of Sinuessa (situated between Rome and Capua) could have any pretension to authenticity, this Synod must have taken place about the beginning of the fourth century, in 303. It says: The Emperor Diocletian had pressed Marcellinus Bishop of Rome to sacrifice to the gods. At first stedfast, the bishop had finally allowed himself to be dragged into the temple of Vesta and of Isis, and there offered incense to the idols. He was followed by three priests and two deacons, who fled the moment he entered the temple, and spread the report that they had seen Marcellinus sacrificing to the gods. A Synod assembled, and Marcellinus denied the fact. The inquiry was continued in a crypt near Sinuessa, on account of the persecution. There were assembled many priests, no fewer than three hundred bishops; a number quite impossible for that country, and in a time of persecution. They first of all condemned the three priests and the two deacons for having abandoned their bishop. As for the latter, although sixty-two witnesses had sworn against him, the Synod would not pronounce judgment: it simply demanded that he should confess his fault, and judge himself; or, if he was not guilty, that he should pronounce his own acquittal. On the morrow fresh witness arose against Marcellinus. He denied again. The third day the three hundred bishops assembled, once more condemned the three priests and the two deacons, called up the witnesses again, and charged Marcellinus in God's name to speak the truth. He then threw himself on the ground, and covering his head with ashes, loudly and repeatedly acknowledged his sin, adding that he had allowed himself to be bribed by gold. The bishops, in pronouncing judgment, formally added: Marcellinus has condemned himself, for the occupant of the highest see cannot be judged by any one (prima sedes non judicatur a quoquam). The consequence of this Synod was, that Diocletian caused many bishops who were present at it to be put to death, even Pope Marcellinus himself, on the 23d of August 303.

This account is so filled with improbabilities and evidently false dates, that in modern times Roman Catholics and Protestants have unanimously rejected the authenticity of it. Before that, some Roman Catholics were not unwilling to appeal to this document, on account of the proposition, prima sedes non judicatur a quoquam. The Roman breviary itself has admitted the account of Marcellinus' weakness, and of the sacrifice offered by him. But it is beyond all doubt that this document is an amplification of the falsehood spread by the Donatists about the year 400. They maintain that during Diocletian's persecution Marcellinus had delivered up the Holy Scriptures, and sacrificed to the idols,—a falsehood which Augustine and Theodoret had already refuted.

SEC. 11. Synod of Cirta (305)

If the Donatists have invented the Synod of Sinuessa, which never took place, they have, on the other hand, contested the existence of a Council which was certainly held in 305 at Cirta in Numidia. This Synod took place on the occasion of the installation of a new bishop of this town. Secundus Bishop of Tigisium, the oldest of the eleven bishops present, presided over the assembly. A short time before, an edict of Diocletian had enacted that the sacred writings should be given up; and a multitude of Christians, and even bishops, had proved weak, and had obeyed the edict. Most of the bishops present at Cirta were accused of this fall; so that the president could say to almost all of them, when questioning them according to their rank, Dicitur te tradidisse. They acknowledged themselves to be guilty, adding, one that God had preserved him from sacrificing to the idols (which would have been doubtless a much greater fall); another, that instead of the sacred books he had given up books of medicine; a third, that he had been forced by violence, and so forth. All implored grace and pardon. The president then demanded of Purpurius Bishop of Limata, if it was true that he had killed two of his nephews. The latter answered, "Do you think you can terrify me like the others? What did you do then yourself, when the curator commanded you to give up the Holy Scriptures?" This was to reproach him with the crime for which he was prosecuting the others; and the president's own nephew, Secundus the younger, addressed his uncle in these words: "Do you hear what he says of you? He is ready to leave the Synod, and to create a schism: he will have with him all those whom you wish to punish, and I know that they have reasons for condemning you." The president asked counsel from some of the bishops: they persuaded him to decide that "each one should render an account to God of his conduct in this matter (whether he had given up the Holy Scriptures or not)." All were of the same opinion, and shouted, Deo gratias!

This is what is told us in the fragment of the synodical acts preserved by S. Augustine in the third book of his work against the Donatist Cresconius. We also learn from this fragment, that the Synod was held in a private house belonging to Urbanus Donatus, during the eighth consulate of Diocletian and the seventh of Maximian, that is to say, in 303. Optatus of Mileve, on the other hand, gives to this Donatus the surname of Carisius, and tells us that they chose a private house because the churches of the town had not yet been restored since the persecution. As for the chronological question, S. Augustine says in another place, that the copy of the synodical acts, which was carefully examined on occasion of the religious conference of Carthage with the Donatists, was thus dated: post consulatum Diocletiani novies et Maximiani octies, tertio nonas Martis, that is to say, March 5, 305. That is, in fact, the exact date, as Valesius has proved in his notes upon the eighth book of the History of the Church by Eusebius, ch. 2. Natalis Alexander has also written a special dissertation upon this subject in his History of the Church.

When the affair respecting the bishops who had yielded up the Holy Scriptures had been decided, they proceeded to the election of the new Bishop of Cirta. The bishops nominated the deacon Silvanus, although, as is proved by a fragment of the acts preserved by S. Augustine, he had delivered up the sacred books in 303, together with his bishop Paul. This Silvanus and some others among the bishops assembled at Cirta, after having been so indulgent towards themselves, afterwards became the chiefs of the rigorous and exaggerated party of the Donatists, who saw traditores everywhere, even where there were none.

SEC. 12. Synod of Alexandria (306)

Almost at the same period, perhaps a year later, a synod was held at Alexandria, under the presidency of Peter, then archbishop of that place. The Bishop of Lycopolis, Meletius, author of the Meletian schism, was, as S. Athanasius tells us, deposed by this Synod for different offences; and among others, for having sacrificed to idols. These last words show that this Synod took place after the explosion of Diocletian's persecution, consequently after 303. S. Athanasius further adds, in his Epistola ad episcopos: "The Meletians were declared schismatics more than fifty-five years ago." This letter having been written in 356 or in 361, the latter date would give the year 306 as that of the Synod; and this is the date which we adopt For on the other hypothesis (reckoning from the year 356) we should be brought to 301, when the persecution of Diocletian had not begun.

To the beginning of the fourth century belongs the

SEC. 13. Synod of Elvira (305 or 306)

This Synod has been, more than any other, an occasion for many learned researches and controversies. The principal work on the subject is that by the Spaniard Ferdinand de Mendoza, in 1593; it comprises three books, the title of which is, de confirmando concilio Illiberitano ad Clementem VIII. The best text of the acts of this Council is found in the Collectio canonum Ecclesiæ Hispanæ, by Franc. Ant. Gonzalez, librarian (Madrid 1808, in folio). It was compiled from nine ancient Spanish manuscripts. Bruns has reproduced it in his Biblioth eccles.

Pliny the elder speaks of two towns named Illiberis: the one in Gallia Narbonensis, which is now called Collioure, in Roussillon (now French); the other in the south of Spain, in the province Bœtica, now Andalusia. As it is a Spanish council, there can be no question but that it was the latter town, as Illiberis in Narbonne had been demolished long before the time of Constantine the Great. Mendoza relates, that in his day the remains of walls bearing the name of Elbira might still be seen on a mountain not far from Granada; and the gate of Granada, situated in this direction, is called the gate of Elbira. There is also another Eliberis, but it dates only from the conquest of the Goths. Illiberris, with a double l and a double r, is the true one, according to Mendoza.

The synodical acts, whose genuineness could be doubted only by hypercriticism, mention nineteen bishops as present at the Council. According to a Codex Pithöanus of its acts, their number must have reached forty-three. The nineteen are: Felix of Acci (Cadiz), who, probably as being the eldest, was nominated president of the Synod; Hosius of Corduba, afterwards so famous in the Arian controversy as Bishop of Cordova; Sabinus of Hispalis (Seville), Camerismus of Tucci, Sinaginis of Epagra (or Bigerra), Secundinus of Castulo, Pardus of Mentesa, Flavian of Eliberis, Cantonius of Urci, Liberius of Emerita, Valerius of Cæsaraugusta (Saragossa), Decentius of Legio (Leon), Melantius of Toledo, Januarius of Fibularia (perhaps Salaria in Hispania Tarraconensis), Vincent of Ossonoba, Quintianus of Elbora, Successus of Eliocroca, Eutychian of Basti (Baza), and Patricius of Malacca, There were therefore bishops from the most different parts of Spain; so that we may consider this assembly as a synod representing 'the whole of Spain. The acts also mention twenty-four priests, and say that they were seated at the Synod like the bishops, whilst the deacons and the laity stood up. The decrees proceeded only from the bishops; for the synodical acts always employed this formula: EPISCOPI universi dixerunt.

1. As for the date of this Synod, the acts tell us that it was celebrated, which means opened, at the Ides of May; that is, on the 15th May. The inscriptions on the acts also give the following particulars: Constantii temporibus editum, eodem tempore quo et Nicæna synodus habita est. Some of the acts add: era 362.

Of course it refers to the Spanish era, which began to be used in Spain in the fifth century: it counted from the thirty-eighth year before Christ, so that the year 362 of the Spanish era corresponds to 324 of our reckoning. This date of 324 answers to that of the Council of Nicæa (325), also mentioned in the inscription on the synodical acts; but the tempore Constantii does not agree with it, at least unless we should read Constantini. But there are very strong objections against this chronological reading.

a. Most of the ancient manuscripts of these synodical acts do not bear any date: one would therefore be led to conclude that this had been added at a later time.

b. Bishop Hosius of Corduba, named among the bishops present at the Synod, was not in Spain in 324: he passed the whole of that year either at the Emperor's court (in Nicomedia) or at Alexandria. Constantine the Great, with whom he was, after the defeat of Licinius, consequently in the autumn of 323 or in the spring of 324, sent him to that place in order to try to settle the Arian strife. Hosius not being able to succeed, in his mission, returned to the Emperor as counsellor on ecclesiastical matters, and immediately afterwards he took part in the first Œcumenical Council of Nicæa, in 325.

c. A long time previous to 323 and 324 Hosius had left Spain, and he generally resided with the Emperor. It is known that after the close of the Council of Arles, in 314, the Donatists appealed from the judgment of the Council to the Emperor Constantine the Great. The sentence given by the Emperor in 316 having been against them, they spread the report that it was Hosius of Cordova who had influenced the Emperor in his judgment. Augustine, in relating this fact, adds that Hosius had, on the contrary, suggested to the Emperor more moderate measures than the Donatists deserved. Hosius was then at the imperial court, at the latest, in 316: a decree which Constantine addressed to Cecilian Bishop of Carthage in 313, and in which he mentions Osius, would even lead us to conclude that the Spanish bishop was with Constantine in 313.

d. We must also notice, that the purport of several canons of Elvira cannot agree with this date of 324.

(α.) Several of these canons appear, indeed, to have been compiled during or soon after a violent persecution, in which several Christians had apostatized. We say during, or soon after; but it is more likely that it was soon after: for during a persecution, bishops from the most distant provinces of Spain, from the north and the south, could hardly assemble in the same place. Now the last persecution of the Spanish Christians by the Emperors was that of Diocletian and of Maximianus Herculeus, from 303 to 305.

(β.) The decisions of Elvira about the lapsi are much more rigorous than those of Nicæa: thus the first canon of Elvira forbids that the holy communion should be administered to the lapsi, even in articulo mortis. This severity evidently indicates a date prior to that of the Synod of Nicæa. Such severity during a persecution, or immediately after, could be explained, but not so twenty years later.

2. It was indeed this severity of the canons of Elvira with regard to the lapsi which suggested to the oratorian Morinus the hypothesis which he propounds in his book de Pœnitentia, viz. that the Synod of Elvira must have assembled before the origin of the Novatian schism, about 250; otherwise the Fathers of Elvira, by their first canon, must have taken the side of the Novatians. But the severity of the Novatians is very different from that of the Synod of Elvira. The Novatians pretended that the Church had not the right to admit to the communion a Christian who had apostatized: the Fathers of Elvira acknowledged this right; they wished only that in certain cases, for reasons of discipline, she should suspend the exercise of this right, and delay the admission, non desperatione veniæ, sed rigors disciplinæ. We must add, that about 250 Hosius and the other bishops present at the Council of Elvira were not yet born, or at least they were not at any rate among the clergy.

3. The hypothesis of the Magdeburg Centuriators, which places the Synod of Elvira in the year 700, is still more unfortunate. To give such dates, is to make Hosius and his

colleagues of Elvira into true Methuselahs of the new covenant.

4. Following the Fasti of Onuphrius, Hardouin has adopted the date 313, giving especially as his reason, that the canons of the Council of Arles in 314 have much in common with those of Elvira. But this is extremely feeble reasoning; for they might easily profit by the canons of Elvira at Arles, even if they were framed ten or twenty years previously. Besides, Hosius, as we have seen above, appears to have left his native country, Spain, in 313.

5. Baluze has propounded another theory. At the Council of Sardica (eleventh canon in Greek, fourteenth canon in Latin), Hosius proposed a law (on the subject of the Sunday festival), which had been before proposed in a former council (superiore concilio). This is an allusion to the twenty-first canon of the Council of Elvira. Baluze remarks, that since Hosius calls the Council of Elvira superius concilium, this Council must have taken place before the Council of Nicæa, which, with Hosius, when the Council of Sardica was held, was only the concilium postremum. The reasoning of Baluze can be maintained up to this point; but afterwards, from some other indications, he wishes to conclude that the Synod of Elvira took place after those of Ancyra and of Neocæsarea; consequently between 314 and 325. This latter part of his proof is very feeble; and besides, he has entirely forgotten that Hosius was not in Spain between 314 and 325.

6. Mansi thinks that the Synod of Elvira took place in 309. It is said in the acts, he remarks, that the Council was held in the Ides of May. Now in 309 these Ides fell on a Sunday;

and at this period they began to hold synods on a Sunday, as the example of Nicæa shows. This last observation is not exact. The Council of Nicæa requires, in the fifth canon, that two synods should be celebrated annually,—one during Lent, the other in the autumn; but there is nowhere any mention of Sunday. The apostolic canons, No. 36 (38), give the same meaning: "The first synod shall be held in the fourth week after Pentecost; the second on the 12th of the month Hyperberataios." Here also, then, there is no mention of Sunday; the 12th of the month Hyperberataios might fall upon any day of the week. In the statutes of the Synod of Antioch in 341, Sunday is not prescribed more than any other day.

7. The calculation of Mendoza, of Natalis Alexander, of Tillemont, of d'Aguirre, of Rémi Ceillier, etc., appears to us more defensible: they all proceed upon the fact that Valerius Bishop of Saragossa, who, we know from the acts, was present at the Synod, was persecuted in 304, with his deacon Vincent, by the Roman prætor Dacian. The deacon was put to death, and Valerius exiled; afterwards he also was martyred, if we may believe an ancient tradition. They concluded from this, that the Council of Elvira could not have taken place before 304, that is to say, before the arrest of Bishop Valerius; and they only disagreed upon the point whether the Council took place at the commencement of the year 300 or 301: d'Aguirre even mentions the commencement of 303. The difficulty is, that they place the Council of Elvira before the outbreak of the persecution; whilst, as has been said before, several of the canons were evidently written just after a persecution, and consequently could not have been promulgated between 300 and 304.

8. The opinion, then, which appears to us the most probable in this question, is the following: In May 305 Diocletian and Maximianus Herculeus had abdicated; and Constantius, celebrated for his benevolence towards the Christians, became sovereign ruler of Spain. The persecution, therefore, having ceased, the Spanish bishops could assemble at Elvira to deliberate, first, respecting the treatment of the lapsi, which was the chief subject of the canons which they formed, and also to seek for means against the invasion of moral corruption.

But it will be said, Was not Valerius of Saragossa dead in 305? I do not think so. To prove it, Rémi Ceillier appeals to Prudentius; but the latter does not say a word of the martyrdom of Valerius, either in his poem upon all the martyrs of Saragossa in general, or in his poem upon Vincent in particular. If Valerius had really been martyred, he would certainly not have failed to say so. Then, if Valerius was living at the time of the abdication of Diocletian and Maximian, he was undoubtedly recalled from exile by Constantius; and he could thus take part in the Synod of Elvira, which we therefore place in the autumn of 305, or in 306. Baronius, Binius in Mansi, and others, accept 305, but on other grounds than ours, whilst Pagi leaves the question undecided. The eighty-one canons of the Synod of Elvira are the following:—

CAN. 1. De his qui post baptismum idolis immolaverunt

Placuit inter nos: Qui post fidem baptismi salutaris adulta ætate ad templum idoli idolaturus accesserit, et fecerit, quod est crimen capitale, quia est summi sceleris, placuit nee in finem eum communionem accipere.

"If an adult who has been baptized has entered an idol's temple, and has committed a capital crime, he cannot be received into communion, even at the end of his life."

Several interpreters of this canon, among others Dr. Herbst, who has explained the canons of Elvira in the Tübinger Quartalschrift, have erroneously thought that we must understand here by communio, not eucharistic communion, but only communion with the Church, or sacramental absolution. This is a mistake: the word communio does not mean only communion with the Church, but sacramental communion as well. If any one is excluded from the Church, and if they cannot receive sacramental absolution, neither can they receive the holy Eucharist.

CAN. 2. De sacerdotibus gentilium qui post baptismum immolaverunt

Flamines, qui post fidem lavacri et regenerationis sacrificaverunt, eo quod geminaverint scelera accedente homicidio, vel triplicaverint facinus cohærente mœchia, placuit eos nec in finem accipere communionem.

CAN. 3. De eisdem si idolis munus tantum dederunt

Item flamines qui non immolaverint, sed munus tantum dederint, eo quod se a funestis abstinuerint sacrificiis, placuit in finem eis præstare communionem, acta tamen legitima pœnitentia. Item ipsi si post pœnitentiam fuerint mœchati placuit ulterius his non esse dandam communionem, ne illusisse de dominica communione videantur.

CAN. 4. De eisdem si catechumeni adhuc immolant quando baptizentur

Item flamines si fuerint catechumeni et se a sacrificiis abstinuerint, post triennii tempora placuit ad baptismum admitti debere.

The office of a flamen in the provinces of the Roman Empire consisted either in offering sacrifices to the gods, or in preparing the public games. It was hereditary in many families; and as it entailed many expenses, he who was legally bound to fill it could not give it up, even if he became a Christian, as is proved by the Code of Justinian, and S. Jerome's work De Vita Hilarionis. It followed from this, that the members of these families of flamines kept their office even when they were catechumens or had been baptized; but they tried to give up the duties which it imposed, especially the sacrifices. They consented still to continue to prepare the public games. In the time of a persecution, the people generally wished to oblige them to offer sacrifices also. This Synod decided on what must be done with these flamines in the different cases which might arise.

a. If they had been baptized, and if they had consented to fulfil all their duties, they had by that act alone (α) sacrificed to idols; (β) they had taken part in murders, by preparing for the games (in the games of gladiators), and in acts of immorality (in the obscene acts of certain plays). Their sin was therefore double and triple. Then they must be refused the communion as long as they lived.

b. If they had been baptized, but if, without sacrificing, they had only given the games, they might be received into communion at the close of their life, provided that they should have first submitted to a suitable penance. But if, after having begun to do penance (that is the sense, and not after the accomplishment of the penance), they should again be led into any act of immorality (that is to say, if as flamines they should allow themselves to organize obscene plays), they should never more receive the communion.

c. If a flamen was only a catechumen, and if, without sacrificing, he had fulfilled his duties (perhaps also given the games), he might be baptized after three years of trial.

CAN. 5. Si domina per zelum ancillam occiderit

Si qua fœmina furore zeli accensa flagris verberaverit ancillam suam, ita ut intra tertium diem animam cum cruciatu effundat, eo quod incertum sit voluntate an casu occiderit; si voluntate, post septem annos, si casu, post quinquennii tempora, acta legitima pœnitentia, ad communionem placuit admitti; quod si intra tempora constituta fuerint infirmata, accipiat communionem.

"If, in anger, a woman should strike her servant, so that the latter should die at the end of three days, the guilty woman shall undergo a seven years' penance if she struck so violently on purpose, and a five years' penance if she did not do so on purpose to kill: she shall not be received into communion till after this delay. If she should fall ill during the time of her penance, she may receive the communion."

This canon was inserted in the Corpus juris can.

CAN. 6. Si quicunque per maleficium hominem interfecerit

Si quis vero maleficio interficiat alteram, eo quod sine idololatria perficere scelus non potuit, nee in finem impertiendam illi esse communionem.

By maleficio is here to be understood the deceits of magic or sorcery, which they considered necessarily connected with idolatry.

The following canon needs no explanation.

CAN. 7. De pœnitentibus mœchiæ si rursus mœchaverint

Si quis forte fidelis post lapsum mœchiæ, post tempora constituta, acta pœnitentia, denuo fuerit fornicatus, placuit nec in finem habere eum communionem.

CAN. 8. De fœminis quæ relictis viris suis aliis nubunt

Item fœminæ, quæ nulla præcedente causa reliquerint viros suos et alteris se copulaverint, nec in finem accipiant communionem.

Some interpreters have thought that the question here was that only of a Christian woman leaving her husband, still a pagan, without any reason; for under no pretext could she leave a Christian husband to marry another. But the following canon proves conclusively that the eighth canon speaks of a Christian couple. If it adds without reason, that does not mean that there exist any cases in which a woman could leave her husband to marry another: the canon decrees only a more severe punishment if she should abandon her husband without reason; whilst the following canon prescribes what punishment to inflict in case she should leave her husband not entirely without a cause (if, for example, the husband is an adulterer).

The ninth canon, which has also been inserted in the Corpus juris canon, is thus worded:—

CAN. 9. De fœminis quæ adulteros maritos relinquunt et aliis nubunt

Item fœmina fidelis, quæ adulterum maritum reliquerit fidelem et alteram ducit, prohibeatur ne ducat; si duxerit, non prius accipiat communionem, nisi quem reliquit de sæculo exierit, nisi forsitan necessitas infirmitatis dare compulerit.

The following canons are much more difficult to explain.

CAN. 10. De relicta catechumeni si alterum duxerit

Si ea quam catechumenus relinquit duxerit maritum, potest ad fontem lavacri admitti: hoc et circa fœminas catechumenas erit observandum. Quodsi fuerit fidelis quæ ducitur ab eo qui uxorem inculpatam relinquit, et quum scierit illum habere uxorem, quam sine causa reliquit, placuit in finem hujusmodi dari communionem.

CAN. 11. De catechumena si graviter ægrotaverit

Intra quinquennii autem tempora catechumena si graviter fuerit infirmata, dandum ei baptismum placuit non denegari.

These two canons are difficult to explain, because the section between the two does not occupy its proper place. They treat, of two quite different cases, and each of these cases is subdivided into two others.

1. a. If a catechumen, without any cause, should leave his wife, who has not yet been baptized, and if the latter should marry another husband, she may be baptized.

b. In the same way, if a female catechumen should, without reason, leave her husband, still unbaptized, and that he should marry again, he may be baptized.

Such is the first case. It supposes that the party who is left without cause is not baptized. Here the tenth canon should stop. What follows treats of another question, viz. if the party who has unlawfully left the other can be married again. The canon does not mention whether the party to be married is baptized, or only a catechumen, and it establishes the following:—

2. a. If a Christian woman marries a man whom she knows to have illegally divorced his wife, she may communicate only on her deathbed. As a Christian, she ought to have known that, according to S. Paul, a Christian (and the catechumen is here considered as such) cannot put away his partner, though an unbeliever, if the latter wishes to continue to live with him.

b. If a female catechumen marries a man who has illegally divorced his wife, her baptism shall be put off five years longer (a further period of trial), and she can be baptized before that time only in case of a serious illness.

We think we have thus clearly and accurately explained the sense of these two canons, which have given so much trouble to commentators.

CAN. 12. De mulieribus quæ lenocinium fecerint

Mater vel parens vel quælibet fidelis, si lenocinium exercuerit eo quod, alienum vendiderit corpus vel potius suum, placuit eam nec in finem accipere communionem.

We might have remarked on the two preceding canons, that their titles are not quite adapted to their contents. It is the same with this one. It threatens with perpetual excommunication those fathers and mothers who should give up their children to prostitution, as well as all those who follow this shameful trade. The words vel potius suum corpus, etc., however, evidently apply only to the parents of the young prostitute: in fact, they sell their own flesh and blood in selling their daughter.

CAN. 13. De virginibus Deo sacratis si adulteraverint

Virgines quæ se Deo dicaverunt, si pactum perdiderint virginitatis atque eidem libidini servierint, non intelligentes quid admiserint, placuit nee in finem eis dandam esse communionem. Quod si semel persuasæ aut infirmi corporis lapsu vitiatæ omni tempore vitæ suæ hujusmodi fœminæ egerint pœnitentiam, ut abstineant se a coitu, eo quod lapsæ potius videantur, placuit eas in finem communionem accipere debere.

When virgins consecrated to God (whether nuns properly so called, or young girls who have consecrated their youth to God, still remaining in their families) have committed a carnal sin without acknowledging their offence, and so continuing obstinately in their blindness (for it is thus that we must understand non intelligentes quid admiserint), they must remain permanently excommunicated; but if they should acknowledge their sin, and do perpetual penance, without falling again, they may receive the communion at the end of their life. This canon was inserted in the Corpus juris can.

CAN. 14. De virginibus sæcularibus si mœchaverint

Virgines quæ virginitatem suam non custodierint, si eosdem qui eas violaverint duxerint et tenuerint maritos, eo quod solas nuptias violaverint, post annum sine pœnitentia reconciliari debebunt; vel si alios cognoverint viros, eo quod mœchatæ sunt, placuit per quinquennii tempora, acta legitima pœnitentia, admitti eas ad communionem oportere.

If a young girl who has made no vows has committed a carnal sin, and if she marries him with whom she has been led away, she shall be reconciled at the end of one year, without being condemned to penance; that is to say, that she may receive the communion at the end of one year, because she has violated only the marriage law, the rights of which she usurped before they were conferred upon her.

Some manuscripts read, post pœnitentiam unius anni reconcilientur; that is to say, that one year's penance should be imposed upon her. The difference between this reading and ours is not important, for our reading also imposes on the guilty one minor excommunication for a year; that is to say, privation of the communion, which we know was also a degree of penance, namely, the fourth. The canon only exempts her from the most severe degrees of excommunication, to which were attached positive works of penance. The other reading says nothing more. If this woman should marry any one except him with whom she had fallen, she would commit a sort of adultery, and ought to submit to five years of penance.

The three following canons forbid to marry pagans, Jews, or heretics, and require no explanation:—

CAN. 15. De conjugio eorum qui ex gentilitate veniunt

Propter copiam puellarum gentilibus minime in matrimonium dandæ sunt virgines Christianæ, ne ætas in flore tumens in adulterium animæ resolvatur.

CAN. 16. De puellis fidelibus ne infidelibus conjungantur

Hæretici si se transferre noluerint ad Ecclesiam catholicam, nec ipsis catholicas dandas esse puellas; sed neque Judæis neque hæreticis dare placuit, eo quod nulla possit esse societas fideli cum infideli: si contra interdictum fecerint parentes, abstineri per quinquennium placet.

CAN. 17. De his qui filias suas sacerdotibus gentilium conjungunt

Si qui forte sacerdotibus idolorum filias suas junxerint, placuit nec in finem iis dandam esse communionem.

CAN. 18. De sacerdotibus et ministris si mœchaverint

Episcopi, presbyteres (!) et diacones si in ministerio positi detecti fuerint quod sint mœchati, placuit propter scandalum et propter profanum crimen nec in finem eos communionem accipere debere.

We must here, as in other places, understand by mœchare, not only adultery in specie, but all fornication in general.

CAN. 19. De clericis negotia et mundinas sectantibus

Episcopi, presbyteres (!) et diacones de locis suis negotiandi causa non discedant, nec circumeuntes provincias quæstuosas nundinas sectentur: sane ad victum sibi conquirendum aut filium aut libertum aut mercenarium aut amicum aut quemlibet mittant, et si voluerint negotiari, intra provinciam negotientur.

S. Cyprian, in his work de Lapsis, also complains that many bishops left their churches and went into foreign provinces for the sake of merchandise, and to give themselves up to trade.

CAN. 20. De clericis et laicis usurariis

Si quis clericorum detectus fuerit usuras accipere, placuit eum degradari et abstineri. Si quis etiam laicus accepisse probatur usuras, et promiserit correptus jam se cassaturum nec ulterius exacturum, placuit ei veniam tribui: si vero in ea iniquitate duraverit, ab ecclesia esse projiciendum.

When we consider the seventeenth Nicene canon, which also forbids lending money at interest, we shall speak of the judgment of the ancient Church on this matter. The first part of our canon has been inserted by Gratian in the Corpus juris canon.

CAN. 21. De his qui tardius ad ecclesiam accedunt

Si quis in civitate positus tres dominicas ad ecclesiam non accesserit, pauco tempore abstineatur, ut correptus esse videatur.

As we have said before, Hosius proposed and had passed at the Council of Sardica a like statute against those who neglected to go to church. It is the eleventh canon of the

Greek and the fourteenth of the Latin text of the decrees of Sardica.

CAN. 22. De catholicis in hæresim transeuntibus, si revertantur

Si quis de catholica Ecclesia ad hæresim transitum fecerit rursusque recurrerit, placuit huic pœnitentiam non esse denegandam, eo quod cognoverit peccatum suum; qui etiam decem annis agat pœnitentiam, cui post decem annos præstari communio debet; si vero infantes fuerint transducti, quod non suo vitio peccaverint incunctanter recipi debent.

CAN. 23. De temporibus jejuniorum

Jejunii superpositiones per singulos menses placuit celebrari, exceptis diebus duorum mensium Julii et Augusti propter quorumdam infirmitatem.

The superponere (ὑπερτίθεσθαι), or the superpositio (ὑπέρθεσις), was an extension or prolongation of the fast beyond the usual duration (until the evening). It consisted in eating absolutely nothing for a whole day.

CAN. 24. De his qui in peregre baptizantur, ut ad clerum non veniant

Omnes qui in peregre fuerint baptizati, eo quod eorum minime sit cognita vita, placuit ad clerum non esse promovendos in alienis provinciis.

None could be admitted into the ranks, of the clergy out of the province in which he had been baptized. This canon passed into the Corpus jur. can.

CAN. 25. De epistolis communicatoriis confessorum

Omnis qui attulerit literas confessorias, sublato nomine confessoris, eo quod omnes sub hac nominis gloria passim concutiant simplices, communicatoriæ ei dandæ sunt litteræ.

This canon has been interpreted in three ways. Mendoza, Baronius, and others, when commenting upon it, thought of the letters of peace (libelli pacis) which the martyrs and confessors gave to the lapsi, to procure for them a speedy reception into the Church. These libelli pacis, indeed, induced many a bishop to admit a lapsus too promptly; but our canon does not speak of this abuse: it does not complain that these letters deceived the bishops: it says, concutiant simplices. If the canon had been intended to warn the bishops against these libelli pacis, it would certainly not have said that they should give to the lapsis communicatorias literas; for this was what was wrong, that they were admitted too soon to communion. Aubespine and Herbst were of the opinion that the canon had reference to some Christians who, before going a journey, did not ask for letters of communion from their bishop, but preferred letters of recommendation given by their confessor, regarding these as more important, and that this practice was forbidden by one synod. This, again, is a mistake. The meaning of the canon is this: "If a Christian, wishing to take a journey, submits to his bishop the draught of a letter of recommendation, in which it is said that the bearer is a confessor, the bishop must erase the word confessor, sublato nomine confessoris, because many simple people are deceived by this title, and the bishop shall give common letters communicatorias."

CAN. 26. Ut omni sabbato jejunetur

Errorem placuit corrigi, ut omni sabbati die superpositiones celebremus.

The meaning of this canon also is equivocal. The title seems to imply that it orders a severe fast every Saturday, and the suppression of the contrary practice followed up to that time. It is thus explained by Garsias in Binius and Mendoza. However, as the sixty-fifth apostolic canon prescribes that, except Holy Saturday, no Saturday should be a fast-day, our canon may also mean, "The ancient error of fasting strictly every Saturday must be abolished:" that is to say, the superpositio is ordered only for Holy Saturday; and for other Saturdays, as for Fridays, the statio only, that is to say, the half-fast is ordered. But in comparing this canon with the forty-third, where the same expressions are again found, we see that the ut determines what was to he henceforth observed, and not in what the error consisted. According to that, our decree would mean that the superpositio must be observed every Saturday, and we must adopt the explanation of Garsias.

CAN. 27. De clericis ut extraneas fœminas in domo non habeant

Episcopus vel quilibet alius clericus aut sororem aut filiam virginem dicatam Deo tantum secum habeat; extraneam nequaquam habere placuit.

This canon is more severe than the third similar canon of the Council of Nicæa. It allows the clergy to have with them in their house (a) only their sisters, or their own daughters; (b) and also that these must be virgins, and consecrated to God, that is, having vowed their virginity to God.

CAN. 28. De oblationibus eorum qui non communicant

Episcopum placuit ab eo, qui non communicat, munus accipere non debere.

In the same way as in the first canon, we must here understand by those qui non communicant, Christians who, like penitents or catechumens, are not in the communio (community), and who therefore do not receive the holy Eucharist. The meaning of the canon is: "The bishop cannot accept at the altar the offerings (oblata) of those who do not communicate."

CAN. 29. De energumenis qualiter habeantur in ecclesia

Energumenus qui ab erratico spiritu exagitur, hujus nomen neque ad altare cum oblatione esse recitandum, nec permittendum ut sua manu in ecclesia ministret.

This canon, like the seventy-eighth apostolic canon, excludes demoniacs possessed by the evil spirit from active participation in divine service: they cannot present any offerings; their names cannot be read among those who are inscribed in the diptychs as offering the sacrifice (diptychis offerentium); and they must not be permitted to hold any office in the Church.

CAN. 30. De his qui post lavacrum mœchati sunt, ne subdiacones fiant

Subdiaconos eos ordinari non debere qui in adolescentia sua fuerint mœchati, eo quod postmodum per subreptionem ad altiorem gradum promoveantur: vel si qui sunt in præteritum ordinati, amoveantur.

CAN. 31. De adolescentibus qui post lavacrum mœchati sunt

Adolescentes qui post fidem lavacri salutaris fuerint mœchati, cum duxerint uxores, acta legitima pœnitentia placuit ad communionem eos admitti.

These two canons need no explanation.

CAN. 32. De excommunicatis presbyteris ut in nccessitate communionem dent

Apud presbyterum, si quis gravi lapsu in ruinam mortis inciderit, placuit agere pœnitentiam non debere, sed potius apud episcopum: cogente tamen infirmitate necesse est presbyterem (!) communionem præstare debere, et diaconem si ei jusserit sacerdos.

This canon is quite in conformity with the ancient custom, according to which the bishop only, and not a priest, could receive a penitent into the Church. It was only in a case of extreme necessity that a priest, or, according to the orders of a priest, a deacon, could give a penitent the communion, that is, could administer to him the eucharistic bread in sign of reconciliation: deacons often gave the communion in the ancient Church. The title of the canon is evidently wrong, and ought to be thus worded: De presbyteris ut excommunicatis in necessitate, etc. It is thus, indeed, that Mansi read it in several manuscripts.

CAN. 33. De episcopis et ministris ut ab uxoribus abstineant

Placuit in totum prohibere episcopis, presbyteris et
diaconibus vel omnibus clericis positis in ministerio
abstinere se a conjugibus suis et non generare filios:
quicunque vero fecerit, ab honore clericatus exterminetur.

This celebrated canon contains the most ancient command
of celibacy. The bishops, priests, and deacons, and in
general all the clergy, qui in ministerio positi sunt, that is,
who are specially employed in the service of the altar, ought
no longer to have any conjugal intercourse with their wives,
under pain of deposition, if they were married when they
took orders. The history of the Council of Nicæa will give
us the opportunity of considering the question of celibacy
in the primitive Church. We will only add here, that the
wording of our canon is defective: prohibere abstinere et
non generare. The canon seems to order what, on the
contrary, it would prohibit, viz.: "It is forbidden that the
clergy should abstain from their wives." A similarly inexact
expression is found in the eightieth canon.

CAN. 34. Ne cerei in cœmeteriis incendantur

Cereos per diem placuit in cœmeterio non incendi,
inquietandi enim sanctorum spiritus non sunt. Qui hæc non
observaverint arceantur ab Ecclesiæ communione.

It is forbidden to light wax candles during the day in
cemeteries, for fear of troubling the spirits of the saints.
Garsias thus explains this canon: "for fear of troubling and
distracting the faithful, who pray in the cemeteries." He
thus makes sancti the synonym of faithful. Binterim has
taken it in the same sense: sanctorum with him is
synonymous with sancta agentium; and he translates it, "so
that the priests, who fulfil their holy offices, may not be

distracted." Baronius, on the contrary, says: "Many neophytes brought the custom from paganism, of lighting many wax candles upon tombs. The Synod forbids this, because metaphorically it troubles the souls of the dead; that is to say, this superstition wounds them." Aubespine gives a fourth explanation. He begins with the supposition that the bishops of Elvira partook of the opinion, then very general, that the souls of the dead hovered over their tombs for some time. The Synod consequently forbade that wax candles should be lighted by day, perhaps to abolish a remnant of paganism, but also to prevent the repose of the souls of the dead from being troubled.

CAN. 35. Ne fæminœ in cœmeteriis pervigilent

Placuit prohiberi ne fœminæ in cœmeterio pervigilent, eo quod sæpe sub obtentu orationis latenter scelera committunt.

CAN. 36. Ne picturæ in ecclesia fiant

Placuit pictures in ecclesia esse non debere, ne quod colitur et adoratur in parietibus depingatur.

These canons are easy to understand: we have elsewhere explained why the ancient Church did not tolerate images. Binterim and Aubespine do not believe in a complete exclusion: they think that the Church in general, and the Synod of Elvira in particular, wished to proscribe only a certain kind of images. Binterim believes that this Synod forbade only one thing,—namely, that any one might hang images in the Church according to his fancy, and often therefore inadmissible ones. Aubespine thinks that our canon forbids only images representing God (because it says adoratur), and not other pictures, especially those of saints. But the canon also says colitur, and the prohibition is conceived in very general terms.

CAN. 37. De energumenis non baptizatis

Eos qui ab immundis spiritibus vexantur, si in fine mortis fuerint constituti, baptizari placet: si fideles fuerint, dandam esse communionem. Prohibendum etiam ne lucernas hi publice accendant; si facere contra interdictum voluerint, abstineatur a communione.

This canon, like the 29th, speaks of demoniacs. If they are catechumens, they may be baptized when at the point of death (in articulo mortis), but not before that. If they are baptized, the communion may be administered to them when at the point of death, but not before. However, as the 29th canon had before forbidden any ministry in the Church to demoniacs, ours particularly adds that they could not fulfil the least service in the Church, not even light the lamps. Perhaps it may have been the custom to have the lamps of the Church lighted by those who were to be baptized, or by those who were to communicate, on the day when they were to receive this sacrament; and the Synod forbids that demoniacs should do so, even if, in spite of their illness, they were able to receive a sacrament. The inscription of the canon does not correspond to its whole tenor.

CAN. 38. Ut in necessitate et fideles baptizent

Loco peregre navigantes aut si ecclesia proximo non fuerit, posse fidelem, qui lavacrum suum integrum habet nec sit bigamus, baptizare in necessitate infirmitatis positum, catechumenum, ita ut si supervixerit ad episcopum eum perducat, ut per manus impositionem perfici possit.

During a sea voyage, or in general, if no church is near, a layman who has not soiled his baptismal robe (by apostasy), and is not a bigamist, may baptize a catechumen who is at the point of death; the bishop ought afterwards to lay hands on the newly baptized, to confirm him.

CAN. 39. De gentilibus si in discrimine baptizari expetunt

Gentiles si in infirmitate desideraverint sibi manum imponi, si fuerit eorum ex aliqua parte honesta vita, placuit eis manum imponi et fieri Christianos.

This canon has been interpreted in two different ways. Binius, Katerkamp, and others, hold that the imposition of hands spoken of in this canon does not mean confirmation, but a ceremony by means of which any one was admitted into the lowest class of catechumens. These interpreters appeal principally to the pretended seventh canon of the second Œcumenical Council. We there read: "We admit them only as pagans: the first day we make them Christians (in the widest sense); the second, catechumens; the third, we exorcise them," etc. etc. According to that, our canon would say: "When a heathen, having a good name, desires during an illness that hands should be laid upon him, it ought to be done, that he may become a Christian." That is to say, he ought by the imposition of hands to be admitted among those who wish to be Christians, consequently among the Christians in the widest sense. The forty-fifth canon also takes the word catechumenus as synonymous with Christian. Besides, we find Constantine the Great received the imposition of hands at the baths of

Helenopolis before his baptism: a ceremony of this kind then preceded the reception of the first sacrament. Relying upon these considerations, the commentators we mentioned say that the canon of Elvira does not speak of baptism, because this could not be administered until after much longer trial. The provost of the Cathedral at Köln, Dr. München, gives another explanation in his dissertation upon the first Synod of Arles. According to him,—

a. As the thirty-seventh canon allows the baptism of demoniacs, it is not probable that they would be more severe with respect to ordinary sick persons in the thirty-ninth canon. On the contrary, the Church has always been tender towards the sick: she has always hastened to confer baptism upon them, because it is necessary to salvation; and for that reason she introduced clinical baptism.

b. In the thirty-eighth canon the Church allows a layman to baptize one who should fall seriously ill during a sea voyage, but not to confirm him. She certainly, then, would allow this sick person to be confirmed if a bishop were present in the ship.

c. As for one who should fall ill upon land, he could easily call a bishop to him; and therefore the case foreseen by the thirty-eighth canon does not apply to him: it would be easy to confer baptism and confirmation on him.

d. The thirty-ninth canon, then, means: "Whoso shall fall ill upon land, and who can summon a bishop to him, may receive baptism and confirmation at the same time."

e. Understood in this way, the canon is more in unison with the two preceding, and with the practice of the ancient Church towards the sick.

CAN. 40. Ne id quod idolothytum est fideles accipiant

Prohibere placuit, ut quum rationes suas accipiunt possessores, quidquid ad idolum datum fuerit, accepto non ferant; si post interdictum fecerint, per quinquennii spatia temporum a communione esse arcendos.

That is to say: When the proprietors of lands and houses receive their rents (rationes),—for example, fruits from their farmers, who perhaps are still pagans,—they ought not to admit anything which had been sacrificed to the gods, under pain of five years' excommunication.

CAN. 41. Ut prohibeant domini idola colere servis suis

Admoneri placuit fideles, ut in quantum possunt prohibeant ne idola in domibus suis habeant; si vero vim metuunt servorem, vel se ipsos puros conservent; si non fecerint, alieni ab ecclesia habeantur.

The preceding canon had shown that many Christians had farmers who were pagans; the present canon supposes the case of a Christian having heathen slaves, and it enacts:

a. That he ought not, even in this case, to tolerate idols in his house.

b. That if he cannot conform to this rule, and must fear the slaves on account of their number, he may leave them their idols; but he must so much the more keep at a distance from them, and watch against every approach to idolatry.

CAN. 42. De his qui ad fidem veniunt quando baptizentur

Eos qui ad primam fidem credulitatis accedunt, si bonæ
fuerint conversationis, intra biennium temporum placuit ad
baptismi gratiam admitti debere, nisi infirmitate
compellente coegerit ratio velocius subvenire periclitanti vel
gratiam postulanti.

He who has a good name, and wishes to become a
Christian, must be a catechumen for two years: then he may
be baptized. If he should fall ill, and desire the grace of
baptism, it may be granted to him before the expiration of
two years.

CAN. 43. De celebratione Pentecostes

Pravam institutionem emendari placuit juxta auctoritatem
Scripturarum, ut cuncti diem Pentecostes celebremus, ne si
quis non fecerit, novam hæresim induxisse notetur.

Some parts of Spain had allowed the bad custom of
celebrating the fortieth day after Easter, not the fiftieth;
consequently the Ascension of Christ, and not Pentecost.
Several ancient manuscripts, indeed, contain this addition:
non quadragesimam. The same addition is found in an
ancient abridgment of the canons of Elvira, with which
Mansi makes us acquainted: post Pascha quinquagesima
teneatur, non quadragesima. We learn also from Cassian,
that in the primitive Church some Christians wished to
close the paschal season with the feast of the Ascension,
that is, at the fortieth day. They regarded all Easter-time
only as a remembrance of Christ's sojourn among His
disciples during the forty days which followed His
resurrection; and therefore they wished to close this period

with the feast of the Ascension. Herbst supposes that a Montanist party in Spain wished to suppress the feast of Pentecost altogether, because the Montanists believed that the Holy Spirit did not descend until He came in Montanus, who was regarded by his followers as the Comforter.

CAN. 44. De meretricibus paganis si convertantur

Meretrix quæ aliquando fuerit et postea habuerit maritum, si postmodum ad credulitatem venerit; incunctanter placuit esse recipiendam.

If a pagan courtezan has given up this abominable way of life, and is married, being still a pagan, there is no particular obstacle to her admission into the Church. She ought to be treated as other pagan women.

CAN. 45. De catechumenis qui ecclesiam non frequentant

Qui aliquando fuerit catechumenus et per infinita tempore, nunquam ad ecclesiam accesserit, si eum de clero quisque cognoverit esse Christianum, aut testes aliqui extiterint fideles, placuit ei baptismum non negari, eo quod veterem hominem dereliquisse videatur.

The case is here imagined of a catechumen who has not been to church for a long time, probably because he did not wish to be known as a Christian during a time of persecution; but afterwards his conscience awakes, and he asks to be baptized. The canon ordains that if he is known to the clergy of the Church to which he belongs, and they know him to be a Christian, or if some of the faithful can attest this, he shall be admitted to baptism, because he appears to have put off the lukewarmness of the old man.

Aubespine gives another interpretation which appears forced, and shows that he most probably had not the text before him. According to him, the meaning of the canon would be: "When a catechumen has fallen away for a long time, and still after all desires baptism and to become a Christian, if he should suddenly lose speech, for example, from illness (the canon says not a word of all that), he may be baptized, provided a clergyman or several of the laity attest that he has desired baptism, and has become a real Christian." The Abbé Migne has placed this explanation in his Dictionary of the Councils.

CAN. 46. De fidelibus si apostaverint quamdiu pœniteant

Si quis fidelis apostata per infinita tempora ad ecclesiam non accesserit, si tamen aliquando fuerit reversus nec fuerit idolator, post decem annos placuit communionem accipere.

The sin of a Christian who should absent himself from church for a long time was naturally much greater than that of a catechumen. For this reason, the baptized Christian who has in fact apostatized is only received to the communion after a ten years' penance, and even then if he has not sacrificed to the gods. It appears to us that this canon alludes to the time of Diocletian's persecution; for during that terrible time more than one cowardly Christian did not go to church, gave no sign of Christian life, and thus apostatized in fact, without positively offering sacrifice to the idols.

CAN. 47. De eo qui uxorem habens sæpius mœchatur

Si quis fidelis habens uxorem non semel sed sæpe fuerit mœchatus in fine mortis est conveniendus: quod si se promiserit cessaturum, detur ei communio: si resuscitatus rursus fuerit mœchatus, placuit ulterius non ludere eum de communione pacis.

If a Christian who is married, and has been often guilty of adultery, is near death, they must go to see him (est conveniendus), and ask him whether, if he should recover, he promises to amend his ways. If he promises, the holy communion should be administered to him; if he should recover, and should again be guilty of adultery, the holy communion must not be allowed to be thus despised, it must henceforth be refused to him, even in articulo mortis. The sixty-ninth and seventy-eighth canons complete the meaning of this one.

CAN. 48. De baptizatis ut nihil accipiat clerus

Emendari placuit ut hi qui baptizantur, ut fieri solebat, numos in concha non mittant, ne sacerdos quod gratis accepit pretio distrahere videatur. Neque pedes eorum lavandi sunt a sacerdotibus vel clericis.

This canon forbids at the same time two things relative to baptism:

1. It was the custom in Spain for the neophytes, at the time of their baptism, to put an offering into the shell which had been used at the baptism. This offering, afterwards called the stole-rights, was to be suppressed.

2. The second part of the canon shows that there was the same custom in certain parts of Spain as at Milan and in Gaul, but which, from the testimony of St. Ambrose, did not exist at Rome, viz. that the bishop and clergy should

wash the feet of the newly baptized when they left the baptismal font. Our Synod forbids this, and this canon has passed into the Corp. jur. can.

CAN. 49. De frugibus fidelium ne a Judæis benedicantur

Admoneri placuit possessores, ut non patiantur fructus suos, quos a Deo percipiunt cum gratiarum actione, a Judæis benedici, ne nostram irritam et infirmam faciant benedictionem: si quis post interdictum facere usurpaverit, penitus ab ecclesia abjiciatur.

The Jews were so numerous and so powerful in Spain during the first centuries of the Christian era, that they might at one time have hoped to be able to Judaize the whole country. According to the monuments—which, however, are of doubtful authority—they established themselves in Spain in the time of King Solomon. It is more likely that they crossed from Africa to the Spanish peninsula only about a hundred years before Christ. There they soon increased in number and importance, and could energetically carry on their work of proselytizing. This is the reason that the Synod of Elvira had to forbid to the priests and the laity all intimate intercourse with Jews (can. 50), and especially marriage (can. 16); for there is no doubt that at this period many Christians of high rank in Spain became Jews, as Jost shows in his work.

CAN. 50. De Christianis qui cum Judæis vescuntur

Si vero quis clericus vel fidelis cum Judæis cibum sumpserit, placuit eum a communione abstineri, ut debeat emendari.

CAN. 51. De hæreticis ut ad clerum non promoveantur

Ex omni hæresi fidelis si venerit, minime est ad clerum promovendus: vel si qui sunt in præteritum ordinati, sine dubio deponantur.

These canons are easy to understand.

CAN. 52. De his qui in ecclesia libellos famosos ponunt

Hi qui inventi fuerint libellos famosos in ecclesia ponere anathematizentur.

This canon forbids the affixing of satires (libellos famosos) in churches, or the reading of them. It has been inserted in the Corp. jur. can.

CAN. 53. De episcopis qui excommunicato alicno communicant

Placuit cunctis ut ab eo episcopo quis recipiat communionem a quo abstentus in crimine aliquo quis fuerit; quod si ælius episcopus præsumpserit eum admitti, illo adhuc minime faciente vel consentiente a quo fuerit communione privatus, sciat se hujusmodi causas inter fratres esse cum status sui periculo præstaturum.

One excommunicated by a bishop can only be restored by the bishop who condemned him. Another bishop receiving him into communion, unless the first bishop acts at the same time, or approves of the reconciliation, must answer for it before his brethren, that is to say, before the provincial synod, and must run the danger of being deprived of his office (status).

CAN. 54. De parentibus qui fidem sponsaliorum frangunt

Si qui parentes fidem fregerint sponsaliorum, triennii tempore abstineantur; si tamen idem sponsus vel sponsa in gravi crimine fuerint deprehensi, erunt excusati parentes; si in iisdem fuerit vitium et polluerint se, superior sententia servetur.

If the parents of those who are betrothed fail to keep the promises made at the betrothal, these parents shall be excluded from the communion for three years, unless either of the betrothed persons be convicted of a very serious fault. In this case, the parents may break the engagement. If the betrothed have sinned together, the first arrangement continues; that is, the parents cannot then separate them. This canon is found in the Corp. juris can.

CAN. 55. De sacerdotibus gentilium qui jam non sacrificant

Sacerdotes qui tantum coronas portant, nec sacrificant nec de suis sumptibus aliquid ad idola præstant, placuit post biennium accipere communionem.

It may be asked whether the word sacerdotes is to be understood as referring to pagan priests who wished to be admitted as Christians, or to Christians who, as we have seen above (can. 2), still bore the office of flamines. Aubespine is of the latter opinion, and according to him the canon would have this meaning: "The Christian who bears the office of flamen, and wears the distinctive sign—that is, the crown—without having sacrificed himself, or having contributed money to pagan sacrifices, must be excluded from eucharistic communion for two years." Aubespine gives the two following reasons in support of his explanation: (a.) When a pagan priest wished to become a Christian, he was not kept longer or more strictly than others as a catechumen, even when he had himself offered sacrifice. (b.) If it had referred to a pagan priest wishing to become a Christian, the Synod would have said, placuit post biennium accepere lavacrum (baptism), and not accipere communionem. This latter expression is used only for those who have been excluded for some time from the Church, and are admitted afresh into her bosom.

For our part, we think that this fifty-fifth canon is nothing but a complement of the second and third canons, and that it forms with them the following gradation:—

Can. 2. Christians who, as flamincs, have sacrificed to idols, and given public pagan games, cannot receive the communion, even when at the point of death.

Can. 3. If they have not offered sacrifices, but have had the games celebrated, they may communicate at the close of their life, after a previous penance.

Can. 55. If they have not offered sacrifice, nor contributed by their fortune to pagan sacrifices (and to such public games), they may receive the communion after two years of penance.

This gradation is continued in the two following canons, the fifty-sixth and fifty-seventh: they refer to Christians who have not been flamines, but who have borne other offices in a heathen state, and so have been brought into relation with paganism.

The fifty-fifth canon evidently alludes to a former and not far distant time of persecution, during which Christians feared to refuse the office of flamines which fell to their lot, and by a half compliance wore the distinctive mark of their office, the crown, in order to pass uninjured through the time of persecution.

CAN. 56. De magistratibus et duumviris

Magistratus vero uno anno quo agit duumviratum, prohibendum placet ut se ab ecclesia cohibeat.

What the consuls were at Rome, the duumviri were, on a small scale, in the Roman municipalities: their office also lasted only a year. These duumviri were obliged, by virtue of their office, to watch over pagan priests personally, and the temples of the town; they had to preside at public solemnities, in processions, etc., which, like all the other national feasts of the Romans, had always more or less a semi-religious and pagan character. For this reason the Synod forbade the duumviri to enter the Church as long as they were in office. In limiting itself to this prohibition, it gave proof of great moderation and of wise consideration, which we ought to appreciate. An absolute prohibition to hold this office would have given up the charge of the most important towns to pagans. But the Council is much more severe in the following canon.

CAN. 57. De his qui vestimenta ad ornandam pompam dederunt

Matronæ vel earum mariti vestimenta sua ad ornandam sæculariter pompam non dent; et si fecerint, triennio abstineantur.

This canon is directed against Christians who should lend their garments for worldly shows, i.e. for public, halfheathenish religious processions. They are punished with three years of excommunication. But why are they treated so much more severely than the duumviri? Because these men and women were not obliged to lend their attire, whilst the duumviri were fulfilling their public duty as citizens. Perhaps also some gave their garments, that they might not be suspected during the persecutions.

CAN. 58. De his qui communicatorias litteras portant, ut de fide interrogentur

Placuit ubique et maxime in eo loco, in quo prima cathedra constituta est episcopatus, ut interrogentur hi qui communicatorias litteras tradunt an omnia recte habeant suo testimonio comprobata.

In Africa no metropolitan rights were attached to particular towns: they always belonged to the oldest bishop of the province, whose bishopric was then called prima sedes. Carthage only was the metropolitan see. It appears to have been the same in Spain before Constantine the Great divided that country into seven political provinces, which entailed the division into ecclesiastical provinces. This may explain why the Bishop of Acci presided at the Synod of Elvira: he was probably the oldest of all the bishops present. What is elsewhere called prima sedes in our canon is prima cathedra; and the bishops of the prima cathedra were to question Christian travellers about their respective dioceses, the latter were to present their recommendatory letters, and were to be asked if they could affirm that all was in a satisfactory state.

CAN. 59. De fidelibus ne ad Capitolium causa sacrificandi ascendant

Prohibendum ne quis Christianus ut gentilis ad idolum
Capitolii causa sacrificandi ascendat et videat; quod si
fecerit, pari crimine teneatur: si fuerit fidelis, post decem
annos acta pœnitentia recipiatur.

Like Rome, many municipalities had a capitol, in the court
of which sacrifices were offered to the gods, and many
Christians were present at the ceremonies of the pagan
worship. Was it from curiosity? was it in order to shelter
themselves from inquiry, not to be known during the
persecution, and to pass for heathen? This is what we are
unable to decide. At any rate, the Synod declared that—

a. Any Christian, either baptized or a catechumen, who
should be present at the sacrifices, should be considered as
having offered sacrifice himself.

b. Consequently any Christian who has been present at
these sacrifices shall be excommunicated and a penitent for
ten years. The Synod says nothing about the punishment of
guilty catechumens: in every case they were in general
punished less severely than the faithful, and perhaps the
fourth canon was applied to them by analogy.

CAN. 60. De his qui destruentes idola occiduntur

Si quis idola fregerit et ibidem fuerit occisus, quatenus in
Evangelio scriptum non est neque invenietur sub apostolis
unquam factum, placuit in numero eum non recipi
martyrum.

It happened sometimes that too zealous Christians would
destroy the idols, and have to pay for their boldness with
their life. The Synod decrees that they must not be

considered as martyrs, for the gospel does not require deeds of this kind, and the apostles did not act in this way; but they considered it praiseworthy if a Christian, whom they might wish to oblige to offer sacrifice to an idol, should overthrow the statue, and break it, as Prudentius Clemens relates with commendation of Eulalia, who suffered martyrdom in Spain in 304, and therefore a short time previous to this Synod.

CAN. 61. De his qui duabus sororibus copulantur

Si quis post obitum uxoris suæ sororem ejus duxerit et ipsa fuerit fidelis, quinquennium a communione placuit abstineri, nisi forte velocius dari pacem necessitas coegerit infirmitatis.

When S. Basil the Great ascended the archiepiscopal throne of Cæsarea, he forbade that a husband, after the death of his wife, should marry her sister; and when some one, of the name of Diodorus, reproached him upon this subject, Basil defended himself in a letter, which has been preserved, and proved that such marriages had always been prohibited at Cæsarea. The Spanish Fathers of Elvira shared S. Basil's opinions, as also did the Synod of Neocæsarea of 314, can. 2, as we shall see hereafter. It is well known that, according to canon law, these marriages are both forbidden and declared to be invalid.

CAN. 62. De aurigis et pantomimis si convertantur

Si auriga aut pantomimus credere voluerint, placuit ut prius artibus suis renuntient, et tunc demum suscipiantur, ita ut ulterius ad ea non revertantur, qui si facere contra interdictum tentaverint, projiciantur ab ecclesia.

The "Apostolical Constitutions" contain the same decree. On the subject of the repugnance of the ancient Church for all these pantomimic scenes, cf. Hefele, "Rigorismus in dem Leben und den Ansichten der alten Christen" (Severity in the Lives and Opinions of the early Christians), an essay published in the Tübinger Theol. Quartalschrift, 1841 (S. 396 ff.).

The following series of canons treats of carnal sins:—

CAN. 63. De uxoribus quæ filios ex adulterio necant

Si qua per adulterim absente marito suo conceperit, idque post facinus occiderit, placuit nec in finem dandam esse communionem, eo quod geminaverit scelus.

CAN. 64. De fœminis quæ usque ad mortem cum alienis viris adulterant

Si qua usque in finem mortis suæ cum alieno viro fuerit mœchata, placuit, nec in finem dandam ei esse communionem. Si vero eum reliquerit, post decem annos accipiat communionem acta legitima pœnitentia.

CAN. 65. De adulteris uxoribus clericorum

Si cujus clerici uxor fuerit mœchata et scierit eam maritus suus mœchari et non eam statim projecerit, nec in finem accipiat communionem, ne ab his qui exemplum bonæ conversationis esse debent, ab eis videantur scelerum magisteria procedere.

The Shepherd of Hermas had before, like this canon, stringently commanded not only the clergy, but all Christians, not to continue to live conjugally with an adulterous spouse, who would not amend his ways, but would persevere in sin. Dr. Herbst says, that what made the sixty-fifth canon necessary was probably the very frequent case of married men having taken orders, and not being able to have conjugal intercourse with their wives, who were therefore on that very account easily tempted to forget themselves.

The series of canons against carnal sins is continued in the following, which forbids marriage with a daughter-in-law:—

CAN. 66. De his qui privignas suas ducunt

Si quis privignam suam duxerit uxorem, eo quod sit incestus, placuit nec in finem dandam esse communionem.

CAN. 67. De conjugio catechumenœ fœminœ

Prohibendum ne qua fidelis vel catechumena aut comatos aut viros cinerarios habeant: quæcumque hoc fecerint, a communione arceantur.

If we attach any importance to the title of this canon, it must be thought to indicate that Christian women, whether catechumens or baptized, were forbidden to marry those designated by the name of cinerarios and comatos. In other manuscripts we read comicos and cenicos. If the latter reading is the true one, the meaning of the canon is very clear—"A Christian woman must not marry an actor;" and this prohibition would explain the aversion of the ancient Church to the theatre, which has been before mentioned. But it is probable that, not having been able to find out the meaning of the words comati and cinerarii, later copyists have altered them, and changed them into comici and scenici. Imagining that here was a prohibition of marriage, they could not understand why a Christian woman was not to marry a man having long hair, or even a hairdresser. We believe that Aubespine is right when he reminds us that many pagan women had foreign slaves, and especially hairdressers, in their service, who ministered not only to the needs of luxury, but to the secret satisfaction of their passions. Perhaps these effeminate slaves—these spadones—encouraging the licentiousness of their mistresses, wore long hair, or, coming from foreign countries—for instance, from Gallia comata—where long hair was always worn, they introduced this name of comati. Tertullian speaks of the cinerarii (peregrinæ proceritatis), and describes them as foreigners, with slight figures, and forming part of the suite of a woman of the world. He mentions them in connection with the spadones, who were ad licentiam secti, or, as S. Jerome says, in securam libidinem exsecti.

Juvenal has not forgotten to signalize these relations of Roman women with eunuchs: "Sunt, quas eunuchi imbelles et mollia semper Oscula delectent."

Martial denounces them, if possible, still more energetically. Perhaps these eunuchs wore long hair like women in order that they might be called comati. Let us finally remark, that in the Glossary cinerarius is translated by δοῦλος ἑταίρας.

If this second explanation of the sixty-seventh canon is accepted, it can be easily imagined why it should be placed in a series of canons treating of carnal sins.

CAN. 68. De catechumena adultera quæ filium necat

Catechumena, si per adulterium conceperit et præfocaverit, placuit eam in fine baptizari.

If a catechumen should conceive by an adulterer, and should procure the death of the child, she can be baptized only at the end of her life.

CAN. 69. De viris conjugatis postea in adulterium lapsis

Si quis forte habens uxorem semel fuerit lapsus, placuit eum quinquennium agere debere pœnitentiam et sic reconciliari, nisi necessitas infirmitatis coegerit ante tempus dari communionem: hoc et circa fœminas observandum.

Adultery committed once was punishable with five years of penance.

CAN. 70. De fœminis quæ consciis maritis adulterant

Si cum conscientia mariti uxor fuerit mœchata, placuit nec in finem dandam ei communionem; si vero eam reliquerit, post decem annos accipiat communionem, si eam cum sciret adulteram aliquo tempore in domo sua retinuit.

If a woman should violate conjugal fidelity with her husband's consent, the latter must not be admitted to communion, even at the end of his life. If he separated from his wife, after having lived with her at all since the sin was committed, he was excluded for ten years.

CAN. 71. De stupratoribus puerorum

Stupratoribus puerorum nec in finem dandam esse communionem.

Sodomites could not be admitted to communion, even on their deathbeds.

CAN. 72. De viduis mœchis si eumdem postea maritum duxerint

Si qua vidua fuerit mœchata et eumdem postea habuerit maritum, post quinquennii tempus acta legitima pœitentia, placuit eam communioni reconciliari: si alium duxerit relicto illo, nec in finem dandam esse communionem; vel si fuerit ille fidelis quem accepit, communionem non accipiet, nisi post decem annos acta legitima pœnitentia, vel si infirmitas coegerit velocius dari communionem.

When a widow had sinned, and had married her accomplice, she was condemned to five years of penance; if she should marry another man, she could never be admitted to communion, even on her deathbed; and if her husband were baptized, he was subject to a penance for ten years, for having married a woman who, properly speaking, was no longer free. This canon was inserted in the Corp. jur. can.

The following canons treat of informers and false witnesses.

CAN. 73. De delatoribus

Delator si quis extiterit fidelis, et per delationem ejus aliquis fuerit proscriptus vel interfectus, placuit eum nec in finem accipere communionem; si levior causa fuerit, intra quinquennium accipere poterit communionem; si catechumenus fuerit, post quinquennii tempora admittetur ad baptismum.

This canon has been inserted in the Corp. jur. can.

CAN. 74. De falsis testibus

Falsus testis prout est crimen abstinebitur; si tamen non fuerit mortale quod objecit, et probaverit quod non (other manuscripts have diu) tacuerit, biennii tempore abstinebitur: si autem non probaverit convento clero, placuit per quinquennium abstineri.

A false witness must be excluded from the communion for a time proportionate to the crime of which he has given false witness. Should the crime be one not punishable with death, and if the guilty one can demonstrate that he kept silence for a long time (diu), that is, that he did not willingly bear witness, he shall be condemned to two years of penance; if he cannot prove this, to five years. The canon is thus explained by Mendoza, Rémi Ceillier in Migne's Dictionary, etc., all preferring the reading diu. Burchard had previously read and quoted the canon with this variation, in his Collectio canonum. But Aubespine divides it into three quite distinct parts. The first, he says, treats of false witnesses; the second, of those who are too slow in denouncing a crime. They must be punished, but only by two years of penance, if they can prove that they have not (non) kept silence to the end. The third condemns those to five years of penance, who, without having borne false witness, still cannot prove what they affirm.

We confess that none of these explanations is quite satisfactory: the first would be the most easily admissible; but it is hardly possible to reconcile it with the reading non tacuerit, which, however, is that of the best manuscripts.

CAN. 75. De his qui sacerdotes vel ministros accusant nec probant

Si quis autem episcopum vel presbyterum vel diaconum falsis criminibus appetierit et probare non potuerit, nec in finem dandam ei esse communionem.

CAN. 76. De diaconibus si ante honorem peccasse probantur

Si quis diaconum se permiserit ordinari et postea fuerit detectus in crimine mortis quod aliquando commiserit, si sponte fuerit confessus, placuit eum acta legitima pœnitentia post triennium accipere communionem; quod si alius eum detexerit, post quinquennium acta pœnitentia accipere communionem laicam debere.

If any one should succeed in being ordained deacon, and it should be subsequently discovered that he had before that committed a mortal sin:

a. In case he was the first to make known his fault, he must be received into communion (as a layman) at the end of three years of penance.

b. In case his sin was discovered by another, at the end of five years. In both cases he was for ever suspended from his office of deacon.

CAN. 77. De baptizatis qui nondum confirmati moriuntur

Si quis diaconus regens plebem sine episcopo vel presbytero aliquos baptizaverit, episcopus eos per benedictionem perficere debebit: quod si ante de sæculo recesserint, sub fide qua quis credidit poterit esse justus.

When Christianity spread from the large towns, where it had been at first established, into the country, the rural churches at first formed only one parish with the cathedral church of the town. Either priests, or Chorepiscopi, or simple deacons, were sent to these rural assemblies, to exercise, within certain limits, the ministerial power. The solemnity of consecrating the Eucharist, and all that had reference to penance, was reserved for the bishop of the town.

The 77th canon refers to such deacons, and it ordains:

a. That baptism administered by the deacon ought to be completed, finished by the bishop's benediction (that is to say, by χειροτονία, or confirmation).

b. That if one who had been baptized by a deacon should die before having received this benediction from the bishop, he may notwithstanding be saved, by virtue of the faith which he professed on receiving baptism.

CAN. 78. De fidelibus conjugatis si cum Judæa vel gentili mœchatæ (i) fuerint

Si quis fidelis habens uxorem cum Judæa vel gentili fuerit mœchatus, a communione arceatur: quod si alius eum detexerit, post quinquennium acta legitima pœnitentia poterit dominicæ sociari communioni.

The 47th and 69th canons have already treated of adultery between Christians: the present canon speaks of a particular case of adultery committed with a Jewish or pagan woman, and decrees a penance of five years if the guilty one has not confessed himself. If he has made a spontaneous confession, the canon only gives this vague and general command, Arceatur, that is, that he should be excommunicated, but it does not say for how long a time: it might be supposed for three years, according to the analogy with the 76th canon. However, it would be strange that adultery with a Jewish or pagan woman should be punished only by three years of penance, while the 69th canon decrees, in a general way, five years' punishment to every adulterer. It is still more difficult to explain why real adultery should be less severely punished in the 78th canon than the evidently less criminal offence of a widow with a man whom she afterwards marries.

CAN. 79. De his qui tabulam ludunt

Si quis fidelis aleam, id est tabulam, luserit numis, placuit eum abstineri; et si emendatus cessaverit, post annum poterit communioni reconciliari.

The thimbles of the ancients had not any points or figures upon their sides (tabula), like ours, but drawings, pictures of idols; and whoever threw the picture of Venus, gained all, as Augustus says in Suetonius: quos tollebat universos, qui Venerem jecerat. It is on this account that the ancient Christians considered the game of thimbles to be not only immoral as a game of chance, but as having an essentially pagan character.

CAN. 80. De libertis

Prohibendum ut liberti, quorum patroni in sæculo fuerint, ad clerum non promoveantur.

He who should give a slave his freedom remained his patron; he had certain rights and a certain influence over him. The freedman continued to be dependent upon his former master; for this reason freedmen whose patrons were heathens could not take orders. This canon was placed in the Corp. jur. can.

CAN. 81. De fœminarum epistolis

Ne fœminæ suo potius absque maritorum nominibus laicis scribere audeant, quæ (qui) fideles sunt vel literas alicujus pacificas ad suum solum nomen scriptas accipiant.

If we should read qui instead of quæ, as Mendoza makes it, on the authority of several manuscripts, our canon is easy to understand. It then divides itself into two parts:

a. Women must not write in their own name to lay Christians, laicis qui fideles sunt; they may do so only in the name of their husbands.

b. They must not receive letters of friendship (pacificas) from any one, addressed only to themselves. Mendoza thinks that the canon means only private letters, and that it is forbidden in the interests of conjugal fidelity.

Aubespine gives quite another sense to the word litteras: he supposes that the Council wishes only to forbid the wives of bishops giving litteras communicatorias to Christian travellers in their own name, and that it also forbids them to receive such addressed to them instead of to their husbands.

If we read quæ, we must attach the words quæ fideles sunt to fœminæ, and the meaning continues on the whole the same.

Besides these eighty-one authentic canons, some others are attributed to the Council of Elvira: for instance, in the Corp. jur. can. (c. 17, causa xxii. q. 4; also c. 21, dist. ii. de consecrat., and c. 15, causa xxii. q. 5), there is evidently a mistake about some of these canons, which, as Mendoza and Cardinal d'Aguirre have remarked, belong to a Synodus Helibernensis or Hibernensis. We will remark finally, that whilst Baronius thinks little of the Synod of Elvira, which he wrongfully suspects of Novatian opinions, Mendoza and Natalis Alexander defend it eloquently.

SEC. 14. Origin of the Schism of the Donatists, and the first Synods held on this account in 312 and 313

The schism of the Donatists occasioned several synods at the beginning of the fourth century. Mensurius was bishop of Carthage during Diocletian's persecution. He was a worthy and serious man, who on the one side encouraged the faithful to courage and energy during the persecution, but on the other side strongly reproved any step which could increase the irritation of the heathen. He especially blamed certain Christians of Carthage, who had denounced themselves to the heathen authorities as possessors of sacred books (even when this was not really the case), in order to obtain martyrdom by their refusal to give up the Holy Scriptures. Nor would he grant the honours of martyrdom to those who, after a licentious life, should court martyrdom without being morally improved. We see, by a letter of Mensurius, how he himself behaved during the persecution. He relates, that when they required the sacred books from him, he hid them, leaving in the church only heretical books, which were taken away by the persecutors. The proconsul had soon discovered this cunning; but, however, did not wish to pursue Mensurius further. Many enemies of the bishop, especially Donatus Bishop of Casæ-Nigræ in Numidia, falsely interpreted what had passed: they pretended that Mensurius had, in fact, delivered up the Holy Scriptures; that, at any rate, he had told a sinful falsehood; and they began to excite disturbance in the Church of Carthage. However, these troubles did not take the form of a miserable schism till after the death of Mensurius. A deacon named Felix, being persecuted by the heathen, took refuge in the house of Bishop Mensurius. As the latter refused to give him up, he was taken to Rome, to answer in person for his resistance before Maxentius, who since Diocletian's abdication had possessed himself of the imperial power in Italy and in Africa. Mensurius succeeded in obtaining an acquittal; but he died on the way back to Carthage, and before arriving there, in 311. Two celebrated priests of Carthage, Botrus and Celestius, aspired to the vacant throne, and thought it their interest to invite to the election and ordination of the future bishop only the neighbouring prelates, and not those of Numidia. It is doubtful whether this was quite according to order. Inasmuch as Numidia formed a separate ecclesiastical province, distinct from the province of proconsular Africa, of which Carthage was the metropolis, the bishops of Numidia had no right to take part in the election of a Bishop of Carthage. But as the metropolitan (or, according to African language, the primate) of Carthage was in some sort the patriarch of the whole Latin Church of Africa; and as, on this account, Numidia was under his jurisdiction, the bishops of Numidia might take part in the appointment of a Bishop of Carthage. On the other side, the Donatists were completely in the wrong, when subsequently they pretended that the primate of Carthage ought to be consecrated by that metropolitan whose rank was the nearest to his own (primas, or primæ sedis episcopus or senex); consequently the new Bishop of Carthage ought to have been consecrated by Secundus Bishop of Tigisis, then metropolitan (Primas) of Numidia: and it is with reason that S. Augustine replied to them in the name of the whole African episcopate, during a conference held at Carthage in 411, that even the Bishop of Rome was not consecrated by the primate nearest to him in rank, but by the Bishop of Ostia. The two priests mentioned above found themselves deceived at the time of the election, which took place at Carthage: for the people, putting them on one side, elected Cecilian, who had been archdeacon under Mensurius; and Felix Bishop of Aptunga, suffragan of Carthage, consecrated him immediately. The consecration was hardly ended, when some priests and some of the laity of Carthage resolved to unite their efforts to ruin the new bishop. On his departure for Rome, Mensurius had confided the treasures of his church to the care of some Christians: at the same time he had given the list of everything entrusted to them into the hands of a pious woman, charging her, "in case he should not return, to remit this list to his successor." The woman fulfilled her commission; and the new bishop, Cecilian, claimed the property of the church from those with whom it had been left. This demand irritated them against him: they had hoped that no one would have known of this deposit, and that they might divide it amongst themselves.

Besides these laymen, the two priests mentioned above arrayed themselves against Cecilian. The soul of the opposition was a very rich lady, who had a great reputation for piety, named Lucilla, and who thought she was most grievously wronged by Cecilian. She had been in the habit, every time she communicated, of kissing the relics of a martyr not accounted such by the Church. Cecilian, who was at that time a deacon, had forbidden the worship of these relics not recognised by the Church, and the pharisaical pride of the woman could not pardon the injury.

Things were in this state when Secundus Bishop of Tigisis, in his office of episcopus primæ sedis of Numidia, sent a commission to Carthage to appoint a mediator (interventor) nominally for the reconciliation of the parties. But the commission was very partial from the beginning: they entered into no relation with Cecilian or his flock; but, on the contrary, took up their abode with Lucilla, and consulted with her on the plan to follow for the overthrow of Cecilian. The malcontents, says Optatus, then asked the Numidian bishops to come to Carthage to decide about the election and the consecration of Cecilian, and in fact Secundus of Tigisis soon appeared with his suffragans. They took up their abode with the avowed opponents of Cecilian, and refused to take part in the assembly or synod which he wished to call, according to custom, to hear the Numidian bishops; and, instead, they held a conciliabulum of their own, at which seventy met, and in a private house in Carthage, before which they summoned Cecilian to appear (312). Cecilian did not attend, but sent word "that if they had anything against him, the accuser had only to appear openly and prove it." No accusation was made; and besides, they could bring forward nothing against Cecilian, except having formerly, as archdeacon, forbidden the visiting of the martyrs in prison and the taking of food to them. Evidently, says Dupin, Cecilian had only followed the counsel of S. Cyprian, in forbidding the faithful to go in crowds to the prisons of the martyrs, for fear of inciting the pagans to renewed acts of violence. Although Cecilian was perfectly right in this respect, it is possible that in the application of the rule, right in itself, he may have acted with some harshness. This is at least what we must conclude if only the tenth part of the accusations raised against him by an anonymous Donatist have any foundation. He says, for instance, that Cecilian would not even allow parents to visit their captive sons and daughters, that he had taken away the food from those who wished to take it to the martyrs, and had given it to the dogs, and the like. His adversaries laid still greater stress on the invalidity of Cecilian's consecration, because his consecrator, Felix of Aptunga, had been a Traditor (i.e. had given up the sacred books) during the persecution of Diocletian. No council had heretofore ordained that the sacraments were valid, even when administered by heinous sinners; therefore Cecilian answered, with a sort of condescension towards his enemies, "that if they thought that Felix had not rightfully ordained him, they had only themselves to proceed to his ordination." But the bishops of Numidia did doubly wrong in thus setting themselves against Felix of Aptunga. First, the accusation of his having given up the sacred books was absolutely false, as was proved by a judicial inquiry made subsequently, in 314. The Roman officer who had been charged to collect the sacred books at Aptunga attested the innocence of Felix; whilst one Ingentius, who, in his hatred against Felix, had produced a false document to ruin him, confessed his guilt. But apart from this circumstance, Secundus and his friends, who had themselves given up the Holy Scriptures, as was proved in the Synod of Cirta, had hardly the right to judge Felix for the same offence. Besides, they had at this same Synod of Cirta consecrated Silvanus bishop of that place, who was also convicted of having been a Traditor. Without troubling themselves with all these matters, or caring for the legality of their proceeding, the Numidians proclaimed, in their unlawful Council, the deposition of Cecilian, whose consecration they said was invalid, and elected a friend and partisan of Lucilla's, the reader Majorinus, to be Bishop of Carthage. Lucilla had bribed the Numidian bishops, and promised to each of them 400 pieces of gold.

This done, the unlawful Numidian Council addressed a circular letter to all the churches of Africa, in which they related what had passed, and required that they should cease from all ecclesiastical communion with Cecilian. It followed from this, that Carthage, being in some sort the patriarchal throne of Africa, all the African provinces were implicated in this controversy. In almost every town two parties were formed; in many cities there were even two bishops—a Cecilian and a Majorinian. Thus began this unhappy schism. As Majorinus had been put forward by others, and besides as he died soon after his election, the schismatics did not take his name, but were called Donatists, from the name of Donatus Bishop of Casæ Nigræ, who had much more influence than Majorinus, and also afterwards on account of another Donatus, surnamed the Great, who became the successor of Majorinus as schismatical Bishop of Carthage. Out of Africa, Cecilian was everywhere considered the rightful bishop, and it was to him only that letters of communion (epistolæ communicatoriæ) were addressed. Constantine the Great, who meanwhile had conquered Maxentius in the famous battle at the Milvian Bridge, also recognised Cecilian, wrote to him, sent him a large sum of money to distribute among his priests, and added, "that he had heard that some unruly spirits sought to trouble the Church; but that he had already charged the magistrates to restore order, and that Cecilian had only to apply to them for the punishment of the agitators." In another letter, addressed to the proconsul of Africa, Anulinus, he exempted the clergy of the Catholic Church of Carthage, "whose president was Cecilian," from all public taxes.

Soon afterwards, the opponents of Cecilian, to whom many of the laity joined themselves, remitted two letters to the proconsul of Africa, begging him to send them to the Emperor. Anulinus accordingly did so. The title of the first letter, which S. Augustine has preserved to us, viz. libellus Ecclesiæ Catholicæ (that is to say, of the Donatist Church) criminum Cæciliani, suffices to show its tenor; the second entreated the Emperor, on account of the divisions among the African bishops, to send judges from Gaul to decide between them and Cecilian. This latter letter, preserved by Optatus, is signed by Lucian, Dignus, Nasutius, Capito, Fidentius, et cæteris episcopis partis Donati. In his note upon this passage, Dupin has proved by quotations from this letter, as it is found in S. Augustine, that the original was partis Majorini, which Optatus changed into Donati, according to the expression commonly used in his time.

We see from the preceding that the Donatists deserved the reproach which was cast upon them, of being the first to call for the intervention of the civil power in a purely ecclesiastical case; and the Emperor Constantine himself, who was then in Gaul, openly expressed his displeasure on this subject, in a letter which he addressed to Pope Melchiades (Miltiades). However, to restore peace to Africa, he charged three bishops of Gaul—Maternus of Cöln, Reticius of Autun, and Marinus of Arles—to make arrangements with the Pope and fifteen other Italian bishops to assemble in a synod which was held at Rome in 313.

Synod at Rome (313)

Cecilian was invited to be present at this Synod, with ten bishops of his obedience. His adversaries were to send an equal number; and at their head stood Donatus of Casæ Nigræ. The conferences began at the Lateran Palace, belonging to the Empress Fausta, on October 2, 313, and lasted three days. The first day Donatus and his friends were first of all to prove their accusations against Cecilian; but they could produce neither witnesses nor documents: those whom Donatus himself had brought to witness against Cecilian, declared that they knew nothing against the bishop, and therefore were not brought forward by Donatus. On the contrary, it was proved that, when Cecilian was only a deacon, Donatus had excited divisions in Carthage; that he had re-baptized Christians who had been baptized before; and, contrary to the rules of the

Church, had laid hands on fallen bishops to reinstate them in their offices. The second day the Donatists produced a second accusation against Cecilian; but they could no more prove their assertions than on the previous day. The continuation of an inquiry already begun concerning the unlawful Council of Carthage of 312, which had deposed Cecilian, was interrupted. As Donatus was totally unable on the third day, as on the two preceding, to produce a single witness, Cecilian was declared innocent, and Donatus condemned on his own confession. No judgment was pronounced on the other bishops of his party. The Synod, on the contrary, declared that if they would return to the unity of the Church, they might retain their thrones; that in every place where there was a Cecilian and a Donatist bishop, the one who had been the longest ordained should remain at the head of the Church, whilst the younger should be set over another diocese. This decision of the Synod was proclaimed by its president the Bishop of Rome, and communicated to the Emperor.

After the close of the Synod, Donatus and Cecilian were both forbidden to return to Africa at once. Cecilian was detained at Brescia for a time. Some time afterwards, however, Donatus obtained permission to go to Africa, but not to Carthage. But the Pope, or perhaps the Synod before closing, sent two bishops, Eunomius and Olympius, to Africa, to proclaim that that was the catholic party for which the nineteen bishops assembled at Rome had pronounced. We see from this that the mission of the two bishops was to promulgate the decisions of the Synod; we also think, with Dupin, that their journey, the date of which is uncertain, took place immediately after the close of the

Synod of Rome. The two bishops entered into communion with Cecilian's clergy at Carthage; but the Donatists endeavoured to prevent the bishops from accomplishing their mission; and some time after, as Donatus had returned to Carthage, Cecilian also returned to his flock.

New troubles soon agitated Africa, and the Donatists again brought complaints of Cecilian before the Emperor. Irritated with their obstinacy, Constantine at first simply referred them to the decision of the Synod of Rome; and when they replied by protesting that they had not been sufficiently listened to at Rome, Constantine decided, first, that a minute inquiry should be made as to whether Felix of Aptunga had really given up the Holy Scriptures (we have given above the result of this inquiry); next, that the whole controversy should be definitely settled by a great assembly of the bishops of Christendom; and consequently he called the bishops of his empire together for the 1st of August 314, to the Council of Arles in Gaul.

SEC. 15. Synod of Arles in Gaul (314)

Cecilian and some of his friends, as well as some deputies of the party of the Donatists, were invited to this Council, and the officials of the empire were charged to defray the expenses of the voyage of these bishops. Constantine specially invited several bishops, amongst others the Bishop of Syracuse. According to some traditions, there were no fewer than 600 bishops assembled at Arles. Baronius, relying on a false reading in S. Augustine, fixes the number at 200. Dupin thought there were only thirty-three bishops at Arles, because that is the number indicated by the title of the letter of the Synod addressed to Pope Silvester, and by the list of persons which is found in several MSS. Notwithstanding this comparatively small number, we may say that all the provinces of Constantine's empire were represented at the Council. Besides these thirty-three bishops, the list of persons also mentions a considerable number of priests and deacons, of whom some accompanied their bishops, and others represented their absent bishops as their proxies. Thus Pope Silvester was represented by two priests, Claudianus and Vitus, two deacons, Eugenius and Cyriacus. Marinus of Arles, one of the three judges (judices ex Gallia), who had been appointed beforehand by the Emperor, appears to have presided over the assembly: at least his name is found first in the letter of the Synod. With Marinus the letter mentions Agrœcius of Trier, Theodore of Aquileia, Proterius of Capua, Vocius of Lyons, Cecilian of Carthage, Reticius of Autun (one of the earlier judices ex Gallia), Ambitausus (Imbetausius) of Reims, Merokles of Milan, Adelfius of London, Maternus of Cöln, Liberius of Emerita in Spain, and others; the last named having already been present at the Synod of Elvira.

It is seen that a great part of Western Christendom was represented at Arles by some bishops; and the Emperor Constantine could truly say: "I have assembled a great number of bishops from different and almost innumerable parts of the empire." We may look on the assembly at Arles as a general council of the West (or of the Roman patriarchate). It cannot, however, pass for an œcumenical council, for this reason, that the other patriarchs did not take any part in it, and indeed were not invited to it; and those of the East especially, according to S. Augustine, ignored almost entirely the Donatist controversy. But has not S. Augustine himself declared this Council to be œcumenical? In order to answer this question in the affirmative, an appeal has been made to the second book of his treatise, De Baptismo contra Donatistas, where he says: "The question relating to re-baptism was decided against Cyprian, in a full council of the whole Church" (plenarium concilium, concilium universæ Ecclesiæ). But it is doubtful whether S. Augustine meant by that the Council of Arles, or whether he did not rather refer to that of Nicæa, according to Pagi's view of the case. It cannot, however be denied that S. Augustine, in his forty-third letter (vii. No. 19), in speaking of the Council of Arles, calls it plenarium Ecclesiæ universæ concilium. Only it must not be forgotten that the expression concilium plenarium, or universale, is often employed in speaking of a national council; and that in the passage quoted S. Augustine refers to the Western Church (Ecclesia universa occidentalis), and not to the universal Church (universalis) in the fullest sense.

The deliberations of the Council of Arles were opened on the 1st of August 314. Cecilian and his accusers were present; but these were no more able than before to prove their accusations. We unfortunately have not in full the acts of the Council; but the synodical letter already quoted informs us that the accusers of Cecilian were aut damnati aut repulsi. From this information we infer that Cecilian was acquitted; and this we know to have been the actual result of the Donatist controversy. The Council, in its letter to the Pope, says, "that it would have greatly desired that the Pope (Silvester) had been able to assist in person at the sessions, and that the judgment given against Cecilian's accusers would in that case certainly have been more severe." The Council probably alluded to the favourable conditions that it had accorded to the Donatist bishops and priests, in case they should be reconciled to the Church.

The letter of the Council contains no other information relating to the affairs of the Donatists. At the time of the religious conference granted to the Donatists in 411, a letter of the African bishops was read, in which they said, that, "dating from the commencement of the schism (ab ipsius separationis exordio), consent had been given that every Donatist bishop who should become reconciled to the Church should alternately exercise the episcopal jurisdiction with the Catholic bishop: that if either of the two died, the survivor should be his sole successor; but in the case in which a church did not wish to have two bishops, both were to resign, and a new one was to be elected." From these words, ab ipsius separationis exordio, Tillemont concluded that it is to the Synod of Arles that this decision should be referred; for, as we have already seen, other proposals of reconciliation were made at Rome. It is not known whether the Synod of Arles decided anything else in the matter of the Donatists. But it is evident that two, perhaps three, of its twenty-two canons (Nos. 13, 14, and 8), refer to the schism of the African Church, which we shall show in examining them one by one.

The Synod of Arles was not satisfied, as their synodal letter tells us, merely to examine and judge the business of the Donatists: it wished to lend its assistance in other points relating to the necessities of the Church, especially to solve the paschal controversy, the question of the baptism of heretics, and to promulgate various rules for discipline.

Convinced that it acted under the inspiration of the Holy Ghost, it used the formula, Placuit ergo, præsente Spiritu sancto et angelis ejus; and begged the Pope, who had the government of the larger diocese (majoris diœceseos gubernacula) under his control, to promulgate its decrees universally. The Synod also sent him the complete collection of its twenty-two canons, while in the letter previously quoted it had given only a short extract from them: consequently it may be maintained, with the brothers Ballerini, that the Synod addressed two letters to the Pope, of which the first, commencing with the enumeration of the bishops present, dwelt chiefly on the affairs of the Donatists, and gave but a short sketch of the other decisions; while the second included literally and exclusively all the decrees, and addressed itself to the Pope only in the words of introduction, and in the first canon. The Benedictines of S. Maur have published the best text of this second synodical letter, and of the canons of the Council of Arles, in the first volume of their Collectio conciliorum Galliæ of 1789, of which the sequel unfortunately has not appeared. We shall adopt this text:

Domino sanctissimo fratri Silvestro Marinus vel cœtus episcoporum qui adunati fuerunt in oppido Arelatensi. Quid decrevimus communi consilio caritati tuæ significamus, ut omnes sciant quid in futurum observare debeant.

CAN. 1. Ut uno die et tempore Pascha celebretur

Primo loco de observatione Paschæ Domini, ut uno die et uno tempore per omnem orbem a nobis observetur et juxta consuetudinem literas ad omnes tu dirigas.

By this canon the Council of Arles wished to make the Roman computation of time with regard to Easter the rule everywhere, and consequently to abolish that of Alexandria, and all others that might differ from it, taking for granted that the bishops of the Council knew the difference that existed between these and the Roman computation. We will not here give the details relating to the paschal controversy, but further on in the history of the Council of Nicæa, so as the better to grasp the whole meaning.

CAN. 2. Ut ubi quisque ordinatur ibi permaneat

De his qui in quibuscumque locis ordinati fuerint ministri, in ipsis locis perseverent.

The twenty-first canon contains the same decision, with this difference, that the former speaks only of the inferior ministers of the Church (ministri), while the latter speaks of the priests and deacons; and both express the view of the ancient Church, in accordance with which an ecclesiastic attached to one church ought not to change to another. We find the same prohibition even in the apostolic canons (Nos. 13 and 14, or 14 and 15); and in the fifteenth canon of Nicæa it is questioned whether this canon of Arles forbids only passing from one diocese to another, or if it forbade moving from one church to another in the same diocese. Dr. München understood the canon in the latter sense, founding his opinion on the seventy-seventh canon of the Synod of Elvira, which shows that each church in a diocese had its own minister. Of course the prohibition as to a change of churches in the same diocese, necessarily applies to moving from one diocese to another.

CAN. 3. Ut qui in pace arma projiciunt excommunicentur

De his qui arma projiciunt in pace, placuit abstineri eos a communione.

This canon has been interpreted in no less than four ways. Ivo of Chartres read, instead of in pace, in prælio; and an ancient manuscript, which was compared by Surius, read in bello. In this case the sense would be: "He who throws down his arms in war is excommunicated." Sirmond tried a second explanation, taking the view that arma projicere is not synonymous with arma abjicere, and signifies arma in alium conjicere. Thus, according to him, the canon forbids the use of arms except in case of war. Dr. München has developed this explanation, by applying the sentence arma projicere in pace to the fights of the gladiators, and he has considered this canon as a prohibition of these games. Constantine the Great, he says, forbade on the 1st October 325 the games of the gladiators in nearly the same terms: Cruenta spectacula in otio civili et domestica quiete non placent; quapropter omnino gladiatores esse prohibemus. Besides these, adds München, the two following canons are directed against the spectacula which were so odious to the early Christians; and this connection also justifies the opinion that canon 3 refers to the spectacula, that is to say, to the fights of the gladiators. Aubespine has tried a fourth explanation. Many Christians, says he, under the pagan emperors, had religious scruples with regard to military service, and positively refused to take arms, or else deserted. The Synod, in considering the changes introduced by Constantine, set forth the obligation that Christians have to serve in war, and that because the Church is at peace (in pace) under a prince friendly to Christians. This explanation has been adopted, amongst others, by Rémi Ceillier, by

Herbst, in the Dictionnaire des conciles of Abbé Migne, and in Abbé Guetté's recently published Histoire de l'église de France. We, however, prefer Dr. München's view of the matter.

CAN. 4. Ut aurigæ dum agitant excommunicentur

De agitatoribus qui fideles sunt, placuit eos quamdiu agitant a communione separari.

These agitators are the jockeys and grooms of the courses, identical with the aurigœ of the sixty-second canon of the Council of Elvira. In the same way that the preceding canon interdicted the games of the gladiators, which were celebrated at the amphitheatre, so this prohibits the racing of horses and chariots, which took place in the circus.

CAN. 5. Ut theatrici quamdiu agunt excommunicentur

De theatricis, et ipsos placuit quamdiu agunt a communione separari.

This canon excommunicates those who are employed in the theatres.

CAN. 6. Ut in infirmitate conversi manus impositionem accipiant

De his qui in infirmitate credere volunt, placuit iis debere manum imponi.

The thirty-ninth canon of Elvira expresses itself in the same manner; and in commenting upon it, we have said that the words manum imponi were understood by one party as a simple ceremony of admission to the order of catechumens without baptism; by others, especially by Dr. München, as expressing the administration of confirmation.

CAN. 7. De fidelibus qui præsides fiunt vel rem publicam agere volunt

De præsidibus qui fideles ad præsidatum prosiliunt, placuit ut cum promoti fuerint literas accipiant ecclesiasticas communicatorias, ita tamen ut in quibuscumque locis gesserint, ab episcopo ejusdem loci cura illis agatur, et cum cœperint contra disciplinam agere, tum demum a communione excludantur. Similiter et de his qui rempublicam agere volunt.

Like the preceding one, this canon repeats a similar statute of the Synod of Elvira. The fifty-sixth canon of Elvira had decreed that a Christian invested with a public office should abstain from appearing in church during the term of these duties, because these necessarily brought him into contact with paganism. But since the Council of Elvira an essential change had taken place. Constantine had himself gone over to Christianity; the Church had obtained full liberty; and if even before this time Christians had often been invested with public offices, this would henceforth be much more frequently the case. It was necessary that, under a Christian emperor and altered circumstances, the ancient rigour should be relaxed, and it is for this reason that the canon of Arles modified the decree of Elvira. If a Christian, it says, becomes præses, that is to say, governor, he is not, as heretofore, obliged to absent himself from church; on the contrary, letters of recommendation will be given him to the bishop of the country which is entrusted to his care (the governors were sent out of their native country, that they might rule more impartially). The bishop was bound to extend his care over him, that is to say, to watch over him, assist him with his advice, that he might commit no injustice in an office which included the jus gladii. If he did not listen to the warnings of the bishop, if he really violated Christian discipline, then only was he to be excluded from the Church. The same line of conduct was adhered to in regard of the municipal authorities as towards the imperial officers. Baronius has erroneously interpreted this canon, in making it exclude heretics and schismatics from holding public offices.

CAN. 8. De baptismo eorum qui ab hæresi convertuntur

De Afris quod propria lege sua utuntur ut rebaptizent, placuit ut si ad Ecclesiam aliquis de hæresi venerit, interrogent eum symbolum; et si perviderint eum in Patre et Filio et Spiritu sancto esse baptizatum, manus ei tantum imponatur ut accipiat Spiritum sanctum. Quod si interrogatus non responderit hanc Trinitatem, baptizetur.

We have already seen that several African synods, held under Agrippinus and Cyprian, ordered that whoever had been baptized by a heretic, was to be re-baptized on re-entering the Church. The Council of Arles abolished this law (lex) of the Africans, and decreed that those who had received baptism from heretics in the name of the holy Trinity were not to be again baptized, but simply to receive the imposition of hands, ut accipiat Spiritum sanctum. Thus, as we have already said, the imposition of hands on those converted was ad pænitentiam and ad confirmationem. The Council of Arles promulgated in this eighth canon the rule that has always been in force, and is still preserved in our time, with regard to baptism conferred by heretics: it was adopted and renewed by the nineteenth canon of the Œcumenical Council of Nicæa.

In several mss. Arianis is read instead of Afris; but it is known that at the time of the first Synod of Arles the sect of the Arians did not yet exist. Binius has thought, and perhaps with some reason, that this canon alluded to the Donatists, and was intended to refute their opinion on the ordination of Cecilian by Felix of Aptunga, by laying down this general principle: "That a sacrament is valid, even when it has been conferred by an unworthy minister." There is, however, no trace of an allusion to the Donatists: it is the thirteenth canon which clearly settles the particular case of the Donatists, as to whether a Traditor, one who has delivered up the Holy Scriptures, can validly ordain.

CAN. 9. Ut qui confessorum litteras afferuut, alias accipiant

De his qui confessorum literas afferunt, placuit ut sublatis iis literis alias accipiant communicatorias.

This canon is a repetition of the twenty-fifth canon of the Synod of Elvira.

CAN. 10. Ut is cujus uxor adulteraverit aliam illa vivente non accipiat

De his qui conjuges suas in adulterio deprehendunt, et iidem sunt adolescentes fideles et prohibentur nubere, placuit ut in quantum possit consilium iis detur, ne viventibus uxoribus suis licet adulteris alias accipiant.

In reference to the ninth canon of Elvira, the Synod of Arles has in view simply the case of a man putting away his adulterous wife; whilst, on the contrary, the Council of Elvira refers to the case of a woman leaving her adulterous husband. In both cases the two Councils alike depart from the existing civil law, by refusing to the innocent party the right of marrying again. But there is the noteworthy difference, that the right of re-marrying is forbidden to the woman, under penalty of permanent excommunication (can. 9 of Elvira); while the man is only strongly advised (in quantum possit consilium iis detur) not to marry again. Even in this case marriage is not allowed, as is shown by the expression et prohibentur nubere. This Synod will not allow that which has been forbidden, but only abstains from imposing ecclesiastical penance. Why is it more considerate to the man? Undoubtedly because the existing civil law gave greater liberty to the husband than to the wife, and did not regard the connection of a married man with an unmarried woman as adultery.

It may be observed that Petavius, instead of et prohibentur nubere, prefers to read et non prohibentur nubere, which would mean that, while they were not prohibited from marrying, they should be strongly recommended not to do so.

CAN. 11. De puellis quæ gentilibus junguntur

De puellis fidelibus quæ gentilibus junguntur placuit, ut aliquanto tempore a communione separentur.

This canon is evidently related to the fifteenth canon of Elvira, with, however, this difference, that the canon of Elvira chiefly relates to the parents, while that of Arles rather concerns daughters. This, too, enforces a penalty, which the other does not.

CAN. 12. Ut clerici fœneratores excommunicentur

De ministris qui fœnerant, placuit eos juxta formam divinitus datam a communione abstineri.

This canon is almost literally identical with the first part of the twentieth canon of Elvira.

CAN. 13. De iis qui Scripturas sacras, vasa dominica, vel nomina fratrum tradidisse dicuntur

De his qui Scripturas sanctas tradidisse dicuntur vel vasa dominica vel nomina fratrum suorum, placuit nobis ut quicumque eorum ex actis publicis fuerit detectus, non verbis nudis, ab ordine cleri amoveatur; nam si iidem aliquos ordinasse fuerint deprehensi, et hi quos ordinaverunt rationales subsistunt, non illis obsit ordinatio. Et quoniam multi sunt qui contra ecclesiasticam regulam pugnare videntur et per testes redemptos putant se ad accusationem admitti debere, omnino non admittantur, nisi, ut supra diximus, actis publicis docuerint.

The Emperor Diocletian had ordered, by his first edict for persecution in 303, first, that all the churches were to be destroyed; secondly, that all sacred books were to be burnt; thirdly, that Christians were to be deprived of all rights and all honours; and that when they were slaves, they were to be declared incapable of acquiring liberty. Consequently Christians were everywhere required to give up the holy books to be burnt, and the sacred vases to be confiscated by the treasury (ad fiscum). This canon mentions these two demands, and, besides these, the traditio nominum. It may be that, according to the first edict, some Christians, and especially the bishops, were required to remit the lists of the faithful belonging to their dioceses, in order to subject them to the decree which deprived them of all rights and honour. However, Dr. München thinks that the traditio nominum was first introduced in consequence of Diocletian's second edict. This edict ordered that all ecclesiastics should be imprisoned, and compelled to sacrifice. Many tried to escape the danger by flight; but it also happened that many were betrayed, and their names (nomina fratrum) given up to the heathen. The thirteenth canon orders the deposition of these Traditores, if they are ecclesiastics. But this penalty was only to be inflicted in case the offence of traditio was proved, not merely by private denunciations (verbis nudis), but by the public laws, by writings signed by officers of justice (ex actis publicis), which the Roman officers had to draw up in executing the Emperor's edict.

The Synod occupied itself with this question: "What must be done if a traditor bishop has ordained clergy?" This was precisely the principal question in the controversy with the Donatists; and the Synod decided "that the ordination should be valid, that is, that whoever should be ordained by such a bishop should not suffer from it" (non illis obsit ordinatio). This part of the passage is very plain, and clearly indicates the solution given by the Council; but the preceding words, et hi, quos ordinaverunt, rationales subsistunt, are difficult to explain. They may very well mean, "If those who have been ordained by them are worthy, and fit to receive holy orders;" but we read in a certain number of MSS., et de his, quos ordinaverint, ratio subsistit, that is to say, "If those are in question who have been ordained by them."

This canon has another conclusion which touches the Donatist controversy; namely: "Accusers who, contrary to all the Church's rules, procured paid witnesses to prove their accusations, as the adversaries of Felix of Aptunga have done, ought not at all to be heard if they cannot prove their complaints by the public acts."

CAN. 14. Ut qui falso accusant fratres suos usque ad exitum excommunicentur

De his qui falso accusant fratres suos, placuit eos usque ad exitum non communicare.

This canon is the sequel to the preceding: "If it is proved that any one has made a positively false and unwarrantable accusation against another (as a traditor), such a person will be excommunicated to the end of his life." This canon is worded in so general a manner, that it not only embraces the false denunciations on the particular case of the traditio, but all false denunciations in general, as the seventy-fifth canon of the Synod of Elvira had already done.

CAN. 15. Ut diacones non offerant

De diaconibus quos cognovimus multis locis offerre, placuit minime fieri debere.

During the persecution of Diocletian, a certain number of deacons seem to have assumed to themselves the right of offering the holy sacrifice, especially when there was no bishop or priest at hand. The Synod of Arles prohibited this. It will be seen that in this canon we translate offerre as "to offer the holy sacrifice," in the same sense as this word is used in the nineteenth canon. Binterim gives another interpretation. By offerre he understands the administration of the Eucharist to the faithful; and he explains the canon in this sense: "The deacons ought not to administer the communion to the faithful in various places, but only in the churches which are assigned to them." We must allow that offerre has sometimes this meaning; for example, in S. Cyprian, de Lapsis: Solemnibus adimpletis calicem diaconus offerre præsentibus cœpit; but,

a. It is difficult to suppose that the Synod of Arles should have employed the expression offerre in two senses so essentially different—in the fifteenth canon, where it would mean to administer the Eucharist, and in the nineteenth canon, where it would mean to offer the holy sacrifice—without having in either pointed out this difference more clearly.

b. The Synod evidently wished to put an end to a serious abuse, as it says, Minime fieri debere. Now it could not have been a very grave offence on the part of the deacons, if, in consequence of the want of clergy, they had administered the communion in several places: after all, they would only have done what they performed ex officio in their own churches.

CAN. 16. Ut ubi quisque fuit excommunicatus, ibi communionem consequatur

De his qui pro delicto suo a communione separantur, placuit ut in quibuscumque locis fuerint exclusi in iisdem communionem consequantur.

The fifty-third canon of the Synod of Elvira had already given the same order. This canon should be compared with the fifth canon of the Synod of Nicæa, the second and sixth of Antioch (in 341), and with the sixteenth of Sardica.

CAN. 17. Ut nullus episcopus alium conculcet episcopum

Ut nullus episcopus alium episcopum inculcet.

A bishop could in many ways inconvenience, molest (inculcare) a colleague; especially—

a. If he allowed himself to exercise various episcopal functions in any diocese other than his own; for example, to ordain clergy, which the Synod of Antioch forbade, in 341, by its thirteenth canon.

b. If he stayed a long time in a strange town, if he preached there, and so threw into the shade the bishop of the place, who might be less able, less learned than himself, for the sake of obtaining the other's see; which the eleventh canon (fourteenth in Latin) of Sardica also forbids.

CAN. 18. De diaconibus urbicis ut sine conscientia presbyterorum nihil agant

De diaconibus urbicis ut non sibi tantum præsumant, sed honorem presbyteris reservent, ut sine conscientia ipsorum nihil tale faciant.

The canon does not tell us in what these usurpations of the suburban deacons consisted (in opposition to the deacons of the country churches, who, being farther from the bishop, had less influence). The words honorem presbyteris reservent seem to imply that the Council of Arles referred to the deacons who, according to the evidence of the Council of Nicæa, forgot their inferiority to the priests, and took rank and place amongst them, which the Synod of Nicæa also forbade. The Synod of Laodicæa also found it necessary to order deacons to remain standing in the presence of priests, unless invited to sit down. The last words of our canon indicate that here also the allusion is to the functions that deacons were generally authorized to exercise in virtue of their charge, such as baptizing and preaching, but which they were not to discharge unless with the consent of the priests who were set over them.

CAN. 19. Ut peregrinis episcopis locus sacrificandi detur

De episcopis peregrinis qui in urbem solent venire, placuit iis locum dare ut offerant.

The seventeenth canon having forbidden bishops to exercise episcopal functions in a strange diocese, the nineteenth canon declares that the celebration of the holy sacrifice is not comprised in this prohibition, and consequently that a bishop should be allowed to offer the holy sacrifice in a strange diocese, or, as we should say, should be permitted to say Mass.

CAN. 20. Ut sine tribus episcopis nullus episcopus ordinetur

De his qui usurpant sibi quod soli debeant episcopos ordinare, placuit ut nullus hoc sibi præsumat nisi assumptis secum aliis septem episcopis. Si tamen non potuerit septem, infra tres non audeat ordinare.

The Synod of Nicæa, canon 4, made the same regulation, that all bishops should not singly ordain another bishop, and orders that there be at least three bishops for this purpose.

CAN. 21. Ut presbyteri aut diacones qui ad alia loca se transferunt deponantur

De presbyteris aut diaconibus qui solent dimittere loca sua in quibus ordinati sunt et ad alia loca se transferunt, placuit ut iis locis ministrent quibus præfixi sunt. Quod si relictis locis suis ad alium se locum transferre voluerint, deponantur.

Cf. the second canon, above, p. 185.

CAN. 22. De apostatis qui in infirmitate communionem pctunt

De his qui apostatant et nunquam se ad ecclesiam repræsentant, ne quidem pœnitentiam agere quærunt, et postea infirmitate accepti petunt communionem, placuit iis non dandam communionem nisi revaluerint et egerint dignos fructus pœnitentiæ.

The Council of Nicæa, in its thirteenth canon, softened this order, and allowed the holy communion to be administered to all sinners at the point of death who should desire it.

Besides, these twenty-two canons of the first Synod of Arles, which are certainly genuine, Mansi found six more in a MS. at Lucca. He thought, however, that these last must have been decreed by another Council of Arles. They are the following:—

CAN. 1 (24)

Placuit ut quantum potest inhibeatur viro, ne dimissa uxore vivente liceat ut aliam ducat super eam: quicumque autem fecerit alienus erit a catholica communione.

CAN. 2 (25)

Placuit ut mulierem corruptam clericus non ducat uxorem, vel is, qui laicus mulierem corruptam duxerit, non admittatur ad clerum.

CAN. 3 (26)

De aliena ecclesia clericum ordinare alibi nullus episcopus usurpet; quod si fecerit, sciat se esse judicandum cum inter fratres de hoc fuerit appetitus.

CAN. 4 (27)

Abstentum clericum alterius ecclesiæ alia non admittat; sed pacem in ecclesia inter fratres simplicem tenere cognoscat.

CAN. 5 (28)

Venientem de Donatistis vel de Montensibus per manus impositionis suscipiantur, ex eo quod contra ecclesiasticum ordinem baptizare videntur.

CAN. 6 (29)

Præterea, quod dignum, pudicum et honestum est, suademus fratribus ut sacerdotes et levitæ cum uxoribus suis non coeant, quia ministerio quotidiano occupantur. Quicumque contra hanc constitutionem fecerit, a clericatus honore deponatur.

If we consider, again, the occasion of this Synod—namely, the schism of the Donatists—we see that as soon as the Synod had pronounced its sentence upon them, they appealed anew to the Emperor, while the Catholic bishops asked permission of him to return to their homes. Constantine thereupon wrote a beautiful and touching letter to the bishops, thanking God for His goodness to him, and the bishops for the equitable and conciliatory judgment that they had pronounced. He complained of the perverseness, the pride, and obstinacy of the Donatists, who would not have peace, but appealed to him from the judgment of the Church, when the sentence of the priests ought to be regarded as that of the Lord Himself (sacerdotum judicium ita debet haberi, ac si ipse Dominus residens judicet). "What audacity, what madness, what folly!" he exclaims; "they have appealed from it like heathens." At the end of his letter he prays the bishops, after Christ's example, to have yet a little patience, and to stay some time longer at Arles, so as to try and reclaim these misguided men. If this last attempt failed, they might return to their dioceses; and he prayed them to remember him, that the Saviour might have mercy upon him. He said that he had ordered the officers of the empire to send the refractory from Arles, and from Africa as well, to his court, where great severity awaited them.

These threats caused a great number of Donatists to return to the Church; others persevered in their obstinacy, and, according to Constantine's order, were brought to the imperial court. From that time there was no longer any occasion for the Catholic bishops to remain at Arles, and in all probability they returned to their dioceses. Arrived at court, the Donatists again prayed the Emperor to judge their cause himself. Constantine at first refused, but, for reasons with which we are not acquainted, ended by consenting to their demand. He summoned Cecilian, the Catholic Bishop of Carthage, as well as his Donatist adversaries, to appear before him at Rome, where he was staying, in August 315. Ingentius, the false accuser of Felix of Aptunga, was to be there to prove to the Donatists that they had improperly called in question the consecration of Cecilian; but Cecilian, for some unknown reason, did not appear. S. Augustine himself did not know why; and the Donatists profited by this circumstance, and urged the Emperor to condemn Cecilian for disobedience. Constantine, however, contented himself with granting him a delay, at the end of which Cecilian was to appear at Milan, which so exasperated many of the Donatists, that they fled from the court to Africa. The Emperor for some time thought of going himself into Africa to judge the cause of the Donatists in their own country. He accordingly sent back some Donatist bishops into Africa, and warned the others by letter of his project, adding, that if they could prove but one of their numerous accusations against Cecilian, he would consider such proof as a demonstration of all the rest.

The Emperor afterwards gave up this scheme, and returned to that which had been first proposed, and in November 316 caused the contending parties to appear before him at Milan. Cecilian presented himself before the Emperor, as well as his antagonists. The Emperor heard both sides, examined their depositions, and finally declared that Cecilian was innocent, that his adversaries were calumniators, and sent a copy of his decision to Eumalius, his vicar in Africa. The Donatists were thus condemned three times, by the two Synods of Rome and of Arles, and finally by the Emperor himself. In spite of this, to weaken the effect of the late sentence, they spread the rumour that the celebrated Hosius Bishop of Corduba, a friend of Cecilian, had prejudiced the Emperor against them.

The subsequent history of the schism of the Donatists does not belong to this place; and we have now to consider two other synods which were held in the East about the same time as that of Arles, and which merit all our attention. They are those of Ancyra and Neocæsarea.

SEC. 16. The Synod of Ancyra in 314

Maximilian having died during the summer of 313, the Church in the East began to breathe freely, says Eusebius. He says nothing further about these Synods; but one of the first, and certainly the most celebrated, of these Councils, was that of Ancyra, the capital of Galatia, which was held for the purpose of healing the wounds inflicted on the Church by the last persecution, and especially to see what could be done on the subject of the lapsi.

The best Greek MSS. of the canons of Ancyra contain a very ancient preface, which shows, without further specification, that the Council of Ancyra was held before that of Nicæa. The presence of Vitalis Bishop of Antioch at the Council of Ancyra proves that it was held before the year 319, which is the year of the death of that bishop. It is, then, between 313 and 319 that it was held. Binius believes he has discovered a still more exact date, in the fact of the presence of Basil Bishop of Amasia at our Synod.

According to his opinion, this bishop suffered martyrdom in 316, under the Emperor Licinius; but Tillemont has proved that he was probably not martyred till 320.

It appears from the sixth canon of Ancyra that the Council was held, conformably to the apostolic canons, No. 38 (36), in the fourth week after Easter. Maximin having died during the summer of 313, the first Pentecost after his death fell in 314; and it is very probable that the Christians immediately availed themselves of the liberty which his death gave them to come to the aid of the Church.

This is also what the words of Eusebius clearly indicate. Baronius, Tillemont, Rémi Ceillier, and others, were therefore perfectly right in placing the Synod of Ancyra after the Easter which followed the death of Maximin; consequently in 314.

We have three lists of the bishops who were present at the Synod of Ancyra. They differ considerably from one another. That which, in addition to the bishops and the towns, names the provinces, is evidently, as the Ballerini have shown, of later origin: for (α) no Greek MS. contains this list; (β) it is wanting in the most ancient Latin translations; (γ) the lists of the provinces are frequently at variance with the civil division of the province at this time. For instance, the list speaks of a Galatia prima, of a Cappadocia prima, of a Cilicia prima and secunda, of a Phrygia Pacatiana, all divisions which did not then exist. Another list of the bishops who were present at Ancyra, but without showing the provinces, is found in the Prisca and in the Isidorian collection. Dionysius the Less does not give a list of the persons: one of this kind has not, until lately, been attached to his writings.

In this state of things, it is evident that none of these lists are of great value, as they vary so much from each other even as to the number of the bishops, which is left undecided, being put down between twelve and eighteen. In the longest list the following names are found: Vitalis of Antioch, Agricolaus of Cæsarea in Palestine, Marcellus of Ancyra, who had become so famous in the Arian controversy, Lupus of Tarsus, Basil of Amasia, Philadelphius of Juliopolis in Galatia, Eustolius of Nicomedia, Heraclius of Tela in Great Armenia, Peter of Iconium, Nunechius of Laodicea in Phrygia, Sergianus of Antioch in Pisidia, Epidaurus of Perga in Pamphilia, Narcissus of Neronias in Cilicia, Leontius of Cæsarea in Cappadocia, Longinus of Neocæsarea in Pontus, Amphion of Epiphania in Cilicia, Salamenus of Germanicia in Cœlesyria, and Germanus of Neapolis in Palestine. Several of these were present, eleven years after, at the first Œcumenical Council of Nicæa. They belonged, as we see, to such different provinces of Asia Minor and Syria, that the Synod of Ancyra may, in the same sense as that of Arles, be considered a concilium plenarium, that is, a general council of the Churches of Asia Minor and Syria. From the fact that Vitalis of Antioch is mentioned first (primo loco), and that Antioch was the most considerable seat of those who were represented at Ancyra, it is generally concluded that Vitalis presided over the Synod; and we admit this supposition, although the Libellus synodicus assigns the presidency to Marcellus of Ancyra.

CAN. 1

Πρεσβυτέρους τοὺς ἐπιθύσαντας, εἶτα ἐπαναπαλαίσαντας μήτε ἐκ μεθόδου τινὸς ἀλλ' ἐξ ἀληθείας, μήτε προκατασκευάσαντας καὶ ἐπιτηδεύσαντας, καὶ πείσαντας ἵνα δόξωσι μὲν βασάνοις ὑποβάλλεσθαι, ταύτας δὲ τῷ δοκεῖν καὶ τῷ σχήματι προσαχθῆναι· τούτους ἔδιξε τῆς μὲν τιμῆς τῆς κατὰ τὴν καθέδραν μετέχειν, προσφέρειν δὲ αὐτοὺς ἢ ὁμιλεῖν ἢ ὅλως λειτουργεῖν τι τῶν ἱερατικῶν λειτουργιῶν μὴ ἐξεῖναι.

"Priests who sacrificed (during the persecution), but afterwards repenting, resumed the combat not only in appearance, but in reality, will continue to enjoy the honours of their office, but they may neither sacrifice or preach, nor fulfil any priestly office."

In this translation we have left out a great incidental proposition (from μήτε προκατασκευάσαντας to προσαχθῆναι), because to be understood it requires some previous explanations. Certain priests who had sacrificed to idols, wishing to be restored to favour, performed a sort of farce to deceive the bishop and the faithful. They bribed some officers and their subordinates, then presented themselves before them as Christians, and pretended to submit to all kinds of tortures, which were not really, but only apparently applied to them, according to the plan which had been previously arranged. The Council also says: "Without having made any arrangements, and without its being understood and agreed that they should appear to submit to tortures which were only to be apparently inflicted on them."

It was quite justifiable, and in accordance with the ancient and severe discipline of the Church, when this Synod no longer allowed priests, even when sincerely penitent, to discharge priestly functions. It was for this same reason that the two Spanish bishops Martial and Basilides were deposed, and that the judgment given against them was confirmed in 254 by an African synod held under S. Cyprian. The first canon, together with the second and third, was inserted in the Corpus juris can.

CAN. 2

Διακόνους ὁμοίως θύσαντας, μετὰ δὲ ταῦτα ἀναπαλαίσαντας τὴν μὲν ἄλλην τιμὴν ἔχειν, πεπαῦσθαι δὲ αὐτοὺς πάσης τῆς ἱερᾶς λειτουργίας, τῆς τε τοῦ ἄρτον ἢ ποτήριον ἀναφέρειν ἢ κηρύσσειν, εἰ μέντοι τινὲς τῶν ἐπισκόπων τούτοις συνίδοιεν κάματόν τινα ἢ ταπείνωσιν πρᾴτητος καὶ ἐθέλοιεν πλεῖόν τι διδόναι ἢ ἀφαιρεῖν, ἐπ᾽ αὐτοῖς εἶναι τὴν ἐξουσίαν.

"In the same manner, the deacons who may have sacrificed, but have afterwards returned to the fight, shall keep the dignities of their office, but shall no longer fulfil any holy function, shall no longer offer the bread and wine (to the celebrant or to the communicants), shall no longer preach. But if any bishops, out of regard to their efforts (for their ardent penitence), and to their humiliation, wish to grant them more privileges, or to withdraw more from them, they have power to do so."

According to this, such deacons could no longer exercise their ministry in the Church, but they continued their offices as almoners to the poor, and administrators of the property of the Church, etc. etc. It is doubtful what is meant by "to offer the bread and the chalice." In the primitive Church, S. Justin testifies that the deacons distributed the holy communion to the laity. It is possible that the canon refers to this distribution. Van Espen, however, thinks that, at the time of the Synod, deacons no longer distributed the consecrated bread to the faithful, but only the chalice, according to a prescription of the Apostolic Constitutions, and an expression of Cyprian; so that ἀναφάτρειν ἄρτον ἢ ποτήριον (because there is mention of ἄρτον, bread) must here relate to the presentation of the bread and the chalice made by the deacon to the bishop or priest who celebrated at the time of the offertory. But it seems from the eighteenth canon of Nicæa, that this primitive custom, in virtue of which deacons also distributed the eucharistic bread as well as wine, had not entirely disappeared at the beginning of the fourth century, and consequently at the time of the Synod of Ancyra.

The word κηρύσσειν, to proclaim, needs explanation. It means in the first place the act of preaching; it is declared to be forbidden to diaconis lapsis. But deacons had, and still have, other things to proclaim (κηρύσσειν). They read the Gospel, they exclaimed: Flectamus genua, Procedamus in pace, Ne quis audientium, Ne quis infidelium; and these functions were also comprised in the κηρύσσειν.

Finally, the canon directs bishops to take into consideration the circumstances and the worth of the diaconi lapsi in adding to or deducting from the measures decreed against them.

CAN. 3

Τοὺς φεύγοντας καὶ συλληφθέντας ἢ ὑπὸ οἰκείων παραδοθέντας ἢ ἄλλως τὰ ὑπάρχοντα ἀφαιρεθέντας ἢ ὑπομείναντας βασάνους ἢ εἰς δεσμωτήριον ἐμβληθέντας

βοῶντάς τε ὅτι εἰσὶ Χριστιανοὶ καὶ περισχισθέντας
(περισχεθέυτας) ἤτοι εἰς τὰς χεῖρας πρὸς βίαν ἐμβαλλόντων
τῶν βιαζομένων ἢ βρῶμά τιπρὸς ἀνάγκην δεξαμένους,
ὁμολογοῦυτας δὲ διόλου ὅτι εἰσὶ Χριστιανοὶ, καὶ τὸ πένθος
τοῦ συμβάυτος ἀεὶ ἐπιδεικνυμένους τῇ πάσῃ καταστολῇ καὶ
τῷ σχήματι καὶ τῇ βίου ταπεινόητι· τούτους ὡς ἔξω
ἁμαρτήματος ὄντας τῆς κοινωνίας μὴ κωλύεσθαι εἰ δὲ καὶ
ἐκωλύθησαν ὑπό τινος, περισσοτέρας ἀκριβέας ἕνεκεν ἢ καὶ
τινων ἀγνοίᾳ, εὐθὺς προσδεχθῆναι· τοῦτο δὲ ὁμοίως ἐπί τε
τῶν ἐκ τοῦ κλήρου καὶ τῶν ἄλλων λαϊκῶν, προσεξητάσθη δὲ
κἀκεῖνο, εἰ δύνανται καὶ λαικοὶ τῇ αὐτῇ ἀνάγκῃ ὑποπεσόντες
προσάγεθαι εἰς τάξιν· ἔδοξεν οὖν καὶ τούτους ὡς μηδὲν
ἡμαρτηκότας, εἰ καὶ ἡ προλαβοῦσα εὑρίσκοιτο ὀρθὴ τοῦ
βίου πολιτεία, προχειρίζεσθαι.

"Those who fled before persecution, but were caught, or
were betrayed by those of their own houses, or in any other
way, who have borne with resignation the confiscation of
their property, tortures, and imprisonment, declaring
themselves to be Christians, but who have subsequently
been vanquished, whether their oppressors have by force
put incense into their hands, or have compelled them to
take in their mouth the meat offered to idols, and who, in
spite of this, have persevered in avowing themselves
Christians, and have evinced their sorrow for what had
befallen them by their dejection and humility,—such, not
having committed any fault, are not to be deprived of the
communion of the Church; and if they have been so treated
by the over-severity or ignorance of their bishop, they are
immediately to be reinstated. This applies equally to the
clergy and to the laity. In the same way it was to be inquired
if the laity, to whom violence has been used (that is to say,

who have been physically obliged to sacrifice), might be promoted to the ministry (τάξις, ordo); and it was decreed that, not having committed any fault (in the case of these sacrifices), they might be elected, provided their former life was found to be consistent."

The meaning of this canon is clear: "Physical constraint relieves from responsibility." That there had been physical constraint was proved in the following ways:—

(a.) By the previous endurance with which they had borne confiscation, tortures, and imprisonment.

(β.) By this, that during their sufferings they had always declared themselves Christians.

Among the expressions of this canon the word περισχισθέντας of the textus vulgatus presents the chief difficulties. Zonaras translates it thus: "If their clothes have been torn from their bodies:" for περισχίζω means to tear away, and with τινὰ to tear off the clothes from any one. But the true reading is περισχεθέντας, which Routh has found in three MSS. in the Bodleian Library, and which harmonizes the best with the versions of Dionysius the Less and of Isidore. We have used this reading (περισχεθέντας) in our translation of the canon; for περιέχω means to surround, to conquer, to subdue.

CAN. 4

Περὶ τῶν πρὸς βίαν θυσάντων, ἐπὶ δὲ τούτοις καὶ τῶν δειπνησάντων εἰς τὰ εἴδωλα, ὅσοι μὲν ἀπαγόμενοι καὶ σχήματι φαιδροτέρῳ ἀνῆλθον καὶ ἐσθῆτι ἐχρήσαντο πολυτεστέρᾳ καὶ μετέσχον τοῦ παρασκευασθέντος δείπνου ἀδιαφόρως, ἔδοξεν ἐνιαυτὸν ἀκροᾶσθαι, ὑποπεσεῖν δὲ τρία ἔτη, εὐχῆς δὲ μόνης κοινωνῆσαι ἔτη δύο, καὶ τότε ἐλθεῖν ἐπὶ τὸ τέλειον.

"As to those who have been forced to sacrifice, and who have besides eaten the meats consecrated to the gods (that is to say, who have been forced to take part in the feasts off the sacrifices), the Council decrees, that those who, being forced to go to the sacrifice, have gone cheerfully, dressed in their best, and without any sorrow (as if there was no difference between this and other meals), and shall there have eaten of it, shall remain one year amongst the audientes (second class of penitents), three years among the substrati (third class of penitents), shall take part in the prayers (fourth class) for two years, and then finally be admitted to the complete privileges of the Church (τὸ τέλειον), that is, to the communion."

CAN. 5

Ὅσοι δὲ ἀνῆλθον μετὰ ἐσθῆτος πενθικῆς καὶ ἀναπεσόντες ἔφαγον μεταξὺ δι᾽ ὅλης τῆς ἀνακλίσεως δακρύοντες, εἰ ἐπλήρωσαν τὸν τῆς ὑποπτώσεως τριετῆ χρόνον χωρὶς προσφορᾶς δεχθήτωσαν· εἰ δὲ μὴ ἔφαγον, δύο ὑποπεσόντες ἔτη τῷ τρίτῳ κοινωνησάτωσαν χωρὶς προσφορᾶς, ἵνα τὸ τέλειον τῇ τετραετίᾳ λάβωσι, τοὺ δὲ ἐπισκόπους ἐξουσίαν ἔχειν τὸν τρόπον τῆς ἐπιστροφῆς δοκιμάσαντας φιλανθρωπεύεσθαι ἢ πλείονα προστιθέναι χρόνον· πρὸ πάντων δὲ καὶ ὁ προάγων βίος καὶ ὁ μετὰταῦτα ἐξεταζέσθω, καὶ οὕτως ἡ φιλανθρωπία ἐπιμετρείσθω.

"Nevertheless, those who have appeared there (that is, at the feast of the sacrifices) in mourning habits, who have been full of grief during the repast, and have wept during the whole time of the feast, shall be three years amongst the substrati, and then be admitted, without taking part in the offering; but if they have not eaten (and have merely been present at the feast), they are to be substrati for two years, and the third year they shall take part in the offering (in the degree of the consistentes, σύστασις), so as to receive the complement (the holy communion) in the fourth year. The bishops will have the power, after having tried the conduct of each, to mitigate the penalties, or to extend the time of penitence; but they must take care to inquire what has passed before and after their fall, and their clemency must be exercised accordingly."

We may see that this canon is closely allied to the preceding one, and that the one explains the other: there only remains some obscurity arising from the expression χωρὶς προσφορᾶς. Aubespine thought that there is here a reference to the offerings which were presented by penitents, in the hope of obtaining mercy; but Suicer remarks that it is not so, and that the reference here is certainly to those offerings which are presented by the faithful during the sacrifice (at the offertory). According to Suicer, the meaning of the canon would be: "They may take part in divine worship, but not actively;" that is, "they may mingle their offerings with those of the faithful:" which corresponds with the fourth or last degree of penitence. But as those who cannot present their offerings during the sacrifice are excluded from the communion, the complete meaning of this canon is: "They may be present at divine service, but may neither offer nor communicate with the faithful." Consequently χωρὶς προσφορᾶς also comprises the exclusion from the communion; but it does not follow from this that προσφορά means the sacrament of the altar, as Herbst and Routh have erroneously supposed. The eucharistic service has, we know, two parts: it is, in the first place, a sacrifice; and then, as a reception of the eucharistic bread, it is a sacrament. And the whole act may be called προσφορά; but the mere reception of the communion cannot be called προσφορά. The canon does not clearly point out the time during which penitents were to remain in the fourth degree of penitence, except in the case of those who had not actually eaten of the sacrificed meats. It says, that at the end of a year they could be received in full, that is to say, at the eucharistic table. The time of penitence is not fixed for those who had actually eaten the sacrificed meats: perhaps it was also a year; or it may be they were treated according to the fourth canon, that is to say, reduced for two years to the fourth degree of penitence. The penitents of the fifth canon, less culpable than those of the fourth, are not, as the latter, condemned to the second degree of penitence.

CAN. 6

Περὶ τῶν ἀπειλῇ μόνον εἰξάνρων κολάσεως καὶ ἀφαιρέσεως ὑπαρχόντων ἢ μετοικίας καὶ θυσάντων καὶ μέχρι τοῦ παρόντος καιροῦ μὴ μετανοησάντων μηδὲ ἐπιστρεψάντων, νῦν δὲ παρὰ τὸν καιρὸν τῆς συνόδου προσελθόντων καὶ εἰς διάνοιαν τῆς ἐπιστροφῆς γενομένων, ἔδοξε μέχρι τῆς μεγάλης ἡμέρας εἰς ἀκρόασιν δεχθῆναι, καὶ μετὰ τὴν μεγάλην ἡμέραν ὑποπεσεῖν ταῖα ἔτη καὶ μετὰ ἄλλα δύο ἔτη κοινωνῆσαι χωρὶς προσφορᾶς, καὶ οὕτως ἐλθεῖν ἐπὶ τὸ τέλειον, ὥστε τὴν πᾶσαν ἐξαετίαν πληρῶσαι· εἰ δέ τινες πρὸ τῆς συνόδου ταύτης ἐδέχθησαυ εἰς μετάνοιαν, ἀπ᾽ ἐκείνον τοῦ χρόνου λελογίσθαι αὐτοῖς τὴν ἀρχὴν τῆς ἐξαετίας· εἰ μέντοι κίνδυνς καί θανάτου προσδοκία ἐκ νόσου ἤ ἄλλης τινὸς προφάσεως συμβαίη, τούτους ἐπὶ ὅρῳ δεχθῆναι.

"As to those who yielded on the first threat of punishment and of the confiscation of their property, or of exile, and who have sacrificed, and to this day have not repented or returned, but who on the occasion of this Synod have repented, and shall resolve to return, it is decreed, that until the great feast (Easter) they shall be admitted to the degree of audientes; that they shall after the great feast be substrati for three years; then that they shall be admitted, but without taking part in the sacrifice for two years, and that then only they shall be admitted to the full service (to the communion), so that the whole time will be six years. For those who have been admitted to a course of penitence previous to this Synod, the six years will be allowed to date from the moment of its commencement. If they were exposed to any danger, or threatened with death following any illness, or if there was any other important reason, they would be admitted, conformably to the present prescription (ὅρος)."

The meaning of the last phrase of the canon is, that if the sick regain their health, they will perform their penance, according to what is prescribed. Zonaras thus very clearly explains this passage. This canon is made intelligible by the two preceding. A similar decision is given in the eleventh Nicene canon.

As we have previously remarked (sec. 16), there is a chronological signification in the expression "till the next

Easter," compared with that of "the six years shall be accomplished." According to the thirty-sixth (thirty-eighth) apostolic canon, a synod was to be held annually in the fourth week after Easter. If, then, a penitent repented at the time of the synod, and remained among the audientes till the next Easter, he had done penance for nearly a year. And adding three years for the degree of the substratio, and two for the last degree, the six years were completed. It is then with good reason that we have deduced from the sixth canon that the Council of Ancyra was held shortly after Easter, and very probably in the fourth week after this feast, that is, in the time prescribed by the apostolic canons.

CAN. 7

Περὶ τῶν συνεστιαθέντων ἐν ἑορτῇ ἐθνικῇ ἐν τόπῳ ἀφωροσμένῳ τοῖς ἐθνικοῖ, ἴδια βρώματα ἐπικομισαμένων καὶ φαγντων, ἔδοξε διετίαν ὑποπεσόντας δεχθῆναν Τὸ δὲ εἰ χρὴ μετὰ τῆς προσφορᾶς ἕκαστον τῶν ἐπιακόπων δοκιμάσαι καὶ τὸν ἄλλον βίον ἐφ᾽ ἑκάστου ἀξιῶσαι.

"As to those who, during a heathen festival, have seated themselves in the locality appointed for that festival, and have brought and eaten their food there, they shall be two years substrati, and then admitted. As to the question of their admission to the offering, each bishop shall decide thereon, taking into consideration the whole life of each person."

Several Christians tried, with worldly prudence, to take a middle course. On the one hand, hoping to escape persecution, they were present at the feasts of the heathen sacrifices, which were held in the buildings adjoining the temples; and on the other, in order to appease their consciences, they took their own food, and touched nothing that had been offered to the gods. These Christians forgot that S. Paul had ordered that meats sacrificed to the gods should be avoided, not because they were tainted in themselves, as the idols were nothing, but from another, and in fact a twofold reason: 1st, Because, in partaking of them, some had still the idols in their hearts, that is to say, were still attached to the worship of idols, and thereby sinned; and 2dly, Because others scandalized their brethren, and sinned in that way. To these two reasons a third may be added, namely, the hypocrisy and the duplicity of those Christians who wished to appear heathens, and nevertheless to remain Christians. The Synod punished them with two years of penance in the third degree, and gave to each bishop the right, either at the expiration of this time to admit them to communion, or to make them remain some time longer in the fourth degree.

CAN. 8

Οἱ δὲ δεύτερον καὶ τρίτον θύσαντες μετὰ βίας, τετραρτίαν ὑοπεσέτωσαν, δύο δὲ ἔτη χωρὶς προσφορᾶς κοινωνησάτωσαν, καὶ τῷ ἑβδόμῳ τελείως δεχθήτωσαν.

"Those who, being compelled, have sacrificed two or three times, shall remain substrati for four years; they shall take part in the worship, without presenting any offering, for two years (as consistentes of the fourth degree); the seventh they shall be admitted to the communion."

CAN. 9

Ὅσοι δὲ μὴ μόνον ἀπέστησαν ἀλλὰ καὶ ἐπανέστησαν καὶ ἠσάγκασαν ἀδελφοὺς καὶ αἴτιοι ἐγένοντο τοῦ ἀναγκασθῆναι, οὗτοι ἔτη μὲν τρία τὸν τῆς ἀκροάσεως δεξάσθωσαν τόπον, ἐν δὲ ἄλλῃ ἑξαετίᾳ τὸν τῆς ὑποπτώσεως, ἄλλον δὲ ἐνιαυτὸν κοινωνησάτωσαν χωρὶς προσφορᾶς, ἵνα τὴν δεκαετίαν πληρώσαντες τοῦ τελείου μετάσχωσιν· ἐν μέντοι τούτῳ χρόνῳ καὶ τὸν ἄλλον αὐτῶν ἐπιτηρεῖσθαι βίον.

"Those who have not only apostatized, but have become the enemies of their brethren, and have compelled them (to apostasy), or have been the cause of the constraint put upon them, shall remain for three years among the audientes (second degree), then six years with the substrati; they shall then take part in the worship, without offering (in quality of consistentes), for one year; and not until the expiration of ten years shall they receive full communion (the holy Eucharist). Their conduct during all this time shall also be watched."

CAN. 10

Διάκονοι ὅσοι καθίστανται, παρ᾽ αὐτὴν τὴν κατάστασιν εἰ ἐμαρτύραντο καὶ ἔφασαν χρῆναι γαμῆσαι, μὴ δυνάμενοι οὕτως μένειν, οὗτοι μετὰ ταῦτα γαμήσαντες ἔστωσαν ἐν τῇ ὑπηρεσίᾳ διὰ τὸ ἐπιτραπῆναι αὐτοὺς ὑπὸ τοῦ ἐπισκόπου· τοῦτο δὲ εἴ τινες σιωπήσαντες καὶ καταδεξάμενοι ἐν τῇ χειροτονίᾳ μένειν οὕτως μετὰ ταῦτα ἦλθον ἐπὶ γάμον, πεαῦσθαι αὐτοὺς τῆς διακονίας.

"If deacons, at the time of their appointment (election), declare that they must marry, and that they cannot lead a celibate life, and if accordingly they marry, they may continue their offices, because the bishop (at the time of their institution) gave them leave to marry; but if at the time of their election they have not spoken, and have agreed in taking holy orders to lead a celibate life, and if later they marry, they shall lose their diaconate."

This canon has been inserted in the Corpus juris canonici.

CAN. 11

Τὰς μνηστευθείσας κόρας καὶ μετὰ ταῦτα ὑπ' ἄλλων ἁρπαγείσας ἔδοξεν ἀποδίδοσθαι τοῖς προμνηστευσαμένοις, εἰ καὶ βίανὑπ' αὐτῶν πάθοιεν.

"Damsels who are betrothed, who are afterwards carried off by others, shall be given back to those to whom they are betrothed, even when they have been treated with violence."

This canon treats only of betrothed women (by the sponsalia de futuro), not of those who are married (by the sponsalia de præsenti). In the case of the latter there would be no doubt as to the duty of restitution. The man who was betrothed was, moreover, at liberty to receive his affianced bride who had been carried off, or not. It was thus that S. Basil had already decided in canon 22 of his canonical letter to Amphilochius.

CAN. 12

Τοὺς πρὸ τοῦ βαπτίσματος τεθυκότας καὶ μετὰ ταῦτα βαπτισθέντας ἔδοξεν εἰς τάξιν προάγεσθαι ὡς ἀπολουσαμένους.

"Those who have sacrificed to the gods before their baptism, and who have afterwards been baptized, may be promoted to holy orders, as (by baptism) they are purified from all their former sins."

This canon does not speak generally of all those who sacrificed before baptism; for if a heathen sacrificed before having embraced Christianity, he certainly could not be reproached for it after his admission. It was quite a different case with a catechumen, who had already declared for Christianity, but who during the persecution had lost courage, and sacrificed. In this case it might be asked whether he could still be admitted to the priesthood. The Council decided that a baptized catechumen could afterwards be promoted to holy orders.

The fourteenth canon of Nicæa also speaks of the catechumens who have committed the same fault.

CAN. 13

Χωρεπισκόπους μὴ ἐξεῖναι πρεσβυτέρους ἢ διακόνους ξειροτονεῖν, ἀλλὰ μηδὲ πρεσβυτέρους χωρὶς τοῦ ἐπιτραπῆναι ὑπὸ τοῦ ἐπισκόπου μετὰ γραμμάτων ἐν ἑτέρᾳ παροικίᾳ.

The literal translation of the Greek text is as follows:—

"It is not permitted to the chorepiscopi to ordain priests and deacons; neither is this permitted to the priests of the towns in other parishes (dioceses) without the written authority of the bishop of the place."

In our remarks on the fifty-seventh canon of the Council of Laodicea, where it is forbidden to appoint chorepiscopi (or country bishops) for the future, we shall explain what must be understood by this office, which is here mentioned for the first time. Compare also the eighth and tenth canons of the Synod of Antioch in 341, and the second proposition of the sixth canon of the Council of Sardica. If the first part of the thirteenth canon is easy to understand, the second, on the contrary, presents a great difficulty; for a priest of a town could not in any case have the power of consecrating priests and deacons, least of all in a strange diocese. Many of the most learned men have, for this reason, supposed that the Greek text of the second half of the canon, as we have read it, is incorrect or defective. It wants, say they, ποιεῖν τι, or aliquid agere, i.e. to complete a religious function. To confirm this supposition, they have appealed to several ancient versions, especially to that of Isidore: sed nec presbyteris civitatis sine episcopi præcepto amplius aliquid imperare, vel sine auctoritate literarum ejus in unaquaque (some read ἐν ἑκάστῃ instead of ἐν ἑτέρᾳ) parochia aliquid agere. The ancient Roman MS. of the canons, Codex canonum, has the same reading, only that it has provincia instead of parochia. Fulgentius Ferrandus, deacon of Carthage, who long ago made a collection of canons, translates in the same way in his Breviatio canonum: Ut presbyteri civitatis sine jussu episcopi nihil jubeant, nec in unaquaque parochia aliquid agant. Van Espen has explained this canon in the same way.

Routh has given another interpretation. He maintained that there was not a word missing in this canon, but that at the commencement one ought to read, according to several MSS., χωρεπισκόποις in the dative, and further down ἀλλὰ μὴν μηδὲ instead of ἀλλὰ μηδὲ, then πρεσβυτέρους (in the accusative) πόλεως, and finally ἑκάστῃ instead of ἑτέρᾳ; and that we must therefore translate, "Chorepiscopi are not permitted to consecrate priests and deacons (for the country), still less (ἀλλὰ μὴν μηδὲ) can they consecrate priests for the town without the consent of the bishop of the place." The Greek text, thus modified according to some mss., especially those in the Bodleian Library, certainly gives a good meaning. Still ἀλλὰ μὴν μηδὲ does not mean, but still less: it means, but certainly not, which makes a considerable difference.

Besides this, it can very seldom have happened that the chorepiscopi ordained priests and deacons for a town; and if so, they were already forbidden (implicite) in the first part of the canon.

CAN. 14

Τοὺς ἐν κλήρῳ πρεσβυτέρους ἢ διακόνους ὄντας καὶ ἀπεχομένους κρεῶν ἔδοξεν ἐφάπτεσθαι, καὶ οὕτως, εἰ βούλοιντο, κρατεῖν ἑαυτῶν εἰ δὲ βούλοιντο (βδελύσσοιντο), ὡς μηδὲ τὰ μετὰ κρεῶν βαλλόμενα λάχανα ἐσθίειν, καὶ εἰ μὴ ὑπείκοιεν τῷ κανόνι, πεπαῦσθαι αὐτοὺς τῆς τάξεως.

"Those priests and clerks who abstain from eating meat ought (during the love-feasts) to eat it (taste it); but they may, if they will, abstain from it (that is to say, not eat it). If they disdain it (βδελύσσοιντο), so that they will not eat even vegetables cooked with meat, and if they do not obey the present canon, they are to be excluded from the ranks of the clergy."

The fifty-second apostolic canon had already promulgated the same law with reference to the false Gnostic or Manichean asceticism, which declared that matter was satanic, and especially flesh and wine. Zonaras has perceived and pointed out that our canon treated of the agapæ, or love-feasts, of the primitive Christians. He shows, besides, that ἐφάπτεσθαι means, to touch the meats, in the same sense as ἀπογεύεσθαι, to taste. Matthæus Blastares agrees with Zonaras. Finally, Routh has had the credit of contributing to the explanation of this canon, inasmuch as, relying on three MSS., the Collectio of John of Antioch and the Latin versions, he has read εἰ δὲ βδελύσσοιντο instead of εἰ δὲ βούλοιντο, which has no meaning here. If βούλοιντο is to be preserved, we must, with Beveridge, insert the negation μὴ. But the reading βδελύσσοιντο has still in its favour that the fifty-second apostolic canon, just quoted, and which treats of the same question, has the expression βδελυσσόμενος in the same sense as our canon. Let us add that κρατεῖν ἑαυτῶν ought to be taken in the sense of ἐγκρατεῖν, that is, to abstain.

CAN. 15

Περὶ τῶν διαφερόντων τῷ κυριακῷ, ὅσα ἐπισκόπου μὴ ὄντος πρεσβύτεροι ἐπώλησαν, ἀναβαλεῖσθαι (ἀνακαλεῖσθαι) τὸ κυριακὸν, ἐν δὲ τῇ κρίσει τοῦ ἐπισκόπου εἶναι, εἴπερ προσήκει ἀπολαβεῖν τὴν τιμὴν εὅτε καὶ μὴ, διὰ τὸ πολλάκις τὴν εἴσοδον (πρόσοδον) τῶν πεπραμένων ἀποδεδωκέναι αὐτοῖς τούτοις πλείονα τὴν τιμήν.

"If the priests, during the vacancy of an episcopal see, have sold anything belonging to the Church, she (the Church) has the right to reclaim it (ἀνακαλεῖσθαι); and it is for the bishop to decide whether they (the buyers) are to receive the price given for the purchase, seeing that often the temporary use of the article sold to them has been worth more than the price paid for it."

If the purchaser of ecclesiastical properties has realized more by the temporary revenue of such properties than the price of the purchase, the Synod thinks there is no occasion to restore him this price, as he has already received a sufficient indemnity from the revenue, and that, according to the rules then in force, interest drawn from the purchase money was not permitted. Besides, the purchaser hall done wrong in buying ecclesiastical property during the vacancy of a see (sede vacante). Beveridge and Routh have shown that in the text ἀνακαλεῖσθαι and πρόσοδον must be read.

CAN. 16

Περὶ τῶν ἀλογευσαμένων ἢ καὶ ἀλογευομένων, ὅσοι πρὶν εἰκοσαετεῖς γενέσθαι ἥμαρτον, πέντε καὶ δέκα ἔτεσιν ὑποπεσόντες κοινωνίας τυγχανέτωσαν τῆς εἰς τὰς προσευχὰς, εἶτα ἐν τῇ κοινωνίᾳ διατελέσαντες ἔτη πέντε, τότε καὶ τῆς προςφορᾶς ἐφαπτέσθωσαν ἐξεταζέσθω δὲ αὐτῶν καὶ ὁ ἐν τῇ ὑποπτώσει βίος, καὶ οὕτως τυγχανέτωσαν τῆς φιλανθρωπίας εἰ δέ τινες κατακόρως ἐν τοῖς ἁμαρτήμασι γεγόνασι, τὴν μακρὰν ἐχέτωσαν ὑπόπτωσιν ὅσοι δὲ ὑπερβάντες τὴν ἡλικίαν ταύτην γυναῖκας ἔχοντες περιπεπτώκασι τῷ ἁμαρτήματι, πέντε καὶ εἴκοσι ἔτη ὑποπεσέτωσαν καὶ κοινωνίας τυγχανέτωσαν τῆς εἰς τὰς προσευχὰς, εἶτα ἐκτελέσαντες πέντε ἔτη ἐν τῇ κοινωνίᾳ τῶν εὐχῶν τυγχανέτωσαν τῆς προσφορᾶς εἰ δέ τινες καὶ γυναῖκας ἔχοντες καὶ ὑπερβάντες τὸν πεντηκονταετῆ χρόνον ἥμαρτον, ἐπὶ τῇ ἐξόδῳ τοῦ βίου τυγχανέτωσαν τῆς κοινωίας.

"Those who have been or are. now guilty of lying with beasts, supposing they are not twenty years old when they commit this sin, ought to be substrati for five years; they should then be allowed to join in the prayers, without offering the sacrifice (and would consequently live in the fourth degree of penitence); and after that time they might assist at the holy sacrifice. An examination must also be made of their conduct while they were substrati, and also notice taken of the lives they led. As for those who have sinned immoderately in this way (i.e. who have for a long time committed this sin), they must undergo a long substratio (no allowance will be made in their case). Those who are more than twenty, and have been married, and have nevertheless fallen into this sin, ought to be allowed to share in the prayers only after a substratio of twenty-five years; and after five years' sharing in the prayers, they should be allowed to assist at the holy sacrifice. If married men more than fifty years old fall into this sin, they shall receive the communion only at the end of their lives."

On the expressions substrati, participation in prayers and in the sacrifice, cf. the remarks above on canons 4 and 5.

CAN. 17

Τοὺς ἀλογευσαμένους καὶ λεπροὺς ὄντας ἤτοι λεπρώσαντας, τούτους προσέταξεν ἡ ἁγία σύνοδος εἰς τοὺς χειμαζομένους εὔχεσθαι.

It is not easy to give the real meaning of this canon. It may perhaps mean: "Those who have committed acts of bestiality, and, being lepers themselves, have now (ἤτοι) made others so, must pray among the χειμαζομένοις."

Others translate it: "Those who have committed acts of bestiality, and are or have been lepers (λεπρώσαντας, i.e. having been leprous), shall pray among the χειμαζομένοις." This last translation seems to us inexact; for λεπρώσαντας does not come from λεπράω, but from λεπρόω, which has a transitive meaning, and signifies "to make leprous." But even if we adopt the former translation without hesitation, it is still asked if the leprosy of which the canon speaks is the malady known by that name, and which lepers could communicate to others especially by cohabitation; or if it means spiritual leprosy, sin, and especially the sin of bestiality, and its wider extension by bad example. Van Espen thinks that the canon unites the two ideas, and that it speaks of the real leprosy caused precisely by this bestial depravity. By the word χειμαζόμενοι some understand those possessed. This is the view of Beveridge and Routh. Others, particularly Suicer, think that the Council means by it penitents of the lowest degree, the flentes, who had no right to enter the church, but remained in the porch, in the open air, exposed to all inclemencies (χειμών), and who must ask those who entered the church to intercede for them.

As, however, the possessed also remained in the porch, the generic name of χειμαζόμενοι was given to all who were there, i.e. who could not enter the church. We may therefore accept Suicer's explanation, with whom agree Van Espen, Herbst, etc. Having settled this point, let us return to the explanation of λέπρα. It is clear that λεπρώσαντας cannot possibly mean "those who have been lepers;" for there is no reason to be seen why those who were cured of that malady should have to remain outside the church among the flentes. Secondly, it is clear that the words λεπροὺς ὄντας, etc., are added to give force to the expression ἀλογευσάμενοι. The preceding canon had decreed different penalties for different kinds of ἀλογευσάμενοι. But that pronounced by canon 17 being much severer than the preceding ones, the ἀλογευσάμενοι of this canon must be greater sinners than those of the former one. This greater guilt cannot consist in the fact of a literal leprosy; for this malady was not a consequence of bestiality. But their sin was evidently greater when they tempted others to commit it. It is therefore λέπρα in the figurative sense that we are to understand; and our canon thus means: "Those who were spiritually leprous through this sin, and tempting others to commit it made them leprous."

CAN. 18

Εἴ τινες ἐπίσκοποι κατασταθέντες καὶ μὴ δεχθέντες ὑπὸ τῆς παροικίας ἐκείνης, εἰς ἣν ὠνομάσθησαν, ἑτέραις βούλοιντο παροικίαις ἐπιέναι καὶ βιάζεσθαι τοὺς καθεστεῶτας καὶ στάσεις κινεῖν κατ' αὐτῶν, τούτους ἀφορίζεσθαι ἐὰν μέντοι βούλοιντο εἰς τὸ πρεσβυτέριον καθέξεσθαι, ἔνθα ἦσαν πρότερον πρεσβύτεροι, μὴ ἀποβάλλεσθαι αὐτοὺς τῆς τιμῆς· ἐὰν δὲ διαστασιάζωσι πρὸς τοὺς καθεστῶτας ἐκεῖ ἐπισκόπους, ἀφαιρεῖσθαι αὐτοὺς καὶ τὴν τιμὴν τοῦ πρεσβυτερίου καὶ γίνεσθα αὐτοὺς ἐκκηύκτους.

"If bishops, when elected, but not accepted by the parish for which they are nominated, introduce themselves into other parishes, and stir up strife against the bishops who are there instituted, they must be excommunicated. But if they (who are elected and not accepted) wish to live as priests in those places where they had hitherto served as priests, they need not lose that dignity. But if they stir up discord against the bishop of the place, they shall be deprived of their presbyterate, and be shut out from the Church."

As long as the people collectively had a share in the election of bishops, it often happened in the primitive Church that a bishop, regularly elected, was either expelled or rejected by a rising of the people. Even although, at the time of his election, the majority were in his favour, yet the minority often put a stop to it; just as we saw in 1848 and 1849, how a very small minority tyrannized over whole towns and countries, and even drove out persons who displeased them. The thirty-fifth apostolical canon (thirty-sixth or thirty-seventh according to other reckonings) and the eighteenth of Antioch (A.D. 341) spoke also of such bishops driven from their dioceses.

When one of these bishops tried by violence or by treachery to drive a colleague from his see, and to seize upon it, he was to incur the penalty of ἀφορίζεσθαι. Van Espen understood by that, the deprivation of his episcopal dignity; but the ἀφορισμὸς of the ancient Church signified more than that: it signified excommunication, at least the minor excommunication, or exclusion from the communion of the Church.

But the canon adds, if a bishop not accepted by his Church does not make these criminal attempts, but will live modestly among the priests of his former congregation, he can do so, and "he shall not lose his dignity." Is it here a question of the title and dignity of a bishop, but without jurisdiction; or does the word τιμὴ signify here only the rank of a priest? Dionysius the Less (Exiguus) has taken it in the latter sense, and translated it, "If they will, as presbyters, continue in the order of the priesthood" (si voluerint in presbyterii ordine ut presbyteri residere). The Greek commentators Zonaras and others have taken it in the same sense. This canon was added to the Corp. jur. can. (c. 6, dist. 92).

CAN. 19

Ὅσοι παρθενίαν ἐπαγγελλόμενοι ἀθετοῦσι τὴν ἐπαγγελίαν, τὸν τῶν διγάμων ὅρον ἐκπληρούτωσαν. Τὰς μέντοι συνερχομένας παρθένους τισὶν ὡς ἀδελφὰς ἐκωλύσαμεν.

"All who have taken a vow of virginity, and have broken that vow, are to be considered as bigamists (literally, must submit to the decrees and prescriptions concerning bigamists). We also forbid virgins to live as sisters with men."

The first part of the canon regards all young persons—men as well as women—who have taken a vow of virginity, and who, having thus, so to speak, betrothed themselves to God, are guilty of a quasi bigamy in violating that promise. They must therefore incur the punishment of bigamy (successiva), which, according to S. Basil the Great, consisted in one year's seclusion. This canon, which Gratian adopted (c. 24, causa 27, quæst. 1), speaks only of the violation of the vow by a lawful marriage, whilst the thirteenth canon of Elvira speaks of those who break their vow by incontinence. In the second part the canon treats of

the συνείσακτοι. On this point we refer to our remarks on
the third canon of Nicæa, and on the twenty-seventh of
Elvira.

CAN. 20

Ἐάν τινος γυνὴ μοιχευθῇ ἢ μοιχεύσῃ τις, ἐν ἑπτὰ ἔτεσι δοκεῖ
(δεῖ) αὐτὸν τοῦ τελείου τυχεῖν κατὰ τοὺς βαθμοὺς τοὺς
προάγοντας.

"If any one has violated a married woman, or has broken
the marriage bond, he must for seven years undergo the
different degrees of penance, at the end of which he will be
admitted into the communion of the Church."

The simplest explanation of this canon is, "that the man or
woman who has violated the marriage bond shall undergo a
seven years' penance;" but many reject this explanation,
because the text says αὐτὸν τύχειν, and consequently can
refer only to the husband. Fleury and Routh think the
canon speaks, as does the seventieth of Elvira, of a woman
who has broken the marriage tie with the knowledge and
consent of her husband. The husband would therefore in
this case be punished for this permission, just as if he had
himself committed adultery. Van Espen has given another
explanation: "That he who marries a woman already
divorced for adultery is as criminal as if he had himself
committed adultery." But this explanation appears to us
more forced than that already given; and we think that the
Greek commentators Balsamon and Zonaras were right in
giving the explanation we have offered first as the most
natural. They think that the Synod punished every adulterer,
whether man or woman, by a seven years penance. There is

no reason for making a mistake because only the word αὐτὸν occurs in the passage in which the penalty is fixed; for αὐτὸν here means the guilty party, and applies equally to the woman and the man: besides, in the preceding canon the masculine ὅσοι ἐπαγγελόμενοι includes young men and young women also. It is probable that the Trullan Synod of 692, in forming its eighty-seventh canon, had in view the twentieth of Ancyra. The sixty-ninth canon of Elvira condemned to a lighter punishment—only five years of penance—him who had been only once guilty of adultery.

CAN. 21

Περὶ τῶν γυναικῶν τῶν ἐκπορνευουσῶν καὶ ἀναιρουσῶν τὰ γεννώμενα καὶ σπουδαζουσῶν φθόρια ποιεῖν ὁ μὲν πρότερος ὅρος μέχρις ἐξόδου ἐκώλυσεν, καὶ τούτῳ συντίθενται φιλανθρωπότερον δὲ τι εὑρόντες ὡρίσαμεν δεκαετῆ χρόνον κατὰ τοὺς βαθμοὺς τοὺς ὡρισμένους (adde πληρῶσαι).

"Women who prostitute themselves, and who kill the children thus begotten, or who try to destroy them when in their wombs, are by ancient law excommunicated to the end of their lives. We, however, have softened their punishment, and condemned them to the various appointed degrees of penance for ten years."

The sixty-third canon of Elvira had forbidden the communion to be administered to such women even on their death-beds; and this was the canon which the Synod of Ancyra had probably here in view. The expression καὶ τούτῳ συντίθενται is vague: τινὲς may be understood, and it might be translated, "and some approve of this severity;" or we might understand αἱ, and translate with Routh, "The same punishment will be inflicted on those who assist in causing miscarriages:" the words then mean, "and those who assist them." We think, however, the first explanation is the easier and the more natural. Gentianus Hervetus and Van Espen have adopted it, translating thus: et ei quidam assentientur.

CAN. 22

Περὶ ἑκουσίων φόνων, ὑποπιπτέτωσαν μὲν, τοῦ δὲ τελείου ἐν τῷ τέλει τοῦ βίου καταξιούσθωσαν.

"As to wilful murderers, they must be substrati, and not allowed to receive the communion as long as they live."

CAN. 23

Ἐπὶ ἀκουσίων φόνων, ὁ μὲν πρότερος ὅρος ἐν ἑπταετίᾳ κελεύει τοῦ τελείου μετασχεῖν κατὰ τοὺς ὡρισμένους βαθμούς· ὁ δὲ δεύτερος τὸν πενταετῆ χρόνον πληρῶσαι.

"As to unpremeditated murder, the earlier ordinance allowed communion (to the homicide) at the end of a seven years' penance; the second required only five years."

Of the first and second ordinances referred to in this canon nothing further is known; as to the terms ὅρος, τέλειον, and βαθμοὶ, see the canons of Ancyra already explained.

CAN. 24

Οἱ καταμαντευόμενοι καὶ ταῖς συνηθείαις τῶν χρόνων (ἐθνεῶν) ἐξακολουθοῦντες ἢ εἰσάγοντές τινας εἰς τοὺς ἑαυτῶν οἴκους ἐπὶ ἀνευρέσει φαρμακειῶν ἢ καὶ καθάρσει, ὑπὸ τὸν κανόνα πιπτέτωσαν τῆς πενταετίας κατὰ τοὺς βαθμοὺς ὡρισμένους, τρία ἔτη ὑποπτώσεως καὶ δύο ἔτη εὐχῆς χωρὶς προσφορᾶς.

"Those who foretell the future, and follow pagan customs, or admit into their houses people (magicians) in order to discover magical remedies, or to perform expiations, must be sentenced to a five years' penance, to three years of substratio, and to two years of attendance at prayers without the sacrifice (non-communicating attendance)."

We must refer to the explanations we have given under canon 4 on the different degrees of penance. It has long been known (as witnesses we have the old Greek commentators Balsamon and Zonaras, and the old Latin interpreters Dionysius the Less and Isidore, confirmed by Routh) that the correct reading is ἐθνῶν instead of χρονῶν. The canon threatens equally diviners and those who consult them and summon them to their houses to prepare magical remedies and perform expiations.

CAN. 25

Μνηστευσάμενός τις κόρην προσεφθάρη τῇ ἀδελφῇ αὐτῆς, ὡς καὶ ἐπιφορέσαι αὐτὴν ἔγημε δὲ τὴν μνηστὴν μετὰ ταῦτα, ἡ δὲ φθαρεῖσα ἀπήγξατο οἱ συνειδότες ἐκελεύσθησαν ἐν δεκαετίᾳ δεχθῆναι εἰς τοὺς συνεστῶτας κατὰ τοὺς ὡρισμένος βαθμούς.

"A certain person who had betrothed himself to a girl, had connection with her sister, so that she became pregnant: he then married his betrothed, and his sister-in-law hanged herself. It was determined that all his accomplices should be admitted among the sistentes (i.e. to the fourth degree of penance), after passing through the appointed degrees for ten years."

The Council here decides, as we see, a particular case which was submitted to it; and it condemned not only the particular offender, but all the accomplices who had assisted him to commit the crime, who had advised him to leave her he had seduced, and to marry her sister, or the like. The punishment inflicted was very severe, for it was only at the end of ten years (passed in the three first degrees of penance) that the offenders were admitted to the fourth degree. It is not stated how long they were to remain in that degree before admission to the communion. The Greek verb προσφθείρομαι generally means, "to do anything to one's hurt:" joined to γυναικὶ or some other similar word, it has the meaning we have given it. We have rendered ἀπήγξατο by "hanged herself;" we ought, however, to note that ἀπάγχω signifies every kind of suicide.

SEC. 17. Synod of Neocæsarea (314–325)

According to the title which the ancient Greek MSS. give to the canons of the Synod of Neocæsarea in Cappadocia, this Synod was held a little later than that of Ancyra, but before that of Nicæa. The names of the bishops who assisted at it seem to furnish a second chronological support to this view. They are for the most part the same as those who are named at the Council of Ancyra, Vitalis of Antioch at their head (the Libellus Synodicus reckons twenty-four of them); but neither the Greek MSS. nor Dionysius the Less have these names. Tillemont and other writers have for this reason raised doubts as to the historical value of these lists, and the brothers Ballerini have not hesitated to disallow their authenticity. It remains, however, an incontestable fact, that the Synod of Neocæsarea took place at about the same time as that of Ancyra, after the death of Maximin the persecutor of the Christians (313), and before the Synod of Nicæa (325). Ordinarily the same date is assigned to it as to that of Ancyra, 314 or 315; but to me it seems more probable that it took place several years later, because there is no longer any question about the lapsed. The Synod of Ancyra had devoted no fewer than ten canons (1–9 and 12) to this subject, as a persecution had then just ceased; the Synod of Neocæsarea did not touch on these matters, probably because at the time when it assembled the lapsed had already received their sentence, and there were no more measures necessary to be taken on that subject. The Libellus Synodicus, it is true, states that the Synod of (Neo) Cæsarea occupied itself with those who had sacrificed to the gods or abjured their religion, or had eaten of sacrifices offered to idols, and during the persecution; but the canons of the Council say not a word of them. It is probable that the late and very inaccurate Libellus Synodicus confounded, on this point, the Synod of Neocæsarea with that of Ancyra. It has, without any grounds, been alleged that the canons of Neocæsarea which spoke of the lapsi have been destroyed.

CAN. 1

Πρεσβύτερος ἐὰν γήμῃ, τῆς τάξεως αὐτὸν μετατίθεσθαι, ἐὰν δὲ πορνεύσῃ ἢ μοιχεύσῃ, ἐξωθεῖσθαι αὐτὸν τέλεον καὶ ἄγεσθαι αὐτὸν εἰς μετάνοιαν.

"If a priest marry, he shall be removed from the ranks of the clergy; if he commit fornication or adultery, he shall be excommunicated, and shall submit to penance."

The meaning is as follows: "If a priest marry after ordination, he shall be deposed from his priestly order, and reduced to the communio laicalis; if he is guilty of fornication or adultery, he must be excommunicated, and must pass through all the degrees of penance in order to regain communion with the Church." We have seen above, in canon 10 of Ancyra, that in one case deacons were allowed to marry after ordination,—namely, when they had announced their intention of doing so at the time of their election. In the case of priests neither the Council of Ancyra nor that of Neocæsarea made any exception. This first canon has been inserted in the Corp. jur. can.

CAN. 2

Γυνὴ ἐὰν γήμηται δύο ἀδελφοῖς, ἐξωθείσθω μέχρι θανάτου, πλὴν ἐν τῷ θανάτῳ, διὰ τὴν φιλανθρεπίαν, εἰποῦσα ὡς ὑλιάνασα λύσει τὸν γάμον, ἕξει τὴν μετάνοιαν• ἐὰν δὲ τελευτήσῃ ἡ γυνὴ ἐν τοιούτῳ γάμῳ οὖσα ἤτοι ὁ ἀνὴρ, δυσχερὴς τῷ μείναντι ἡ μετάνοια.

"If a woman has married two brothers, she shall be excommunicated till her death; if she is in danger of death, and promises in case of recovery to break off this illegitimate union, she may, as an act of mercy, be admitted to penance. If the woman or husband die in this union, the penance for the survivor will be very strict."

This is a question of marriage of the first degree of affinity, which is still forbidden by the present law. The canon punishes such marriages with absolute excommunication; so that he who had entered into such should not obtain communion even in articulo mortis, unless he promised in case of recovery to break this union. This promise being given, he can be admitted to penance (ἕξει τὴν μετάνοιαν). Zonaras thus correctly explains these words: "In this case he shall receive the holy communion in articulo mortis, provided he promises that, if he recovers, he will submit to penance." Canon 6 of Ancyra was explained in the same way.

CAN. 3

Περὶ τῶν πλείστοις γάμοις περιπιπτόντων ὁ μὲν χρόνος σαφὴς ὁ ὡρισμένος, ἡ δὲ ἀναστροφὴ καὶ ἡ πίστις αὐτῶν συντέμνει τὸν χρόνον.

"As for those who have been often married, the duration of their penance is well known; but their good conduct and faith may shorten that period."

As the Greek commentators have remarked, this canon speaks of those who have been married more than twice. It is not known what were the ancient ordinances of penitence which the Synod here refers to. In later times, bigamists were condemned to one year's penance, and trigamists from two to five years. S. Basil places the trigamists for three years among the audientes, then for some time among the consistentes. Gratian has inserted this third canon of Neocæsarea in the c. 8, causa 31, quæst. 1, in connection with canon 7 of the same Synod.

CAN. 4

Ἐὰν πρόθηταί τις ἐπιθυμῆσαι (ἐπιθυμήσας) γυναικὸς συγκαθευδῆσαι μετ' αὐτῆς (αὐτῇ), μὴ ἔλθη δὲ εἰς ἔργον αὐτοῦ ἡ ἐνθύμησις, φαίνεται ὅτι ὑπὸ τῆς χάριτος ἐρρύσθη.

"If a man who burns with love for a woman proposes to live with her, but does not perform his intention, it is to be believed that he was restrained by grace."

Instead of ἐπιθυμῆσαι we must read, with Beveridge and Routh, who rely upon several MSS., ἐπιθυμήσας. They also replace μετ' αὐτῆς by αὐτῇ. The meaning of this canon is, that "he who has sinned only in thought must not undergo a public penance."

CAN. 5

Κατηχούμενος, ἐὰν εἰσερχόμενος εἰς (τὸ) κυριακὸν ἐν τῇ τῶν κατηχουμένων τάξει στήκη, οὗτος δὲ (φανῇ) ἁμαρτάνων, ἐὰν μὲν γόνυ κλίνων, ἀκροάσθω μηκέτι ἁμαρτάνων· Ἐὰν δὲ καὶ ἀκροώμενος ἔτι ἁμαρτάνη, ἐξωθείσθε.

"If a catechumen, after being introduced into the Church, and admitted into the ranks of the catechumens, acts as a sinner, he must, if he is genuflectens (i.e. to say, in the second degree of penance), become audiens (the lowest degree), until he sins no more. If, after being audiens, he continues to sin, he shall be entirely excluded from the Church."

Routh, on good critical grounds, recommends the introduction into the text of τὸ and φανῇ. The form στήκη and the verb στήκω, to stand up, do not occur in classical Greek, but are often found in the New Testament, e.g. in S. Mark 11:25, and are formed from the regular perfect ἕστηκα. Hardouin thinks the canon has in view the carnal sins of catechumens; and ἁμάρτημα has elsewhere this meaning, e.g. in canons 2, 9, and 14 of Nicæa.

CAN. 6

Περὶ κυοφορούσης, ὅτι δεῖ φωτίζεσθαι ὁπότε βούλεται· οὐδὲν γὰρ ἐν τούτῳ κοινωνεῖ ἡ τίκτουσα τῷ τικτομένῳ, διὰ τὸ ἑκάστου ἰδίαν τὴν προαίρεσιν τὴν ἐπὶ τῇ ὁμολογίᾳ δείκνυσθαι.

"A woman with child may be illuminated (i.e. to say, baptized) whenever she demands it; for she who bears has nothing on this account in common with him who is borne, since each party must profess his own willingness (to be baptized) by his confession of faith."

Some thought that when a woman with child is baptized, the grace of the sacrament is given to the fruit of her womb, and so to baptize this child again after its birth is in a manner to administer a second baptism; and they conclude that they ought not to baptize a pregnant woman, but that they must wait till her delivery.

CAN. 7

Πρεσβύτερον εἰς γάμους διγαμούντων (διγαμοῦντος) μὴ ἑστιᾶσθαι, ἐπεὶ μετάνοιαν αἰτοῦντος τοῦ διγάμου, τίς ἔσται ὁ πρεσβύτερος, ὁ διὰ τῆς ἑστιάσεως συγκατατιθέμενος τοῖς γάμοις;

"No priest shall eat at the marriage feast of those who are married for the second time; for if such a bigamist should (afterwards) ask leave to do penance, how stands the priest who, by his presence at the feast, had given his approval to the marriage?"

We have already seen by canon 3, that in the East that successive bigamy (bigamia successiva) which is here in question, as Beveridge thinks, and not bigamy properly so called, was punished in the East by a year's penance. The meaning of the canon is as follows: "If the bigamist, after contracting his second marriage, comes to the priest to be told the punishment he has to undergo, how stands the priest himself, who for the sake of the feast has become his accomplice in the offence?"

CAN. 8

Γυνή τινος μοιχευθεῖσα λαϊκοῦ ὄντος, ἐὰν ἐλεγχθῇ φανερῶς, ὁ τοιοῦτος εἰς ὑπηρεσίαν ἐλθεῖν οὐ δύναται· ἐὰν δὲ καὶ μετὰ τὴν χειροτονίαν μοιχευθῇ, ὀφείλει ἀπολῦσαι αὐτήν· ἐὰν δὲ συζῇ, οὐ δέναται ἔχεσθαι τῆς ἐγχειρισθείσης αὐτῷ ὑπηρεσίας.

"If the wife of a layman has been unfaithful to her husband, and she is convicted of the sin, her (innocent) husband cannot be admitted to the service of the Church; but if she has violated the law of marriage after her husband's ordination, he must leave her. If, in spite of this, he continues to live with her, he must resign the sacred functions which have been entrusted to him."

The Corp. jur. can. has adopted this canon. The reason for this ordinance evidently consists in this, that through the close connection between a man and his wife, a husband is dishonoured by an adulterous wife, and a dishonoured man cannot become an ecclesiastic. The Pastor of Hermas had already shown that a husband must leave his adulterous wife.

CAN. 9

Πρεσβύτερος, ἐὰν προημαρτηκὼς σώματι προαχθῇ καὶ ὁμολογήσῃ ὅτι ἥμαρτε πρὸ τῆς χειροτονίας, μὴ προσφερέτω, μένων ἐν τοῖς λοιποῖς διὰ τὴν ἄλλην σπουδήν• τὰ γὰρ λοιπὰ ἁμαρτήματα ᾿φασαν οἱ πολλοὶ καὶ τὴν χειροθεσίαν ἀφιέναι• ἐὰν δὲ αὐτὸς μὴ ὁμολογῇ, ἐλεγχθῆναι δὲ φανερῶς μὴ δυνηθῇ, ἐπ᾿ αὐτῷ ἐκείνῳ ποιεῖσθαι τὴν ἐξουσίαν.

"A priest who has committed a carnal sin before being ordained, and who of his own accord confesses that he has sinned before ordination, must not offer the holy sacrifice; but he may continue his other functions if he is zealous, for many think that other sins (except that of incontinence) were blotted out by his ordination as priest. But if he does not confess it, and he cannot clearly be convicted, it shall be in his own power to act (as he will, i.e. to offer the sacrifice, or to refrain from offering)."

Cf. can. 22 of the Council in Trullo, and can. 1, causa 15, quæst. 8, in the Corp. jur. can.

CAN. 10

Ὁμοίως καὶ διάκονος, ἐὰν ἐν τῷ αὐτῷ ἁμαρτήματι περιπέσῃ, τὴν τοῦ ὑπηρέτου τάξιν ἐχέτω.

"In the same way, the deacon who has committed the same sin must only have the office of an inferior minister."

The preposition ἐν before τῷ αὐτῷ is struck out by Routh, on the authority of several MSS. By ministri (ὑπήρεται) are meant the inferior officers of the Church—the so-called minor orders, often including the sub-deacons. This canon, completely distorted by false translations (of the Prisca and Isidore), was made into one canon with the preceding in the Corp. jur. can.

CAN. 11

Πρεσβύτερος πρὸ τῶν τριάκοντα ἐτῶν μὴ χειροτονείσθω, ἐὰν καὶ πάνυ ᾖ ὁ ἄνθρωπος ἄξιος, ἀλλὰ ἀποτηρείσθω· ὁ γὰρ Κύριος Ἰησοῦς Χριστὸς ἐν τῷ τριακοστῷ ἔτει ἐφωτίσθη καὶ ἤρξατο διδάσκειν.

"No one is to be ordained priest before he is thirty years old. Even although he be in every respect worthy, he must wait; for our Lord Jesus Christ, when thirty years old, was baptized, and began (at that age) to teach."

We know that, in the primitive Church, φωτίζεσθαι, to be illuminated, means to be baptized. We find this canon in the Corp. jur. can.

CAN. 12

Ἐὰν νοσῶν τις φωτισθῇ, εἰς πρεσβύτερον ἄγεσθαι οὐ δύναται,—οὐκ ἐκ προαιρέσεως γὰρ ἡ πίστις αὐτοῦ, ἀλλ' ἐξ ἀνάγκης,—εἰ μὴ τάχα διὰ τὴν μετὰ ταῦτα αὐτοῦ σπουδὴν καὶ πίστιν καὶ διὰ σπάνιν ἀνθρώπων.

"If a man is baptized when he is ill, he cannot be ordained priest; for it was not spontaneously, but of necessity (through fear of death), that he made profession of the faith—unless, perhaps, he has displayed great zeal and faith, or if the supply of candidates fails."

All commentators, except Aubespine, say that this canon, which was received into the Corp. jur. can., speaks of those who, by their own fault, have deferred the reception of baptism till their deathbed. Aubespine thinks that it refers to catechumens who have not received baptism earlier through no fault of their own, but who, finding themselves smitten by a severe sickness, are baptized before the usual time, i.e. before receiving all the necessary instruction. It was, he added, on account of this want of instruction that they were forbidden to enter the priesthood if they regained their health. But the forty-seventh canon of Laodicea tells us that in the primitive Church it was the duty of such catechumens to receive instruction even after baptism, and this alone overthrows Aubespine's conjecture.

CAN. 13

Ἐπιχώριοι πρεσβύτεροι ἐν τῷ κυριακῷ τῆς πόλεως προσφέρειν οὐ δύνανται παρόντος ἐπισκόπου ἢ πρεσβυτέρων πόλεως, οὔτε μὴν ἄρτον διδόναι ἐν εὐχῇ οὐδὲ ποτήριον· ἐὰν δὲ ἀπῶσι καὶ εἰς εὐχὴν κληθῇ μόνος, δίδωσιν.

"Country priests must not offer the holy sacrifice in the town church (the cathedral) when the bishop or the town priests are present: they must not do more than distribute, with prayer, the bread and the chalice. But if the bishop and his priests are absent, and if the country priest be invited to celebrate, he may administer holy communion."

Instead of κληθῇ μόνος, the old Latin translators of the canons, Dionysius the Less and Isidore, read κληθῶσι, μόνοι; that is to say, "If they are asked, then only can they administer the Lord's Supper;" and Routh recommends this reading. This canon is contained in the Corp. jur. can.

CAN. 14

Οἱ δὲ χωρεπίσκοποι εἰσὶ μὲν εἰς τύπον τῶν ἑβδομήκοντα· ὡς δὲ συλλειτουργοὶ διὰ τὴν σπουδὴν (τὴν) εἰς τοὺς πτωχοὺς προσφέρουσι τιμώμενοι.

"The chorepiscopi represent the seventy disciples of Christ as fellow-workers; and on account of their zeal for the poor, they have the honour of offering the sacrifice."

A function is here assigned to the chorepiscopi which is denied to country priests, namely, the offering of the holy sacrifice in the cathedral, in the presence of the bishop and the town priests. On the chorepiscopi, compare c. 13 of Ancyra, and our remarks below on canon 57 of Laodicea. Many MSS. and editions have canons 13 and 14 in one.

CAN. 15

Διάκονοι ἑπτὰ ὀφείλουσιν εἶναι κατὰ τὸν κανόνα, κἂν πάνυ μεγάλη ἔη ἡ πόλις· πεισθήσῃ δέ ἀπὸ τῆς βίβλου τῶν Πράξεων.

"In even the largest towns there must be, as a rule, no more than seven deacons. This may be proved from the Acts of the Apostles."

This canon was given in the Corp. jur. can.

BOOK II
THE FIRST ŒCUMENICAL COUNCIL OF
NICÆA, A.D. 325

CHAPTER I
PRELIMINARY

SEC. 18. The Doctrine of the Logos prior to Arianism

FROM the beginning, two points concerning the Logos
and His relation to the Father have stood as divinely
revealed in the consciousness of the Church. On the one
hand, His real divinity and equality with the Father; on the
other, His personal distinction from the Father. But before
the Council of Nicæa this sure doctrine of the faith had not
been set forth in a sufficiently definite or positive manner;
whilst some of the ancient Fathers, in expounding the faith
of the Church, had, without thoroughly mastering the
formula of Nicæa, perfectly understood and taught its
meaning. Others selected less happy expressions, and
sometimes erroneous ones—such as would, in their
consequences, even lead to heresy. These same Fathers
have, in different portions of their writings, expressed
themselves sometimes with theological accuracy, sometimes
with less accuracy. Thus, for example, S. Irenæus, Clement
of Alexandria, S. Gregory Thaumaturgus of Neocæsarea,
and Methodius, did not always choose their expressions
carefully, but in substance they incontestably maintained
the true doctrine. It is the same with Justin, Athenagoras,
and Theophilus, who expressed themselves irreproachably
on the chief dogmatic points, but differ in some of their
inferences from the rule of the Church. The Apologists,
above all others, to make themselves more acceptable and

intelligible to the heathen who were accustomed to the Platonic philosophy, made a less clear and exact declaration of the doctrine of the Logos. In this endeavour they have too often brought the Christian idea of the Logos near to that of Plato and Philo, and so have too often degraded the Son in His dignity and power, attributed a beginning to His existence, and consequently have not recognised His equality with the Father (thus, among the orthodox Fathers, Athenagoras and Theophilus; among the more heterodox, Tatian, Tertullian, and especially Origen), and have emphasized too much the personal distinction between the Father and the Son.

On the other hand, they also tried to establish the second point of the traditional doctrine, the true divinity of the Son, and His equality with the Father, by declaring that the Logos was not a creature, and by saying that He came from the substance of the Father, and not from nothing, as the creatures do. They sometimes deny that the Logos was subsequent to the Father in His existence, which they affirm in other places. Attaching themselves to the distinction established by Philo between the λόγος ἐνδιάθετος and προφορικός, several of the ancient Fathers, philosophizing on the Son of God in the sense of the Logos προφορικός (that is, as He is personally distinct from the Father), speak of this Logos as of a being subordinate, and having an existence subsequent in time to that of the Father. In other places, on the contrary, they seem to suppress the distinction, purely nominal, between ἐνδιάθετος and προφορικός, and include the Logos completely in the divine substance. These last passages correct all that is exaggerated in the others, and positively support the ancient Fathers on the solid basis of the Church.

In certain cases, the two principal points of the doctrine of the Logos—the unity of the Son with the Father, and the distinction between the Father and the Son—have been regarded as contradictory propositions; and instead of preserving each in its theological entirety and relation to the other, they have thought to annihilate the one by the other. Out of this arose Sabellianism. This heresy, while maintaining the proper Godhead of the Son, in order the better to establish His equality with the Father, destroyed the personal distinction between the Father and the Son. But as one extreme leads to another, Sabellianism necessarily produced Subordinationism as its natural reaction; i.e. the theory which, in endeavouring to preserve the personal distinction between the Father and the Son, like Emanationism, subordinates in glory and in dignity Him who is begotten—that is to say, the Son—to Him who is unbegotten, and thus approximates Him more or less to the creatures. The celebrated Dionysius the Great, Bishop of Alexandria, is the most remarkable in this contest. About the year 260, in his dogmatic letter to Ammonius and Euphranor, as is well known, he expressed himself very indefinitely; and in order to mark more forcibly the distinction between the Father and the Son, he spoke of the latter as a ποίημα τοῦ Θεοῦ. He added, "that the Son in substance is alien from the Father (ξένον κατ᾽ οὐσίαν), as the vine plant and the vinedresser are distinct one from the other in substance;" and "as He is a ποίημα, He could not have been before He was made (οὐκ ἦν, πρὶν γένηται)." Thus in words, though not by intention, Dionysius had placed the Son on a par with the creatures. His excuse is found in the uncertain and vacillating language of his time, even apart from his well-intended opposition to Sabellianism, since other orthodox writers also describe the derivation of the Son from the Father promiscuously by such expressions as ποιεῖν, γεννᾶν, γένεσθαι, condere, and generare.

Pope Dionysius and his Synod were more clearsighted than these theologians. When several African bishops complained to him of the errors of Dionysius of Alexandria, the Pope held a Synod about the year 260; and after having deliberated with the members of the Synod on the dogma in question, he addressed to his colleague in Alexandria, and probably at the same time to other bishops of Egypt and Libya, a letter very remarkable in the history of the true faith, the greater part of which has been preserved for us by S. Athanasius. In it he protests against three errors: first, against the tritheistic, "which, diametrically opposed to Sabellius, divides the divine monarchy into three separate powers or hypostases, and plainly teaches that there are three Gods." Baur supposed that the accusers of Dionysius of Alexandria had supported the doctrine of tritheism. Dorner, on the other hand, believes that tritheism was the result of a mixture of Sabellianism and Marcionitism; but he has not proved that this amalgamation existed during that period. Secondly, the Pope condemned, briefly and casually, Sabellianism; and, thirdly and lastly, he spoke at some length against those who called the Son a creature, when Holy Scripture declares that He was begotten. "Had He been created," said he, "there would have been a period when He did not exist.

Now the Son has always existed (ἀεὶ ἦν)." The Pope then
explains critically those passages in the Bible which
seemingly speak of a creation of the Son; and against these
he brings forward those which speak of His generation and
of His eternity. He closes with these words: "The admirable
and holy unity (of God) cannot in consequence be divided
into three Godheads; and the dignity and incomparable
greatness of the Lord ought not to be lowered by the
expression creature being applied to Him. It is necessary to
believe in God the Father Almighty, and in Jesus Christ His
Son, and in the Holy Ghost, and that the Logos is united to
the God of the universe." The Bishop of Rome here clearly
professes the doctrine of Nicæa; and that Dionysius the
Great of Alexandria also professed it, is proved by two
letters which he then sent to Rome to justify himself, and
which S. Athanasius quoted in order to prove that the
Arians had done wrong in numbering Dionysius as one of
their party. Dionysius says, in his letters, that his accusers
had falsely charged him with denying the equality of the
substance of the Father and the Son; and if he had said that
nowhere in the Bible the word ὁμοούσιος could be found,
the argument of which he made use, and which his
adversaries had passed over in silence, was in complete
agreement with that expression. He had, indeed, compared
the relation between God the Father and God the Son with
those between parents and children, as children are of the
same substance as their parents. He had also employed
other analogous arguments, e.g. the example of the plant
and its root or its seed, between which there was an evident
identity of substance. To the same effect was his
comparison of the river and its source. He says, in another
part of his letter of justification: "There has never been a

moment when God was not the Father, and the Son is eternal; but He has His being, not of Himself, but of the Father." Also in a third place he declares "he does not believe the Logos is a creature, and that he has not called God Creator (ποιητής), but Father, to express the relation that He has to the Son. If, however, in the course of his speech (and without intending it) he has once called the Father ποιητὴς to express His relation to the Son, he may be excused, seeing that the learned Greeks call themselves also ποιηταὶ, as being fathers of their works, and that the Bible itself does not always employ the word in the sense of creator, but sometimes also in the sense of originator: for instance, when it says we are the ποιηταὶ of the movements of our hearts."

After Dionysius the Great, the most illustrious doctors of the Church of Alexandria, Theognostus, Pierius, and Bishop Peter, professed also the orthodox doctrine of the Logos. The first of these, who was chief of the catechetical school of this town from 270 to about 280, states explicitly, in a fragment preserved by S. Athanasius: "The substance of the Son came not from without, neither was it produced from nothing: it proceeds from the substance of the Father, as brilliancy proceeds from light, vapour from water." If in a fragment of Theognostus, preserved by Photius, the Son is called a κτίσμα, Photius presumes this expression comes from a questioner; as the work from which it is taken is a dialogue: anyhow, the formal declaration quoted above proves that he could not have used the word κτίσμα in an Arian sense. His successor, the priest Pierius, professes the same doctrine of the Logos. Photius says of him: "It is true he called the Father and the Son two substances (οὐσίας) instead of persons or hypostases; but, however, he spoke of the two εὐσεβῶς, that is, in an orthodox manner." And this testimony of Photius is the more convincing to us, from the decided manner in which he blames Pierius in another passage on account of his doctrine of the Holy Ghost: if his teaching on the Logos had not been orthodox, Photius would have blamed him for this too.

The third great Alexandrian of that time was Bishop Peter; and although the fragment attributed to him in the Chronicon Paschale is probably not genuine, two other fragments prove that he attributed to the Son the same nature and Godhead as to the Father.

It was different at Antioch, where the efforts to uphold the unity of God degenerated into the doctrine of Paul of Samosata, who considered the Logos as impersonal, and not distinct from the Father, and saw in Christ only a man in whom the divine Logos had dwelt and operated. A fellow-countryman of Paul's, who shared his sentiments, Lucian, priest of Antioch, defended for some time this heretical doctrine of the Trinity, and for that reason was excommunicated for a time. Later, however, he acquired great distinction, by the publication of a corrected copy of the Septuagint, and by the firmness with which he suffered martyrdom under Maximin. The restoration of Lucian to the Church proves that eventually he renounced the doctrine of Paul of Samosata; but being still convinced that the Church did not maintain with sufficient firmness the dogma of the unity of God, he imagined another hypothesis of the Trinity, which is not perfectly known to us for lack of sufficient information, but which, according to Alexander Bishop of Alexandria, came out in the heresy of the Exucontians, and more particularly in that of his disciple Arius. Arius himself traced his doctrine to the school of Lucian, in greeting his friend Eusebius of Nicomedia, who shared his opinion, with the name of Συλλουκιανιστής (fellow-Lucianist). This being the case, it is of little importance to decide whether Arius was personally a disciple of Lucian at Antioch, or whether his opinion was formed from his writings only. In the letter from Arius to Eusebius of Nicomedia, just quoted, one sees that the principles of Lucian were widely spread in Asia; for Arius not only speaks of Eusebius as sharing his opinions, but also of a great many other bishops of Asia, who had all proclaimed that the Son was not eternal equally with the Father. The denial of the co-eternity of the Father and the Son seems therefore to have been a fundamental point in the doctrine of Lucian.

Besides, S. Epiphanius says: "Lucian and his followers all denied that the Son of God had taken a human soul, attributing to Him only a human body, for the sake of endowing the Logos with human feelings, such as sorrow, joy, and the like; and they also declared Him a being inferior to God—a creature, in fact." Arius and his partisans made great use of the σῶμα Χριστοῦ ἄψυχον, and thereby again revealed their affinity with the school of Lucian. We know also that Lucian was looked upon as the author of the creed that the Eusebians (that is, the friends of Arius) submitted to the Synod of Antioch in 341, in which, as we shall see, the teaching was not positively heretical, but in which all sharp precision of dogma is intentionally avoided.

SEC. 19. Arius

The Subordinationist theology of Antioch was transplanted to Alexandria by Arius, the oft-named disciple of the school of Lucian; and on this new ground it gained strength and importance. The mind of Arius was disposed to this purely rationalistic theology; and from his point of view of mere natural intelligence, it became impossible for him to reconcile theoretically these two apparently contradictory dogmas of the equality of the Logos with the Father, and of His distinction from Him. "Arius," says Dorner with justice, "takes part with pleasure and skill in the relative sphere: he handles the lower categories of logic with dialectic skill; but he never rises above it: he applies it to everything. He is quite incapable of rising to speculative science, properly so called." But he would certainly not have created so much disturbance in the minds of the people, had he not found in Alexandria a field well prepared to receive this theory of subordination, even so far back as the time of Origen. A certain hostility had been created against the theology of equality (the doctrine of the equality of the Son with the Father), which was taught by Theognostus, Pierius, and Bishop Peter, and now anew by Bishop Alexander. The representatives of the old Alexandrian tendency naturally linked themselves with pleasure to Arius; and thus it was that in later times the Arians earnestly appealed to the authority of Origen, and protected themselves under his name, and pretended to proceed directly from him. Athanasius carefully refuted this. Besides, the Church of Alexandria was a specially prepared soil for this new growth: she had been for more than a century the philosophizing Church of Christianity (ἐκκλησία φιλοσοφικωτάτη). She readily threw herself into all philosophical and theological controversies. Being in close proximity to the native country of Sabellianism, she felt constantly called upon to combat it, and so was led imperceptibly into the other extreme. Arius himself was Libyan by birth, consequently a compatriot of Sabellius; thus he might have considered himself specially called on to combat the Sabellian theory, which annihilated all distinction between the Father and the Son. Philonism, of which Alexandria was the hotbed, seems also to have exercised some influence over the development of Arianism; and as the following details will prove, Arius built on the base of this philosophy. Thus,

(α.) Like Philo, he exaggerated the distinction between the world and God, and considered the supreme God much too sublime to enter into direct relation with the world, and the world much too low to bear any direct action of God. Now Athanasius proves that Arius, and his friends Eusebius and Asterius, had appropriated to themselves this fundamental proposition of Philo's philosophy.

(β.) Like Philo, Arius admitted an intermediate being, who, being less than God, was the divine organ of the creation of the world (like the created gods of Plato): this intermediate being was the Logos. Thus the Arian Logos resembled that of Philo: they are each declared inferior to the Father; and Philo, who in general considered him as personal, gives to him the name of ὑπηρέτης Θεοῦ.

(γ.) Now the intermediate and inferior being could not be equal in substance and equal in eternity (consubstantial and co-eternal) with the supreme and only true God. It may thus be seen how all the other Subordinationist predicates of the Logos arise of themselves from the fundamental propositions of Philo.

Arius completely failed to perceive the contradiction which springs from the adoption of an intermediate being. According to his view, the supreme God could not create anything imperfect; yet He makes the Son imperfect. If God can create only perfect beings, it becomes necessary that the plenitude of perfection, and consequently of divinity, be found in the Son; if not, the supreme God could create imperfect beings: thus He could equally have created the world.

The analogy between the intermediate being of the Arians and the Gnostic Demiurge is evident, but the difference which existed between the two must not be overlooked. They resemble each other, inasmuch as neither can produce perfect beings. But whilst the Gnostic Demiurge only presides over a period of the world's existence, the Arian Logos does not cease to act as long as the world exists. The age of the Emperor Constantine was undeniably very favourable for the rise and rapid propagation of the doctrine of Subordination; for after the conversion of the Emperor, many learned heathens entered the Church without a real vocation, and there spread on all sides religious theories much more favourable to half-pagan Subordinationism than to the profoundly Christian doctrine of the equality of the Father and of the Son.

We know but little of the life of Arius before he set forth his errors, and what is known of him is not very certain. He embraced at Alexandria the side of the Meletians at first, but afterwards abandoned it, and was ordained deacon by

Peter Bishop of Alexandria. At a later period, having taken the side of the Meletians, he was excommunicated by Bishop Peter; but his successor Achillas (A.D. 312) reconciled him to the Church, and ordained him priest. Soon after, Arius was. put at the head of a Church called Baucalis, as the large number of Christians in Alexandria had rendered necessary the division of the town into districts, corresponding with what are now called parishes.

Arius was tall and thin; a learned man and a clever logician; of austere appearance and serious bearing, and yet of very fascinating manners; at the same time proud, ambitious, insincere, and cunning. Epiphanius calls him a perfidious serpent. Bishop Alexander reproaches him with his avarice, and speaks of his following composed of women, in such a way that later historians believed—wrongfully, no doubt— that disgraceful inferences might be drawn against his private life. Two statements by Theodoret, on the ambition and arrogance of Arius, have led to the belief that, after the death of Achillas (towards the end of 312), Arius strove for the Episcopal dignity; but seeing his old colleague Alexander preferred to him, he conceived a deep hatred against him. The Arian historian Philostorgius, on the contrary, asserts that Arius himself made over to Alexander the votes which were offered to himself. Neither of these assertions seems to have been true. Theodoret is nearer the truth when he says, that in the beginning Alexander highly esteemed Arius. Chronology confirms this statement; for the discussion between Arius and his bishop did not, as it would seem, take place until 318 or 320, when Alexander had been Bishop of Alexandria for more than six years, and until then apparently the most profound good feeling had

existed between Arius and him. But whilst admitting that a
certain antipathy existed between them, it must not
therefore be concluded that it gave rise to the doctrinal
controversy: this was simply the result of different
theological convictions. Socrates thus relates the manner in
which this difference first arose: "Bishop Alexander of
Alexandria one day spoke, in presence of his priests and
clergy, of the mystery of the Trinity, and insisted especially
on the Unity in the Trinity, philosophizing on this grave
subject, and thinking he was gaining honour by his
argument. But Arius, who was eager for dispute, professed
to discover Sabellianism in the bishop's doctrine. He
opposed it vehemently, and asserted that if the Father had
begotten the Son, he who was begotten had a beginning of
his being (ἀρχὴν ὑπάρξεως), and consequently there was a
time when he could not have been (ἦν, ὅτε οὐκ ἦν); that it
also followed that the Son had his beginning from nothing
(ἐξ οὐκ ὄντων ἔχει τὴν ὑπόστασιν)."

All history posterior to Arianism proves that Arius was
unjust in accusing his bishop of Sabellianism; but that
which chiefly proves it is the conduct of Alexander at the
Council of Nicæa, and likewise his letters and those of
Arius, which we shall soon have occasion to examine.

Arius admitted, with the orthodox Fathers, that the term
"begotten" was the palladium which could alone save the
doctrine of the personal existence of the Son against
Sabellianism. He therefore took the idea of "begotten" as
the groundwork of his argument; but he transferred the
idea of time, which rules every human generation, to the
divine generation, and drew from that, as he thought, with
logical necessity, the proposition that the Son could not be

co-eternal with the Father. He did not, however, wish to speak of a priority in time, properly so called, but only of priority similar to a priority in time, of the Father to the Son; for, according to Arius, time began with the creation, and thus the Son, by whom all things were created, and who, consequently, was before the creation, was born also before all time. Other theologians had, before Arius, already developed this argument; but he afterwards went beyond it, and thought that the distinction he had established between the Father and the Son would fade away if he admitted that the Son is begotten of the substance of the Father. This fear has apparently been justified by the history of the word "consubstantial" (ὁμοούσιος); for this word, as we have already seen, was rejected by the Synod of Antioch, held in 269. But Arius not only avoided this definite expression, but all others similar to it used by the holy Fathers to show that the Son emanated from the substance of the Father. He not only rejected the expression, but the thing expressed, by positively declaring that he was made ἐξ οὐκ ὄντων, which was diametrically opposed to the ὁμοούσιος, and thus went further than any one else among the ancients. He positively made the Logos a "creature" in the special sense of the word.

Arius had another motive for not admitting that the Son was begotten of the substance of the Father. He believed that by so doing the divine substance would be divided, whilst God is essentially indivisible; and, in point of fact, the Arians constantly reproached their adversaries with considering the divine substance as something corporeal, and dividing it. They believed that their doctrine of the

Logos alone maintained, not only the indivisibility and immateriality of God, but likewise His immutability. The creation of temporal things would, according to them, have wrought a change in the Creator; for if the supreme God had made the world, He would have lost His immutability, which is contrary to the idea we have of God. On the contrary, there was no danger in denying the immutability of the Son, as being declared to be a creature who took part in the creation of the world. They said, then, "By nature the Son is not unchangeable, but only by His own will."

Arius first appeared on the scene with these opinions between 318 and 320. This date, though uncertain, has every appearance of probability. Sozomen, Theodoret, and Epiphanius relate, as did Socrates, with slight differences of detail only, the beginning of the Arian controversy. Socrates does not say that Bishop Alexander gave rise to the discussion by a sermon; according to him, it was Arius who began of himself to spread his errors. The bishop was blamed for tolerating the beginning of it. He did not, however, wish to use his authority against Arius: he preferred to call together his clergy, and made them argue in his presence with Arius; and they proclaimed the Son ὁμοούσιος and συναίδιος (consubstantial and co-eternal with the Father). In the beginning of the discussion Alexander did not take either side; but towards the end he approved of those who had defended the consubstantiality and co-eternity of the Son, and commanded Arius to retract his error. Epiphanius maintains, but it is difficult to admit the assertion, that the chief adversary and opposer of Arius was Bishop Meletius, the chief of the schismatics, of whom we have already spoken. Arius was little disposed to submit to the orders of his bishop; on the contrary, he sent to several bishops a written confession of faith, and begged them, if they approved of it, to send him their adhesion, and to intercede with Bishop Alexander in his favour. In a short time he made many friends, especially the celebrated Eusebius of Nicomedia, who, being then bishop in the household of Constantine and his sister Constantia, exercised great influence over them, and over many of the other bishops. He interested himself actively with them on behalf of Arius, and sent him his adhesion in writing. He, like Arius, was a disciple of Lucian, and accepted in general the propositions of Arianism.

"One only," he thought, "the Father, is unbegotten; the other (the Son) is truly (that is to say, in the full sense of the word) created, and not of the substance of the Father (οὐκ ἐκ τῆς οὐσίας αὐτοῦ γεγονώς). The Son does not participate in the substance (οὐσία) of the unbegotten; He differs from Him in nature and in power, although He was created in perfect resemblance to the nature and power of His Creator. No one can express in words His beginning, or even understand it in thought." The letter to Bishop Paulinus of Tyre, in which Eusebius expresses these opinions, is at the same time a proof of the zeal he displayed in favour of Arius and his cause; for he reproaches this bishop with not having declared in favour of Arius, although at heart he shared his opinions. He exhorts him to repair his fault, and above all to write (as he no doubt had already done himself) to Bishop Alexander, and set forth the true doctrine, namely, that of Subordination. He proposed Eusebius of Cæsarea to him as a model, the celebrated church historian, who, without being a decided Arian, was visibly in favour of this party. Besides these two, Eusebius and Paulinus of Tyre, there were the bishops, Theodotus of Laodicea, Athanasius of Anazarbus, Gregory of Berytus, and Ætius of Lydda (or Diospolis), who interested themselves in favour of Arius. Very shortly others showed themselves on the same side: among the most remarkable were the two Africans, Secundus Bishop of Ptolemais in Libya, and Theonas of Marmarica, both of whom belonged to the province of Alexandria, and openly took part with Arius. Besides, from the Alexandrian and Mareotic clergy, there were added to the heretical party the two priests Chares and Pistus, and the thirteen following deacons,—Achillas, Euzoius, Aithalas, Lucius, Sarmates, Julius, Menas, Helladius, Serapion, Paramnon, Zosimus, Irenæus, and a second Arius. Among them also are named Carponas and Eusebius, without mention of the order to which they belonged. These names are given by Bishop Alexander himself in three lists, made at different times, for which reason they do not all agree. Epiphanius, on the contrary, speaks of seven priests, twelve deacons, and seven hundred virgins consecrated to God (Egypt had a great many such) who took part with Arius. It is probable that, in so grave a matter, Alexander early consulted with other bishops; at least this may be concluded from some passages contained in a letter which he wrote later, and which is found in Theodoret. But it is also certain that at the beginning Alexander endeavoured to keep the matter as quiet and peaceable as possible; and that, in connection with his clergy, he addressed remonstrances not only by word, but in writing, to Arius and his partisans.

SEC. 20. The Synod of Alexandria in 320, and its Consequences

Bishop Alexander, seeing the uselessness of his efforts, in 320 or 321 convoked a large ecclesiastical assembly in Alexandria, at which were present nearly a hundred Egyptian and Libyan bishops. The matter of their deliberations has not reached us; we only know that Arius and his partisans were anathematized. His partisans, said Alexander in two letters, were the two bishops Theonas and Secundus, and the majority of the deacons recently named. Arius wished to prove that Eusebius of Cæsarea, Theodotus of Laodicea, Paulinus of Tyre, and, in one word, the greater number of the bishops in Asia, were condemned with him by the Synod of Alexandria; but that was a false inference. It is likely that the Synod, after having excommunicated by name the African Arians, and especially those of Alexandria, pronounced a general anathema against the partisans of this heresy; and from this Arius drew the conclusions which suited him.

Although excommunicated, Arius continued to hold congregations for divine service; and Bishop Alexander speaks of several churches (which he designates as dens of thieves) where the Arians habitually met, and offered night and day outrages against Christ, and against the bishop. He mentions, in the same letter, how they sought in different towns to attract adherents by their lectures and writings, and especially sought to deceive women by their flatteries and falsehoods. They went so far, says he, that they stirred up against the orthodox the populace and the civil authorities (still principally heathen, for Egypt depended on Licinius), and endeavoured, when all was peace, to excite a new persecution. Alexander saw himself obliged, by the insolence and constant machinations of the Arians, as well as by the open partisanship of Eusebius of Nicomedia, to inform all the bishops of the position of affairs in elaborate letters. For the same purpose he convoked a new assembly of the Alexandrian and Mareotic clergy, and asked all the united clergy (among them Athanasius, then a deacon) to sign his Epistola encyclica. After a very fine introduction on the unity of the Church, Alexander especially complained of Eusebius of Nicomedia, who had undertaken to protect the heresy, and who recommended Arius and his partisans everywhere by his writings and letters. This conduct obliged him to speak openly. He afterwards enumerated the names of the apostates, and exposed their chief errors, which were the following:—

1. "God was not always Father; there was a time when He was not Father (ἦν, ὅτε ὁ Θεὸς πατὴρ οὐκ ἦν).

2. "The Logos of God has not always been (οὐκ ἀεὶ ἦν); He was created from nothing; God, the self-existent, created from nothing Him who is not self-existent (the ὢν Θεὸς— the μὴ ὄντα).

3. "Consequently there was a time when He was not; for

4. "The Son is a creature, a κτίσμα and a ποίημα.

5. "He is not of the same substance as the Father (οὔτε ὅμοιος κατ᾽ οὐσίαν); He is not truly and according to His nature the Word and the Wisdom of God (οὔτε ἀληθινὸς κατ᾽ οὐσίαν τοῦ πατρὸς λόγος ἐστὶν, οὔτε ἀληθινὴ σοφία αὐτοῦ ἐστιν); but one of the works, and of the creatures of

God (εἷς τῶν ποιημά των καὶ γενητῶν). He is only by an abuse (καταχρηστικῶς) called the Logos; He was created by the true Logos (ἰδίῳ τοῦ Θεοῦ λόγῳ), and by the inner (ἐν τῷ Θεῷ) Wisdom of God (the λόγος ἐνδιάθετος of Philo).

"It is by this inner Wisdom (λόγος ἐνδιάθετος) that God created Him (the λόγος προφορικὸς) and all things.

6. "Thus it is that by nature He is subject to change (τρεπτὸς, that is to say, by nature liable to sin).

7. "He is a stranger to the divine οὐσία, and differs from it (ξένος τε καὶ ἀλλότριος). He does not know God perfectly; He does not even know His own nature perfectly.

8. "He was created for us, so that God might create us by Him as His instrument; and He would not have existed (οὐκ ἂν ὑπέστη), had He not been called into existence by God through love for us."

Bishop Alexander afterwards refutes these Arian doctrines by texts from the Holy Scriptures; and at the end he implores the bishops not to admit the Arians into the communion of the Church, and to have no confidence in Eusebius and others like him.

Theodoret has preserved a second letter of Alexander's (and of his Synod), addressed, according to the title given by Theodoret, to Alexander Bishop of Constantinople. But not only is this title wanting in three ancient manuscripts; but besides, at the time the letter was written, the name Constantinople did not exist. Moreover, this letter was not addressed to one, but to several bishops, as the contents prove. It is said in the letter, that Arius and his friend

Achillas went further than Colluthus had done, who had
previously founded a sect in Alexandria. Even Colluthus at
this time blamed the conduct of the Arians, who did not
submit to the Church, who held meetings in their dens of
robbers, denied the Godhead of our Saviour,
misinterpreted those texts of Scripture for their own
purpose which speak of the humiliation of Christ, which
was for our salvation, and endeavoured to stir the people
up against the orthodox, and to excite persecutions against
them by calumnious pamphlets written by disorderly
women. After having been for these several causes
excluded from the Church, the Arians endeavoured by
falsehoods, and by concealing their errors, to bring other
bishops over to their side, and many of them had
succeeded in being admitted into the communion of the
Church. Consequently it became necessary to unveil
without delay their errors, which consisted in maintaining:

"That there was a period when the Son of God did not
exist;

"That, not existing at first, He was later called into
existence;

"That He was created out of nothing, like everything else,
reasonable or unreasonable, and consequently was by
nature liable to change, capable of goodness and of sin;

"But that God, knowing that He (the Son) would not deny
Him, chose Him above all created beings, although by
nature He had no higher claim than the other sons of God,
that is, than other virtuous men. If Peter and Paul had
sought to reach the same perfection as Christ, their relation

to God would have been absolutely the same as that in which Christ stood."

Then Bishop Alexander again refuted the Arians by texts of Scripture: he compared them to the Ebionites, to Artemas and Paul of Samosata; he called them Exucontians (οἱ ἐξ οὐκ ὄντων), a title which in later times was frequently employed; he complained that three Syrian bishops urged the Arians to still graver excesses; then returned afresh to biblical proof against the Arians, and developed the orthodox faith, saying that the Son was not subject to any change, and is in all things like the Father, perfect as He is perfect, and in one point only subordinate to the Father—in not being unbegotten. In other respects the Son is the exact image of the Father. He is from all eternity; but from this it must not be concluded, as the Arians have wrongfully done, and as they falsely accuse those who are orthodox of doing, that the Son was not begotten: for those two terms, "Being from all eternity," and "not begotten," are not identical; there is a difference between them. The Son, being in all things the image of the Father, should be worshipped as God. The Christian recognises also, with the Father and the Son, the Holy Ghost, who worked in the holy men of the Old Testament, and on the holy teachers of the New.

Bishop Alexander continued to set forth the other articles of the faith, and employed the term which became celebrated later in Christian controversy, the "Mother of God" (θεοτόκος). In conclusion, he exhorted the bishops to admit no Arian into the communion of the Church, and to act as did the bishops of Egypt, Libya, Asia, Syria, etc., who had sent him written declarations against Arianism, and signed his τόμος, that is to say, his treatise (perhaps the encyclical letter of which we have already spoken). He hopes they will send him similar declarations, as perhaps the number of the bishops might convert the Arians. He adds in the appendix the names of the ecclesiastics of Alexandria who were excommunicated along with Arius.

SEC. 21. Arius obliged to leave Alexandria; his Letters and his Thalia

Driven from Alexandria by his bishop, Arius went first to Palestine, and from thence addressed a letter to his powerful protector, Eusebius of Nicomedia. In it he complains of the persecution which he had to suffer at the hands of Alexander, particularly of being driven from the town; and accuses Alexander of maintaining "that the Father and the Son co-existed always together, that the Son was not begotten, that He was begotten from all eternity, that He was unbegotten Begotten, that the Father was not one moment anterior to the Son, and that He is of God Himself." (It may be seen how Arius misrepresents some of the doctrinal propositions of Alexander, as we have already found, because he could not reconcile the eternity of the Son with His divine generation.) Further, Arius asserts that Eusebius of Cæsarea, Theodotus of Laodicea, Paulinus of Tyre, etc., and all the Eastern bishops, were anathematized by Alexander because they taught that the Father existed before the Son. Only three Eastern bishops were not excommunicated, he adds: these are Philogonius, Hellanicus, and Macarius, because they have in an impious manner called the Son, the one an eructation of the Father (ἐρυγή, according to the forty-fourth Psalm, ver. 2), the other a projection (προβολή), the third co-begotten (συναγέννητον). Arius could not, he said, admit such impiety, even if the heretics threatened him a thousand times with death. As to the Arians, he says, they teach "that the Son is not begotten, and that He is not a part of the Unbegotten (with reference to the sense in which ὁμοούσιος was rejected at Antioch); that He was not created of anything which existed before Him; but that He was called into being by the will and according to the plan (of God), before time and before the world (that is to say, He was before the world was made, but that He was not eternal), and as full God (πλήρης Θεός), only-begotten (μονογενής), and unchangeable (ἀναλλοίωτος). Before being begotten, or created, or determined, or founded, He was not; for He is not unbegotten." He concludes by being remembered to Eusebius, who, like himself, belonged to the school of Lucian.

The exposition Arius here makes of his doctrine agrees perfectly, one point excepted, with that which was given a little further back by the Bishop of Alexandria. Alexander, in fact, says in his two letters, that Arius made of the Son "a being who, according to His nature, was capable of virtue or of sin." Arius seems to say the contrary in that which precedes this; but this difference is only in appearance. Arius, to be consistent, should have said: "The Son being a κτίσμα, and not of the substance of the Father, is by nature subject to change, as are all the κτίσματα." But he might also, and he did actually, affirm that "de facto the Son was immutable, but that His immutability was the effect of volition, and not by nature." Arius, in like manner, takes the expression πλήρης Θεός in a double sense. He cannot and will not say that the Son is by nature equal in glory to the

Father; he says that He is perfect God only by the will of the Father, that is to say, that the Father has made Him partaker of His divine glory. A careful analysis of the principal work of Arius, called the Thalia, will show, besides, how well-founded was the accusation made by Bishop Alexander, that Arius had here concealed his real sentiments.

Invited, in consequence of this letter, by Eusebius, Arius went a short time after to Nicomedia, and wrote from thence, perhaps at the instigation of Eusebius, a polite letter to his former bishop Alexander, in order to be on as good terms as possible with him. First, he sets forth in his letter a kind of creed which should explain the faith, as Arius and his friends had received it from their predecessors, and even from the Bishop Alexander himself, as follows:—

1. "There is only one true God, alone uncreate, alone eternal, alone without beginning, alone wise, good, and powerful; one only Judge and King, and alone unchangeable.

2. "Before all time He begot His only Son, and by Him created the world and all things.

3. "He did not only beget Him in appearance" (Arius believed in the eternal generation as being only in appearance, and imputed all real generation to time), "but He actually called Him into existence by His own will, as an unchangeable and immutable being.

4. "The Son is a perfect creature of God (κτίσμα τοῦ Θεοῦ τέλειον), but yet distinct from all other creatures; He is begotten, yet again He differs from all that is begotten.

5. "He is not, as is asserted by Valentinus, a projection (προβολή), nor yet, as the Manichæans assert, a substantial part of the Father (μέρος ὁμοούσιον τοῦ πατρός); nor, as the Sabellians wish, the Son-Father; nor, as is said by Hieracas, light of light, or one torch emanating from another; nor had He a previous existence, and was afterwards begotten and made the Son,—a thing which Bishop Alexander himself" (whom Arius still addresses as μακάριε πάπα) "had often publicly controverted, and with reason.

6. "He was created by the will of God before time, and before all worlds. He has received His life and His being from the Father, who also has communicated His glory to Him; and without taking from Himself, has given Him the heritage of all things.

7. "There are three persons: God, who is the cause of all things, who is unique, and without beginning; the Son, who is begotten of the Father before all things, created and established before the worlds. He was not until He was begotten; but He was begotten before all time, before all things, and He alone was called by the Father (immediately) into being. He is not, however, eternal or unbegotten, like the Father. He had not His being at the same time as the Father, as some say, who thus introduce two unbegotten principles; but as God is the monad and the beginning, or the principle of all things, He is therefore before all things, and consequently also before the Son, as Bishop Alexander himself has declared in the Church.

8. "The Son having received His being from God, who gave Him glory, life, and all things, so God must be His

principle (ἀρχή), and must rule Him (ἄρχει αὐτοῦ) as His God, and as being before Him.

9. "In conclusion, it is attempted to show that the biblical expressions, the Son is of the Father, ex utero, etc., do not refer to similarity of substance."

During his stay in Nicomedia, Arius wrote his principal work, called Θάλεια, that is, "The Banquet." Only fragments of it remain. They are preserved in the works of S. Athanasius. The book, it appears, was partly in prose and partly in verse. The ancients compared it to the songs of the Egyptian poet Sotades, and pronounced it highly effeminate and overwrought. According to Athanasius, there were some of these "Thalias" already among the heathen, which were read at their banquets for the promotion of gaiety. Arius selected this light form, it seems, to familiarize the masses with the doctrine taught in his book. With the same intention he afterwards wrote songs for sailors, carpenters, and travellers. Athanasius says the Thalia was held in great honour by the friends of Arius, and that they venerated it as a second Bible. In reality, it contains Arianism in its strongest form, and at the same time shows clearly its Philonian foundation. In one of these fragments Arius boasts of being very celebrated (περικλυτὸς), having had much to suffer for the glory of God (that is, because he gave the Father the glory due to Him, as opposed to the Son); and he goes on: "God has not always been Father; there was a moment when He was alone, and was not yet Father: later He became so. The Son is not from eternity; He came from nothing, etc. When God wished to create us, He first created a being which He called the Logos, Sophia, and Son, who should create us as an instrument. There are two Sophias: one is in God (i.e. ἐνδιάθετος), by which even the Son was made. It is only by sharing (μετέχει) the nature of this inner Sophia of God that the Son was also called Wisdom (σοφία προφορικός). So also, besides the Son, there is another Logos—he who is in God; and as the Son participates in this Logos, He also is by grace (κατὰ χάριν) called Logos and Son."

In the second fragment, the Thalia sets forth that with which, as we have seen, Bishop Alexander had reproached Arius,—namely, "that the Logos did not perfectly know the Father; that he could not even entirely understand his own nature; that the substance (οὐσίαι) of the Father, the Son, and the Holy Ghost are entirely different the one from the other. These three persons are, in their essence and glory (δόξα), thoroughly and infinitely dissimilar (ἀνόμοιοι πάμπαν ... ἐπ' ἄπειρον)."

In the third fragment Arius says, after the Philonian manner, from the beginning: "God is ἄρρητος (ineffable), and nothing (therefore not even the Son) is equal to or like Him, or of the same glory. This eternal God made the Son before all creatures, and adopted Him for His Son (ἤνεγκεν εἰς υἱόν).... The Son has nothing in his own nature akin to God, and is not like to Him in essence. The invisible God is also invisible to the Son, and the Son can see Him only so far as is permitted by the will of the Father. The Three Persons of the Trinity are not equal in glory, the Hypostases (Persons) are not confounded, and one is infinitely more glorious than the other. God could create a being like unto the Son, but He cannot create a being more glorious or more great. That which the Son is, He is through the Father and the mighty God (ἰσχυρὸς Θεὸς). He (the Son) adores Him who is more glorious than Himself."

SEC. 22. Synod in Bithynia—Intervention of the Emperor Constantine

Sozomen speaks of a Synod in Bithynia which supported the Arians by an encyclical addressed to all the bishops, asking them to receive the Arians into the communion of the Church. This Synod was held by the partisans of Arius, probably during his stay in Nicomedia, and perhaps even in that town. The part espoused by so many bishops did not bring about peace in the Church: the struggle, on the contrary, became more intense; and there arose so much division among Christians, and such grievous schisms in all towns, and even in the villages, that the heathens everywhere turned it into ridicule on the stage. S. Athanasius shows us how much occasion the Arians gave to the heathens for such derision, by describing their proselytism, which was as improper as it was ridiculous: for example, how they gained women to their side by asking sophistical questions, such as, "Hast thou had a son before thou didst bear?" in order to win them over to their opinion of the later origin of the Son.

The political events which then arose undoubtedly increased the trouble in Egypt and in the East, the seat of Arianism. The Emperor Licinius, to whom Egypt and Asia belonged, after being vanquished by Constantine in 315, had concluded a definite peace with him; and in consequence of this treaty he lived several years on the best terms with his father-in-law and the Christians. But towards the end of 322 Licinius took advantage of Constantine's crossing the frontiers of his empire, in pursuit of the Sarmatians, to break with him; and in 323 entered into a war, which towards the autumn of the year ended in the total defeat of Licinius by sea and land. This war accounts for the increase of the confusion and divisions in the Church, as well as for the lack of all authentic history of Arianism during this period (322–323). Another circumstance which may thus be explained is the boldness of Arius in returning to Alexandria. In his struggle against Constantine, Licinius became the champion of heathenism, and oppressed the Church, particularly the bishops. Arius had no further cause to fear Alexander, and the principal obstacle to his return was thus removed. The actual return of Arius to Alexandria is proved by Sozomen, and still better by a letter from the Emperor Constantine, of which we shall shortly speak. Sozomen says that "Arius sent messages to the Bishops Paulinus of Tyre, Eusebius of Cæsarea, and Patrophilus of Scythopolis, asking permission to officiate as formerly, and to do so even in Alexandria. As is understood from the tenor of the letter, these bishops summoned their colleagues to a council, and allowed Arius and his adherents to hold, as formerly, private religious assemblies, without, however, withdrawing themselves from the submission due to Bishop Alexander, and on the condition of asking for peace and communion."

Constantine, now master of the whole empire, consequently also of Egypt and the other provinces disturbed by Arianism, considered it his duty to re-establish religious as well as civil peace, and took the necessary measures as soon as he had returned to Nicomedia. He sent first a long letter to Arius and Bishop Alexander, the purport of which Eusebius has preserved entire, but which Socrates only gives in fragments. He says in this letter, that "he has learnt with great sorrow that sharper controversies than those of Africa (the Donatist disputes) have arisen at Alexandria, although it appears to him that they are questions respecting things of no importance and of no use, which Alexander ought not to have excited, and about which Arius ought to have kept his different views to himself. They were questions which the human mind was too weak to solve correctly; and therefore both Arius and Alexander should forgive each other, and do that which he, their fellow-servant, advised them. He thought that they could easily be reconciled, as they did not disagree on any main point of the law, nor on any innovation in divine service, and were therefore substantially at one; that philosophers of the same school had often differed in accessories: we should be able to bear such differences, but bring them as little as possible before the people. That was vulgar, puerile, and unworthy of priests. That, therefore, they ought to agree, and free him from so great a cause of anxiety."

It is evident that the Emperor was not at that time aware of the importance of the Arian controversy, and that his letter does not merit the great praise it received from Eusebius and others. Constantine sent this letter, in the contents of which Eusebius of Nicomedia perhaps had a hand, to Alexandria by the celebrated Bishop Hosius of Cordova. This venerable man, whom the Emperor usually consulted, was sixty-seven years of age. He had been a confessor during the persecution of Diocletian; and the Emperor hoped that his presence would bring about a reconciliation.

It is uncertain what Hosius did at Alexandria: it is only known that he opposed Sabellianism there, proving the Christian doctrine of the nature and persons of the Holy Trinity, probably to make clear the difference between the Sabellian and the orthodox doctrine. It is not known if he was present at the Synod of Alexandria, which deposed Colluthus. Perhaps this Council was held later. Unhappily Hosius did not succeed in his mission to Alexandria. Philostorgius relates that later he met the Bishop of Alexandria at a synod at Nicomedia, where he approved of the term ὁμοούσιος, and excommunicated Arius. The statement is not probable.

However, the Emperor's letter and Hosius' mission remaining alike without result, and the Paschal controversy continuing to disturb many eastern provinces (the custom of the Quartodecimans existed still in Syria, Cilicia, and Mesopotamia), the Emperor, perhaps advised by Hosius, thought there could be no better means to re-establish the peace of the Church than the calling of an œcumenical council.

CHAPTER II
THE DISCUSSIONS AT NICÆA

SEC. 23. The Synodal Acts

THE first and principal source from which we draw our information respecting the deliberations at Nicæa, must of course be the acts of the Synod. Unhappily we possess only three portions of them—the Creed, the twenty Canons, and the Synodal Decree; and the question arises, whether this is all which ever existed; in other words, whether the separate discussions and debates at Nicæa were committed to writing, and subsequently lost, or whether they neglected to take minutes of the proceedings. Vague rumours of later times have reported that minutes were taken; and it is asserted in the preface to the Arabic edition of the Canons, that the acts of the Nicene Synod fill no fewer than forty volumes, and have been distributed throughout the whole world. To a similar effect is that which the pseudo-Isidore writes, in the preface to his well-known collection. "He had learnt," he says, "from the Orientals, that the acts of Nicæa were more voluminous than the four Gospels." At the Synod of Florence, in the fifteenth century, one of the Latin speakers asserted that Athanasius had asked and obtained a genuine copy of the acts of Nicæa from the Roman bishop Julius, because the Oriental copies had been corrupted by the Arians. Some went so far as even to indicate several collections of archives in which the complete acts of Nicæa were preserved. Possevin, for instance, professed to know that a copy was in the archiepiscopal library at Ravenna. As a matter of fact, this library had only a manuscript of the Nicene Creed, which was written in purple and gold letters. At an earlier period,

Pope Gregory x. had written to the King and to the Catholicus of the Armenians, to ask for a copy of the acts, which were said to exist in Armenia, but in vain. Others professed to know, or offered as a conjecture, that the documents in request were at Constantinople or Alexandria, or rather in Arabia. In fact, they discovered, in the sixteenth century, in old Arabic MSS., besides the twenty Canons of Nicæa already mentioned, which were well known before, a great number of other ecclesiastical ordinances, constitutions, and canons, in an Arabic translation, which all, it was said, belonged to the Nicene Council We shall demonstrate beyond a doubt, at sec. 41, the later origin of these documents.

The same must be said of an alleged collection of minutes of a disputation held at Nicæa between some heathen philosophers and Christian bishops, which S. Gelasius of Cyzicus, in the fifth century, inserted in his History of the Council of Nicæa, of which we shall presently have something more to say. They are also spurious, and as apocryphal as the pretended minutes of a disputation between Athanasius and Arius. Those who know this history of S. Gelasius only by hearsay, have taken it for an additional and more complete collection of the Synodal Acts of Nicæa, and thereby have strengthened the vague rumour of the existence of such. As a matter of fact, however, there is no evidence of any one ever having seen or used those acts. An appeal cannot be made to Balsamon on this point; for when this celebrated Greek scholar of the twelfth century refers, in his explanation of the first canon of Antioch, to the Nicene acts, he is evidently thinking simply of the Synodal Decree of Nicæa.

We believe we can also show, that from the first no more acts of Nicæa were known than the three documents already named—the Creed, the twenty Canons, and the Synodal Decree. This is indicated by Eusebius, when he says, in his Life of Constantine: "That which was unanimously adopted was taken down in writing, and signed by all." So early as the year 350, Athanasius could give no other answer to a friend who wished to learn what passed at Nicæa. If a complete copy of the acts had existed, Athanasius would certainly have known of it, and would have directed his friend to that Baronius maintains that Athanasius himself speaks of the complete acts of Nicæa, in his work de Synodis Arim. et Seleuc. c. 6; but the Cardinal was led into error by an incorrect Latin translation of the passage which he quoted, for the Greek text does not speak of acts properly so called: it says only, that "if we wish to know the true faith, there is no need for another council, seeing we possess τὰ τῶν πατέρων (that is to say, the decisions of the Nicene Fathers), who did not neglect this point, but set forth the faith so well, that all who sincerely follow their γράμματα may there find the scriptural doctrine concerning Christ." To see in these words a proof of the existence of detailed acts of the Council, is certainly to give much too wide a meaning to the text, as Valesius has remarked, and Pagi also: it is most likely that Athanasius, when writing this passage, had in view only the Creed, the Canons, and the Synodal Decree of Nicæa.

In default of these acts of the Council of Nicæa, which do not exist, and which never have existed, besides the three authentic documents already quoted, we may consider as historical the accounts of the ancient Church historians,

Eusebius, Socrates, Sozomen, Theodoret, and Rufinus, as well as some writings and sayings of S. Athanasius', especially in his book de Decretis synodi Nicænæ, and in his Epistola ad Afros. A less ancient work is that by Gelasius Bishop of Cyzicus in the Propontis, who wrote in Greek, in the fifth century, a History of the Council of Nicæa, which is to be found in all the larger collections of the councils. In the composition of this work Gelasius made use of the works mentioned above, and had also other ancient documents at his disposal, which had been carefully collected by his predecessor, Bishop Dalmasius. We shall see hereafter that he admitted things which were improbable, and evidently false. Gelasius, however, has in Dorscheus a defender against the too violent attacks to which he has been subjected.

The work of Gelasius is divided into three books, the first of which is only the life of the Emperor Constantine the Great, and contains absolutely nothing relative to the Council of Nicæa. The whole of the second book, on the contrary, is devoted to the history of that assembly. The third is wholly composed of three letters of Constantine's; but we may presume that it was formerly larger, and contained particularly the account of Constantine's baptism, which Photius borrowed from Gelasius, but which was subsequently mutilated, in order that the honour of having been the place where the great Emperor received baptism might not be taken from the city of Rome. However, no sort of proof is given in support of this suspicion.

An anonymous Copt undertook a similar work to that of Gelasius. This writer probably lived a short time after the

Council of Nicæa, and composed a sort of history of this
Synod (Liber synodicus de concilio Nicæno) in the Coptic
language. Four fragments of this work, which was lost,
were discovered more than fifty years ago by the learned
archæologist George Zoëga (Danish consul at Rome, a
convert to Roman Catholicism, and interpreter at the
Propaganda, who died in 1809), and were published in the
Catalogus codicum Copticorum manuscriptorum musei
Borgiani. Unfortunately the proof sheets of this work were
almost all lost, in consequence of the death of Zoëga and of
his Mæcenas happening immediately after its completion,
and from a lawsuit entered into by the heirs. The learned
French Benedictine Cardinal Pitra has just published these
four fragments afresh, with a Latin version and notes, in
the first volume of his Spicilegium Solesmense (Paris 1852,
p. 509 sqq.).

1. The first and largest of these fragments contains the
Nicene Creed, with the anathemas pronounced against
Arius. Only the first lines are wanting. Then come some
additions by the author of the Liber Synodicus. The first
runs thus: "This is the faith proclaimed by our" fathers
against Arius and other heretics, especially against Sabellius,
Photinus (? who lived long after Nicæa), and Paul of
Samosata; and we anathematize those adversaries of the
Catholic Church who were rejected by the 318 bishops of
Nicæa. The names of the bishops are carefully preserved,
that is to say, of the Eastern ones; for those of the West
had no cause for anxiety on account of this heresy."

This addition had been for a long time in Hardouin's
collection in Latin, and in Mansi's, and it was generally
attributed to Dionysius the Less. The second addition is a

more detailed exposition of the Catholic faith, also proceeding from the pen of the author of the Liber Synodicus. It says: "We adore not only one divine person, like Sabellius; but we acknowledge, according to the confession of the Council of Nicæa, one Father, one Son, one Holy Ghost. We anathematize those who, like Paul of Samosata, teach that the Son of God did not exist before the Virgin Mary—not before He was born in the flesh, etc. We anathematize also those who hold that there are three Gods, and those who deny that the Logos is the Son of God (Marcellus of Ancyra and Photinus of Sirmium)." The author puts next to these two additions a document which has been handed down to us, the first half of the list of bishops present, at Nicæa, containing one hundred and sixty-one names.

2. The second and shortest of the fragments contains the second part of the Nicene Creed, not quite accurately repeated by one or more later believers. To the words Spiritus sanctus are already added Qui procedit a Patre, an interpolation which could not have been added till after the second Œcumenical Council. Then comes a further Expositio fidei, which endeavours to work out the consequences of the Nicene Creed, and is especially directed against Sabellius and Photinus.

3. The third fragment gives us next the end of this Expositio fidei. It is followed by two additions, attributed to an Archbishop Rufinus, otherwise unknown. The first expresses the joy which the orthodox doctrine gives to the author; the second tells us that each time the bishops rose at Nicæa they were three hundred and nineteen in number, and that they were only three hundred and eighteen when

they took their seats. They could never discover who the three hundred and nineteenth was, for he was sometimes like one, sometimes like another; at last it was manifest that it was the Holy Spirit. Rufinus then writes a certain number of Sententiæ synodi sanctæ; but some of these judgments are on points which were not brought before the Nicene Council, especially on man's free-will. They are undoubtedly somewhat similar to the Expositio fidei orthodoxæ, which is contained in the second and third fragments.

4. The fourth fragment contains the Coptic translation of the second, third, fourth, fifth, and sixth canons of Nicæa. It is more or less according to the original Greek text, without the principal meaning ever being altered.

These four Coptic fragments certainly possess interest to the historian of the Nicene Council, who is anxious to know all the sources of information; but they have not so much value and importance as Zoëga and Pitra have attributed to them. We shall again speak of each of these fragments in their proper place in the history of the Council of Nicæa.

The anonymous author of the book entitled τὰ πραχθέντα ἐν Νικαίᾳ, several manuscripts of which are in existence, pretends to be a contemporary of the Nicene Council. This small treatise, published by Combefis, and of which Photius has given extracts, contains palpable errors,—for instance, that the Nicene Council lasted three years and six months. It is generally of small importance.

We may say the same of the λόγος of a priest of Cæsarea, named Gregory, upon the three hundred and eighteen Fathers of Nicæa. Combefis, who has also published this document, supposes that the author probably lived in the seventh century. He, however, calls the book opus egregium; but, with the exception of some biographical accounts of one of the bishops present at Nicæa, Gregory gives only well-known details, and improbable accounts of miracles. Although the value of these latter small treatises is not great, Hardouin and Mansi, coming after Combefis, ought to have inserted them in their collections of the Councils. These Collections contain all the other known documents relative to the history of the Council of Nicæa, and they form the basis of the account which we have to give of it. We shall hereafter speak of the numerous canons attributed to the Council of Nicæa, and of another pretended creed directed against Paul of Samosata.

SEC. 24. The Convocation by the Emperor

The letters of invitation sent by the Emperor Constantine the Great to the bishops, to ask them to repair to Nicæa, do not unfortunately now exist, and we must content ourselves with what Eusebius says on the subject. "By very respectful letters (τιμητικοῖς γράμμασι) the Emperor begged the bishops of every country (ἀπανταχόθεν) to go as quickly as possible to Nicæa." Rufinus says that the Emperor also asked Arius. It is not known whether invitations were sent to foreign bishops (not belonging to the Roman Empire). Eusebius says that the Emperor assembled an œcumenical council (σύνοδον οἰκουμενικὴν); but it is not at all easy to determine the value of the word οἰκουμένη. However it may be, Eusebius and Gelasius affirm that some foreign bishops took part in this great Council. The former says: "A bishop even from Persia was present at the Council, and Scythia itself was represented among the bishops." Gelasius does not mention a Scythian bishop—that is to say, a Goth; but he begins his work with these words: "Not only bishops from every province of the Roman Empire were present at the Council, but even some from Persia." The signatures of the members of the Council which still remain (it is true they are not of incontestable authenticity) agree with Eusebius and Gelasius; for we there find one John Bishop of Persia, and Theophilus the Gothic metropolitan. Socrates also mentions the latter, who, he says, was the predecessor of Ulphilas.

It is impossible to determine whether the Emperor Constantine acted only in his own name, or in concert with the Pope, in assembling the bishops. Eusebius and the most ancient documents speak only of the Emperor's part in the Council, without, however, a positive denial of the participation of the Pope. The sixth Œcumenical Synod, which took place in 680, says, on the contrary: "Arius arose as an adversary to the doctrine of the Trinity, and Constantine and Silvester immediately assembled (συνέλεγον) the great Synod at Nicæa." The Pontifical of Damasus affirms the same fact. From that time, the opinion that the Emperor and the Pope had agreed together to assemble the Council became more and more general; and with whatever vivacity certain Protestant authors may have arrayed themselves against this supposition, it certainly seems probable that in such an important measure the Emperor would have thought it necessary not to act without the consent and co-operation of him who was recognised as the first bishop of Christendom. Let us add that Rufinus had already expressly said that the Emperor assembled the Synod ex sacerdotum sententia. If he consulted several bishops upon the measure which he had in view, he certainly would have taken the advice of the first among them; and the part of the latter in the convocation of the Council must certainly have been more considerable than that of the other bishops, or the sixth Council would doubtless have expressed itself in another way. The testimony of this Council is here of real importance. If it had been held in the West, or even at Rome, what it says might appear suspicious to some critics; but it took place at Constantinople, at a period when the bishops of this city were beginning to be rivals to those of Rome. The Greeks formed greatly the majority of the members of the Council, and consequently their testimony in favour of Rome, more especially in favour of the co-operation of Silvester, is very important.

In order to make the journey to Nicæa possible to some, and at least easier to others, the Emperor placed the public conveyances and the beasts of burden belonging to the Government at the disposal of the bishops; and while the Council lasted, he provided abundantly for the entertainment of its members. The choice of the town of Nicæa was also very favourable for a large concourse of bishops. Situated upon one of the rivers flowing into the Propontis on the borders of Lake Ascanius, Nicæa was very easy to reach by water for the bishops of almost all the provinces, especially for those of Asia, Syria, Palestine, Egypt, Greece, and Thrace: it was a much frequented commercial city, in relation with every country, not far distant from the imperial residence in Nicomedia, and after the latter the most considerable city in Bithynia. After the lapse of so many centuries, and under the oppressive Turkish rule, it is so fallen from its ancient splendour, that under the name of Isnik it numbers now scarcely 1500 inhabitants. This is fewer than the number of guests it contained at the time when our Synod was held.

SEC. 25. Number of the Members of the Council

Eusebius says that there were more than two hundred and fifty bishops present at the Council of Nicæa; and he adds that the multitude of priests, deacons, and acolytes who accompanied them was almost innumerable. Some later Arabian documents speak of more than two thousand bishops; but it is probable that the inferior orders of the clergy were reckoned with them, and perhaps all together they reached that number. Besides, there must have been more bishops at Nicæa than Eusebius mentions; for S. Athanasius, who was an eye-witness, and a member of the Council, often speaks of about three hundred bishops, and in his letter ad Afros he speaks expressly of three hundred and eighteen. This number was almost universally adopted; and Socrates himself, who always follows Eusebius in his details respecting the commencement of the Nicene Synod, and copies him often word for word, nevertheless adopts the number three hundred and eighteen; also Theodoret, Epiphanius, Ambrose, Gelasius, Rufinus, the Council of Chalcedon, and Sozomen, who speaks of about three hundred bishops.1 In fact, the number of bishops present varied according to the months: there were perhaps fewer at the beginning; so that we may reconcile the testimonies of the two eye-witnesses Eusebius and Athanasius, if we

suppose that they did not make their lists at the same time.
The number of three hundred and eighteen being admitted,
it is natural that we should compare it with the three
hundred and eighteen servants of Abraham.1 S. Ambrose,1
and several others after him, notice this parallel. Most of
these three hundred and eighteen bishops were Greeks:
among the Latins we find only Hosius of Cordova, Cecilian
of Carthage, Marcus of Calabria, Nicasius of Dijon,
Domnus of Stridon (in Pannonia), the two Roman priests
Victor and Vincent, representatives of Pope Silvester.1
With Hosius of Cordova, the most eminent members of
the Council were those of the apostolic sees, Alexander of
Alexandria, Eustathius of Antioch, and Macarius of
Jerusalem: then came the two bishops of the same name,
Eusebius of Nicomedia and of Cæsarea; Patamon of
Heraclea in Egypt, who had lost one eye in the last
persecution; Paphnutius of the higher Thebaïs, and
Spiridion of Cyprus, both celebrated for their miracles.
Paphnutius had one eye bored out and his legs cut off
during Maximin's persecution. Another bishop, Paul of
Neocæsarea, had had his hands burnt by the red-hot irons
that Licinius had commanded to be applied to them. James
of Nisibis was honoured as a worker of miracles: it was said
that he had raised the dead. There was also seen among the
foremost, Leontius of Cæsarea, a man endowed with the
gift of prophecy, who during the journey to Nicæa had
baptized the father of S. Gregory of Nazianzus; besides
Hypatius of Gangra, and S. Nicolas of Myra in Asia Minor,
so well known for his generosity, that Eusebius could say
with truth: "Some were celebrated for their wisdom, others
for the austerity of their lives and for their patience, others
for their modesty; some were very old, some full of the

freshness of youth." Theodoret adds: "Many shone from apostolic gifts, and many bore in their bodies the marks of Christ."

It is no wonder if, considering their circumstances, there were some unlearned among so large a number of bishops; but Bishop Sabinus of Heraclea in Thrace, a partisan of Macedonius, was quite wrong when, shortly afterwards, he laughed at the general ignorance of the members of the Council of Nicæa. After having given vent to his hatred as a heretic, he did not hesitate to copy one of these Nicene Fathers, Eusebius, the father of ecclesiastical history. Socrates has shown that the same Sabinus fell into other contradictions.

Among the auxiliaries of the bishops of Nicæa, he who became by far the most celebrated was Athanasius, then a young deacon of Alexandria, who accompanied his bishop Alexander. He was born about the year 300, at Alexandria, and had been consecrated to the service of the Church in a very peculiar manner. Rufinus relates the fact in the following manner:—According, he says, to what he heard at Alexandria from those who knew Athanasius, Alexander Bishop of Alexandria one day saw on the sea-shore several children imitating the ceremonies of the Church. They did not do it at all as children generally do in play; but the bishop remarked that they followed every ecclesiastical rite very exactly, and especially that Athanasius, who represented the bishop, baptized several catechumens from among the children. Alexander questioned them, and what he heard convinced him, and also his clergy, that Athanasius had really administered the sacrament of baptism to his little playfellows, and that it only required the confirmation of the Church. Probably the young officiant had not intended to play, but to do well quod fieri vult ecclesia. According to the bishop's advice, all these children were consecrated to the work of the ministry; and Alexander soon took the young Athanasius to be with him, ordained him deacon in 319, and placed so much confidence in him that he raised him above all the other clergy, and made him an archdeacon, although scarcely twenty years of age. It is probable that Athanasius took part in the Arian controversy from the commencement; at least Eusebius of Nicomedia, or other adversaries of his, attribute Alexander's persevering refusal of reconciliation with Arius to his influence. "At Nicæa," says Socrates, "Athanasius was the most vehement opponent of the Arians." He was at the same time the man of highest intelligence in the Synod, and an able logician. This aptness for controversy was particularly valuable in the conflict with such sophists as the Arians. The bishops had even brought learned laymen and accomplished logicians with them, who, like Athanasius and others who were present, not being bishops, took a very active part in the discussions which preceded the deliberations and decisions properly so called.

SEC. 26. Date of the Synod

All the ancients agree in saying that the Synod took place under the consulship of Anicius Paulinus and Anicius Julianus, 636 years after Alexander the Great, consequently 325 A.D. They are not equally unanimous about the day and the month of the opening of the Council. Socrates says: "We find from the minutes that the time of the Synod (probably of its commencement) was the 20th May." The acts of the fourth Œcumenical Council give another date.

In the second session of that assembly, Bishop Eunomius of Nicomedia read the Nicene Creed; and at the commencement of his copy were these words: "Under the consulship of Paulinus and Julianus, on the 9th of the Greek month Dasius, that is, the 13th before the Kalends of July, at Nicæa, the metropolis of Bithynia." The Chronicle of Alexandria gives the same date, xiii Cal. Jul., and consequently indicates the 19th June. In order to reconcile the data of Socrates with those of the Council of Chalcedon, we may perhaps say that the Council opened on the 20th May, and that the Creed was drawn up on the 19th June. But Athanasius expressly says that the Fathers of Nicæa put no date at the commencement of their Creed; and he blames the Arian bishops Ursacius and Valens, because their Creed was preceded by a fixed date. Consequently the words placed at the top of the copy of the Nicene Creed read at Chalcedon must have proceeded, not from the Synod of Nicæa, but from some later copyist. But neither can we establish, as Tillemont and some other historians have tried to do, that this date signifies, not the day when the Creed was drawn up, but that of the opening of the Synod. Even if the Synod had affixed no date to its Creed, we may well suppose that this date was placed there at a later period, and continue to believe that the Council opened on the 20th of May 325, and that it published the Creed on the 19th of June. Baronius found a third chronological datum in an ancient manuscript, attributed to Atticus Bishop of Constantinople, according to which the Synod lasted from the 14th June to the 25th August. But we may reconcile this date with the other two, on the theory that the Synod was called together for the 20th of May. The Emperor being absent at that time, they held only

less solemn discussions and deliberations until the 14th
June, when the session properly so called began, after the
arrival of the Emperor; that on the 19th the Creed was
drawn up; and that the other business, such as the Easter
controversy, was then continued, and the session
terminated on the 25th August.

Valesius and Tillemont think otherwise. The former rejects
the date given by Socrates, and thinks that the Council
could not have assembled so early as the 20th May 325. He
calculates that, after the victory of Constantine over
Licinius and the Emperor's return, the mission of Hosius to
Alexandria, his sojourn there, then the preparations for the
Synod, and finally the journeys of the bishops to Nicæa,
must have taken a longer time; and he regards it as more
probable that the Synod commenced on the 19th June. But
Valesius erroneously supposes that the great battle of
Chalcedon (or Chrysopolis), in which Constantine defeated
Licinius, took place on the 7th September 324; whilst we
have more foundation for believing that it was a year
previously, in 323. But if we admit that Constantine
conquered Licinius in September 324, and that the next
day, as Valesius says, he reached Nicomedia, there would
remain from that day, up to the 20th May 325, more than
eight months; and this would be long enough for so
energetic and powerful a prince as Constantine was, to take
many measures, especially as the re-establishment of peace
in religion appeared to him a matter of extreme importance.
Besides, in giving the 19th June as the commencement of
the Synod, Valesius gains very little time: a month longer
would not be sufficient to overcome all the difficulties
which he enumerates.

Tillemont raises another objection against the chronology which we adopt. According to him, Constantine did not arrive at Nicæa till the 3d July, whilst we fix the 14th June for the opening of the solemn sessions of the Council in the presence of the Emperor. Tillemont appeals to Socrates, who relates that, "after the termination of the feast celebrated in honour of his victory over Licinius, he left for Nicæa." This feast, according to Tillemont, could have been held only on the anniversary of the victory gained near Adrianopolis the 3d July 323. But first, it is difficult to suppose that two special feasts should be celebrated for two victories so near together as those of Adrianopolis and of Chalcedon: then Socrates does not speak of an anniversary feast, but of a triumphal feast, properly so called; and if we examine what this historian relates of the last attempts of Licinius at insurrection, we are authorized in believing that Constantine celebrated no great triumphal feast till after he had repressed all these attempts, and even after the death of Licinius. Eusebius expressly says that this feast did not take place till after the death of Licinius. We need not examine whether the reports spread abroad respecting the last insurrections of Licinius were true or not; for if Constantine caused false reports to be spread about the projects of Licinius, it is natural that he should wish to confirm them afterwards by giving a public feast. It is true we do not know the exact date of the execution of Licinius; but it was probably towards the middle of 324, according to others not until 325: and therefore the triumphal feast of which we are speaking could easily have been celebrated a short time before the Council of Nicæa.

SEC. 27. The Disputations

In the interval which separated the opening of the Synod (20th May) and the first solemn session in the presence of the Emperor, the conferences and discussions took place between the Catholics, the Arians, and the philosophers, which are mentioned by Socrates and Sozomen. Socrates says expressly, that these conferences preceded the solemn opening of the Synod by the Emperor; and by comparing his account with those of Sozomen and Gelasius, we see that Arius was invited by the bishops to take part in them, and that he had full liberty there to explain his doctrine. We find, too, that many of his friends spoke in his favour, and that he reckoned as many as seventeen bishops among his partisans, particularly Eusebius of Nicomedia, Theognis of Nicæa, Maris of Chalcedon, Theodorus of Heraclea in Thrace, Menophantus of Ephesus, Patrophilus of Scythopolis, Narcissus of Cilicia, Theonas of Marmarica, Secundus of Ptolemais in Egypt, and up to a certain point Eusebius of Cæsarea. Besides, a good many priests, and even laymen, took his side; for, as Socrates says, many learned laymen and distinguished dialecticians were present at these conferences, and took part, some for Arius, others against him. On the orthodox side it was chiefly Athanasius and the priest Alexander of Constantinople, vested with power by his old bishop, who did battle against, the Arians.

Sozomen also mentions these conferences, in which some wished to reject every innovation in matters of faith; and others maintained that the opinion of the ancients must not be admitted without examination. He adds, that the most able dialecticians made themselves renowned, and were remarked even by the Emperor; and that from this time

Athanasius was considered to be the most distinguished member of the assembly, though only a deacon. Theodoret praises Athanasius equally, who, he says, "won the approbation of all the orthodox at the Council of Nicæa by his defence of apostolic doctrine, and drew upon himself the hatred of the enemies of the truth." Rufinus says: "By his controversial ability (suggestiones) he discovered the subterfuges and sophisms of the heretics (dolos ac fallacias)."

Rufinus, and Sozomen, who generally follows him, mention some heathen philosophers as being present at the Synod and at these conferences, either in order to become better acquainted with Christianity, or to try their controversial skill against it. What Gelasius relates is not very probable: he affirms that Arius took these heathen philosophers with him, that they might help him in his disputations. He gives an account, at a disproportionate length, of the pretended debates between the heathen philosopher Phædo, holding Arian opinions, and Eustathius Bishop of Antioch, Hosius of Cordova, Eusebius of Cæsarea, etc., the result of which, he says, was the conversion of the philosopher. According to Valesius, this account is entirely false, and what Rufinus relates about the philosophers is, to say the least, singular. One of these philosophers, he says, could not be overcome by the most able among the Christians, and always escaped like a serpent from every proof which was given him of the error of his doctrines. At last a confessor, an unlearned and ignorant man rose and said: "In the name of Jesus Christ, listen, O philosopher, to the truth. There is one God, who created heaven and earth, who formed man of clay, and gave him a soul. He created everything visible and invisible by His Word: this Word, whom we call the Son, took pity on human sinfulness, was born of a virgin, delivered us from death by His sufferings and death, and gave us the assurance of eternal life by His resurrection. We expect Him now to be the Judge of all our actions. Dost thou believe what I say, O philosopher?" The philosopher, wonderfully moved, could no longer hold out, and said: "Yes; surely it is so, and nothing is true but what thou hast said." The old man replied: "If thou believest thus, rise, follow me to the Lord, and receive the seal of His faith." The philosopher turned towards his disciples and hearers, exhorted them to embrace the faith of Christ, followed the old man, and became a member of the holy Church. Sozomen and Gelasius repeat the account of Rufinus. Socrates also relates the principal part of the story; but he does not say that the philosophers who took part in these conferences were heathens: his words seem rather to refer to Christian controversialists who took the side of Arius.

SEC. 28. Arrival of the Emperor—Solemn Opening of the Council—Presidency

During these preparatory conferences the Emperor arrived; and if Socrates is correct, the Synod was solemnly opened the very day following the discussion with the philosopher. From the account given by Sozomen at the beginning of the nineteenth chapter of his first book, one might conclude that the solemn session in the presence of the Emperor, which we are now to describe, did not take place till after all the discussions with Arius; but Sozomen, who certainly made use of the narrative of Eusebius, tells us that the Synod was inaugurated by this solemnity (ἡμέρας ὁρισθείσης τῇ συνόδῳ). Eusebius thus describes it: "When

all the bishops had entered the place appointed for their
session, the sides of which were filled by a great number of
seats, each took his place, and awaited in silence the arrival
of the Emperor. Ere long the functionaries of the court
entered, but only those who were Christians; and when the
arrival of the Emperor was announced, all those present
rose. He appeared as a messenger from God, covered with
gold and precious stones,—a magnificent figure, tall and
slender, and full of grace and majesty. To this majesty he
united great modesty and devout humility, so that he kept
his eyes reverently bent upon the ground, and only sat
down upon the golden seat which had been prepared for
him when the bishops gave him the signal to do so. As
soon as he had taken his place, all the bishops took theirs.
Then the bishop who was immediately to the right of the
Emperor arose, and addressed a short speech to him, in
which he thanked God for having given them such an
Emperor. After he had resumed his seat, the Emperor, in a
gentle voice, spoke thus: 'My greatest desire, my friends,
was to see you assembled. I thank God, that to all the
favours He has granted me He has added the greatest, that
of seeing you all here, animated with the same feeling. May
no mischievous enemy come now to deprive us of this
happiness! And after we have conquered the enemies of
Christ, may not the evil spirit attempt to injure the law of
God by new blasphemies! I consider disunion in the
Church an evil more terrible and more grievous than any
kind of war. After having, by the grace of God, conquered
my enemies, I thought I had no more to do than to thank
Him joyfully with those whom I had delivered. When I was
told of the division that had arisen amongst you, I was
convinced that I ought not to attend to any business before

this; and it is from the desire of being useful to you that I have convened you without delay. But I shall not believe my end to be attained until I have united the minds of all—until I see that peace and that union reign amongst you which you are commissioned, as the anointed of the Lord, to preach to others. Do not hesitate, my friends—do not hesitate, ye servants of God; banish all causes of dissension—solve controversial difficulties according to the laws of peace, so as to accomplish the work which shall be most agreeable to God, and cause me, your fellow-servant, an infinite joy.' "

Constantine spoke in Latin. An assistant placed at his side translated his discourse into Greek, and then the Emperor gave place to the presidents of the Council (παρεδίδου τὸν λόγον τοῖς τῆς συνόδου προέδροις). The Emperor had opened the Council as a kind of honorary president, and he continued to be present at it; but the direction of the theological discussions, properly speaking, was naturally the business of the ecclesiastical leaders of the Council, and was left to them. We thus arrive at the question of the presidency; but as we have already spoken of it in detail in the Introduction, we may be satisfied with recalling here the conclusion then arrived at, that Hosius of Cordova presided at the assembly as Papal legate, in union with the two Roman priests Vito (Vitus) and Vincentius.

SEC. 29. Mutual Complaints of the Bishops

When the Emperor had yielded the direction of the assembly to the presidents (προέδροις), Eusebius tells us that the disputations and mutual complaints began. By this he means that the Arians were accused of heresy by the orthodox, and these in their turn by the Arians. Other authors add, that for several days divers memorials were sent to the Emperor by the bishops accusing one another, and by the laity criminating the bishops; that on the day fixed to decide these quarrels the Emperor brought to the Synod all the denunciations which had been sent to him, sealed with his signet, and, with the assurance that he had not read them, threw them into the fire. He then said to the bishops: "You cannot be judged by men, and God alone can decide your controversies." According to Socrates, he added: "Christ has commanded man to forgive his brother, if he would obtain pardon for himself."

It is possible that all this account, drawn from more recent sources, may be only an amplification of what Eusebius relates of the complaints and grievances which were brought forward; and this suggestion has the greater probability when we consider that Eusebius, who tries on every occasion to extol his hero the Emperor, would certainly not have passed this act over in silence. However, it is impossible absolutely to throw aside the account by Rufinus and his successors, which contains nothing intrinsically improbable.

SEC. 30. Manner of Deliberation

We possess but few sources of information respecting the manner of deliberation which was adopted, from the solemn opening of the Synod by the Emperor up to the promulgation of the creed. Eusebius, after having mentioned the grievances brought by the bishops against one another, merely continues thus: "Grievances were numerous on both sides, and there were at the beginning many controversies, accusations, and replies. The Emperor listened to both sides with much patience and attention. He assisted both sides, and pacified those who were too violent. He spoke in Greek, in an extremely gentle voice, answered some with arguments, praised others who had spoken well, and led all to a mutual understanding; so that, in spite of their previous differences, they ended by being of the same mind."

Socrates describes the discussions almost in the same words as Eusebius, so also Sozomen; and we may conclude from their testimony, and still more from the account by Rufinus, that the discussions between the Arians and the orthodox, which had commenced before the first solemn session of the Council, continued in the Emperor's presence. As to the time during which these debates lasted, Gelasius tells us that "the Emperor sat with the bishops for several months;" but it is evident that he confuses the discussions which took place before the solemn opening of the Synod by the Emperor with the deliberations which followed (he speaks of the philosophers for the first time after the opening), and he imagines that the Emperor was present not only at the later, but also at the preliminary deliberations.

Rufinus maintains further, "that they then held daily sessions, and that they would not decide lightly or prematurely upon so grave a subject; that Arius was often called into the midst of the assembly; that they seriously discussed his opinions; that they attentively considered what there was to oppose to them; that the majority rejected the impious system of Arius; and that the confessors especially declared themselves energetically against the heresy." It is nowhere said whether those who were not bishops were admitted to these later debates and disputations, as they had been to the first Sozomen speaks only of the bishops who had discussed; Eusebius says nothing of such a limitation; and it is probable that men like Athanasius, and the priest Alexander of Constantinople, might speak again upon so important a question. Amongst the bishops, Marcellus of Ancyra signalized himself as an opponent of the Arians.

The analogy which we may suppose to have existed between the Nicene and later Synods has caused the admission that at Nicæa the members of the Synod were divided into commissions or private congregations, which prepared the materials for the general sessions. But we find no trace of this fact in the ancient documents; and the accounts of Eusebius and others leave us rather to suppose that there were no such commissions, but only general sessions of the bishops.

Our information respecting these sessions is unfortunately very slight and defective; and except the short intimations that we have already seen in Eusebius and his successors, few details have reached us. Gelasius himself, elsewhere so prolix, says no more than Eusebius and Rufinus; for what he relates of the discussions of the heathen philosophers can only have occurred at the commencement of the Council, if it happened at all. We should have been very much indebted to him, if, instead of the long, dry, and improbable discussions of the heathen philosopher Phædo, he had transmitted to us something of the discussions of the theologians.

SEC. 31. Paphnutius and Spiridion

Some further details furnished by Rufinus give no more information respecting the doctrinal discussions with the Arians, but have reference to two remarkable bishops who were present at Nicæa. The first was Paphnutius from Egypt, who, he says, was deprived of his right eye, and had his knees cut off, during the persecution by the Emperor Maximin. He had worked several miracles, cast out evil spirits, healed the sick by his prayers, restored sight to the blind, and the power of their limbs to the lame. The Emperor Constantine esteemed him so highly, that he frequently invited him to go to his palace, and devoutly kissed the socket of the eye which he had lost.

The second was Spiridion of Cyprus, who from a shepherd became a bishop, continued to tend his flocks, and made himself famous by his miracles and prophecies. One night, when robbers entered his fold, they were detained there by invisible bonds, and not till the next morning did the aged shepherd perceive the men who had been miraculously made prisoners. He set them free by his prayer, and presented them with a ram, in order that they might not have had useless trouble. Another time he compelled his daughter Irene, after she was buried, to speak to him from her tomb, and tell him where she had placed a deposit which a merchant had entrusted to him; and she gave, in fact, the required information. Such is the account given by Rufinus, who is followed by Socrates and Gelasius.

SEC. 32. Debates vrith the Eusebians. The ὁμοούσιος

Athanasius gives us some details respecting the intervention of a third party, known under the name of Eusebians. It was composed, at the time of the Council, of about twelve or fifteen bishops, the chief of whom was Eusebius of Nicomedia, who gave them his name. Theodoret says of them: "They attempted to conceal their impiety, and only secretly favoured the blasphemies of Arius." Eusebius of Cæsarea often sided with them, although he was rather more adverse to Arianism than the Eusebians, and stood nearer to the orthodox doctrine. If we wished to employ expressions in use in reference to modern parties and assemblies, we should say: At Nicæa the orthodox bishops formed, with Athanasius and his friends, the right; Arius and some of his friends the left; whilst the left centre was occupied by the Eusebians, and the right centre by Eusebius of Cæsarea.

Athanasius tells us that "the Eusebian intermediate party was very plainly invited by the Nicene Fathers to explain their opinions, and to give religious reasons for them. But hardly had they commenced speaking when the bishops were convinced of their heterodoxy," so strongly was their tendency to Arianism manifested. Theodoret probably alludes to this fact when he quotes from a pamphlet by Eustathius of Antioch, that the Arians, who were expressly called Eusebians in the eighth chapter, laid before the Synod a Creed compiled by Eusebius, but that this Creed was rejected with great marks of dissatisfaction, as tainted with heresy. We know that Valesius, in his notes upon Theodoret, advances the opinion that the Creed in question was compiled, not by Eusebius of Nicomedia, but by Eusebius of Cæsarea; but we shall see further on, that the historian submitted to the Council quite another Creed, which has been highly commended, and which would certainly neither have merited nor provoked such strong dissatisfaction from the bishops. Moreover, S. Ambrose says expressly, that Eusebius of Nicomedia submitted a heterodox writing to the Council.

When the Eusebians saw that the Synod were determined to reject the principal expressions invented by the Arians,— viz.: the Son is ἐξ οὐκ ὄντων, a κτίσμα and ποίημα; that He is susceptible of change (τρεπτῆς φύσεως) and ἦν ὅτε οὐκ ἦν,—they tried to bring it about that in their place biblical expressions should be selected to define the doctrine of the Church, in the hope that these expressions would be sufficiently vague and general to allow another interpretation which might be favourable to their doctrine. Athanasius, who relates this fact, does not say precisely that the Eusebians proposed these biblical expressions, but that they would have rejoiced in them. However, if we consider their habitual conduct, and their continual and oft-repeated complaint that an unbiblical expression had bee selected at Nicæa, we can hardly be wrong in supposing that they actually suggested the use of expressions drawn from the Bible. The Fathers showed themselves disposed to accept such, and to say, "The Logos is from God, ἐκ τοῦ Θεοῦ" (instead of "out of nothing," as the Arians wanted it); the Eusebians consulted together, and said, "We are willing to accept the formula; for all is from God, we and all creatures, as says the apostle." When the bishops found out this falseness and ambiguity, they wished to explain more exactly the words "of God," and added (in their Creed), "The Son is of the substance of God (ἐκ τῆς οὐσίας τοῦ

Θεοῦ);" and they could no longer pretend to misunderstand this. The bishops went on, and said further, "The Logos is the virtue of God, the eternal image of the Father, perfectly like to the Father, immutable and true God;" but they remarked that the Eusebians exchanged signs amongst themselves, to notify that they agreed with these expressions: for in the Bible man is also called an image of God, the "image and glory of God;" even the locusts are called a "power of God." The term immutable applies alike to man; for S. Paul says, "Nothing can separate us from the love of Christ;" and even the attribute of eternal may be applied to man, as we see it in S. Paul.

In order to exclude this dishonest exegesis, and to express themselves more clearly (λευκότερον), the bishops chose, instead of the biblical expressions, the term ὁμοούσιος (that is, of the same substance, or consubstantial). By this expression they meant, "that the Son is not only like to the Father, but that, as His image, He is the same as the Father; that He is of the Father; and that the resemblance of the Son to the Father, and His immutability, are different from ours: for in us they are something acquired, and arise from our fulfilling the divine commands. Moreover, they wished to indicate by this, that His generation is different from that of human nature; that the Son is not only like to the Father, but inseparable from the substance of the Father; that He and the Father are one and the same, as the Son Himself said: "The Logos is always in the Father, and the Father always in the Logos, as the sun and its splendour are inseparable."

Athanasius speaks also of the internal divisions of the Eusebians, and of the discussions which arose in the midst of them, in consequence of which some completely kept silence, thereby confessing that they were ashamed of their errors. As they began more clearly to foresee that Arianism would be condemned, the Eusebians grew colder in its defence; and the fear of losing their offices and dignities so influenced them, that they ended by nearly all subscribing to the ὁμοούσιος and the entire Nicene formula. Eusebius of Nicomedia, in particular, proved himself very feeble and destitute of character; so much so, that even the Emperor, before and afterwards his protector, publicly reproached him for his cowardice, in a letter which we still possess, and related how Eusebius had personally and through others entreated him to forgive him, and allow him to remain in his office.

SEC. 33. The Creed of Eusebius of Cæsarea

Eusebius of Cæsarea made a last attempt to weaken the strong expression ὁμοούσιος, and the force of the stringently defined doctrine of the Logos. He laid before the Council the sketch of a Creed compiled by himself, which was read in the presence of the Emperor, and proposed for adoption by the assembly. After a short introduction, the Creed was conceived in these words: "We believe in one only God, Father Almighty, Creator of things visible and invisible; and in the Lord Jesus Christ, for He is the Logos of God, God of God, Light of Light, life of life, His only Son, the first-born of all creatures, begotten of the Father before all time, by whom also everything was created, who became flesh for our redemption, who lived and suffered amongst men, rose again the third day, returned to the Father, and will come again one day in His glory to judge the living and the dead. We believe also in the Holy Ghost. We believe that each of these three is and subsists: the Father truly as Father, the Son truly as Son, the Holy Ghost truly as Holy Ghost; as our Lord also said, when He sent His disciples to preach: Go and teach all nations, and baptize them in the name of the Father, and of the Son, and of the Holy Ghost." Eusebius added, that this was his true belief; that he always had believed thus; that he always would believe it, and anathematize every heresy. He relates, that after the reading of this formula nobody arose to contradict him; that, on the contrary, the Emperor praised it very highly, declared that he thus believed, exhorted everybody to accept the Creed and to sign it, only adding to it the word ὁμοούσιος. The Emperor, he adds, himself explained this word ὁμοούσιος more exactly: he said it did not signify that there was in God a corporeal substance, nor that the divine substance was divided (between the Father and the Son), and rent between several persons; for material relations cannot be attributed to a purely spiritual being.

After these words of the Emperor, says Eusebius, the bishops might have added the word ὁμοούσιος, and given to the Creed that form in which it might be universally adopted, to the exclusion of every other.

It is possible, indeed, that the Council may have taken the formula of Eusebius as the basis of its own; at least the comparison of the two Creeds speaks in favour of that hypothesis; but even if this were so, it is not the less true that they differ considerably and essentially: the word ὁμοούσιος is the principal point, and moreover it is not correct to say that the Nicene Fathers added no more than this word to the Eusebian formula. The Arians would

perhaps have been able to admit this Creed, whilst that of
Nicæa left them no subterfuge. It is besides evident that in
his account of the matter Eusebius has not spoken the
whole truth, and his account itself explains why he has not
done so. In fact, when they presented the Nicene Creed to
him to sign, he begged a moment for reflection, and then
signed it; and then feared, as having hitherto been a
protector of Arianism, that he would be blamed for having
given his signature. It was in order to explain this conduct
that he addressed a circular letter to his Church, in which
he related what we have just borrowed from him,—namely,
the Creed he had proposed, its acceptation by the Emperor,
etc. After having transcribed the Nicene Creed in extenso,
with the anathemas which are attached to it, he continues,
in order to excuse himself: "When the bishops proposed
this formula to me, I did not wish to consent to it before
having minutely examined in what sense they had taken the
expressions ἐκ τῆς οὐσίας and ὁμοούσιος. After several
questions and answers, they declared that the words ἐκ τοῦ
πατρός did not imply that the Son was a part of the Father;
and that appeared to me to correspond with the true
doctrine, which proclaims that the Son is of the Father, but
not a part of His substance. For the sake of peace, and in
order not to depart from the right doctrine, I would not
resist the word ὁμοούσιος. It is for the same reason that I
admitted the formula, 'He is begotten, and not created,'
after they had explained to me that the word created
designates in general all other things created by the Son,
and with which the Son has nothing in common. He is not
a ποίημα, He is not similar to things created by Himself; but
He is of a better substance than all creatures: His substance
is, according to the teaching of the Scriptures, begotten of

the Father; but the nature of this generation is inexplicable and incomprehensible to the creature." "As to the word ὁμοούσιος," Eusebius continues, "it is supposed that the Son is ὁμοούσιος with the Father, not after the manner of bodies and mortal beings (ζῶα), nor in such a way that the substance and power of the Father are divided and rent, or transformed in any way; for all that is impossible with a nature not begotten of the Father (ἀγένητος φύσις). The word ὁμοούσιος expresses that the Son has no resemblance with the creatures, but is like in all things to the Father who has begotten Him, and that He is of no other hypostasis or substance (οὐσία) than that of the Father. I have agreed to this explanation, as I know that some ancient bishops and celebrated writers have also made use of the word ὁμοούσιος. After these explanations as to the meaning of the Nicene formula, which were supplied in the presence of the Emperor, we have all given our assent, and we have found nothing unacceptable in the anathema attached to the Creed, seeing that it prohibits expressions which are not found in Holy Scripture. In particular, it has seemed to me quite right to anathematize the expression, 'He was not before He was begotten;' for, according to the universal doctrine, the Son of God was before His corporeal birth, as the Emperor himself affirmed: by His divine birth He is before all eternity; and before being begotten de facto (ἐνεργείᾳ) by the Holy Ghost of Mary, He was κατὰ δύναμιν in the Father."

These last words certainly do no honour to the character of Eusebius. He must have known that the Arians did not hold what he attributed to them,—namely, that the Son was not before His appearance in the flesh (by Mary); for the

Arian expression οὐκ ἦν πρὸ τοῦ γεννηθῆναι (He was not
before He was begotten) refers evidently to the generation
of the Son by the Father—a generation anterior to time—
and not to His generation in time by the Holy Ghost in the
womb of the Virgin Mary, as Eusebius sophistically
suggests. He must have known, besides, in what sense the
Council rejected the οὐκ ἦν πρὸ τοῦ γεννηθῆναι: he had
recourse, however, to a dishonest artifice, giving another
meaning to words perfectly clear in the Arian system, and
attributing a gross folly to the old friends he had forsaken.

S. Athanasius has already remarked upon this; and it is
astonishing, after that (not to speak of other writers), that
even Möhler has overlooked the fact. But on the other side
Möhler has with justice pointed out with what partiality
Eusebius everywhere puts forward the Emperor's
intervention, as if the Nicene Creed had been his work, and
not the bishops'. According to his account, one should
imagine that the Emperor hindered free discussion by his
presence, whilst S. Ambrose and S. Athanasius both assure
us of the contrary. The latter particularly asserts: "All the
Nicene bishops condemned this heresy; ... and they were
not constrained to this by anybody, but they quite
voluntarily vindicated the truth as they ought."

The zeal displayed by the Emperor Constantine for the
ὁμοούσιος, and of which he gave proofs by the deposition
of the Arians, contrasts strongly with the manner in which
he regards the controversy at the beginning, and which he
expressed before the Synod in his letter to Alexander
Bishop of Alexandria, and to Arius. Constantine had been
at that time, according to all appearance, under the
influence of the bishop of his residence, Eusebius of

Nicomedia, so much the more as he was only a layman, and in fact only a catechumen himself. But during the Council Hosius doubtless helped him to understand the question more thoroughly, and the subterfuges of the Arians certainly also contributed to give the Emperor a strong aversion to a cause which was defended by such evil means.

SEC. 34. The Nicene Creed

Tillemont, relying upon a passage of S. Athanasius, has thought he might venture to attribute to Bishop Hosius the greatest influence in the drawing up of the Nicene Creed. But the assertion of S. Athanasius applies only to the part taken by Hosius in the development of the faith of Nicæa: he does not speak in any way of a special authorship in the compilation of the formula of Nicæa. It is the same with the expression of S. Hilary: Hujus igitur intimandæ cunctis fidei, Athanasius in Nicæna synodo diaconus, vehemens auctor exstiterat. Here also only the great influence which S. Athanasius had in the deliberations of the Nicene Council is spoken of; but it is not said that he gave the notion of the Creed. We know, in fine, from S. Basil, that Hermogenes, then a deacon, subsequently Bishop of Cæsarea in Cappadocia, acted as secretary to the Synod, and that he wrote and read the Creed.

This Creed, the result of long deliberations, many struggles, and scrupulous examination, as the Emperor himself said, has been preserved to us, with the anathema which was affixed to it, by Eusebius, in a letter which he wrote to his Church, and which we have mentioned above: also by Socrates, Gelasius, and others. It is as follows:

Πιστεύομεν εἰς ἕνα Θεὸν Πατέρα παντοκράτορα, πάντων ὁρατῶν τε καὶ ἀοράτων ποιητήν• καὶ εἰς ἕνα Κύριον Ἰησοῦν Χριστὸν τὸν Υἱὸν τοῦ Θεοῦ, γεννηθέντα ἐκ τοῦ Πατρὸς μονογονῆ, τουτέστιν ἐκ τῆς οὐσίας τοῦ Πατρὸς, Θεὸν ἐκ Θεοῦ, φῶς ἐκ φωτὸς, Θεὸν ἀληθινὸν ἐκ Θεοῦ ἀληθινοῦ, γεννηθέντα, οὐ ποιηθέντα, ὁμοούσιον τῷ Πατρὶ, δι' οὗ τὰ πάντα ἐγένετο, τά τε ἐν τῷ οὐρανῷ καὶ τὰ ἐν τῇ γῇ• τὸν δ' ἡμᾶς τοὺς ἀνθρώπους καὶ διὰ τὴν ἡμετέραν σωτηρίαν κατελθόντα καὶ σαρκωθέντα, ἐνανθρωπήσαντα, παθόντα καὶ ἀναστάντα τῇ τρίτῃ ἡμέρᾳ, ἀνελθόντα εἰς οὐρανοὺς, καὶ ἐρχόμενον κρῖναι ζῶντας καὶ νεκρούς. Καὶ εἰς τὸ Ἅγιον Πνεῦμα. Τοὺς δὲ λέγοντας, ἦν ποτὲ ὅτε οὐκ ἦν, καὶ πρὶν γεννηθῆναι οὐκ ἦν, καὶ ὅτι ἐξ οὐκ ὄντων ἐγένετο, ἢ ἐξ ἑτέρας ὑποστάσεως ἢ οὐσίας φάσκοντας εἶναι, ἢ κτιστὸν ἢ τρεπτὸν ἢ ἀλλοιωτὸν τὸν Υἱὸν τοῦ Θεοῦ, ἀναθεματίζει ἡ καθολικὴ Ἐκκλεσία.

"We believe in one GOD, the Father Almighty, Creator of all things visible and invisible; and in one Lord JESUS Christ, the Son of GOD, only-begotten of the Father, that is, of the substance of the Father. GOD of GOD, light of light, very GOD of very GOD, begotten, not made, being of the same substance with the Father, by whom all things were made in heaven and in earth, who for us men and for our salvation came down from heaven, was incarnate, was made man, suffered, rose again the third day, ascended into the heavens, and He will come to judge the living and the dead. And in the Holy Ghost. Those who say, There was a time when He was not, and He was not before He was begotten, and He was made of nothing (He was created), or who say that He is of another hypostasis, or of another substance (than the Father), or that the Son of God is created, that He is mutable, or subject to change, the Catholic Church anathematizes."

All the bishops, with the exception of five, declared themselves ready immediately to subscribe to this Creed, under the conviction that the formula contained the ancient faith of the apostolic Church. This was so clear, that even the Novatian bishop Acesius, although separated from the Church on points of discipline, gave witness to its dogmatic truth, and adopted the Creed unconditionally, saying, "The Council has introduced nothing new in this act, O Emperor; this has been the universal belief since apostolic times." The five bishops who at first refused to sign were: Eusebius of Nicomedia, Theognis of Nicæa, Maris of Chalcedon, Theonas of Marmarica, and Secundus of Ptolemais. They even ridiculed the term ὁμοούσιος, which could only refer, they said, to substances emanating from other substances, or which came into existence by division, separation, and the like. In the end, however, all signed except Theonas and Secundus, who were anathematized together with Arius and his writings. They were also excommunicated. But a writer on their own side, Philostorgius, says that these three bishops did not act honestly in their subscription; for he relates that, by the advice of the Emperor, they wrote, instead of ὁμοούσιος, the word ὁμοιούσιος (similar in substance, instead of one in substance), which has almost the same sound and orthography. We see, indeed, from the beginning that the signatures of these three bishops were not considered sincere; for Bishop Secundus, when he was exiled, said to Eusebius of Nicomedia: "Thou hast subscribed in order not to be banished; but I hope the year will not pass away before thou shalt have the same lot."

SEC. 35. The Signatures

It appears that, at the time of S. Epiphanius (cir. 400), the signatures of all the 318 bishops present at Nicæa still existed. But, in our own time, we have only imperfect lists of these signatures, disfigured by errors of copyists, differing from each other, and containing the names of only 228 bishops. Moreover, the names of several bishops are omitted in these lists whom we know to have been present at Nicæa; for instance, those of Spiridion and Paphnutius. The name even of Marcellus of Ancyra is inaccurately given as Pancharius of Ancyra. But in spite of these faults of detail, the lists may be regarded as generally authentic. They are, it is true, in Latin, but they bear evident traces of translation from the Greek. What proves their antiquity still more, is the circumstance that the members of the Council are grouped in them by provinces, as in other ancient Synods; for instance, at those of Arles and Chalcedon. That, however, which is of greatest importance, is the fact that the provinces named in these lists perfectly agree with their political division at the time of the Nicene Council; and particularly that those provinces whose limits were assigned at a later period are not mentioned. The bishops of these countries (e.g. Euphratesia, Osrhoëne, etc.) are, on the contrary, classed quite correctly according to the names of the ancient provinces. This is why the Ballerini have with justice defended the authenticity of the lists of signatures at the Nicene Council against some objections made by Tillemont.

Zoëga has discovered a new list of this kind in an ancient
Coptic manuscript, and Pitra published it in the Spicilegium
Solesmense. He has given not only the Coptic text, but by
comparing it with the Latin lists still exant he has made out
a new list of Nicene bishops distributed equally in
provinces, and thus corrected and completed the lists
known up to the present time.

Even before Zoëga, Selden had given another list translated
from the Arabic, which numbers altogether 318 persons,
but includes the names of several priests, and frequently of
many bishops, for one and the same town; so much so, that
Labbe and Tillemont have decidedly rejected this list as
apocryphal. Another shorter list, given by Labbe, and after
him by Mansi, does not belong at all to the Nicene Council,
but to the sixth Œcumenical. In fine, Gelasius gives the
shortest list: it mentions only a few bishops who sign for all
the ecclesiastical provinces.

SEC. 36. Measures taken by the Emperor against the Arians

When the formula of the Synod was laid before the
Emperor, he looked upon it as inspired by God, as a
revelation from the Holy Spirit dwelling in men so holy,
and he threatened to banish any one who would not sign it.
We have already seen the effect produced by these threats.
But the Emperor fulfilled them without delay, and exiled to
Illyria Arius and the two bishops Secundus and Theonas,
who had refused to subscribe, as well as the priests who
were attached to them. At the same time he ordered the
books of Arius and his friends to be burned, and he
threatened all who concealed them with pain of death. He
even wished to annihilate the name of Arians, and ordered

them in future to be called Porphyrians, because Arius had imitated Porphyry in his enmity to Christianity.1 Subsequently Eusebius of Nicomedia and Theognis of Nicæa were also deposed and banished, because, while admitting the Creed, they would not recognise the deposition of Arius, and had admitted Arians amongst them. At the same time, the churches of Nicæa and Nicomedia were required by the Emperor to elect orthodox bishops in their place. The Emperor particularly blamed Eusebius of Nicomedia, not only for having taught error, but for having taken part in Licinius' persecution of the Christians, as well as plotted intrigues against Constantine himself, and deceived him.

SEC. 37. Decision of the Easter Question

The second object of the Nicene Council was the removal of the difficulties, which had existed up to that time, as to the celebration of the festival of Easter. The old controversy respecting Easter was great and violent; but almost greater and more violent still is that which has been raised among learned men of later times on the Paschal controversy, and on purely accessory questions belonging to it—for example, whether the Primate had gained or lost in this controversy—so that the true point of the controversy has been almost lost from sight.

The first who went most thoroughly into this question was the learned French Jesuit, Gabriel Daniel, in 1724. A German professor, Christopher Augustus Heumann, presented independently, almost at the same time, the result of his studies upon the Easter controversy. Mosheim examined the whole of this question anew, yet only with reference to the work of Daniel (he had not been able to lay his hand on Heumann's dissertation); and the greater number of his successors accepted his conclusions, particularly Walch, in the first volume of his Ketzerhistorie.

The same question has been debated with a new interest in modern times, because of its relation to the criticism of the Gospels; and particularly by the Tübingen school, in the interest of its peculiar theories. But the best work published on this subject is that of Dean Weitzel, at the time a deacon at Kircheim, under the title of Die christl. Passafeier der drei ersten Jahrhunderte (The Christian Paschal Controversy of the Three First Centuries). He has cleared up several points which had remained obscure through want of complete original information.

By the use of these preparatory works, amongst which we must mention the Dissertation of Rettberg, published in Ilgen's Zeitschrift für historische Theologie (Gazette of Historical Theology), and by personally investigating anew the existing sources of original information, we have arrived at the following results:—As the Old Testament is the figure of the New, Christians in all times have recognised in the paschal lamb of the Jews the prototype of Christ, and His great expiatory sacrifice upon the cross. The Messianic passages in the Bible had already compared Christ to a lamb, and in the New Testament S. John the Baptist had explicitly called Him the Lamb of God; besides which, the slaying of the Lamb upon the cross corresponded fully with the slaying of the Jewish paschal lamb. The typical character of the Jewish paschal lamb was so evident in the eyes of the ancient Christians, that the Apostle Paul called our Lord Jesus Christ "our Passover (τὸ πάσχα ἡμῶν)."

All parties unanimously agreed, in the controversy which rose later about the celebration of Easter, that the festival itself had been instituted by the apostles. But the existence of this controversy proves that, if the apostles prescribed the celebration of the festival of Easter, they did not determine how it was to be celebrated, so that different practices arose in different countries.

It is commonly supposed that there were only two separate ways of celebrating Easter—that of Asia Minor, and that of the West; but the most modern researches have established beyond doubt that there were three parties in these divisions, of which two were in the Church herself, and a third belonged to an heretical Ebionite sect.

If we would characterize these three in a general manner, we might say: The latter held, with the continuance of the obligation of the ancient law in general, the validity of the old legal passover: their festival then, properly speaking, was not Christian; it was rather Jewish. The two other parties, both looking from a Christian point of view, believed in the abrogation of the ancient law, and their festival was purely Christian. In their opinion, the prototype—that is to say, the Jewish Easter—had ceased, after having received its accomplishment in Christ; whilst the Ebionites, or the third party, wished still to preserve the type and the typical feast.

But the two parties who regarded the matter equally from a Christian point of view, differed on two points: (a) as to the time of the Easter festival, and (b) as to the fast.

To the one, as to the other, Easter was the great festival of Redemption by Christ. But the great drama of Redemption had two particularly remarkable moments—the death and the resurrection of the Lord; and as the Jewish feast lasted for several days, Christians also prolonged their Easter for several days, so as to comprehend the two great moments of the work of redemption. Thus both sides celebrated (α) the day of death, and (β) the day of resurrection. They were also agreed as to the time of the celebration of the festival, in so far as the two parties were agreed, to the greatest possible extent, as to the date of the death of Christ, and chose, as the first decisive point in deciding the festival, the 14th of Nisan, not because they regarded the Jewish law as binding upon that point, but because Christ's Passion had actually commenced on that date; and thus they formed their conclusions, not on legal, but on historical grounds.

However, even with this common basis, divergences were possible, in that some insisted upon the day of the week, and wished specially to preserve the remembrance of that upon which Christ had died, and also that upon which He had risen again. These—and they were principally the Westerns—consequently always celebrated the anniversary of the death of Christ upon a Friday, and the day of resurrection upon a Sunday, considering this custom as the ἀληθέστερα τάξις (truer order), in opposition to the Jewish ordinance. The others, on the contrary, belonging chiefly to Asia Minor, insisted upon the day of the year and of the month, and wished above all to celebrate the remembrance of the Lord's death exactly upon the day of the month on which it happened, which, according to them, was the 14th Nisan. They believed, as we shall see hereafter—and the Westerns held the same opinion—that Christ had not partaken of the paschal lamb with His disciples in the last year of His life, but that on the 14th of the month Nisan, before the feast of the passover, He had been crucified; consequently they wished to celebrate the Saviour's death on the 14th Nisan, whatever day of the week it fell upon, even were it not a Friday.

Thus the first difference as to the time consisted in this, that the one considered above everything the day of the week upon which Christ died, whilst the others attached the most importance to the day of the month or of the year. But the former did not neglect either the day of the month or of the year: with them also the 14th Nisan ($\iota\delta' = 14$) was decisive; that is to say, they too regulated their festival according to the $\iota\delta'$. When the 14th Nisan fell upon a Friday, the two parties were agreed about the time of the festival, because the day of the week and of the month coincided. But if, for example, the $\iota\delta'$ fell upon a Tuesday, the Asiatics celebrated the death of Christ upon the Tuesday, and the Westerns on the following Friday; and if the $\iota\delta'$ fell upon a Saturday, the Asiatics celebrated the death festival upon that Saturday, whilst the Westerns kept it still on the Friday following.

All this it is needless to discuss; but one point is not certain,—namely, whether, when the $\iota\delta'$ (and consequently their commemoration of the death) did not fall upon a Friday, but, for instance, on a Wednesday, the Asiatics celebrated the feast of the resurrection the third day after the commemoration of the death—in this case on the Friday—or kept it on the Sunday. Weitzel holds the latter opinion; but he has not been able to bring sufficient proofs in support of his decision. All depends here upon the sense given to the words of Eusebius: "The majority of bishops had (in the second century) decreed that the μυστήριον τῆς ἐκ νεκρῶν ἀναστάσεως could be celebrated only on a Sunday." Does he by μυστήριον τῆς ἐκ νεκρ., etc., refer to the mystery of the resurrection? If so, it demonstrates that the feast of the resurrection had until then been celebrated upon other days. To escape this argument, Weitzel takes μυστήριον in the sense of sacrament, that is to say, the reception of the holy communion; and according to him, these bishops ordained the communion of the resurrection to be received only on Sunday; whilst previously the Asiatics had been satisfied to celebrate the feast of the resurrection on Sunday, but had been accustomed to communicate on the day upon which the 14th Nisan fell. We should rather hold the opinion that it was the feast of the resurrection which previously had not been celebrated on Sunday. This question of the communion leads us to the second point of difference between the Asiatics and the Occidentals, that is to say, the fast.

This divergency arose from the different way of conceiving of the day of the death of Christ. The Westerns considered it exclusively as a day of mourning: they looked upon it, so to speak, from the historical side, and were in the same state of mind as the disciples upon the day of the death of Christ, that is, in deepest sorrow. The Orientals, on the contrary, rather considered this day, from its dogmatic or doctrinal side, as the day of redemption; and for this reason it was to them, not a day of mourning, but of joy, dating from the moment when Christ died, and had thus accomplished the work of redemption. Yet the hours of the day preceding the moment of death were spent by them in mourning, in memory of the Passion of Christ. They completed the fast at the moment of the death of Christ—three o'clock in the afternoon—and then they celebrated the feast of the communion, that is to say, the sacred rite of the feast, with the solemn Agape (love-feast) and the δεῖπνον Κυρίου (Supper of the Lord). The Occidentals, on the contrary, considering the whole day as consecrated to mourning, continued the fast, a sign of mourning, and did not end it until the joyful morning of the resurrection. It was upon this day that they celebrated the Easter communion, and not upon the Saturday, as Mosheim has supposed.

It is a secondary question, whether the Eastern Church ended their fast upon the 14th Nisan after the Easter communion, or recommenced it once more, and continued it to the day of the resurrection. The words of Eusebius, impartially considered, are favourable to the first opinion; for his ἐπιλύεσθαι (to loose) and his ἐπίλυσις (loosing) of the fast indicate rather a total completion than a simple suspension. In spite of this, Mosheim has attempted to demonstrate, from a passage of S. Epiphanius, that the Audians, a degenerate branch of the Quartodecimans, of Asia Minor, fasted again after their Easter feast. But even if the Audians did in fact follow this custom, it cannot from this be concluded that it was an universal Eastern custom. In the second place, Mosheim was the first to see in this passage what he wished to demonstrate; and he misunderstood it, as we shall see hereafter when speaking of the sect of the Audians.

This difference respecting the fast was not the only one. Not merely was the day of the end of the fast not the same with the Eastern and Western Churches, but there was no perfect uniformity in the manner (εἶδος) of fasting, and this difference went back to the remotest times. S. Irenæus indicates this in the fragment of his letter to Pope Victor, which Eusebius has preserved: "Some," says he, "fast only one day; others two; others, again, several days." Then come these obscure words, οἱ δὲ τεσσαράκοντα ὥρας ἡμερινάς τε καὶ νυκτερινὰς συμμετροῦσι τὴν ἡμέραν αὐτῶν. If we place a comma after τεσσαράκοντα, the sense is this: "Others fast forty hours, reckoning the hours of the day and night;" that is to say, they fast equally by day and night. Massuet has understood the passage in this way. But if we place no comma after τεσσαράκοντα, the sense is: "Others fast in all forty hours by day and night (perhaps the twenty-four hours of Good Friday and sixteen hours on Saturday)." Valesius and Böhmer defend this interpretation. Gieseler gives a third explanation. He proposes to read τῇ ἡμέρᾳ, or more exactly, σὺν τῇ ἡμέρᾳ, instead of τὴν ἡμέραν, and translates it thus: "Others reckon forty hours in all with their day;" that is, they fast upon the day they consider as the passover, or the day of the death of Christ, and begin with the death-hour (three hours after noon) a new fast of forty hours until the resurrection. We do not think that such a modification of the text, wanting in all critical authority, can be justified; but we cannot absolutely decide between Massuet and Valesius, which is happily unnecessary for our principal purpose. S. Irenæus clearly says that the differences in the manner of celebrating Easter were then of no recent date—that they had also existed in the primitive Church. After Valesius' translation, S. Irenæus concludes that this difference was the result of the negligence of the rulers (κρατούντων) of the Church; but Massuet has proved that this translation was incorrect, and demonstrated that the expression κρατεῖν does not here mean to rule, but to maintain (a custom), and that S. Irenæus intended to say, "who (our ancestors), it appears, have not sufficiently maintained the matter (παρὰ τὸ ἀκριβὲς κρατούντων), and thus have bequeathed to their descendants a custom which arose in all simplicity, and from ignorance."

What we have just said plainly proves, that the two parties of whom we speak, the Asiatic and Western Churches, were both perfectly established upon a Christian and ecclesiastical basis; for Easter was a festival equally important and sacred to both, and their difference had regard, not to the kernel of the matter, but to the shell. It was otherwise, as we have already indicated, with the third party, which, for the sake of brevity, we call the Ebionite or Judaic sect. It had this in common with the Asiatic party, that it determined the celebration of Easter according to the day of the month or of the year (the ιδ'), without regard to the day of the week. Consequently there were two parties of Quartodecimans, if we take this expression in its more extended sense; that is to say, two parties who celebrated their Easter festival upon the 14th Nisan, who were thus agreed in this external and chronological point, but who differed toto cœlo in regard to the essence of the matter.

In fact, the Ebionite party started from the proposition, that the prescription of Easter in the Old Testament was not abolished for Christians, and therefore that these ought, like the Jews, and in the same manner, to eat a paschal lamb in a solemn feast on the 14th Nisan. This Jewish paschal banquet was to them the principal thing. But the other Quartodecimans, regarding the subject in a Christian light,

maintained that the ancient paschal feast was abolished—
that the type existed no longer—that what it had
prefigured, namely, the death of the Lamb upon the cross,
had been realized,—and that therefore the Christian should
celebrate, not the banquet, but the death of his Lord.

The difference between these two parties therefore depends
upon the question as to the perpetual obligatory force of
the Mosaic law. The Ebionite Quartodecimans accepted,
while the orthodox denied this perpetuity; and consequently
the latter celebrated not the Jewish passover, but the day of
the death of Christ. Both parties appealed to the Bible. The
Ebionites said: Christ Himself celebrated the passover on
the 14th Nisan; Christians, then, ought to celebrate it on
that day, and in the same way. The orthodox
Quartodecimans maintained, on the contrary, that Christ
had not eaten the passover in the last year of His earthly
life, but that He was crucified on the 14th Nisan, before the
time of the paschal feast commenced; and that thus the
14th Nisan is the anniversary, not of the feast of the
passover, but of the death of Christ.

Eusebius asserts that Asia was the home of the
Quartodeciman party. But it is not quite clear what he
means by Asia; since the word signifies sometimes a quarter
of the world, sometimes Asia Minor, sometimes only a
portion of the latter, Asia Proconsularis, of which Ephesus
was the capital. Eusebius has not here taken the word Asia
in any of these three acceptations: for (α) the
Quartodeciman party had not its home either in the whole
of Asia Minor or the whole of Asia, since, as Eusebius
himself says, Pontus (in Asia Minor), Palestine, and
Osrhoëne followed another practice; and, on the other side,

(β) it was not confined to proconsular Asia, for we find it also in Cilicia, Mesopotamia, and Syria, as S. Athanasius testifies. S. Chrysostom says even, that formerly it prevailed also at Antioch.

But Eusebius points out his meaning more clearly in the following chapter, where he classes among the Quartodecimans the Churches of Asia (proconsular), "and the neighbouring provinces." We shall see later, that there were amongst these Quartodecimans in Asia Minor, not only orthodox, but Ebionites, particularly at Laodicea. If the Quartodecimans in general formed a minority among Christians, the Ebionites, as it appears, formed but a small group in this minority.

The great majority of Christians regulated the festival of Easter according to the day of the week, so that the resurrection might always be celebrated on a Sunday, and the death of Christ always on a Friday. According to Eusebius, this mode of celebration of the Easter festival "was observed by all other Churches throughout the whole world, with the exception of Asia;" and he particularly mentions Palestine, Rome, Pontus, France, Osrhoëne, Corinth, Phœnicia, and Alexandria. The Emperor Constantine the Great affirms that "all the Churches of the West, the South, and the North, had adopted this practice, particularly Rome, the whole of Italy, Africa, Egypt, Spain, Gaul, Britain, Libya, Achaia (Greece); it had even been adopted in the dioceses of Asia, Pontus, and Cilicia." This can be only partially true of Cilicia and Asia Minor; for the latter was quite the seat of the Quartodecimans, and S. Athanasius distinctly classes Cilicia amongst the Quartodeciman provinces.

It follows from what has been said, that it is not quite correct to call the practice of those who regulated Easter according to the day of the week the Western practice; for a great number of the Eastern provinces also adopted this plan. It might rather be called the common or predominant use; whilst the Quartodeciman custom, which was based on a Jewish theory, should be called the Ebionite; and the second Quartodeciman custom, which rested upon a Christian basis, may be called the Johannean. The orthodox Quartodecimans, indeed, specially appealed to S. John the evangelist, and partly to the Apostle S. Philip, as we see from the letter of their head, Polycrates of Ephesus; and they affirmed that these two great authorities had always celebrated Easter on the 14th Nisan. But the Western or ordinary usage was also based upon the apostolical authority of the prince-apostles SS. Peter and Paul, who, according to them, had introduced this custom.

Besides, all parties preserved the expression of the feast of the passover given in the Old Testament, although it only recalled particularly the passing of the destroying angel over the dwellings of the Israelites; for פֶּסַח, from פָּסַח, signifies passing over. In a more general way this word signifies the deliverance from Egypt; and in this sense it might have been employed figuratively by Christians, as their feast of deliverance from Egypt The Aramaic פַּסְחָא (Pascha) prevailed along with the Hebrew form פֶּסַח (Pesach), and more widely than this; and thus many Gentile Christians, who were unacquainted with Hebrew, were easily led to derive the word Pascha from the Greek verb πάσχειν.

Sometimes by the word Pascha was signified the whole week of the Passion, sometimes the days which they celebrated during that week, or even a particular day in it, especially that of our Lord's death. Tertullian, for instance, in his book de Jejunio, calls the whole week Pascha, but in his work de Oratione only Good Friday. Constantine the Great, in the same way, speaks sometimes of one day, sometimes of several days, in Easter week. He seems also particularly to signify by the word Easter the day of the death of Christ; nevertheless he calls the day of the resurrection not only ἡμέρα ἀναστάσεως, but also πάσχα, as may be seen from the whole tenor of the passage in Eusebius, and from several others quoted by Suicer. Basil the Great, for instance, in his Exhortatio ad Baptismum, identifies the ἡμέρα τοῦ πάσχα with the μνημόσυνον (day of commemoration) τῆς ἀναστάσεως. Subsequently, from what period is uncertain, in order to make a distinction, they call the day of the death πάσχα σταυρώσιμον (passover of crucifixion), and the day of the resurrection πάσχα ἀναστάσιμον (passover of resurrection).

It is clear from a passage in Tertullian,1 that the universal custom of the ancient Church was to celebrate Easter for a whole week. S. Epiphanius says still more plainly,1 "The Catholic Church celebrates not only the 14th Nisan, but the whole week;" and as he certainly emphasized this in opposition to the Quartodecimans, we may presume that the Ebionite Quartodecimans celebrated only the 14th of Nisan as the feast of the passover; that at least the other days were thrown into the shade relatively to this principal feast, which was quite in accordance with their Jewish tendency. The observance of the Mosaic prescription respecting the paschal feast seemed to them far more important than the celebration of the days of the death and resurrection of our Lord.

Although there was a notable difference in the three ways of keeping Easter, the antagonism between the Johannean and the ordinary custom was first noticed; but the higher unity in the spirit and in the essence of the subject made the chronological difference seem less striking and more tolerable. S. Irenæus gives a proof of this when he distinctly says, in a fragment of the synodical letter which he wrote in the name of the Gallican bishops, "that the Roman bishops before Soter, namely Anicetus, Pius, Hyginus, Telesphorus, and Xystus (the latter was living at the beginning of the second century), did not follow the Asiatic custom, nor did they tolerate it amongst their people, but that nevertheless they lived amicably with those who came to Rome from countries where a contrary practice prevailed; and they even sent the holy Eucharist, in token of unity, to the Quartodeciman bishops of those Churches."

The first known debate respecting this difference, and the first attempt made at the same time to put an end to it, took place when S. Polycarp went to Rome to see Pope Anicetus, towards the middle of the eleventh century. We cannot determine exactly in what year this took place. Baronius declares, but with insufficient reason, for the fifth year of Marcus Aurelius, 167 years after Christ. But Polycarp was so advanced in years at this time, that it is difficult to believe he could have undertaken so long a journey; besides, Anicetus had then been in the see of Rome for ten years, and consequently Polycarp might well have visited him before. However, Polycarp went to Rome, and not about the Easter business, as Baronius concludes from an incorrect translation of Eusebius, but about some other slight differences which he wished to compose in concert with Anicetus. He was certainly the most worthy representative of the Johannean or Asiatic opinions, being recognised as the most distinguished bishop of Asia Minor, and certainly the only disciple of S. John then living. We may suppose that he followed the Johannean practice with regard to the celebration of Easter, not only from the fact that he was Bishop of Smyrna in Asia Minor, but also from this, that Polycrates of Ephesus, the ardent defender of the Johannean custom, particularly appealed to Polycarp in his struggle with Pope Victor. Polycarp and Anicetus received each other with the kiss of peace, and held a conference on the subject of Easter, which did not however last long, Anicetus being unable to induce Polycarp to abandon a practice which the latter "had observed in communion with the Evangelist S. John." Neither would Anicetus abandon the custom pursued by his predecessors in the episcopate. In spite of this difference they lived in communion, and Anicetus conferred what was then a very special mark of distinction upon his host, allowing him to celebrate the holy Eucharist in his church and in his presence. After that they separated in peace, and the same feeling continued between the two parties whom they represented.

Some years after Polycarp's journey we meet with the first known movements of the Ebionite Quartodecimans. Melito Bishop of Sardes relates, in a fragment of his work (two books, περὶ τοῦ πάσχα), that "when Servilius Paulus was Proconsul of Asia, and Sagaris Bishop of Laodicea had suffered martyrdom, a warm controversy arose at Laodicea on the subject of Easter." The time in which Melito flourished was probably about the year 170. This fragment does not specify the particular point upon which the controversy turned, but we learn that from another source. Apollinaris of Hierapolis, a contemporary, a friend, and a compatriot of Melito, whose opinions also he held, likewise wrote a work upon Easter; and the two fragments which have been preserved in the Chronicon Paschale assert—(1) "Those are mistaken who hold that our Lord ate the paschal lamb with His disciples upon the 14th Nisan, and that He died upon the great day of unleavened bread (the 15th Nisan). They pretend that S. Matthew affirms it; but such an opinion is not accordant with the (ancient) law, and the Gospels (especially those of S. Matthew and S. John) would thus be contradictory." The second fragment says: "The 14th Nisan is the true passover of our Lord, the great Sacrifice; instead of the lamb, we have here the Lamb of God," etc.

By these fragments we see that Apollinaris belonged to those Christians who held that our Lord did not partake of the passover the last year of His life, but that He was crucified upon the 14th Nisan. Thus the immolation of the lamb, the type, was realized by the death of the Lamb upon the cross upon the same 14th of Nisan, in the week of the Passion. The type was then abolished, and the commemoration of the death of Christ replaced the Jewish (ιδ') feast. He holds that by admitting this theory the evangelists can be harmonized, and that an exact parallelism was established between the facts of the New and the types of the Old Testament. According to the opposite opinion, however, (1) the evangelists are not agreed; and (2) that opinion does not agree with the ancient law. It is not said why, but we may conclude from his words that the following was implied: "If Christ had eaten the paschal lamb upon the 14th Nisan, His death should have taken place upon the 15th Nisan, whilst the type of this death was only upon the 14th; and consequently the resurrection falls upon the 17th Nisan, whilst the type occurs upon the 16th."

The proximity of Hierapolis and of Laodicea, and the fact that Melito and Apollinaris lived at the same time, sanction the presumption that the party attacked by the latter was identical with that of Laodicea, and which Melito attacked; and as Apollinaris and Melito were associated as apologists and lights of their time, they were also certainly associated in the Easter controversy. Apollinaris was, as his fragments prove, a Johannean Quartodeciman; and Melito was the same, for Polycrates expressly appeals to him.

But against whom did Apollinaris write, and what was the character of the party against whom he and Melito contended? Apollinaris does not enter into detail upon this point: he simply indicates, in the first extract, that his opponents celebrated the paschal feast upon the 14th Nisan. They were therefore Quartodecimans; but as he was of that class himself, we must seek elsewhere for the special character of his adversaries; and as in the second extract he strongly insists upon the 14th Nisan "being the true passover of the. Lord, the great sacrifice wherein the Son of God was immolated instead of the Jewish lamb," we may conclude naturally enough that his adversaries were Ebionite Quartodecimans, who also celebrated, it is true, the 14th Nisan, but in a Jewish manner, with the feast of the passover. This is made still more evident by an extract from Hippolytus, of which we shall have to speak hereafter. Moreover, the work of Melito determined Clement of Alexandria to write a λόγος περὶ τοῦ πάσχα, not indeed to refute it, but to complete Melito's work. Of this work of Clement's we have only fragments preserved in the Chronicon Paschale, and the first of these fragments says: "Christ always ate the paschal lamb with His disciples in His earlier years, but not in the last year of His life, in which He was Himself the Lamb immolated upon the cross." The second fragment has the words: "Christ died on the 14th of Nisan; and after His death, on the evening of the same day, the Jews celebrated their passover feast."

Clement here quite agrees with Apollinaris, and his work proves that the same party which Apollinaris opposed still existed after the lapse of many years.

After some time, S. Hippolytus attacked them in two fragments, both preserved in the Chronicon Paschale. He distinctly says: "The controversy still lasts, for some erroneously maintain that Christ ate the passover before His death, and that consequently we ought to do so also. But Christ, when He suffered, no longer ate the legal passover; for He was Himself the passover, previously announced, which was on that day fulfilled in Him." This fragment by Hippolytus is taken from his work against the heresies, and consequently from that time the Ebionite Quartodecimans were rightly considered as heretics. He says again, in the second fragment of his work upon Easter: "Christ did not partake of the passover before His death; He would not have had time for it."

We need not wonder that an Italian bishop like Hippolytus should have thought it necessary to oppose the Ebionite party; for it was not restricted to Phrygia (Laodicea) and the other countries of Asia Minor, but it had found defenders even at Rome, and Hippolytus was a priest of the Roman Church—he was even for some time a schismatical Bishop of Rome. Eusebius indeed says: "Several sects arose in Rome in the time of the Montanists, of which one had for its chief the priest Florinus, another Blastus." He does not tell us their doctrine, but says that Florinus was deposed, and that both of them had seduced many of the faithful. He adds: Irenæus wrote against Florinus a book called de Monarchia, and against Blastus another, de Schismate; but again he does not mention the doctrine taught by Blastus. We have no more account of it than is contained in the apocryphal supplement to Tertullian's book de Prescriptione, where it is said, in the fifty-third chapter: Est præterea his omnibus (to Marcion, to Tatian, etc.) etiam Blastus accedens, qui latenter Judaismum vult introducere. According to this text, Blastus was a Judaizer, having tendencies analogous to those of the Ebionite Quartodecimans of Asia Minor (especially of Laodicea). If Blastus, towards 180, tried to introduce the Ebionite Quartodecimanism into Italy, and even into Rome, the aversion of Pope Victor towards the Quartodecimans in general can be easily explained, and his earnestness in his controversy with Polycrates and the Asiatics.

We thus reach the second period of the Paschal controversy. In the first, we have seen the two customs of the Church—the Johannean custom, and the usual one—existing side by side, each of these opposing only the

Ebionite party. Now, on the contrary, the two purely Christian opinions are to be found in violent conflict. It was probably Pope Victor who was the cause of the struggle: the intrigues of Blastus doubtless resulted in setting him against the Quartodecimans, and leading him to forbid the celebration of the feast on the 14th Nisan. In 196, S. Jerome's Chronicle says that he wrote to the most eminent bishops of every country, asking them to assemble synods in their provinces, and by their means to introduce the Western mode of celebrating Easter. These letters—for example, those to Polycrates of Ephesus—also contained threats in case of resistance. Numerous synods therefore assembled, as we learn from Eusebius; and all, with the exception of those of Asia Minor, unanimously declared "that it was a rule of the Church to celebrate the mystery of the resurrection only on a Sunday." They acquainted all the faithful with this declaration by synodical letters. Eusebius saw several of these synodical letters, especially those from the Synods of Palestine, presided over by Theophilus Bishop of Cæsarea and Narcissus of Jerusalem; also those from the bishops of Pontus, under Palma; from the bishops of Gaul, under Irenæus; from the bishops of Osrhoëne; and, finally, the private letter from Bacchylus Bishop of Corinth. They unanimously pronounced in favour of Victor's opinion, except Polycrates Bishop of Ephesus. The latter had also been president of a synod composed of a great number of the bishops of his province. He said that all approved of the remarkable letter which he proposed to send to Pope Victor, which Eusebius has preserved. In this letter he says, "We celebrate the true day, without adding or subtracting anything;" and he appeals, in justification of his practice, as we have before seen, to the Apostle Philip, who died at Hierapolis, to S. John the Evangelist, to Polycarp, and others, who all kept Easter on the fourteenth day after the new moon. Seven of his own relations had been bishops of Ephesus before him, and had observed the same custom. "As he had attained the age of sixty-five years, Polycrates no longer feared any threatening, he said, for he knew that we ought to obey God rather than men."

Thereupon, says Eusebius, continuing his account, Pope Victor tried to excommunicate (ἀποτέμνειν πειρᾶται) the Churches of Asia and of the neighbouring provinces; and he addressed an encyclical letter to this effect to all the Christians of those countries. The words of Eusebius might also be understood to mean that Victor really launched a sentence of excommunication against these Churches, and they have been taken in this sense by the later Church historian Socrates; but it is more correct to say, as Valesius has shown, that the Pope thought of excommunicating the Asiatics, and that he was kept from carrying out the sentence especially by S. Irenæus. Eusebius says, indeed, "He tried to excommunicate them." He adds: "This disposition of Victor did not please other bishops, who exhorted him rather to seek after peace. The letters in which they blame him are still extant." However, Eusebius gives only the letter of S. Irenæus, who, although born in Asia Minor, declared that the resurrection of the Saviour ought to be celebrated on a Sunday; but also exhorted Victor not to cut off from communion a whole group of Churches which only observed an ancient custom. He reminds him that his predecessors had judged this difference with much more leniency, and that, in particular,

Pope Anicetus had discussed it amicably with Polycarp Bishop of Smyrna.

Eusebius here remarks, that Irenæus, as his name indicates, had become εἰρηνοποῖος, and that he addressed letters on this occasion, not only to Victor, but to other bishops.

Thus this debate did not bring about the uniformity which Victor desired. However, as a consequence of these explanations and negotiations, some Churches of Asia, it appears, renounced their custom, and adopted that of the West, as Massuet and Valesius have concluded from the letter published by Constantine after the close of the Synod of Nicæa, in which he says: "Asia" (doubtless meaning some of its Churches), "Pontus, and Cilicia have adopted the universal custom." This can apply only to a part of Cilicia, seeing that, according to the testimony of S. Athanasius, the custom of the Quartodecimans prevailed there. Thus up to this time the controversy bore only upon these two points: 1st, Was the festival to be held according to the day of the week, or that of the month? 2d, When was the fast to cease?

But in the third century, which we have now reached, a fresh difficulty arose to complicate the debate, which we may call briefly the astronomical difficulty.

We have seen that with the Asiatics, as with the Westerns, Easter was determined by the 14th Nisan, with this difference only, that the Asiatics always celebrated Easter on this day, whilst the Westerns kept it on the Sunday following (with them the Sunday of the resurrection was their greatest festival). But then this question arose: On what precise day of the year does the 14th Nisan fall? or how can the lunar date of the 14th Nisan be reconciled with the solar year? The Jews' ecclesiastical year, the first month of which is called Nisan, commences in the spring. At the beginning of spring, and particularly towards the equinox, barley is ripe in Palestine. For this reason the month Nisan is also called the month of sheaves; and the great festival of the month Nisan, the passover, is at the same time the feast of harvest, in which the first sheaf of barley is offered to God as first-fruits. According to this, the 14th Nisan comes almost at the same time with the full moon after the vernal equinox; and although the lunar year of the Jews is shorter than the solar year, they made up the difference by an intercalary month, so that the 14th Nisan always occurred at the same period. It was also partly determined by the ripeness of the barley.

Many Fathers of the Church relied especially on the fact that the passover had always been kept by the ancient Hebrews, and by the contemporaries of our Saviour, after the equinox, and so ordered that the festival should continue to be celebrated after the commencement of the spring. They remarked that the Jews had always determined the ιδ' in this way until the fall of Jerusalem. The defective practice of not fixing the ιδ' according to the equinox was not introduced among them until after that event.

We may see clearly what resulted from this rule. Whoever observed it, could no longer regulate his Easter according to the 14th Nisan of the Jews, inasmuch as this day occurred after the equinox. If the 14th fell before the equinox with the Jews, the Christians ought to have said: "The Jews this year celebrate the 14th Nisan at a wrong date, a month too soon: it is not the full moon before, but the full moon after the equinox, which is the true full moon of Nisan." We say full moon, for the 14th Nisan was always necessarily at the full moon, since each month among the Jews began with the new moon. In this case the Christians kept their Easter a month later than the Jews, and determined it according to the full moon after the vernal equinox. Hence it resulted—

1. That if a Johannean Quartodeciman acted according to the equinox, he always celebrated his Easter exactly on the day of the full moon after the equinox, without minding on what day of the week it fell, or whether it coincided with the Jewish 14th of Nisan or not.

2. That if a Western acted also according to the equinox, he always celebrated his Easter on the Sunday after the full moon which followed the vernal equinox. If the full moon fell on a Sunday, he kept the festival not on that Sunday, but on the following one, and that because the day of the resurrection (consequently his Easter) ought to be observed not on the very day of the ιδ' (being the day of Christ's death), but after the ιδ'.

We shall presently see that the latter manner of computation for regulating the celebration of the Easter festival was adopted by many, if not all, in the West; but we cannot determine whether many of the Asiatics did the same. The seventh (eighth) of the so-called Apostolic Canons, besides, ordered Easter to be celebrated universally after the vernal equinox.

When abandoning the way of Jewish computation, the Christians had naturally much more difficulty in determining the period of their Easter. It was necessary to make special calculations in order to know when Easter would fall; and the most ancient known calculation on this point is that of Hippolytus, a disciple of S. Irenæus, who was erroneously called Bishop of Pontus, but who was in fact a Roman priest at the commencement of the third century, and was opposition Bishop of Rome about the year 220 to 235. Eusebius says of him, that in his book upon Easter he makes a computation, and bases it upon a canon of sixteen years. Nothing more was known of this calculation or canon until in 1551, on the way to Tivoli, not far from the Church of S. Lawrence, there was discovered a marble statue of a bishop seated on his throne. It is at present in the Vatican Museum. It was recognised as the statue of Hippolytus, because a catalogue of the works of the bishop represented was inscribed upon the back of the throne. Upon the right side of the throne is a table of the Easter full moons, calculated for a period of a hundred and twelve years (from 222 to 333 after Christ). Upon the left side is a table of the Easter Sundays for the same period, and the calculation for both tables is based upon the cycle of sixteen years mentioned by Eusebius: so that, according to this calculation, after sixteen years, the Easter full moon falls on the same day of the month, and not of the week; and after a hundred and twelve years it falls regularly on the same day of the month, and of the week also. Ideler justly remarks that Hippolytus might have abridged his calculation one half, since according to it the full moon fell every eight years on the same day of the month, and that every fifty-six years it fell again on the same day of the month and of the week also.

This point being settled, Hippolytus lays down the following principles:—

1. The fast should not cease till the Sunday. This is expressly said in the inscription on the first table (engraven on the right side of the throne).

2. It is thence established that it is the Sunday which gives the rule, that the communion feast must then be celebrated, and the day of Christ's death on the Friday.

3. As Hippolytus always places the ιδ' after the 18th March, doubtless he considered the 18th March as the equinox, and this day formed the basis of his Easter calculations.

4. If the ιδ' fell on a Friday, he would keep Good Friday on that day. If the ιδ' fell on a Saturday, he would not keep Easter on the following day, but put it off for a week (as occurred in the year 222). In the same way, if the ιδ' fell on a Sunday, it was not that day, but the following Sunday, which was his Easter day (for example, in 227).

As Hippolytus was a disciple of S. Irenæus, and one of the principal doctors of the Church of Rome, we may consider his Easter calculation as exactly expressing the opinion of the Westerns, and especially of the Church of Rome, on the subject.

The Church of Alexandria also did not celebrate Easter until after the equinox. The great Bishop Dionysius expressly says so in an Easter letter, now lost, which is mentioned by Eusebius. According to him, Dionysius must also have published an Easter canon for eight years. At Alexandria, the city of astronomers, it would, besides, have been easy for Bishop Dionysius to make a more exact computation than that of Hippolytus, who had settled the question satisfactorily for only a certain number of years.

But Dionysius was in his turn surpassed by another Alexandrian—Anatolius Bishop of Laodicea in Syria since 270, who wrote a work upon the feast of Easter, a fragment of which has been preserved by Eusebius. He discovered the Easter cycle of nineteen years, and began it with the year 277, probably because in that year his calculation was established.

1. Anatolius proceeds upon the principle that the ancient Jews did not celebrate the passover until after the equinox, and that consequently the Christian's Easter ought never to be kept until after the vernal equinox.

2. He considers the 19th March as the equinox.

3. He says nothing about the old question relating to the fast, and the time when it should close; but evidently, as he was an Alexandrian, he followed the usual custom (and not that of Asia).

This cycle of nineteen years was soon subjected to different modifications, after which it was generally adopted in Alexandria from the time of Diocletian. The chief modification was, that the Alexandrians placed the equinox not on the 19th, but on the 21st March, which was tolerably exact for that period. Besides, when the ιδ' fell on a Saturday, they departed from the systems of Anatolius and

Hippolytus, and celebrated Easter on the following day, as we do now. The completion of this cycle of nineteen years is attributed to Eusebius of Cæsarea.

Such was the state of the question at the commencement of the fourth century. It shows us that the differences in the time for the celebration of Easter were at that time greater than ever.

The introduction of the question about the equinox had added fresh differences to the three former ones. Not only did some of the Asiatics continue the Jewish calculation then in use, so that their Easter might fall before the equinox; but some of the Westerns, not consulting the last astronomical calculations, also celebrated their Easter before the equinox.

Like the Asiatics, the Western Quartodecimans, who did not consider the equinox at all, often celebrated Easter earlier than the rest of Christendom, and therefore called themselves Protopaschites. But also among the Equinoctialists themselves there existed some difference: for the Alexandrians calculated Easter according to the cycle of nineteen years, and took the 21st March as the date of the equinox; whilst the Romans, as they followed Hippolytus, observed the cycle of sixteen years (subsequently that of eighty-four years), and placed the equinox on the 18th March. When the full moon occurred on the 19th March, it was considered by the Latins the Easter full moon, and they celebrated their festival on the following Sunday; whilst with the Alexandrians this full moon was before the equinox, and consequently they waited for another full moon, and celebrated their Easter a month after the day considered right by the Latins.

These serious and numerous differences were indeed very lamentable, and were the cause of many disputes and frequent troubles in countries where these different modes simultaneously existed. They often made the Christians an object of the most bitter ridicule on the part of the heathen. Indeed, the Council of Arles perfectly responded to the exigencies of the times, when in 314 it endeavoured to establish unanimity upon this question. This Synod commanded in its very first canon, that henceforth Easter should be celebrated uno die et uno tempore per omnem orbem, and that, according to custom, the Pope should send letters everywhere on this subject. The Synod therefore wished to make the Roman mode predominant, and to suppress every other, even the Alexandrian (supposing that the difference between the Alexandrian and the Roman calculation was known to the bishops at Arles).

But the ordinances of Arles were not accepted everywhere, and they failed to establish uniformity in the Church. The decision of an œcumenical council became necessary; and, in fact, the first Œcumenical Council of Nicæa was occupied with this business. We are ignorant of the detailed debates on this subject, knowing only the result as we find it in the encyclical letter of the Council, and in the Emperor's circular.

In the former document, the Council thus addresses the Church of Alexandria, and its well-beloved brethren in Egypt, Libya, and Pentapolis: "We give you good news of the unity which has been established respecting the holy passover. In fact, according to your desire, we have happily elucidated this business. All the brethren in the East who formerly celebrated Easter with the Jews, will henceforth keep it at the same time as the Romans, with us, and with all those who from ancient times have celebrated the feast at the same time with us."

The Emperor Constantine made the following announcement in his letter to all who were not present at the Council:

"When the question relative to the sacred festival of Easter arose, it was universally thought that it would be convenient that all should keep the feast on one day; for what could be more beautiful and more desirable, than to see this festival, through which we receive the hope of immortality, celebrated by all with one accord, and in the same manner? It was declared to be particularly unworthy for this, the holiest of all festivals, to follow the custom (the calculation) of the Jews, who had soiled their hands with the most fearful of crimes, and whose minds were blinded. In rejecting their custom, we may transmit to our descendants the legitimate mode of celebrating Easter, which we have observed from the time of the Saviour's Passion to the present day (according to the day of the week). We ought not therefore to have anything in common with the Jews, for the Saviour has shown us another way: our worship follows a more legitimate and more convenient course (the order of the days of the week); and consequently, in unanimously adopting this mode, we desire, dearest brethren, to separate ourselves from the detestable company of the Jews, for it is truly shameful for us to hear them boast that without their direction we could not keep this feast. How can they be in the right,—they who, after the death of the Saviour, have no longer been led by reason, but by wild violence, as their delusion may urge them? They do not possess the truth in this Easter question; for, in their blindness and repugnance to all improvements, they frequently celebrate two passovers in the same year. We could not imitate those who are openly in error. How, then, could we follow these Jews, who are most certainly blinded by error? for to celebrate the passover twice in one year is totally inadmissible. But even if this were not so, it would still be your duty not to tarnish your soul by communications with such wicked people (the Jews). Besides, consider well, that in such an important matter, and on a subject of such great solemnity, there ought not to be any division. Our Saviour has left us only one festal day of our redemption, that is to say, of His holy passion, and He desired (to establish) only one Catholic Church. Think, then, how unseemly it is, that on the same day some should be fasting, whilst others are seated at a banquet; and that after Easter, some should be rejoicing at feasts, whilst others are still observing a strict fast. For this reason, Divine Providence wills that this custom should be rectified and regulated in a uniform way; and every one, I hope, will agree upon this point. As, on the one hand, it is our duty not to have anything in common with the murderers of our Lord, and as, on the other, the custom now followed by the Churches of the West, of the South, and of the North, and by some of those of the East, is the most acceptable, it has appeared good to all, and I have been guarantee for your consent, that you would accept it with joy, as it is followed at Rome, in Africa, in all Italy, Egypt, Spain, Gaul, Britain, Libya, in all Achaia, and in the

dioceses of Asia, of Pontus, and Cilicia. You should
consider not only that the number of churches in these
provinces make a majority, but also that it is right to
demand what our reason approves, and that we should
have nothing in common with the Jews. To sum up in few
words: by the unanimous judgment of all, it has been
decided that the most holy festival of Easter should be
everywhere celebrated on one and the same day, and it is
not seemly that in so holy a thing there should be any
division. As this is the state of the case, accept joyfully the
divine favour, and this truly divine command; for all which
takes place in assemblies of the bishops ought to be
regarded as proceeding from the will of God. Make known
to your brethren what has been decreed, keep this most
holy day according to the prescribed mode; we can thus
celebrate this holy Easter day at the same time, if it is
granted me, as I desire, to unite myself with you; we can
rejoice together, seeing that the divine power has made use
of our instrumentality for destroying the evil designs of the
devil, and thus causing faith, peace, and unity to flourish
amongst us. May God graciously protect you, my beloved
brethren."

We find no further details in the acts. But it is easy to
understand that the Fathers of the Council took as the basis
of their decision the computation which was most generally
admitted among orthodox Christians, that is, the one which
regulated the ιδ' according to the equinox, and Easter
Sunday according to the ιδ'. We have a letter of
Constantine's upon this point, which clearly shows the
mind of the Council; for, according to this letter, the Synod
requires, 1st, that Easter day should always be a Sunday

(and therefore decides against the Quartodecimans); and 2d, that it should never be celebrated at the same time as the feast of the Jews. It results from this second decision, that according to the Synod, if the ιδ' should fall on a Sunday, Easter was not to be celebrated on that Sunday, but a week later. And this for two reasons: (1) Because the ιδ' indicates the day of the Saviour's death, and that the festival of the resurrection ought to follow that day, and not to coincide with it; (2) because in those years when the ιδ' should fall on a Sunday, Christians would be celebrating their Easter at the same time as the Jews, which was what the Synod wished to avoid. The third decision made at Nicæa was (3) to forbid Christians to celebrate Easter twice in one year; that is to say, that the equinox should be considered in all calculations about Easter.

In my opinion, there is no doubt that Constantine, in his letter, which has every appearance of being a synodical letter, mentioned only the decisions really arrived at by the Council. This indubitable fact being once admitted, it must certainly be acknowledged also that the Synod was right in giving rules for determining Easter day. Perhaps it did not explain expressly the principles which formed the basis of the three decisions given above, but undoubtedly all these decisions showed them sufficiently. When Ideler maintains "that the rule clearly enunciated in S. Epiphanius had not been expressly prescribed by the Council of Nicæa," this opinion has no foundation, unless Ideler plays upon the word expressly; for Epiphanius gives, as the basis of his computation, the same three rules already laid down by the Nicene Council and in the letter of Constantine,—the observation of the Equinox, placing the ιδ' after the equinox, and placing the Sunday after the ιδ'. Ideler appears to me to have too easily accepted the theories in the second book of Christian Walch's Decreti Nicæni de Paschale explicatio, which are opposed to our opinions.

It may be asked whether the Council intended to give the preference to the Roman computation, against the Alexandrian. Both rested upon the three rules accepted by the Council; but the Romans considered the 18th March, and the Alexandrians the 21st March, as the terminus a quo of the Easter full moon. According to Ideler, our Synod did not take much notice of this difference, and seemed indeed to entirely ignore it. The acts of the Council, in fact, do not show that it knew of this difference. The tenor of Constantine's letter seems to authorize the opinion expressed by Ideler. The synodical letter indeed says: "In future, all shall celebrate Easter with the Romans, with us, and with all," etc.; and Constantine supposes that the manner of celebrating Easter among the Romans and the Egyptians, and consequently among the Alexandrians, is identical. However, the great importance of the Easter question, and the particular value which it had at the time of the Nicene Council, hardly allow it to be supposed that the differences between the Roman and Alexandrian computations should not have been known in such a large assemblage of learned men, among whom were Romans and Alexandrians. It is much more rational to admit that these differences were well known, but that they were passed over without much discussion. To act thus was indeed an absolute necessity, if they wished to arrive at complete uniformity upon the Easter question; and what we are now saying is not a pure hypothesis, for Cyril of

Alexandria says: "The General Synod has unanimously decreed that, since the Church of Alexandria is experienced in such sciences, she should announce by letter every year to the Roman Church the day on which Easter should be celebrated, so that the whole Church might then learn the time for the festival through apostolical authority" (i.e. of the Bishop of Rome).

Pope Leo. I. expresses himself in the same way in his letter to the Emperor Marcian. He says: "Studuerunt itaque sancti Patres" (he certainly understands by that the Fathers of Nicæa, though he does not expressly say so) "occasionem hujus erroris auferre, omnem hanc curam Alexandrino episcopo delegantes (quoniam apud Ægyptios hujus supputationis antiquitus tradita esse videbatur peritia), per quem quotannis dies prædictæ solemnitatis Sedi apostolicæ indicaretur, cujus scriptis ad longinquiores Ecclesias indicium generale percurreret." If Pope Leo is in the right, this text teaches us two things: (1) That the Synod of Nicæa gave the preference to the Alexandrian computation over the Roman, whilst the contrary had been decreed at Arles; (2) That the Synod found a very good way of smoothing difficulties, by ordaining that the Alexandrian Church should announce the day for Easter to the Church of Rome, and that Rome should make it known to the whole Church.

Another account taken from S. Ambrose agrees very well with what S. Leo says. S. Ambrose tells us, indeed, that according to the advice of several mathematicians, the Synod of Nicæa adopted the cycle of nineteen years. Now this is the Alexandrian cycle; and in fact, in charging the

Church of Alexandria to tell the day for Easter every year to the Church of Rome, it adopted the Alexandrian cycle.

Dupin therefore took useless trouble when he tried to prove that the Fathers of Nicæa had simply given occasion for the adoption of this canon. The Benedictine editions of the works of S. Ambrose have also weakened the meaning of the words of S. Ambrose, by making him say that the Nicene Fathers had indeed mentioned this cycle, but that they had not positively ordered it to be used.

It is rather remarkable that the Synod should not have placed its decision as to the celebration of the festival of Easter among its canons. None of the canons of the Council, not even those of doubtful authenticity, treat of this subject. Perhaps the Synod wished to conciliate those who were not ready to give up immediately the customs of the Quartodecimans. It refused to anathematize a practice which had been handed down from apostolic times in several orthodox Churches.

The differences in the way of fixing the period of Easter did not indeed disappear after the Council of Nicæa. Alexandria and Rome could not agree, either because one of the two Churches neglected to make the calculation for Easter, or because the other considered it inaccurate. It is a fact, proved by the ancient Easter table of the Roman Church, that the cycle of eighty-four years continued to be used at Rome as before. Now this cycle differed in many ways from the Alexandrian, and did not always agree with it about the period for Easter. In fact, (α) the Romans used quite another method from the Alexandrians: they calculated from the epact, and began from the feria prima of January. (β) The Romans were mistaken in placing the full moon a little too soon; whilst the Alexandrians placed it a little too late. (γ) At Rome the equinox was supposed to fall on the 18th March; whilst the Alexandrians placed it on the 21st March. (δ) Finally, the Romans differed in this from the Greeks also: they did not celebrate Easter the next day when the full moon fell on the Saturday.

Even the year following the Council of Nicæa—that is, in 326—as well as in the years 330, 333, 340, 341, 343, the Latins celebrated Easter on a different day from the Alexandrians. In order to put an end to this misunderstanding, the Synod of Sardica in 343, as we learn from the newly discovered festival letters of S. Athanasius, took up again the question of Easter, and brought the two parties (Alexandrians and Romans) to regulate, by means of mutual concessions, a common day for Easter for the next fifty years. This compromise, after a few years, was not observed. The troubles excited by the Arian heresy, and the division which it caused between the East and the West, prevented the decree of Sardica from being put into execution; therefore the Emperor Theodosius the Great, after the re-establishment of peace in the Church, found himself obliged to take fresh steps for obtaining a complete uniformity in the manner of celebrating Easter. In 387, the Romans having kept Easter on the 21st March, the Alexandrians did not do so for five weeks later—that is to say, till the 25th April—because with the Alexandrians the equinox was not till the 21st March. The Emperor Theodosius the Great then asked Theophilus Bishop of Alexandria for an explanation of the difference. The bishop responded to the Emperor's desire, and drew up a chronological table of the Easter festivals, based upon the principles acknowledged by the Church of Alexandria. Unfortunately, we now possess only the prologue of his work.

Upon an invitation from Rome, S. Ambrose also mentioned the period of this same Easter in 387, in his letter to the bishops of Æmilia, and he sides with the Alexandrian computation. Cyril of Alexandria abridged the paschal table of his uncle Theophilus, and fixed the time for the ninety-five following Easters, that is, from 436 to 531 after Christ. Besides this, Cyril showed, in a letter to the Pope, what was defective in the Latin calculation; and this demonstration was taken up again, some time after, by order of the Emperor, by Paschasinus Bishop of Lilybæum and Proterius of Alexandria, in a letter written by them to Pope Leo I. In consequence of these communications, Pope Leo often gave the preference to the Alexandrian computation, instead of that of the Church of Rome. At the same time also was generally established, the opinion so little entertained by the ancient authorities of the Church— one might even say, so strongly in contradiction to their teaching—that Christ partook of the passover on the 14th Nisan, that He died on the 15th (not on the 14th, as the ancients considered), that He lay in the grave on the 16th, and rose again on the 17th. In the letter we have just mentioned, Proterius of Alexandria openly admitted all these different points.

Some years afterwards, in 457, Victor of Aquitaine, by order of the Roman Archdeacon Hilary, endeavoured to make the Roman and the Alexandrian calculations agree together. It has been conjectured that subsequently Hilary, when Pope, brought Victor's calculation into use, in 456, that is, at the time when the cycle of eighty-four years came to an end. In the latter cycle the new moons were marked more accurately, and the chief differences existing between the Latin and Greek calculations disappeared; so that the Easter of the Latins generally coincided with that of Alexandria, or was only a very little removed from it. In cases when the ιδ' fell on a Saturday, Victor did not wish to decide whether Easter should be celebrated the next day, as the Alexandrians did, or should be postponed for a week. He indicates both dates in his table, and leaves the Pope to decide what was to be done in each separate case. Even after Victor's calculations, there still remained great differences in the manner of fixing the celebration of Easter; and it was Dionysius the Less who first completely overcame them, by giving to the Latins a paschal table having as its basis the cycle of nineteen years. This cycle perfectly corresponded to that of Alexandria, and thus established that harmony which had been so long sought in vain. He showed the advantages of his calculation so strongly, that it was admitted by Rome and by the whole of Italy; whilst almost the whole of Gaul remained faithful to Victor's canon, and Great Britain still held the cycle of eighty-four years, a little improved by Sulpicius Severus. When the Heptarchy was evangelized by the Roman missionaries, the new converts accepted the calculation of Dionysius, whilst the ancient Churches of Wales held fast their old tradition. From this arose the well-known British dissensions about the celebration of Easter, which were transplanted by Columban into Gaul. In 729, the majority of the ancient British Churches accepted the cycle of nineteen years. It had before been introduced into Spain, immediately after the conversion of Reccared. Finally, under Charles the Great, the cycle of nineteen years triumphed over all opposition; and thus the whole of Christendom was united, for the Quartodecimans had gradually disappeared.

Before returning to the Quartodecimans, we will here add some details for the completion of what has been said on the Easter question. In ancient times, the entire duration of a year was calculated erroneously. Thus it happened by degrees, that the equinox, instead of falling on the 21st March as announced by the calendar, really fell on the 11th March of the calendar then in use. The calculations upon the lunar months also contained many errors. For this reason, in 1582, Pope Gregory XIII. introduced a calendar improved by Alois Lilius of Calabria, by the Jesuit Clavius, and others. The improvements of this calendar were: 1st, That the morrow of the 4th October 1582 was counted as the 15th October, and the calendar was thus made to agree with astronomical calculations; 2d, The Easter full moon was calculated much more accurately than before, and rules were established for the future prevention of the difficulties which had been previously experienced. Every fourth year was to be leap year, with the exception of the secular year (i.e. the year at the end of the century); yet even in this case, in four secular years, one was to be leap year. Thus the years 1600 and 2000 are leap years, whilst the years 1700 and 1800 and 1900 are not so.

The Gregorian Calendar from this time came into use in all Catholic countries. The Greek Church would not admit it. Protestants accepted it in 1775, after long hesitation and much dissension. In the time of Gregory XIII. the difference between the calendar and the real astronomical year was ten days; if this calendar had not been changed, it would have been eleven days in 1700, and twelve in 1800: for this reason the Russians with their Julian Calendar are now twelve days behind us. But even the Gregorian Calendar itself is not quite exact; for, according to the calculations of Lalande, which are now generally admitted, the duration of a tropical year is shorter by 24 seconds than the Gregorian Calendar, so that after 3600 years it would differ by one day from the astronomical year. Besides this, the Gregorian Calendar has not fixed the months with perfect accuracy. A somewhat defective cycle was selected on account of its greater simplicity; so that, astronomically speaking, the Easter full moon may rise two hours after the time calculated by the calendar: thus, it might be at one o'clock on the Sunday morning, whilst announced by the calendar for eleven o'clock on Saturday night. In this case Easter would be celebrated on that same Sunday, when it ought to be on the following Sunday.

We remark, finally, that the Gregorian Calendar occasionally makes our Christian Easter coincide with the Jewish passover, as for instance in 1825. This coincidence is entirely contrary to the spirit of the Nicene Council; but it is impossible to avoid it, without violating the rule for finding Easter which is now universally adopted.

SEC. 38. The later Quartodecimans

The Council of Nicæa was to find more difficulty in the East than in the West in establishing complete uniformity in the celebration of Easter. Without regard to the synodical decisions, many Quartodecimans continued to celebrate Easter according to their old custom. The Synod of Antioch in 341 was even obliged to threaten them with ecclesiastical penalties if they did not adopt the common rules. It did so in these words, in its first canon: "All those who do not observe the decision respecting the holy festival of Easter made by the holy and great Synod of Nicæa, assembled in the presence of the most pious Emperor Constantine, are to be excommunicated and cut off from the Church if they continue obstinate in rejecting the legal rule." The preceding refers to the laity. But if a pastor of the Church, a bishop, priest, or deacon, acted contrary to this decree, and ventured, to the great scandal of the people, and at the risk of troubling the Church, to Judaize, and to celebrate Easter with the Jews, the Synod considered him as no longer forming part of the Church, seeing that he not only bore the weight of his own sin, but that he was also guilty of the fall of several others. This clergyman is by the very fact itself deposed; and not he alone, but also all those who continue to go to him after his deposition. Such as are deposed have no longer any right to any of the outward honour given them by the sacred office with which they were invested.

These threatenings were not entirely successful. On the contrary, we learn from S. Epiphanius that in his time, about the year 400 after Christ, there were still many Quartodecimans, and that they were even disagreed among themselves. As to their faith, they are orthodox, said S. Epiphanius; but they hold too much to Jewish fables, i.e. they observe the Jewish Easter, and build upon the passage: "Cursed is he who does not celebrate his passover on the

14th Nisan." All that we know respecting these
Quartodecimans may be summed up as follows:—

a. They celebrate one day only, whilst the Catholic Easter
lasts for a whole week.

b. On that day, the day of the ιδ', they fast, and they
communicate: they fast till three o'clock, consequently not a
whole day; which S. Epiphanius disapproves.

c. One party among them (in Cappadocia) always celebrated
Easter on the 25th March, on whatever day of the week it
might fall, according to the (apocryphal) Acta Pilati, which
says that Jesus Christ died on the 25th March.

d. Others did not for that reason abandon the 14th Nisan,
but hoped to make the two dates agree, by celebrating their
Easter on the day of the full moon immediately following
the 25th March.

According to this, the Quartodecimans of S. Epiphanius
fall into three classes, one of which abandons the ιδ', and
consequently separates itself considerably from the Jews. It
is impossible to determine whether the other classes
followed the ancient or the new method of the Jews in their
calculation for Easter; but the praise which S. Epiphanius
gives them for their orthodoxy proves that they were not
Ebionites, but that they were attached to the Johannean
tradition which was for a long time prevalent in Asia Minor.

SEC. 39. The Audians

The Audians, or Odians, are a remarkable branch of the
Quartodecimans: they lived in cloisters, and followed the

rules of the monastic life. Their foundation was derived from a certain Audius of Mesopotamia, about the time of the Synod of Nicæa. Audius had become celebrated by the severity of his asceticism; and Epiphanius, who mentions him in his History of Heretics, treats him with all possible favour, so much so that the ascetic with whom he sympathizes makes him almost forget the schismatic. Audius, he says, had censured the abuses which had been introduced into the Church, particularly the luxury and avarice of several of the bishops and clergy, and had therefore brought upon himself much hatred and persecution. He had borne all with patience, when finally the blows and unworthy treatment of which he was the object, forced him, so to speak, to excommunicate himself, and together with a few partisans, among whom were found some bishops and priests, to form a particular sect.

As for the rest, adds Epiphanius, he had certainly not fallen from the true faith: at most, he could be accused only of having expressed and maintained a singular opinion upon a point of small importance. Like several ancient doctors, e.g. Melito, Audius anthropomorphically considered the resemblance of man to God to be in the body,—an opinion which S. Epiphanius has refuted in a rather long dissertation. Before beginning the refutation of Audius, Epiphanius relates that this ascetic was consecrated bishop after he left the Church, by a bishop who had left the Church with him. He adds that the Audians lived by the work of their hands, and that their whole life was truly praiseworthy.

According to Epiphanius, the second difference between the Audians and the Church was about the celebration of the festival of Easter. From the ninth chapter S. Epiphanius seeks to express very explicitly what he understands by this difference, but his exposition is not clear.

The Audians set out from this fundamental principle: Easter must be celebrated at the same time (but not in the same manner) as with the Jews. This practice had been that of the primitive Church; and it was only from consideration for the Emperor Constantine, and in order to celebrate his birthday, that it had been abolished at Nicæa. Epiphanius refutes this last accusation of the Audians, by showing that, according to the rules of Nicæa, Easter could not always fall on the same day of the month: therefore it could not always fall on the Emperor's birthday.

To support their manner of celebrating Easter, Epiphanius says, that the Audians quoted a sacred book, διατάξεις τῶν ἀποστόλων. This book, we see, bears the same title as our so-called Apostolic Constitutions; but the fragments of it given by S. Epiphanius are not to be found in our text of the Apostolic Constitutions, and especially upon the Easter question they disagree with the contents of these Constitutions. S. Epiphanius spares no praise of the orthodoxy of these διατάξεις: he even finds that as to discipline it is quite conformed to the custom of the Church. Only the Audians interpret it erroneously in what concerns the celebration of the Easter festival. The apostles in these διατάξεις give the following rule: "You (that is, you Gentile Christians) ought to celebrate Easter at the same time as your brethren who have been Jews (ἐκ περιτομῆς)." The apostles meant: You ought to act like the rest of the faithful; whilst the Audians interpreted their words thus: You ought to celebrate Easter with the Jews (οἱ ἐν περιτομῇ). If, however, the apostolic rule meant, in a general way, that they ought to celebrate Easter with other Christians, Epiphanius concludes with reason that the Audians ought now to bow to the commands of the Council of Nicæa; for in speaking thus, the διατάξεις had in view the unity and uniformity of the Church. S. Epiphanius proves that the διατάξεις really only desired unity, and that they gave no directory of their own for the keeping of the festival. He quotes the following passage in support of his sentiments: "Even if those whose manner of celebrating Easter you have adopted should be mistaken in their views, you ought not to regard it." The διατάξεις did not therefore intend to prescribe the best and most correct practice, but to induce the minority to follow the majority; and as Christians who had been Jews formed this majority, they recommended Jewish practice for the establishment of unity.

Up to this S. Epiphanius is clear and intelligible; but what follows is full of difficulties, many of which are perhaps insoluble. Here is all that we can say with any certainty about these riddles of Œdipus, as Petavius calls them in his notes upon Epiphanius.

To prove to the Audians that they should follow the sense and not the letter of the διατάξεις, he seeks to show that, taken in a literal sense, the text contains contradictions. In proof, he gives the following passage in the eleventh chapter: "Whilst the Jews have their festival of joy (the passover), you should weep and fast on their account, because it was on the day of this feast that they nailed the Saviour to the cross. And when they weep and eat unleavened bread with bitter herbs, you should celebrate your festival of joy." Now, as the Jews held this festival on a Sunday, it would follow, according to the διατάξεις, that Christians should weep and fast on the Sunday. But this is forbidden, and the διατάξεις themselves say, "Cursed be he who fasts on the Sunday." Here there is a manifest contradiction; and, looked at closely, there is even a double contradiction: for, 1st, It is commanded to fast, and yet not to fast on the Sunday; and 2d, This precept is in opposition to the other, which the Audians pretend to draw from the διατάξεις, namely, that they ought to celebrate Easter with the Jews. Thus, says Epiphanius, the διατάξεις, according to the opinion of the Audians on the one side, require Easter to be kept with the Jews; and on the other, they require Christians to do the contrary of what the Jews do. S. Epiphanius then tries to smooth this difficulty about the literal sense, and does it in the following way: "When the Jews celebrate their feast after the equinox, you may do so at the same time as they; but if, according to their new and wrong reckoning, they celebrate it before the equinox, you should not imitate them: for in that case there would be two celebrations of Easter in the same year."

S. Epiphanius having this solution in mind, had already made allusion to it at the beginning of the eleventh chapter, by remarking that Easter was calculated according to the sun, the equinox, and the moon, whilst the Jews paid no attention to the equinox. By this remark he interrupts his demonstration of the contradictions contained in the διατάξεις. He had said, indeed, at the end of the tenth chapter: "Even the terms (the terms of the διατάξεις) contain a contradiction, for they contain the command to observe the fast of the vigil during the time of the feast of unleavened bread (μεσαζόντων τῶν ἀζύμων). Now, according to ecclesiastical calculation, that is not possible every year." With Petavius, I think that Epiphanius here simply says the same as in the eleventh chapter: "When the Jews feast, we should fast; but the repast of the Jews often takes place on the Sabbath, during which day it is forbidden to fast." The meaning, then, of the words quoted above is this: "They demand that we should fast on the day of the feast of unleavened bread, that is, on the day of the ιδ' (μεσαζ. ἀζ. = during the time of unleavened bread). But, according to the Church calendar, that is not always possible, because sometimes the ιδ' falls on a Sunday." I regard, then, the last words of the tenth chapter as merely announcing the contradiction which is afterwards shown in the eleventh chapter. Weitzel gives another meaning to these words: "The vigil of Easter (before the festival of the resurrection) should always fall in the middle of the week of unleavened bread, which is not always possible, according to the ecclesiastical calculation." It is quite true that this coincidence could not always take place according to the calculation of Nicæa; but it would have been of no use for Epiphanius to appeal to the Council of Nicæa, as it was no authority to the Audians. With them, on the contrary, the eve of the festival of the resurrection always fell about the middle of the week of unleavened bread, that is to say, at the end of the second day. Besides, the connection between the tenth and eleventh chapters, and the line of argument of S. Epiphanius, render necessary the explanation which we have given of this passage.

In bringing forward these contradictions of the διατάξεις, S. Epiphanius simply wished to refute the exaggerated

Quartodecimanism of the Audians; but he does not mean to say that these same Audians followed all these principles of the διατάξεις. He does not say, "You celebrate Easter with the Jews, and you fast when they are eating the passover." On the contrary, it appears that they were ignorant of these further requirements of the διατάξεις; for Epiphanius does not in the least reproach them with acting in this way. He does not suppose in any way that they so hold it, but he shows them that that is what the διατάξεις teach. All that we know of the way of celebrating Easter in use among the Audians is therefore reduced to this:—

a. They always celebrated Easter with the Jews, consequently on the day of the ιδ'.

b. They did not separate themselves from the Jews, even when the latter kept their passover before the equinox. This twofold practice is entirely in harmony with what we know of the origin and character of the Audians. Before separating from the Church, they shared the sentiments of many Asiatic Christians; that is to say, they were Johannean Quartodecimans, who celebrated their Easter, communicated, and ended their fast on the day of the ιδ'. The orthodoxy of the Church which they left (the Catholic Church of Asia Minor), and the praises of S. Epiphanius of their faith, do not allow us to suppose that they could have been Ebionite Quartodecimans. Epiphanius does not say that they celebrate Easter in the same manner as the Jews, but only that they celebrate it at the same time as the Jews. Neither must we conclude that they were Ebionites because they sometimes kept Easter with the Jews before the equinox. That only proves that they followed the ιδ' closely, simply, and literally, without troubling themselves with astronomical calculations. When the Jews celebrated the ιδ', they kept their Christian feast.

We have seen that they appealed to an apocryphal book. We do not know if they followed the rules of this book on other points. The analysis which Epiphanius makes of all the passages of the διατάξεις shows us that the Audians did not follow entirely the rules given in this work about the celebration of Easter. It is not easy to determine the exact meaning of these rules. As Epiphanius understands them, they set forth the following requirements:—"When the Jews keep their passover after the equinox, you may celebrate Easter at the same time; but if, according to their new and erroneous reckoning, they keep it before the equinox, you ought not to imitate them." Weitzel gives another meaning to this passage: "When the Jews eat," etc. He believes that the διατάξεις wish to establish a middle course between the Western and Eastern practices—that Quartodecimanism is their basis; to which they add the two following directions:—

a. On the day of the ιδ', when the Jews keep their passover, you should fast and weep, because it is the day of Christ's death.

b. But when the Jews are mourning on the days following the passover, or more exactly, on the Mazot days, you should feast, that is to say, you should celebrate your Easter festival on the day of the resurrection.

They therefore preserved on one side the Asiatic practice, which required that Easter should be regulated according to the day of the month; and on the other, they admitted the

Roman custom, which was to fast on the day of Christ's death, and to celebrate the festival on the day of His resurrection. The eve of that day would then be the ἀγρυπνία μεσαζόντων τῶν ἀζύμων spoken of by Epiphanius at the end of the tenth chapter. We have shown above that this latter opinion was without foundation; and besides, Weitzel's hypothesis has also this against it, that it makes the διατάξεις offer a very strange compromise between the Easter usage of the Westerns and that of the Asiatics,—a compromise which is found nowhere else, and which the Audians would not have accepted.

Epiphanius gives the following information upon the after-history of the Audians, and the duration of this sect of the Quartodecimans. As Audius was continually trying to spread his doctrine further, and as he had already gained both men and women to his side, the bishops complained of him to the Emperor, who banished him to Scythia. S. Epiphanius does not say how long he lived there; but he relates that he spread Christianity among the Goths in the neighbourhood (probably those on the borders of the Black Sea); that he founded monasteries among them, which became celebrated for the austerity of their rules and the chastity of their monks; but that he continued to celebrate Easter according to his method, and to maintain his opinion about our likeness to God. The Audians showed the same obstinacy in refusing to communicate with other Christians, or to live even with the most virtuous among them. What appears intolerable to S. Epiphanius is, that they would not content themselves with the general name of Christians, and that they united to it the name of a man in calling themselves Audians. After the death of Audius,

Uranius was their principal bishop in Mesopotamia; but
they had several bishops in the land of the Goths, among
whom Epiphanius mentions Sylvanus. After the death of
Uranius and Sylvanus, the sect became very small. With the
other Christians, they were driven from the country of the
Goths by the pagan king Athanarich (372). "They have also
left our country," adds S. Epiphanius, "and their convent
on Mount Taurus (in the south of Asia Minor), as well as
those in Palestine and Arabia, have been abandoned." S.
Epiphanius concludes his notice with the remark, that the
number of members of this party and of their monasteries
was very small at the time when he wrote, that is, about the
year 400 after Christ; and they then had only two resorts,
one in Chalcis, and the other in Mesopotamia. It is hardly
probable that the anthropomorphic monks of Egypt could
have had any connection with the Audians: the laws of the
Emperors Theodosius II. and Valentinian III. prove that
the latter still existed in the fifth century, for they were then
reckoned among the heretics; but in the sixth century they
altogether disappear.

SEC. 40. Decision on the subject of the Meletian Schism

The third chief business of the Synod of Nicæa was to put
an end to the Meletian schism, which had broken out some
time before in Egypt, and must not be confused with
another Meletian schism which agitated Antioch half a
century later. The imperfect connection, or rather the
contradiction, which exists in the information furnished by
the original documents, hardly allows us to determine what
was the true origin of the Meletian schism of Egypt. These
documents may be divided into four classes, as chief of
which, on account of their importance, we must mention

those discovered more than a century ago by Scipio Maffeï, in a MS. belonging to the chapter of Verona, and printed in the third volume of his Observazioni letterarie. Routh afterwards reprinted them in his Reliquiæ sacræ.

These documents are all in Latin, but they are evidently translated from the Greek; and in order to be understood, must often be re-translated into Greek. But that is not always sufficient: in many places the text is so corrupt as to be perfectly unintelligible. The authenticity of these documents, which are three in number, has been doubted by no one, and their importance has been universally acknowledged. The most important, the largest, and the most ancient of these pieces, is a letter written from their dungeon by the four Egyptian bishops, Hesychius, Pachomius, Theodorus, and Phileas, to Meletius himself. Eusebius relates that these four bishops were seized and martyred under Diocletian. Maffeï presumes s that Phileas Bishop of Thmuis, in Upper Egypt, was the composer of this common letter, because this bishop is known elsewhere as a writer, and is quoted by Eusebius and S. Jerome as a learned man. What adds to the probability of this hypothesis, is the fact that in the letter in question Phileas is mentioned the last, whilst Eusebius and the Acts of the Martyrs, translated into Latin, mention him first, and represent him as one of the most important men in Egypt. Besides, this letter by Phileas, etc., was evidently written at the commencement of the schism of Meletius, and before he had been formally separated from the Church; for the bishops gave him the name of dilectus comminister in Domino. "They have," they say, "for some time heard vague rumours on the subject of Meletius: he was accused of troubling the divine order and ecclesiastical rules. Quite recently these reports had been confirmed by a great number of witnesses, so that they had been obliged to write this letter. It was impossible for them to describe the general sadness and profound emotion occasioned by the ordinations that Meletius had held in strange dioceses. He was, however, acquainted with the law, so ancient and so entirely in conformity with divine and human right, which forbids a bishop to hold an ordination in a strange diocese. But without respect to this law, or to the great bishop and father Peter (Archbishop of Alexandria), or for those who were in prison, he had brought everything into a state of confusion. Perhaps he would say in self-justification, that necessity had obliged him to act thus, because the parishes were without pastors. But this allegation was false, for they had instituted several περιοδευταί and visitors; and in case of these being negligent, he should have brought the matter before the imprisoned bishops. In case they should have told him that these bishops were already executed, he could easily have discovered if it were so; and even supposing that the news of their death had been verified, his duty was still to ask of the chief Father (Peter Archbishop of Alexandria) permission to hold ordinations." Finally, the bishops recommended him to observe the holy rules of the Church for the future.

The second document is a short notice added by an ancient anonymous writer to the preceding letter. It is thus worded: "Meletius having received and read this letter, made no answer to it, nor did he go either to the imprisoned bishops or to Peter of Alexandria. After the death of these bishops as martyrs, he went immediately to Alexandria, where he made partisans of two intriguers, Isidore and Arius, who wished to become priests, and were full of jealousy against their archbishop. They pointed out to him the two visitors appointed by Archbishop Peter: Meletius excommunicated them, and appointed two others in their place. When Archbishop Peter was told of what was passing, he addressed the following letter to the people of Alexandria."

This letter is the third important document, and is thus worded: "Having learned that Meletius had no respect for the letter of the blessed bishops and martyrs (we perceive that Phileas and his companions had been already executed), but that he has introduced himself into my diocese—that he has deposed those to whom I had given authority, and consecrated others—I request you to avoid all communion with him, until it is possible for me to meet him with some wise men, and to examine into this business."

We will thus sum up what results from the analysis of these three documents:—

1st. Meletius, an Egyptian bishop (the other bishops call him comminister) of Lycopolis in the Thebaïs (S. Athanasius gives us this latter information in his Apologia contra Arianos, No. 71), made use of the time when a great number of bishops were in prison on account of their faith, in despite of all the rules of the Church, to hold ordinations in foreign dioceses, probably in those of the four bishops, Phileas, Hesychius, Theodoras, and Pachomius.

2d. Nothing necessitated these ordinations; and if they had been really necessary, Meletius ought to have asked permission to hold them from the imprisoned bishops, or, in case of their death, from Peter Archbishop of Alexandria.

3d. None of these three documents tell where Archbishop Peter was at that time, but the second and third prove that he was not at Alexandria. They show also that he was not imprisoned like his four colleagues, Phileas and the rest. Indeed, it was because Peter could not live at Alexandria that he had authorized commissaries to represent him, but Meletius took advantage of his absence to bring trouble into this city also.

Again, we may conclude that Peter was not imprisoned:

(α.) Even from the letter which he wrote, saying, "He would go himself to Alexandria."

(β.) From the first as well as the second document putting a difference between his situation and that of the imprisoned bishops.

(γ.) Finally, from these words of Socrates: "During Peter's flight, on account of the persecution then raging, Meletius allowed himself to hold ordinations." We will admit, in passing, the fact that Archbishop Peter, like Dionysius the Great and S. Cyprian, had fled during the persecution, and was absent from Alexandria, because it is of great importance in judging of the value of other information from the same sources.

4th. According to the second document, Meletius despised the exhortations of the four imprisoned bishops, and would not enter into relation either with them or with Archbishop Peter; and after the death of these bishops he went himself to Alexandria, where he united with Arius and Isidore, excommunicated the episcopal visitors appointed by Peter, and ordained two others.

5th. Archbishop Peter, being informed of all these things, recommended from his retreat all the faithful not to communicate with Meletius.

The offence of Meletius, then, consisted in his having introduced himself without any right into other dioceses, and in having given holy orders. It was not so much the necessity of the Church as his own arrogance and ambition which impelled him to this step. Epiphanius and Theodoret tell us that Meletius came next in rank to the Bishop of Alexandria, that he was jealous of his primate, and wished to profit by his absence, in order to make himself master and primate of Egypt.

The second source of information upon the origin of the Meletians is composed of some expressions of S. Athanasius, and of the ecclesiastical historian Socrates. Athanasius, who had had much to do with the Meletians, says—

(α.) In his Apology: "The latter (Peter Archbishop of Alexandria) in a synodical assembly deposed Melitius (Athanasius always writes Μελίτιος), who had been convicted of many offences, and particularly of having offered sacrifice to idols. But Melitius did not appeal to another synod, neither did he try to defend himself; but he raised a schism, and to this day his followers do not call themselves Christians, but Melitians. Shortly afterwards he began to spread invectives against the bishops, particularly against Peter, and subsequently against Achillas and Alexander" (who were Peter's two immediate successors).

(β.) The same work of S. Athanasius furnishes us also with the following information: "From the times of the bishop and martyr Peter, the Melitians have been schismatics and enemies of the Church: they injured Bishop Peter, maligned his successor Achillas, and denounced Bishop Alexander to the Emperor."

(γ.) S. Athanasius in a third passage says: "The Melitians are impelled by ambition and avarice." And: "They were declared schismatics fifty-five years ago, and thirty-six years ago the Arians were declared heretics."

(δ.) Finally, in a fourth passage: "The Eusebians knew well how the Melitians had behaved against the blessed martyr Peter, then against the great Achillas, and finally against Alexander of blessed memory."

Socrates agrees so well in all concerning the Meletians with what Athanasius says, that it might be supposed that Socrates had only copied Athanasius.

Here is an epitome of the facts given by both:

1. They accuse Meletius of having offered sacrifice to the gods during the persecution. The three documents analysed above do not say a word of this apostasy, neither does Sozomen mention it; and S. Epiphanius gives such praises to Meletius, that certainly he did not even suspect him of this apostasy. It may also be said with some reason, that such consideration would not have been shown to Meletius

and his followers by the Synod of Nicæa if he had really offered sacrifice to idols.

On the other hand, it cannot be admitted that S. Athanasius should have knowingly accused Meletius of a crime which he had not committed. The whole character of this great man is opposed to such a supposition; and besides, the commonest prudence would have induced him to avoid making an accusation which he knew to be false, in a public work against declared adversaries. It is much more probable that such reports were really circulated about Meletius, as other bishops, e.g. Eusebius of Cæsarea, were subjected to the like calumny. What may perhaps have occasioned these rumours about Meletius, is the fact that for some time this bishop was able to traverse Egypt without being arrested, and ordained priests at Alexandria and elsewhere; whilst bishops, priests, and deacons who were firm in the faith were thrown into prison, and shed their blood for their holy faith.

2. Athanasius and Socrates reproach Meletius with having despised, calumniated, and persecuted the Bishops of Alexandria, Peter, Achillas, and Alexander.

3. By comparing the expressions of S. Athanasius with the original documents analysed above, we are able to determine almost positively the period of the birth of the Meletian schism. Athanasius, indeed, agrees with the three original documents, in affirming that it broke out during the episcopate of Peter, who occupied the throne of Alexandria from the year 300 to 311. S. Athanasius gives us a much more exact date when he says that the Meletians had been declared schismatics fifty-five years before.

Unfortunately we do not know in what year he wrote the work in which he gives this information. It is true that S. Athanasius adds these words to the text already quoted: "For thirty-six years the Arians have been declared heretics." If S. Athanasius is alluding to the condemnation of Arianism by the Council of Nicæa, he must have written this work in 361, that is to say, thirty-six years after the year 325, when the Council of Nicæa was held; but others, and particularly the learned Benedictine Montfaucon, reckon these thirty-six years from the year 320, when the heresy of Arius was first condemned by the Synod of Alexandria. According to this calculation, Athanasius must have written his Epistola ad Episcopos Ægypti in 356. These two dates, 356 and 361, give us 301 or 306 as the date of the origin of the schism of Meletius, since it was fifty-five years before 356 or 361, according to S. Athanasius, that the Meletians were condemned. We have therefore to choose between 301 and 306; but we must not forget that, according to the original documents, this schism broke out during a terrible persecution against the Christians. Now, as Diocletian's persecution did not begin to rage in a cruel manner until between the years 303 and 305, we are led to place the origin of this schism about the year 304 or 305.

4. Our second series of original authorities do not say that Meletius ordained priests in other dioceses, but S. Athanasius mentions that "Meletius was convicted of many offences." We may suppose that he intended an allusion to these ordinations, and consequently it would be untrue to say that Athanasius and the original documents are at variance.

5. Neither can it be objected that S. Athanasius mentions a condemnation of Meletius by a synod of Egyptian bishops, whilst the original documents say nothing about it, for these documents refer only to the first commencement of the Meletian schism. Sozomen, besides, is agreed upon this point with S. Athanasius, in the main at least. He says: "Peter Archbishop of Alexandria excommunicated the Meletians, and would not consider their baptism to be valid; Arius blamed the bishop for this severity." It must be acknowledged that, according to the right opinion respecting heretical baptism, the archbishop was here too severe; but also it must not be forgotten that the question of the validity of baptism administered by heretics was not raised until later, and received no complete and definite solution till 314, at the Council of Arles.

Up to this point, the documents which we have consulted have nothing which is mutually contradictory; but we cannot say as much of the account given us of the Meletian schism by S. Epiphanius. He says: "In Egypt there exists a party of Meletians, which takes its name from a bishop of the Thebaïs called Μελήτιος. This man was orthodox, and in what concerns the faith did not at all separate from the Church.... He raised a schism, but he did not alter the faith. During the persecution he was imprisoned with Peter, the holy bishop and martyr (of Alexandria), and with others.... He had precedence of the other Egyptian bishops, and came immediately after Peter of Alexandria, whose auxiliary he was.... Many Christians had fallen during the persecution, had sacrificed to idols, and now entreated the confessors and martyrs to have compassion on their repentance. Some of these penitents were soldiers; others belonged to the clerical order. These were priests, deacons, etc. There was then much hesitation and even confusion among the martyrs: for some said that the lapsi should not be admitted to penitence, because this ready admission might shake the faith of others. The defenders of this opinion had good reasons for them. We must number among these defenders Meletius, Peleus, and other martyrs and confessors: all wished that they should await the conclusion of the persecution before admitting the lapsi to penitence. They also demanded that those clergy who had fallen should no longer exercise the functions of their office, but for the rest of their lives should remain in lay communion." The holy Bishop Peter, merciful as he ever was, then made this request: "Let us receive them if they manifest repentance; we will give them a penance to be able afterwards to reconcile them with the Church. We will not refuse them nor the clergy either, so that shame and the length of time may not impel them to complete perdition." Peter and Meletius not agreeing upon this point, a division arose between them; and when Archbishop Peter perceived that his merciful proposition was formally set aside by Meletius and his party, he hung his mantle in the middle of the dungeon as a sort of curtain, and sent word by a deacon: "Whoever is of my opinion, let him come here; and let whoso holds that of Meletius go to the other side." Most passed over to the side of Meletius, and only a few to Peter. From this time the two parties were separate in their prayers, their offerings, and their ceremonies. Peter afterwards suffered martyrdom, and the Archbishop Alexander was his successor. Meletius was arrested with other confessors, and condemned to work in the mines of Palestine. On his way to exile Meletius did what he had before done in prison,—ordained bishops, priests, and deacons, and founded churches of his own, because his party and that of Peter would not have communion with each other. The successors of Peter called theirs the Catholic Church, whilst the Meletians named theirs the Church of the Martyrs. Meletius went to Eleutheropolis, to Gaza, and to Aelia (Jerusalem), and everywhere ordained clergy. He must have remained a long time in the mines; and there also his followers and those of Peter would not communicate together, and assembled in different places for prayer. At last they were all delivered. Meletius still lived a long time, and was in friendly relations with Alexander, the successor of Bishop Peter. He occupied himself much with the preservation of the faith. Meletius lived at Alexandria, where he had a church of his own. It was he who first denounced the heresy of Arius to Bishop Alexander.

We see that Epiphanius gives the history of the Meletian schism in quite a different way from S. Athanasius and the original documents. According to him, the origin of this schism was the disagreement between Meletius and Peter on the subject of the admission of the lapsi, and particularly about the clergy who had fallen. In this business Meletius had not been so severe as the Novatians, but more so than his archbishop, who had shown too much mercy,—so much so that the right appeared to be undoubtedly on his side. In order to explain this contrast, it has often been supposed that Epiphanius took a notice composed by a Meletian as the foundation of his own account, and that he was thus led to treat Meletius much too favourably. But it seems to me that it may be explained more satisfactorily. S.

Epiphanius relates, that on his way to the mines, Meletius founded a Church for his party at Eleutheropolis. Now Eleutheropolis was the native country of S. Epiphanius, consequently he must have known many of the Meletians personally in his youth. These fellow-countrymen of S. Epiphanius would doubtless make him acquainted with the origin of their party, placing it in the most favourable light; and subsequently S. Epiphanius would give too favourable an account of them in his work.

It may now be asked, What is the historical value of S. Epiphanius' history? I know that very many Church historians have decided in its favour, and against Athanasius; but since the discovery of original documents, this opinion is no longer tenable, and it must be acknowledged that S. Epiphanius was mistaken on the principal points.

a. According to Epiphanius, Meletius was imprisoned at the same time as Peter. Now the original documents prove that, at the time of the commencement of the schism, neither Peter nor Meletius was in prison.

b. According to S. Epiphanius, Bishop Peter of Alexandria was too merciful towards the lapsi; but the penitential canons of this bishop present him in quite another light, and prove that he knew how to keep a wise middle course, and to proportion the penance to the sin. He who had borne torture for a long time before allowing himself to be conquered by the feebleness of the flesh, was to be less severely punished than he who had only resisted for a very short time. The slave who, by order of his master, and in his stead, had sacrificed to idols, was only punished by a year of ecclesiastical penance, whilst his master was subjected to a penance of three years (canons 6 and 7). The tenth canon particularly forbids that deposed priests should be restored to their cures, and that anything but lay communion should be granted to them. Peter therefore here teaches exactly what S. Epiphanius supposes to be the opinion of Meletius, and what, according to him, Peter refused to admit.

c. S. Epiphanius is mistaken again, when he relates that Peter was martyred in prison, as the original documents, and S. Athanasius, who had the opportunity of knowing the facts, tell us that Peter left his retreat, and excommunicated Meletius in a synod.

d. According to S. Epiphanius, Alexander was the immediate successor of Bishop Peter, whilst in reality it was Achillas who succeeded Peter, and Alexander succeeded him.

e. Finally, according to S. Epiphanius, the schismatic Meletius, although having a separate church at Alexandria, was on the best terms with Archbishop Alexander, and denounced the heresy of Arius to him; but the whole conduct of Meletius towards the Archbishop of Alexandria, and the part taken by the Meletians in the Arian heresy, give much more credibility to the assertion of S. Athanasius. Meletius, according to him, despised and persecuted Bishop Alexander, as he had before done his predecessors on the throne of Alexandria.

We have exhausted the three sources of information already mentioned. Those remaining for us to consult have neither the importance, nor the antiquity, nor the historical value of the three first. Among these documents there are, however, two short accounts by Sozomen and Theodoret, which deserve consideration, and which agree very well with the original documents, and in part with what is said by S. Athanasius. We have already made use of these accounts. As for S. Augustine, he mentions the Meletians only casually, and says nothing as to the origin of the sect; besides, he must have had before him the account of Epiphanius.

The great importance of the Meletian schism decided the Council of Nicæa to notice it, especially as, in the Emperor's mind, the principal object of the Council was to restore peace to the Church. Its decision on this matter has been preserved to us in the synodical letter of the Egyptian bishops, etc., who speak in these terms of the Meletian schism, after having treated of the heresy of Arius: "It has also been necessary to consider the question of Meletius and those ordained by him; and we wish to make known to you, beloved brethren, what the Synod has decided upon this matter. The Synod desired, above all things, to show mercy; and seeing, on carefully considering all things, that Meletius does not deserve consideration, it has been decided that be should remain in his city, but without having any authority there, and without the power of ordination, or of selecting the clergy. He is also forbidden to go into the neighbourhood or into any other town for such an object. Only the simple title of bishop should remain to him; and as for the clergy ordained by him, it is necessary to lay hands upon them again, that they may afterwards be admitted to communion with the Church, to give them their work, and to restore to them the honours which are their due; but in all dioceses where these clergy are located, they should always come after the clergy ordained by Alexander. As for those who, by the grace of God and by their prayers, have been preserved from all participation in the schism, and have remained inviolably attached to the Catholic Church, without giving any cause for dissatisfaction, they shall preserve the right of taking part in all ordinations, of presenting such and such persons for the office of the ministry, and of doing whatever the laws and economy of the Church allow. If one of these clergy should die, his place may be supplied by one newly admitted (that is to say, a Meletian); but on the condition that he should appear worthy, that he should be chosen by the people, and that the Bishop of Alexandria should have given his consent to such election." These stipulations were to be applied to all the Meletians. There was, however, an exception made with Meletius, that is to say, that the rights and prerogatives of a bishop were not retained to him, because they well knew his incorrigible habit of putting everything in disorder, and also his precipitation. Therefore, that he might not continue to do as he had done before, the Council took from him all power and authority.

"This is what particularly concerns Egypt and the Church of Alexandria. If any other decree has been made in the presence of our dear brother of Alexandria, he will acquaint you with it when he returns amongst you; for in all that the Synod has done, he has been a guide and a fellow-worker."

It was probably on account of the Meletians, and to cut short the pretensions of Meletius, who desired to withdraw himself from the authority of the Patriarch of Alexandria, and to set himself up as his equal, that the Synod of Nicæa made this plain declaration in its sixth canon: "The ancient order of things must be maintained in Egypt, in Libya, and in Pentapolis; that is to say, that the Bishop of Alexandria shall continue to have authority over the other bishops, having the same relation as exists with the Bishop of Rome. The ancient rights of the Churches shall also be protected, whether at Antioch or in the other bishoprics. It is evident, that if one should become a bishop without the consent of his metropolitan, he could not, according to the order of the great Synod, retain this dignity; but if, from a pure spirit of contradiction, two or three should oppose an election which the unanimity of all the others renders possible and legal, in such a case the majority must carry the day."

The Synod had hoped to gain the Meletians by gentleness; but it succeeded so little, that after the Nicene Synod they became more than ever enemies to the Church, and by uniting with the Arians, did a thousand times more harm than they had done before. Also, in speaking of this admission of the Meletians into the Church, decreed by the Council of Nicæa, S. Athanasius rightly said, "Would to God it had never taken place!" In the same passage we learn from S. Athanasius, that in order to execute the decree of the Council of Nicæa, Alexander begged Meletius to give him a list of all the bishops, priests, and deacons who formed his party. Alexander wished to prevent Meletius from hastening to make new ordinations, to sell holy orders for money, and thus to fill the Church with a multitude of unworthy clergy, abusing the mercy of the Council of Nicæa. Meletius remitted, indeed, the desired list to the Archbishop of Alexandria, and subsequently Athanasius inserted it in his Apologia against the Arians.

We see from it that the Meletians numbered in Egypt twenty-nine bishops, including Meletius; and at Alexandria, four priests, three deacons, and a military almoner. Meletius himself gave this list to Alexander, who doubtless made these ordinations valid, in obedience to the Council of Nicæa.

According to the ordinance of Nicæa, Meletius remained in "his city," Lycopolis; but after the death of Bishop Alexander, through the mediation of Eusebius of Nicomedia, that alliance was entered into between the Meletians and the Arians which was so unfortunate for the Church, and particularly for S. Athanasius, in which Meletius took part. It is not known when he died. He nominated as his successor his friend John, who, after being maintained in his office by the Eusebians at the Council of Tyre in 335, was driven into exile by the Emperor Constantine. The best known of the Meletians are—Bishop Arsenius, who, it is said, had had one hand cut off by S. Athanasius; Bishop Callinicus of Pelusium, who at the Council of Sardica was a decided adversary of S. Athanasius; the hermit Paphnutius, who must not be mistaken for the bishop of the same name who at the Council of. Nicæa was the defender of the marriage of priests; and the pretended priest Ischyras, who was among the principal accusers and most bitter enemies of S. Athanasius. We shall afterwards have occasion to speak of the part taken by the Meletians in the troubles excited by the heresy of Arius; suffice it here to say, that this schism existed in Egypt until the middle of the fifth century, as is attested by Socrates and Theodoret, both contemporaries. The latter mentions especially some very superstitious

Meletian monks who practised the Jewish ablutions. But after the middle of the fifth century, the Meletians altogether disappear from history.

SEC. 41. Number of the Nicene Canons

The Synod of Nicæa also set forth a certain number of canons or prescriptions on discipline; but there has been much discussion as to the number. We give here our opinion upon this question, which we have before discussed in the Tübinger Theologische Quartalschrift.

Let us see first what is the testimony of those Greek and Latin authors who lived about the time of the Council concerning the number.

a. The first to be consulted among the Greek authors is the learned Theodoret, who lived about a century after the Council of Nicæa. He says, in his History of the Church: "After the condemnation of the Arians, the bishops assembled once more, and decreed twenty canons on ecclesiastical discipline."

b. Twenty years later, Gelasius Bishop of Cyzicus, after much research into the most ancient documents, wrote a history of the Nicene Council. Gelasius also says expressly that the Council decreed twenty canons; and, what is more important, he gives the original text of these canons exactly in the same order, and according to the tenor which we find elsewhere.

c. Rufinus is more ancient than these two historians. He was born near the period when the Council of Nicæa was held, and about half a century after he wrote his celebrated history of the Church, in which he inserted a Latin translation of the Nicene canons. Rufinus also knew only of these twenty canons; but as he has divided the sixth and the eighth into two parts, he has given twenty-two canons, which are exactly the same as the twenty furnished by the other historians.

d. The famous discussion between the African bishops and the Bishop of Rome, on the subject of appeals to Rome, gives us a very important testimony on the true number of the Nicene canons. The presbyter Apiarius of Sicca in Africa, having been deposed for many crimes, appealed to Rome. Pope Zosimus (417–418) took the appeal into consideration, sent legates to Africa; and to prove that he had the right to act thus, he quoted a canon of the Council of Nicæa, containing these words: "When a bishop thinks he has been unjustly deposed by his colleagues, he may appeal to Rome, and the Roman bishop shall have the business decided by judices in partibus." The canon quoted by the Pope does not belong to the Council of Nicæa, as he affirmed; it was the fifth canon of the Council of Sardica (the seventh in the Latin version). What explains the error of Zosimus is, that in the ancient copies the canons of Nicæa and Sardica are written consecutively, with the same figures, and under the common title of canons of the Council of Nicæa; and Zosimus might optima fide fall into an error which he shared with many Greek authors, his contemporaries, who also mixed the canons of Nicæa with those of Sardica. The African bishops not finding the canon quoted by the Pope either in their Greek or in their Latin copies, in vain consulted also the copy which Bishop Cecilian, who had himself been present at the Council of

Nicæa, had brought to Carthage. The legates of the Pope
then declared that they did not rely upon these copies, and
they agreed to send to Alexandria and to Constantinople to
ask the patriarchs of these two cities for authentic copies of
the canons of the Council of Nicæa. The African bishops
desired in their turn that Pope Boniface should take the
same step (Pope Zosimus had died meanwhile in 418), that
he should ask for copies from the Archbishops of
Constantinople, Alexandria, and Antioch. Cyril of
Alexandria and Atticus of Constantinople, indeed, sent
exact and faithful copies of the Creed and canons of Nicæa;
and two learned men of Constantinople, Theilo and
Thearistus, even translated these canons into Latin. Their
translation has been preserved to us in the acts of the sixth
Council of Carthage, and it contains only the twenty
ordinary canons. It might be thought at first sight that it
contained twenty-one canons; but on closer consideration
we see, as Hardouin has proved, that this twenty-first article
is nothing but an historical notice appended to the Nicene
canons by the Fathers of Carthage. It is conceived in these
terms: "After the bishops had decreed these rules at Nicæa,
and after the holy Council had decided what was the
ancient rule for the celebration of Easter, peace and unity
of faith were re-established between the East and the West.
This is what we (the African bishops) have thought it right
to add according to the history of the Church."

The bishops of Africa despatched to Pope Boniface the
copies which had been sent to them from Alexandria and
Constantinople, in the month of November 1419; and
subsequently in their letters to Celestine I. (423–432),

successor to Boniface, they appealed to the text of these documents.

e. All the ancient collections of canons, either in Latin or Greek, composed in the fourth, or quite certainly at least in the fifth century, agree in giving only these twenty canons to Nicæa. The most ancient of these collections were made in the Greek Church, and in the course of time a very great number of copies of them were written. Many of these copies have descended to us; many libraries possess copies: thus Montfaucon enumerates several in his Bibliotheca Coisliniana. Fabricius makes a similar catalogue of the copies in his Bibliotheca Græca to those found in the libraries of Turin, Florence, Venice, Oxford, Moscow, etc.; and he adds that these copies also contain the so-called apostolic canons, and those of the most ancient councils.

The French bishop John Tilius presented to Paris, in 1540, a MS. of one of these Greek collections as it existed in the ninth century. It contains exactly our twenty canons of Nicæa, besides the so-called apostolic canons, those of Ancyra, etc. Elias Ehinger published a new edition at Wittemberg in 1614, using a second MS. which was found at Augsburg; but the Roman collection of the Councils had before given, in 1608, the Greek text of the twenty canons of Nicæa. This text of the Roman editors, with the exception of some insignificant variations, was exactly the same as that of the edition of Tilius. Neither the learned Jesuit Sirmond nor his coadjutors have mentioned what manuscripts were consulted in preparing this edition; probably they were manuscripts drawn from several libraries, and particularly from that of the Vatican. The text of this Roman edition passed into all the following collections, even into those of Hardouin and Mansi; while Justell in his Bibliotheca juris Canonici, and Beveridge in his Synodicon (both of the eighteenth century), give a somewhat different text, also collated from MSS., and very similar to the text given by Tilius. Bruns, in his recent Bibliotheca Ecclesiastica, compares the two texts. Now all these Greek MSS., consulted at such different times, and by all these editors, acknowledge only twenty canons of Nicæa, and always the same twenty which we possess.

The Latin collections of the canons of the Councils also give the same result,—for example, the most ancient and the most remarkable of all, the Prisca, and that of Dionysius the Less, which was collected about the year 500. The testimony of this latter collection is the more important for the number twenty, as Dionysius refers to the Græca auctoritas.

f. Among the later Eastern witnesses we may further mention Photius, Zonaras, and Balsamon. Photius, in his Collection of the Canons, and in his Nomocanon, as well as the two other writers in their commentaries upon the canons of the ancient Councils, quote only and know only of twenty canons of Nicæa, and always those which we possess.

g. The Latin canonists of the middle ages also acknowledge only these twenty canons of Nicæa. We have proof of this in the celebrated Spanish collection, which is generally but erroneously attributed to S. Isidore (it was composed at the commencement of the seventh century), and in that of Adrian (so called because it was offered to Charles the Great by Pope Adrian I.). The celebrated Hincmar

Archbishop of Rheims, the first canonist of the ninth century, in his turn attributes only twenty canons to the Council of Nicæa; and even the pseudo-Isidore assigns it no more.

In the face of these numerous and important testimonies from the Greek Church and the Latin, which are unanimous in recognising only twenty canons of Nicæa, and exactly those which have been handed down to us, we cannot consider authentic the Latin letter which is pretended to have been written to Pope Marcus by S. Athanasius, in which it is said that the Council of Nicæa promulgated first of all forty Greek canons, then twenty Latin canons, and that afterwards the Council reassembled, and unitedly ordained these seventy canons. A tradition, erroneously established in the East, may have caused this letter to be accepted. We know, indeed, that in some Eastern countries it was believed that the Council of Nicæa had promulgated this number of canons, and some collections do contain seventy. Happily, since the sixteenth century we have been in possession of these pretended canons of Nicæa; we can therefore judge them with certainty.

The first who made them known in the West was. the Jesuit J. Baptista Romanus, who, having been sent to Alexandria by Pope Paul IV., found an Arabic MS. in the house of the patriarch of that city, containing eighty canons of the Council of Nicæa. He copied the MS., took his copy to Rome, and translated it into Latin, with the help of George of Damascus, a Maronite archbishop. The learned Jesuit Francis Turrianus interested himself in this discovery, and had the translation of Father Baptista revised and improved by a merchant of Alexandria who was in Rome. About the same time another Jesuit, Alphonso Pisanus, composed a Latin history of the Council of Nicæa, with the help of the work of Gelasius of Cyzicus, which had just been discovered; and at his request Turrianus communicated to him the Latin translation of the Arabic canons. Pisanus received them into his work. In the first edition the testimony of the pretended letter of S. Athanasius to Marcus caused him to reduce the eighty canons to seventy; but in the subsequent editions he renounced this abbreviation, and published all the eighty canons in the order of the Arabic MS. It was in this way that the Latin translation of the eighty so-called Arabic canons of Nicæa passed into the other collections of the Councils, particularly into that of Venice and of Binius. Some more recent collections, however, adopted the text of a later translation, which Turrianus had made.

Shortly after the first edition of Alphonso Pisanus appeared, Turrianus made the acquaintance of a young converted Turk called Paul Ursinus, who knew Arabic very well, and understood Latin and Italian. Turrianus confided to him a fresh translation of the eighty Arabic canons. Ursinus, in preparing it, made use of another ancient Arabian MS., discovered in the library of Pope Marcellus II. (1555). This second MS. agreed so well with that of Alexandria, that they might both be taken for copies from one and the same original. Turrianus published this more accurate translation in 1578. He accompanied it with notes, and added a Proëmium, in which he tried to prove that the Council of Nicæa promulgated more than twenty canons. All the collections of the Councils since Turrianus have considered his position as proved, and have admitted the eighty canons.

In the following century, the Maronite Abraham Echellensis made the deepest researches with reference to the Arabic canons of the Council of Nicæa; and they led him to the opinion that these canons must have been collected from different Oriental nations, from the Syrians, Chaldeans, Maronites, Copts, Jacobites, and Nestorians, and that they had been translated into many Oriental languages. At the same time he started, and with truth, the suggestion that these Oriental collections were simply translations of ancient Greek originals, and that consequently in the Greek Church too they must have reckoned more than twenty canons of Nicæa. After having compared other Arabian MSS. which he had obtained, Echellensis gave a fresh Latin translation of these canons at Paris in 1645. According to these MSS., there were eighty-four canons instead of eighty. However, this difference arose much more from the external arrangement than from the canons themselves. Thus the thirteenth, seventeenth, thirty-second, and fifty-sixth canons of Turrianus were each divided into two in the translation by Abraham Echellensis; on the other hand, the forty-third and eighty-third of Echellensis each formed two canons in the work of Turrianus. The twenty-ninth, thirty-seventh, and forty-first of A. Echellensis are wanting in Turrianus; but, again, Echellensis has not the forty-fifth canon of Turrianus. A superficial study of these two collections of canons would lead to the conclusion that they were almost identical; but it is not so. The corresponding canons in the two translations sometimes have an entirely different meaning. We can but conclude either that the Arabian translators understood the Greek original differently, or else that the MSS. which they used showed considerable variations. The latter supposition is the most probable; it would explain how the eighty-four Arabian canons contain the twenty genuine canons of Nicæa, but often with considerable changes. Without reckoning these eighty-four canons, Echellensis has also translated into Latin, and published, a considerable number of ecclesiastical decrees, διατυπώσεις, constitutiones, also attributed to the Nicene Council. He added to this work a Latin translation of the Arabic preface, which preceded the entire collection in the MS., together with a learned dissertation in defence of the eighty-four canons, with a good many notes. Mansi has retained all these articles, and Hardouin has also reproduced the principal part of them.

It is certain that the Orientals believed the Council of Nicæa to have promulgated more than twenty canons: the learned Anglican Beveridge has proved this, reproducing an ancient Arabic paraphrase of the canons of the first four Œcumenical Councils. According to this Arabic paraphrase, found in a MS. in the Bodleian Library, the Council of Nicæa must have put forth three books of canons: the first containing eighty-four canons, referring to priests, monks, etc.; the second containing the first twenty authentic canons; the third being only a series of rules for kings and superiors, etc. The Arabic paraphrase of which we are speaking gives a paraphrase of all these canons, but Beveridge took only the part referring to the second book, that is to say, the paraphrase of the twenty genuine canons; for, according to his view, which, as we shall show, was perfectly correct, it was only these twenty canons which were really the work of the Council of Nicæa, and all the others were falsely attributed to it. The little that Beveridge gives us of the paraphrase of the first book of the pretended canons shows, besides, that this first book tolerably coincided with the fifteen decrees edited by Echellensis, which concern monks, abbots, and abbesses. Renaudot informs us that the third book of the Arabic paraphrase proves that the third book of the canons contained also various laws by Constantine, Theodosius, and Justinian. Beveridge believed this paraphrase to be the work of an Egyptian priest named Joseph, who lived in the fourteenth century, because that name is given in the MS. accompanied by that chronological date; but Renaudot proves conclusively that the Egyptian priest named Joseph had been only the possessor of the MS. which dated from a much earlier period.

However it may be as to the latter point, it is certain that these Arabic canons are not the work of the Council of Nicæa: their contents evidently prove a much more recent origin. Thus:

a. The thirty-eighth canon (the thirty-third in Turrianus) ordains that the Patriarch of Ephesus should proceed to Constantinople, which is the urbs regia, ut honor sit regno et sacerdotio simul. This decree therefore supposes that Byzantium was then changed into Constantinople, and that it had become the imperial residence. Now this change did not take place until about five years after the Council of Nicæa. At the period when the Council was held, Byzantium was still quite an insignificant town, almost reduced to ruins by a previous devastation. The bishopric of Constantinople was only raised to the dignity of a

patriarchate by the second and fourth Œcumenical
Councils. Therefore this canon, translated into Arabic,
could not have belonged to the Council of Nicæa, and does
not date back further than the fourth Œcumenical Council.

b. The forty-second canon of A. Echellensis (thirty-sixth in
Turrianus) forbids the Ethiopians to elect a patriarch: their
spiritual head was to bear only the title of Catholicus, and
to be under the jurisdiction of the Patriarch of Alexandria,
etc. This canon also betrays a more recent origin than the
time of the Council of Nicæa. At that period, indeed,
Ethiopia had no bishop; hardly had S. Frumentius begun
the conversion of its people; and it was only subsequently,
when S. Athanasius was already Archbishop of Alexandria,
that S. Frumentius made him acquainted with the good
results of his missions, and was consecrated by him bishop
to the new converts. Our canon, on the contrary, supposes
a numerous episcopate to be then existing in Ethiopia, and
its head, the Catholicus, to be desirous to free himself from
the mother church of Alexandria. This canon, as well as
others quoted by Turrianus and by A. Echellensis, assumes
that the institution of patriarchates was then in full vigour,
which was not the case at the time of the Council of Nicæa.

c. Peter de Marca has already proved the forty-third canon
of the text of A. Echellensis (thirty-seventh in Turr.) to be
more recent than the third Œcumenical Council of Ephesus
(431). This Council of Ephesus rejected the pretensions of
the Patriarch of Antioch respecting the choice of the
bishops of Cyprus. According to Marca's demonstration,
this dependence of Cyprus upon the see of Antioch cannot
be verified before the year 900: for in the time of the
Emperor Leo the Wise (911), we know, from the Notitia of

his reign, that Cyprus was not then dependent upon Antioch; whilst this Arabian canon makes out that this submission was already an accomplished fact, disputed by no one.

d. The fifty-third canon (forty-ninth in Turr.), which condemns simony, has its origin from the second canon of the fourth Œcumenical Council of Chalcedon. It is therefore evident that it was not formed at Nicæa.

e. In the thirty-eighth, thirty-ninth, and forty-second canons (c. 33, 34, and 36 in Turr.), the Bishop of Seleucia, Almodajen, is already called Catholicus,—a dignity to which he did not attain until the sixth century, under the Emperor Justinian. In this canon, as Seleucia has the Arabian name of Almodajen, Renaudot concludes that these canons were not formed until the time of Mahomet.

The Constitutiones, edited by Echellensis, still less than the eighty-four canons, maintain the pretension of dating back to the Council of Nicæa.

a. The first division of these Constitutions, that de Monachis et Anachoretis, presupposes an already strong development of monasticism. It speaks of convents for men and women, abbots and abbesses, the management of convents, and the like. But we know that, at the time of the Council of Nicæa, monasticism thus organized had scarcely made its appearance. Even in the first times after our Synod, there were none of those large convents mentioned in the Arabic canons, but only hamlets of monks, consisting of groups of cabins.

b. The second series of Arabian Constitutions comprises nineteen chapters. It also speaks of convents, abbots, the property and possession of convents, etc. (c. 1–10). The eighth canon shows that there were already many monks who were priests. Now this was certainly not the case at the time of the Council of Nicæa, when monasticism was in its infancy. The ninth chapter speaks of Constantinople as the imperial residence (urbs regia), which again betrays a later period.

c. The third series comprises twenty-five chapters. The Nicene Creed, which is contained in it, has here already the addition which was made to it in the second Œcumenical Council. The Arabic Creed, besides, is much longer than the genuine one. The Orientals added several phrases, as Abraham Echellensis has remarked. This Arabic Creed asserts that Jesus Christ is perfectus homo, vera anima intellectuali et rationali præditus; words betraying an intention of opposing Apollinarism, as well as those following: duas habentes naturas, duas voluntates, duas operationes, in una persona, etc., which seem to be a protest against the heresy of the Monophysites and the Monothelites.

Following this Creed, the Arabic text relates, falsely, that Constantine entreated the bishops assembled at Nicæa to give the name of Constantinople to Byzantium, and to raise his bishopric to the rank of an archbishopric, equal to that of Jerusalem.

The decrees of this last series, examined in detail, also show that they are more recent than the Council of Nicæa, by mentioning customs of later origin. Thus the tenth chapter commands the baptism of infants; the twelfth and thirteenth chapters, again, concern monks and nuns; the fourteenth chapter finds it necessary to forbid that children should be raised to the diaconate, and more especially to the priesthood and episcopate.

We may therefore sum up the certain proofs resulting from all these facts, by affirming that these Arabic canons are not genuine; and all the efforts of Turrianus, Abraham Echellensis, and Cardinal d'Aguirre, cannot prevent an impartial observer from coming to this opinion even with regard to some of those canons which they were anxious to save, while abandoning the others. Together with the authenticity of these canons, the hypothesis of Abraham Echellensis also vanishes, which supposes them to have been collected by Jacob, the celebrated Bishop of Nisibis, who was present at the Nicene Synod. They belong to a later period. Assemani offers another supposition, supporting it by this passage from Ebed-jesu: "Bishop Maruthas of Tagrit translated the seventy-three canons of Nicæa." Assemani believes these seventy-three canons to be identical with the eighty-four Arabic canons, but such identity is far from being proved. Even the number of the canons is different; and if it were not so, we know, from what we saw above, that several of the Arabic canons indicate a more recent period than those of Bishop Maruthas. It is probable that Maruthas really translated seventy-three canons, supposed to be Nicene; that is to say, that he had in his hands one of those MSS. spoken of above, which contained various collections of canons falsely attributed to the Council of Nicæa.

It will be asked why in some parts of the East they should have attributed so great a number of canons to the Council of Nicæa. It is not difficult to explain the mistake. We know, indeed, that the canons of various councils were at a very early period collected into one corpus; and in this corpus the canons of Nicæa always had the first place, on account of their importance. It happened afterwards, that either accidentally or designedly, some copyists neglected to give the names of the councils to those canons which followed the Nicene. We have already seen that even at Rome there was a copy containing, sub uno titulo, the canons of Nicæa and those of Sardica. When these copies were circulated in the East, that which might have been foreseen took place in course of time: viz., from a want of the spirit of criticism, all the later canons which followed after the true canons were attributed to the Council of Nicæa.

But it must also be said that certain learned men, especially Baronius and the Spanish Cardinal d'Aguirre, have tried hard to prove, from the only Greek and Latin memorials, and without these Arabic canons, that the Synod of Nicæa published more than twenty canons.

a. The Synod, said Aguirre, certainly set forth a canon on the celebration of Easter; and a proof of this is, that Balsamon, in his commentary upon the first canon of Antioch, mentions this Nicene canon as being in existence. There must therefore, concludes Aguirre, have been above twenty Nicene canons. But it may be answered that the ancient authors make no mention of a canon, but only of a simple ordinance, of the Council of Nicæa respecting the celebration of the Easter festival; and it is indeed certain

that such a rule was given by the Council, as is proved by
the synodical decree. As for Balsamon, he says exactly the
contrary to what Cardinal d'Aguirre maintains,—namely, ἐν
γοῦν τοῖς κανόσι τῶν ἐν Νικαίᾳ πατέρων τοῦτο οὐχ εὕρηται,
εἰς δὲ τὰ πρακτικὰ τῆς πρώτης συνόδου εὑρίσκεται; that is to
say, "which is not to be found in the canons of the Fathers
of Nicæa, but which was there discussed." D'Aguirre
evidently did not consult the Greek text of Balsamon, but
probably made use of the inaccurate Latin translation which
Schelstrate has given of it. But even admitting that some
later writer may have given as a canon the Nicene rule
about Easter, even the nature of things shows that it could
only be a disciplinary measure. Perhaps also a passage of
the Synod held at Carthage in 419 had been misunderstood.
This Synod says that the Council of Nicæa re-established
the antiquus canon upon the celebration of Easter; which
from the context means, and can mean, only this—the
ancient rule for the celebration of Easter was restored by
the Council of Nicæa, to be observed by the generations
following.

b. Cardinal d'Aguirre says, in the second place, that if some
very ancient authors are to be trusted, the acts of the
Council of Nicæa were very voluminous, and he concludes
from this that there must have been more than twenty
canons; but we have explained above that it is very doubtful
whether these acts contained more than the Creed, the
canons, and the synodical letter; and even if the acts were
really very voluminous, it does not necessarily follow that
they contained a larger number of canons. The acts of the
Council of Ephesus are very extensive; but nevertheless
that Council published only six canons, eight at the most, if

we consider as canons two decrees which had a special object.

c. Aguirre suggests further, that the Arians burnt the complete acts of the Council of Nicæa, and allowed only these twenty canons to remain, in order to have it believed that the Council had decreed no others. Baronius also makes a similar supposition, but there is not the slightest proof of such an act on the part of the Arians; and if the Arians had done as he suggests, they would certainly have burnt the Creed of Nicæa itself, which contains their most express condemnation.

d. It is well-nigh superfluous to refute those who have maintained that the Synod of Nicæa lasted three years, and who add that it must certainly have promulgated above twenty canons during all that time. The Synod began and ended in the year 325: it was after the close of it that the Emperor Constantine celebrated his vicennalia. The supposition that the Council lasted for three years is a fable invented subsequently by the Orientals; but even were it true, if the Council really lasted for three years, one could not therefore affirm that it must have promulgated a great number of decrees.

e. The following passage from a letter of Pope Julius I. has been also made use of to prove that the Council of Nicæa published more than twenty canons: "The bishops at Nicæa rightly decided that the decrees of one council may be revised by a subsequent one." This letter is to be found in the works of S. Athanasius. But Pope Julius I. does not say that the Nicene Fathers made a canon of their decision; on the contrary, he appears to consider that it was by their

Charles Joseph Hefele, D.D.

example, in judging afresh the Arian question, already judged at Alexandria, that the Nicene Fathers authorized these revisions.

f. When the Patriarch of Constantinople, Flavian, appealed to Rome against the decision of the Robber-Synod of Ephesus, Pope Leo the Great, in two letters addressed to the Emperor Theodosius, appealed in his turn to a decree of the Council of Nicæa, to show that such appeals were permissible. Cardinal d'Aguirre immediately concludes that Pope Leo there quotes a canon which is not among the twenty authentic ones. The Cardinal did not see that Pope Leo here commits the same mistake as Pope Zosimus, by quoting a canon of Sardica as one of those passed at Nicæa.

g. It is less easy to explain these words of S. Ambrose, quoted by Baronius and Aguirre: Sed prius cognoscamus, non solum hoc apostolum de episcopo et presbytero statuisse, sed etiam Patres in concilio Nicæno tractatus addidisse, neque clericum quemdam debere esse, qui secunda conjugia sortitus. An examination of this text shows, however, that S. Ambrose does not attribute to the Council of Nicæa a canon properly so called; he uses only the expression tractatus. The Benedictines of S. Maur, besides, say very reasonably on this passage of S. Ambrose: "As Pope Zosimus mistook a canon of Sardica for one of Nicæa, so S. Ambrose may have read in his collectio of the Acts of Nicæa some rule de digamis non ordinandis, belonging to another synod, and may have thought that this rule also emanated from the Council of Nicæa."

h. We have to examine an expression of S. Jerome, which it has been said will show that more than twenty canons were

promulgated at Nicæa. S. Jerome says in his Præfatio ad
librum Judith: Apud Hebræos liber Judith inter agiographa
legitur, cujus auctoritas ad roboranda ila, quæ in
contentionem veniunt, minus idonea judicatur.... Sed quia
hunc librum Synodus Nicæna in numero Sanctarum
Scripturarum legitur computasse, acquieri postulationi
vestræ, etc. If we conclude from these words that the
Fathers of Nicæa gave a canon of the genuine books of the
Bible, we certainly draw an inference which they do not
sustain. The meaning seems rather to be this: the Nicene
Fathers quoted this book of Judith, that is to say, made use
of it as a canonical book, and so in fact recognised it. In
this way the Council of Ephesus implicitly acknowledged
the Epistle to the Hebrews, by approving of the anathemas
levelled by Cyril against Nestorius, in which this epistle is
quoted as a book of the Bible. It is true that, in some
memorials left to us by the Council of Nicæa, we find no
such quotation from the book of Judith; but the difficulty
does not lie there: the quotation may have been made vivâ
voce in the Council; and this fact may have been laid hold
of, and preserved in some document composed by a
member of the Council. Besides, S. Jerome said only these
words, "legitur computasse," that is to say, we read that the
Council of Nicæa did so. If the Council had really made a
canon on this subject, S. Gregory of Nazianzus,
Amphilochius, and others, would not have subsequently
refused to reckon the book of Judith in the number of
canonical books. S. Jerome himself in another passage is
doubtful of the canonicity of the book; he therefore can
have attached no great importance to what he said of the
Council of Nicæa on the subject of the book of Judith.
Finally, the Council of Laodicæa, more recent than that of

Nicæa, in its sixtieth canon, does not reckon the book of
Judith among the canonical books: such exclusion would
have been utterly impossible if the pretended canon had
been really promulgated at Nicæa in 325.

i. It has been attempted also to decide the controversy now
under consideration by the high authority of S. Augustine,
who in his 213th epistle (in earlier editions the 110th) says:
"Even in the lifetime of Valerius I was appointed
coadjutor-bishop in Hippo, not being aware that this had
been prohibited by the Council of Nicæa." It has been
said—and Cardinal d'Aguirre especially insisted—that this
prohibition is not to be found in the twenty canons; but he
is mistaken: the prohibition is there; it is very explicit in the
eighth canon.

k. We proceed to an objection taken from Pope Innocent
I., who says in his twenty-third epistle, that at Nicæa it was
forbidden that any one should be ordained priest who had
served in war after his baptism. This prohibition, indeed, is
not to be found in the twenty Nicene canons; but an
attentive reading of Innocent I.'s epistle leads us to ask if
Innocent really considered this prohibition as proceeding
from the Council of Nicæa. He says, in fact: "You know
yourselves the rules of Nicæa about ordination, tamen
aliquam partem, quæ de ordinationibus est provisa,
inserendam putavi." It is not known whether the two words
aliqua pars ought to be understood of a rule of Nicæa, or of
a rule taken from another synod, and treating of the same
subject. Innocent twice mentions this prohibition to ordain
soldiers as priests: once in the forty-third epistle, where he
in no way mentions the Council of Nicæa: the second time
in Ep. i. c. 2, where it is true that in the context there is

reference to the Council of Nicæa; but in the passage itself, where the Pope recalls the prohibition, he does not rest upon the authority of that Council. In the passage the word item evidently means secundo, and not that the rule following is a decree of Nicæa. We might even admit that Pope Innocent intended to quote a Nicene rule, but that would prove nothing contrary to our position. The words quoted by the Pope are those of a Council of Turin, as has been thoroughly shown by Labbe. We must therefore conclude that Innocent made the same mistake as his predecessor Zosimus.

l. Gelasius of Cyzicus gives nine constitutiones, exclusive of the twenty authentic canons; and at the close of Book II. c. 29 he says explicitly, "The bishops of Nicæa gave various similar διατυπώσεις;" hence it has been said that he refutes our thesis. But these constitutiones are purely dogmatical (λόγος διδασκαλικὸς): therefore they are not canons, and could not have increased the number to more than twenty; but—and this is the principal point—they are most certainly spurious: none of the ancient writers are acquainted with them; no one among the moderns has endeavoured to defend their historical value; most do not even mention them—as, for instance, Tillemont and Orsi; and those who quote them content themselves with denying their genuineness.

m. According to Baronius and d'Aguirre, Socrates, the Greek historian of the Church, is erroneously represented as having said that the Council of Nicæa commanded the use of the doxology thus worded, "Glory be to the Father and to the Son," in order to show the equality of the Father and the Son; whilst the Arians proposed this form, "Glory be to the Father through the Son." But in the said passage Socrates simply affirms that there was one party at Antioch which made use of the one form, and another which used the other, and that the Arian Bishop Leontius tried to prevent the praises of God being sung according to the παράδοσις of the Council of Nicæa, that is, to prevent their using forms in accordance with the Nicene doctrine. Valesius also remarks, when translating that passage from Socrates, that the Greek historian nowhere says what Baronius and Aguirre attribute to him. We know, indeed, that before the rise of the Arian heresy the Fathers of the Church often altered the form of the doxology, sometimes saying "by the Son," sometimes "and to the Son." But as the Arians would not use the form "and to the Son," and persisted in saying "by the Son," the orthodox in their turn gained the habit of saying almost exclusively, without there being any rule on the subject, "and to the Son." If there had been a rule, the orthodox bishops would not long subsequently have allowed the form "by the Son" to have been used.

n. Pope Leo appealed repeatedly to the Council of Nicæa to show that the Patriarch of Constantinople wrongfully laid claim to a precedency over the Patriarchs of Alexandria and Antioch. Aguirre hence concludes that the Pope must have had Nicene decrees before him which are not among the twenty canons recognised as authentic. It is easy to reply that S. Leo refers only to the sixth canon of Nicæa, which maintains the Archbishops of Alexandria and Antioch in their rights, and consequently implicitly forbids any other bishop to be placed above them.

o. Notwithstanding the efforts of Cardinal d'Aguirre, it is impossible to make a serious objection of what was said by the second Council of Arles, held about the year 452. This Council expresses itself thus: magna synodus antea constituit—that whoso falsely accused another of great crimes should be excommunicated to their life's end. It is perfectly true, as has been remarked, that the twenty canons of Nicæa contain no such rule; but it has been forgotten that, in making use of the expression magna synodus, the second Council of Arles does not mean the Council of Nicæa: it has in view the first Council of Arles, and particularly the fourteenth canon of that Council.

p. The objection drawn from the Synod of Ephesus is still only specious. The Council of Ephesus relies upon a decision of the Council of Nicæa in maintaining that the Church of Cyprus is independent of the Church of Antioch. Aguirre thought that this was not to be found in the twenty canons; but it is not so, for the Council of Ephesus certainly referred to the sixth canon of Nicæa when it said: "The canon of the Fathers of Nicæa guaranteed to each Church the rank which it previously held."

q. Again, it has been said that Atticus Bishop of Constantinople alludes to a canon not found among the twenty, when he indicates very precisely in a letter who those are, according to the rule of the Council of Nicæa, who ought to have literæ formatæ. But the document bearing the name of Bishop Atticus was unknown to the whole of antiquity; it belongs only to the middle ages, and has certainly no greater value than the pseudo-Isidorian documents. But if this memorial were authentic (Baronius accepts it as such), it would prove nothing against our position; for Baronius himself tells us that the Fathers of Nicæa deliberated very secretly upon the form that the literæ formatæ ought to take, but made no canon upon the subject.

r. The last witness of Aguirre has no greater weight. It is an expression of S. Basil's, who affirms that the Council of Nicæa made rules for the punishment of the guilty, that future sins might be avoided. Now the canons of Nicæa in our possession, as we shall see hereafter, authorize S. Basil to speak in this way. Some other objections of less importance not repeated by Aguirre might be noticed, but they have been sufficiently exposed and refuted by Natalis Alexander.

SEC. 42. Contents of the Nicene Canons

After having determined the number of authentic canons of the Council of Nicæa, we must now consider more closely their contents. The importance of the subject, and the historical value that an original text always possesses, has decided us to give the Greek text of the acts of the Council (according to the editions of Mansi and of Bruns), together with a translation and a commentary intended to explain their meaning.

CAN. 1

Εἴ τις ἐν νόσῳ ὑπὸ ἰατρῶν ἐχειρουργήθη, ἢ ὑπὸ βαρβάρων ἐξετμήθη, οὗτος μενέτω ἐν τῷ κλήρῳ· εἰ δέ τις ὑγιαίνων ἑαυτὸν ἐξέτεμε, τοῦτον καὶ ἐν τῷ κλήρῳ ἐξεταζόμενον πεπαῦσθαι προσήκει, καὶ ἐκ τοῦ δεῦρο μηδένα τῶν τοιούτων χρῆναι προάγεσθαι· ὥσπερ δὲ τοῦτο πρόδηλον, ὅτι περὶ τῶν

ἐπιτηδευόντων τὸ πρᾶγμα καὶ τολμώντων ἑαυτοὺς ἐκτέμνειν
εἴρηται· οὕτως εἴ τινες ὑπὸ βαρβάρων ἢ δεσποτῶν
εὐνουχίσθησαν, εὑρίσκοιντο δὲ ἄλλως ἄξιοι, τοὺς τοιούτους
εἰς κλῆρον προσίεται ὁ κανών.

"If a man has been mutilated by physicians during sickness,
or by barbarians, he may remain among the clergy; but if a
man in good health has mutilated himself, he should resign
his post after the matter has been proved among the clergy,
and in future no one who has thus acted should be
ordained. But as it is evident that what has just been said
only concerns those who have thus acted with intention,
and have dared to mutilate themselves, those who have
been made eunuchs by barbarians or by their masters will
be allowed, conformably to the canon, to remain among the
clergy, if in other respects they are worthy."

This ordinance of Nicæa agrees well with the directions
contained in the apostolic canons 21–24 inclusive (20–23
according to another way of numbering them), and it is to
these apostolic canons that the Council makes allusion by
the expression ὁ κανών. It was not Origen alone who, a
long time before the Council of Nicæa, had given occasion
for such ordinances: we know, by the first apology of S.
Justin, that a century before Origen, a young man had
desired to be mutilated by physicians, for the purpose of
completely refuting the charge of vice which the heathen
brought against the worship of Christians. S. Justin neither
praises nor blames this young man: he only relates that he
could not obtain the permission of the civil authorities for
his project, that he renounced his intention, but
nevertheless remained virgo all his life. It is very probable
that the Council of Nicæa was induced by some fresh

similar cases to renew the old injunctions; it was perhaps the Arian Bishop Leontius who was the principal cause of it. S. Athanasius, and after him Theodoret and Socrates, relate in fact that Leontius, a Phrygian by birth, and a clergyman at Antioch, lived with a subintroducta named Eustolion; and as he could not separate himself from her, and wished to prevent her leaving him, mutilated himself. His bishop, Eustathius, had deposed him, more especially for this last act; but the Emperor Constantine afterwards made him by force Bishop of Antioch. Leontius became afterwards one of the most bitter opponents of S. Athanasius. This ordinance of Nicæa was often renewed in force by subsequent synods and by bishops; and it has been inserted in the Corpus juris canonici.

CAN. 2

Ἐπειδὴ πολλὰ ἤτοι ὑπὸ ἀνάγκης ἢ ἄλλως ἐπειγομένων τῶν ἀνθρώπων ἐγένετο παρὰ τὸν κανόνα τὸν ἐκκλησιαστικὸν, ὥστε ἀνθρώπους ἀπὸ ἐθνικοῦ βίου ἄρτι προσελθόντας τῇ πίστει, καὶ ἐν ὀλίγῳ χρόνῳ κατηχηθέντας εὐθὺς ἐπὶ τὸ πνευματικὸν λουτρὸν ἄγειν, καὶ ἅμα τῷ βαπτισθῆναι προσάγειν εἰς ἐπισκοπὴν ἢ πρεσβυτερεῖον· καλῶς ἔδοξεν ἔχειν, τοῦ λοιποῦ μηδὲν τοιοῦτο γίνεσθαι· καὶ γὰρ καὶ χρόνου δεῖ τῷ κατηχουμένῳ, καὶ μετὰ τὸ βάπτισμα δοκιμασίας πλείονος· σαφὲς γὰρ τὸ ἀποστολικὸν γράμμα τὸ λέγον· Μὴ νεόφυτον, ἵνα μὴ τυφωθεὶς εἰς. κρίμα ἐμπέσῃ καὶ παγίδα τοῦ διαβόλου· εἰ δὲ προϊόντος τοῦ χρόνου ψυχικόν τι ἁμάρτημα εὑρεθῇ περὶ τὸ πρόσωπον, καὶ ἐλέγχοιτο ὑπὸ δύο ἢ τριῶν μαρτύρων, πεπαύσθω ὁ τοιοῦτος τοῦ κλήρου· ὁ δὲ παρὰ ταῦτα ποιῶν, ὡς ὑπεναντία τῇ μεγάλῃ συνόδῳ θρασυνόμενος, αὐτὸς κινδυνεύσει περὶ τὸν κλῆρον.

"Seeing that many things, either from necessity or on account of the pressure of certain persons, have happened contrary to the ecclesiastical canon, so that men who have but just turned from a heathen life to the faith, and who have only been instructed during a very short time, have been brought to the spiritual laver, to baptism, and have even been raised to the office of priest or bishop, it is right that in future this should not take place, for time is required for sound instruction in doctrine, and for further trial after baptism. For it is a wise saying of the apostle, as follows: 'Not a novice, lest through pride he fall into condemnation, and into the snare of the devil.' If hereafter a cleric is guilty of a grave offence, proved by two or three witnesses, he must resign his spiritual office. Any one who acts against this ordinance, and ventures to be disobedient to this great Synod, is in danger of being expelled from the clergy."

It may be seen by the very text of this canon, that it was already forbidden to baptize, and to raise to the episcopate or to the priesthood any one who had only been a catechumen for a short time: this injunction is in fact contained in the eightieth (seventy-ninth) apostolical canon; and according to that, it would be older than the Council of Nicæa. There have been nevertheless certain cases in which, for urgent reasons, an exception has been made to the rule of the Council of Nicæa,—for instance, that of S. Ambrose. The canon of Nicæa does not seem to allow such an exception, but it might be justified by the apostolical canon which says, at the close: "It is not right that any one who has not yet been proved should be a teacher of others, unless by a peculiar divine grace." The expression of the canon of Nicæa, ψυχικὸν τι ἁμάρτημα, is not easy to

explain: some render it by the Latin words animale
peccatum, believing that the Council has here especially in
view sins of the flesh; but, as Zonaras has said, all sins are
ψυχικὰ ἁμαρτήματα. We must then understand the passage
in question to refer to a capital and very serious offence, as
the penalty of deposition annexed to it points out.

These words have also given offence, εἰ δὲ προϊόντος τοῦ
χρόνου; that is to say, "It is necessary henceforward," etc.,
understanding that it is only those who have been too
quickly ordained who are threatened with deposition in case
they are guilty of crime; but the canon is framed, and ought
to be understood, in a general manner: it applies to all other
clergymen, but it appears also to point out that greater
severity should be shown towards those who have been too
quickly ordained. Others have explained the passage in this
manner: "If it shall become known that any one who has
been too quickly ordained was guilty before his baptism of
any serious offence, he ought to be deposed." This is the
interpretation given by Gratian, but it must be confessed
that such a translation does violence to the text. This is, I
believe, the general sense of the canon, and of this passage
in particular: "Henceforward no one shall be baptized or
ordained quickly. As to those already in orders (without any
distinction between those who have been ordained in due
course and those who have been ordained too quickly), the
rule is that they shall be deposed if they commit a serious
offence. Those who are guilty of disobedience to this great
Synod, either by allowing themselves to be ordained or
even by ordaining others prematurely, are threatened with
deposition ipso facto, and for this fault alone." We

consider, in short, that the last words of the canon may be understood as well of the ordained as of the ordainer.

CAN. 3

Ἀπηγόρευσεν καθόλου ἡ μεγάλη σύνοδος μήτε ἐπισκόπῳ μήτε πρεσβυτέρῳ μήτε διακόνῳ μήτε ὅλως τινὶ τῶν ἐν τῷ κλήρῳ ἐξεῖναι συνείσακτον ἔχειν, πλὴν εἰ μὴ ἄρα μητέρα ἢ ἀδελφὴν ἢ θείαν, ἢ ἃ μόνα πρόσωπα πᾶσαν ὑποψίαν διαπέ φευγε.

"The great Synod absolutely forbids, and it cannot be permitted to either bishop, priest, or any other cleric, to have in his house a συνείσακτος (subintroducta), with the exception of his mother, sister, aunt, or such other persons as are free from all suspicion."

In the first ages of the Church, some Christians, clergymen and laymen, contracted a sort of spiritual marriage with unmarried persons, so that they lived together; but there was not a sexual, but a spiritual connection between them, for their mutual spiritual advancement. They were known by the name of συνείσακτοι, ἀγαπηταί, and sorores. That which began in the spirit, however, in many cases ended in the flesh; on which account the Church very stringently forbade such unions, even with penalties more severe than those with which she punished concubinage: for it happened that Christians who would have recoiled from the idea of concubinage permitted themselves to form one of these spiritual unions, and in so doing fell. It is very certain that the canon of Nicæa forbids this species of union, but the context shows moreover that the Fathers had not these particular cases in view alone; and the expression συνείσακτος should be understood of every woman who is introduced (συνείσακτος) into the house of a clergyman for the purpose of living there. If by the word συνείσακτος was only intended the wife in this spiritual marriage, the Council would not have said, any συνείσακτος except his mother, etc.; for neither his mother nor his sister could have formed this spiritual union with the cleric. The injunction, then, does not merely forbid the συνείσακτος in the specific sense, but orders that "no woman must live in the house of a cleric, unless she be his mother," etc. Because this interpretation presents itself naturally to the mind, several ancient authors have read in the Greek text ἐπείσακτον instead of συνείσακτον; for instance, the Emperor Justinian in his Novel 123 (c. 29), and Rufinus in his translation of the canon. Several councils, amongst others the second of Tours (c. 11) and the fourth of Toledo (c. 42), have also received this reading, but wrongly, as is proved by the best Greek manuscripts. Beveridge, S. Basil, and Dionysius the Less read συνείσακτον with us. On the meaning of the last words of this canon, it has been doubted whether the Council allows all persons who are free from suspicion to live in the house of a clerk, as it is understood by Gratian; or whether the true translation is this: "And his sisters and aunts cannot remain unless they be free from all suspicion." Van Espen explains the text in this manner, but this interpretation does not seem altogether in accordance with the original.

Another question has been raised on this subject,—namely, whether it supposes the marriage of priests, or whether it orders celibacy, and then the real wives of clerics would be included in the word συνείσακτοι. This last interpretation is that of Bellarmin; but it is without foundation, for the συνείσακτοι are here forbidden to all clerks, and we know that at this period those in minor orders were permitted to marry. In conclusion, it cannot be overlooked that this canon shows that the practice of celibacy had already spread to a great extent among the clergy; as even Fuchs confesses, and as Natalis Alexander has also remarked. The question of the relation of the Council of Nicæa to celibacy will be considered when we come to the history of Paphnutius.

CAN. 4

Ἐπίσκοπον προσήκει μάλιστα μὲν ὑπὸ πάντων τῶν ἐν τῇ ἐπαρχίᾳ καθίστασθαι· εἰ δὲ δυσχερὲς εἴη τὸ τοιοῦτο, ἢ διὰ κατεπείγουσαν ἀνάγκην ἢ διὰ μῆκος ὁδοῦ, ἐξάπαντος τρεῖς ἐπὶ τὸ αὐτὸ συναγομένους, συμψήφων γινομένων καὶ τῶν ἀπόντων καὶ συντιθεμένων διὰ γραμμάτων, τότε τὴν χειροτονίαν ποιεῖσθαι· τὸ δὲ κῦρος τῶν γινομένων δίδοσθαι καθ' ἑκάστην ἐπαρχίαν τῷ μητροπολίτῃ.

"The bishop shall be appointed by all (the bishops) of the eparchy (province); if that is not possible on account of pressing necessity, or on account of the length of journeys, three (bishops) at the least shall meet, and proceed to the imposition of hands (consecration) with the permission of those absent in writing. The confirmation of what has been done belongs by right, in each eparchy, to the metropolitan."

The Church was not obliged in principle to conform itself to the territorial divisions of the states or of the provinces in establishing its own territorial divisions. If, however, it often accepted these civil divisions as models for its own, it was to facilitate the conduct of business, and to prevent any disruption of received customs. Thus the apostles often passed through the principal cities of one province for the purpose of preaching the gospel there before entering another, and afterwards they treated the faithful of that province as forming one community. For instance, S. Paul writes to the Church of God at Corinth, and to all the faithful of Achaia: he unites, then, in his thoughts all the Christians of the province of Achaia, and at the head of the Churches of that province he places that of Corinth, which was its political capital. He addresses in the same manner another of his letters "to the Churches of the Galatians," again uniting in his mind all the communities of that civil province. The result of this action of the Church was, that the bishops of the same province soon considered that there was a certain bond between them, and the bishop of the capital thus gained insensibly a sort of pre-eminence over his colleagues in the province. This pre-eminence could only be based in some cases on the civil importance of the capital; but it must not be forgotten that the civil capital was often also the ecclesiastical, as being the first city in the province in which a Christian Church was founded, from which the gospel was made known to the other cities in the province. It is especially the civil importance that the Synod of Antioch of 341 had in view when it said, in its ninth canon: "The bishops of each eparchy must understand that it is the bishop of the metropolis (political capital) who has charge of the business of the eparchy, because all meet at the metropolis to transact their business." The word eparchy here most certainly designates the civil province; and evidently the

Synod wished to make the civil divisions the basis of ecclesiastical divisions. The Council of Nicæa follows the same course: it orders in this fourth canon that a bishop shall be chosen by the other bishops of the whole eparchy (political province); and in accordance with the ninth canon of the Synod of Antioch, it decides that the metropolitan shall have charge of the business of the eparchy. The first remark that there is to make on this canon is, then, to point out that the Council of Nicæa accepts the political division as the basis of the ecclesiastical division; but there were afterwards exceptions to this rule.

The second remark relates to the method of proceeding in the election of bishops. In apostolic times the apostles themselves chose the bishops. During the period immediately after apostolic times it was the disciples of the apostles, ἐλλόγιμοι ἄσδρες, as S. Clement calls them. Thus such men as Titus and Timothy nominated bishops; but the election had to be approved by the whole community, συνευδοκησάσης τῆς ἐκκλησίας πάσης, as S. Clement says again; so that here a new agent appears in the choice of a bishop: the community has to make known whether it considers the person elected fitted or unfitted for the charge. After the death of the disciples of the apostles this practice changed; there were no longer any bishops who had such an uncontested ascendency over the others. A letter of S. Cyprian tells us in a very clear manner how episcopal elections and consecrations were then carried on. "In almost all provinces," he writes, "the business is managed in this manner: The nearest bishops in the province meet in the city for which the election is to be held. The bishop is then elected plebe præsente; the people are bound to be present at the election, for singulorum vitam plenissime novit. The episcopal dignity is after that conferred universæ fraternitatis suffragio and episcoporum judicio." Beveridge has explained this very important passage in the following manner. The bishops of the province choose their future colleague, and the fraternitas—that is to say, the people and the clergy of the city—decide whether the choice is acceptable, whether the candidate is worthy of the episcopate. It seems to me that Beveridge thus does violence to the expression suffragio, and does not quite accurately translate judicio. Suffragium is derived from sub and frango. It properly means a fragment—a shred or scrap—and refers to the shell which the ancients used for voting in the assemblies of the people. This expression, then, ought here to signify that the people, the community, had the right of noting, but that the right of deciding—the judicium—was reserved to the bishops of the province. Van Espen gives the same explanation that we do in his canon law. The fraternitas, he says—that is to say, the clergy and people of the community—who are interested in the choice had the right of presentation; the bishops had afterwards to decide. They had then the principal part to perform. In certain cases the bishops elected and consecrated a candidate sine prævia plebis electione—for instance, when the people would undoubtedly have made a bad choice. As it was by the judicium of the bishops that the new bishop was appointed, so it was also their duty to consecrate the newly elected.

The Council of Nicæa thought it necessary to define by precise rules the duties of the bishops who took part in these episcopal elections. It decided, (a) that a single bishop of the province was not sufficient for the appointment of another; (b) three at the least should meet, and (c) they were not to proceed to election without the written permission of the absent bishops; it was necessary (d) to obtain afterwards the approval of the metropolitan. The Council then accepts the ordinary division according to the metropolis: it accepts it as far as the nomination and ordination of bishops is concerned, and it grants certain rights to the metropolitan. The principal result of this division—namely, the provincial synod—will be considered under the next canon.

Meletius was probably the occasion of this canon. It may be remembered that he had nominated bishops without the concurrence of the other bishops of the province, and without the approval of the metropolitan of Alexandria, and had thus occasioned a schism. This canon was intended to prevent the recurrence of such abuses. The question has been raised as to whether the fourth canon speaks only of the choice of the bishop, or whether it also treats of the consecration of the newly elected. We think, with Van Espen, that it treats equally of both,—as well of the part which the bishops of the province should take in an episcopal election, as of the consecration which completes it.

The Council of Nicæa had a precedent in the first apostolic canon, and in the twentieth canon of Arles, for the establishment of this rule. The canon of Nicæa was afterwards in its turn reproduced and renewed by many councils,—by that of Laodicea (c. 12), of Antioch (c. 19), by the fourth Synod of Toledo (c. 19), the second of Nicæa (c. 13): it is also reproduced in the Codex Ecclesiæ Afric. (c.

13). It has been put into execution in the Greek Church as well as in the Latin Church, and inserted in all collections of ecclesiastical laws, especially in the Corpus juris canonici.

It has been, however, interpreted in different ways. The Greeks had learnt by bitter experience to distrust the interference of princes and earthly potentates in episcopal elections. Accordingly, they tried to prove that this canon of Nicæa took away from the people the right of voting at the nomination of a bishop, and confined the nomination exclusively to the bishops of the province. In order to obtain a solid ground for this practice, the seventh Œcumenical Council held at Nicæa (c. 3) interpreted the canon before us in the sense that a bishop could be elected only by bishops; and it threatens with deposition any one who should attempt to gain, by means of the temporal authority, possession of a bishopric. One hundred years later, the eighth Œcumenical Council enforces the same rule, and decides, in accordance "with former councils," that a bishop must not be elected except by the college of bishops. The Greek commentators, Balsamon and others, therefore, only followed the example of these two great Councils in affirming that this fourth canon of Nicæa takes away from the people the right previously possessed of voting in the choice of bishops, and makes the election depend entirely on the decision of the bishops of the province.

The Latin Church acted otherwise. It is true that with it also the people have been removed from episcopal elections, but this did not happen till later, about the eleventh century; and it was not the people only who were removed, but the bishops of the province as well, and the election was conducted entirely by the clergy of the cathedral church. The Latins then interpreted the canon of Nicæa as though it said nothing of the rights of the bishops of the province in the election of their future colleague (and it does not speak of it in a very explicit manner), and as though it determined these two points only: (a) that for the ordination of a bishop three bishops at least are necessary; (b) that the right of confirmation rests with the metropolitan. In the Latin Church this right of confirmation passed in course of time from the metropolitans to the Pope, particularly by the concordats of Aschaffenburg.

CAN. 5

Περὶ τῶν ἀκοινωνήτων γενομένων, εἴτε τῶν ἐν τῷ κλήρῳ εἴτε ἐν λαϊκῷ τάγματι, ὑπὸ τῶν καθ᾽ ἑκάστην ἐπαχίαν ἐπισκόπων κρατείτω ἡ γνώμη κατὰ τὸν κανόνα τὸν διαγορεύοντα, τοὺς ὑφ᾽ ἑτέρων ἀποβληθέντας ὑφ᾽ ἑτέρων μὴ προσίεσθαι. ἐξεταζέθω δέ, μὴ μικροψυχίᾳ ἢ φιλονεικίᾳ ἤ τινι τοιαύτῃ ἀηδίᾳ τοῦ ἐπισκόπου ἀποσυνάγωγοι γεγέννηται. ἵνα οὖν τοῦτο τὴν πρέπουσαν ἐξέτασιν λαμβάνῃ, καλῶς ἔχειν ἔδοξεν, ἑκάστου εὐιαυτοῦ καθ᾽ ἑκάστην ἐπαρχίαν δὶς τοῦ ἔτους συνόδους γίνεσθαι, ἵνα κοινῇ πάντων τῶν ἐπισκόπων τῆς ἐπαρχίας ἐπὶ τὸ αὐτὸ συναγομένων, τὰ τοιαῦτα ζητήματα ἐξετάζοιτο, καὶ οὕτως οἱ ὁμολογουμένως προσκεκρουκότες τῷ ἐπισκόπῳ κατὰ λόγον ἀκοινώνητοι παρὰ πᾶσιν εἶναι δόξωσι, μέχρις ἂν τῷ κοινῷ τῶν ἐπισκόπων δόξῃ τὴν φιλανθρωποτέραν ὑπὲρ αὐτῶν ἐκθέσθαι ψῆφον• αἱ δὲ σύνοδοι γινέσθωσαν, μία μὲν πρὸ τῆς τεσσαρακοστῆς, ἵνα πάσης μικροψυχίας ἀναιρουμένης τὸ δῶρον καθαρὸν προσφέρηται τῷ Θεῷ, δευτέρα δὲ περὶ τὸν τοῦ μετοπώρου καιρόν.

"As regards the excommunicated, the sentence passed by the bishops of each province shall have the force of law, in conformity with the canon which says: He who has been excommunicated by some should not be admitted by others. Care must, however, be taken to see that the bishop has not passed this sentence of excommunication from narrow-mindedness, from a love of contradiction, or from some feeling of hatred. In order that such an examination may take place, it has appeared good to order that in each province a synod shall be held twice a year, composed of all the bishops of the province: they will make all necessary inquiries that each may see that the sentence of excommunication has been justly passed on account of some determined disobedience, and until the assembly of bishops may be pleased to pronounce a milder judgment on them. These synods are to be held, the one before Lent, in order that, having put away all low-mindedness, we may present a pure offering to God, and the second in the autumn."

As we have already remarked, the Council in this canon again takes as a basis divisions by metropolitan provinces, by instituting provincial synods; and it lays down for them one part of the business which should occupy them.

Before the Council of Nicæa, ecclesiastical law had already forbidden that any one who had been excommunicated should be admitted by another bishop; the twelfth (thirteenth) apostolical canon even threatens a bishop who should do so with excommunication. This rule of the

Council of Nicæa, that a sentence of excommunication passed by a bishop should be examined by a provincial synod which had the right to annul it, is found, if not literally, at least in sense, in the thirty-sixth apostolic canon (thirty-eighth), which says that a provincial synod should decide those ecclesiastical questions which are in dispute. This same apostolical canon orders very explicitly that two provincial synods shall be held every year, but it does not appoint the same seasons as the canon of the Council of Nicæa. It might be supposed at first sight, that according to the ordinance of Nicæa, a provincial synod is only required to make inquiries about the force of sentences of excommunication which have been passed; but it may be seen that the Œcumenical Council held at Constantinople has correctly explained this canon, in saying that it entrusts the provincial Council with the care of examining into the whole affairs of the province.

Gelasius has given, in his history of the Council of Nicæa, the text of the canons passed by the Council; and it must be noticed that there is here a slight difference between his text and ours. Our reading is as follows: "The excommunication continues to be in force until it seem good to the assembly of bishops (τῷ κοινῷ) to soften it." Gelasius, on the other hand, writes: μέχρις ἄν τῷ κοινῷ ἤ τῷ ἐπισκόπῳ, κ.τ.λ., that is to say, "until it seem good to the assembly of bishops, or to the bishop (who has passed the sentence)," etc.... Dionysius the Less has also followed this variation, as his translation of the canon shows. It does not change the essential meaning of the passage; for it may be well understood that the bishop who has passed the sentence of excommunication has also the right to mitigate it. But the variation adopted by the Prisca alters, on the contrary, the whole sense of the canon: the Prisca has not τῷ κοινῷ, but only ἐπισκόπῳ: it is in this erroneous form that the canon has passed into the Corpus juris can. The latter part of the canon, which treats of provincial councils, has been inserted by Gratian.

CAN. 6

Τὰ ἀρχαῖα ἔθη κρατείτω τὰ ἐν Αἰγύπτῳ καὶ Λιβύῃ καὶ Πενταπόλει, ὥστε τὸν Ἀλεξανδρείας ἐπίσκοπον πάντων τούτων ἔχειν τὴν ἐξουσίαν, ἐπειδὴ καὶ τῷ ἐν τῇ Ῥώμῃ ἐπισκόπῳ τοῦτο σύνηθές ἐστιν· ὁμοίως δὲ καὶ κατὰ Ἀντιόχειαν καὶ ἐν ταῖς ἄλλαις ἐπαρχίαις τὰ πρεσβεῖα σώζεσθαι ταῖς ἐκκλησίαις· καθόλου δὲ πρόδηλον ἐκεῖνο, ὅτι εἴ τις χωρὶς γνώμης τοῦ μητροπολίτου γένοιτο ἐπίσκοπος, τὸν τοιοῦτον ἡ μεγάλη σύνοδος ὥρισε μὴ δεῖν εἶναι ἐπίσκπον· ἐὰν μέντοι τῇ κοινῇ πάντων ψήφῳ, εὐλόγῳ οὔσῃ καὶ κατὰ κανόνα ἐκκλησιαστικὸν, δύο ἢ τρεῖς δι᾿ οἰκείαν φιλονεικίαν ἀντιλέγωσι, κρατείτω ἡ τῶν πλειόνων ψῆφος.

"The old custom in use in Egypt, in Libya, and in Pentapolis, should continue to exist, that is, that the bishop of Alexandria should have jurisdiction over all these (provinces); for there is a similar relation for the Bishop of Rome. The rights which they formerly possessed must also be preserved to the Churches of Antioch and to the other eparchies (provinces). This is thoroughly plain, that if any one has become a bishop without the approval of the metropolitan, the great Synod commands him not to remain a bishop. But when the election has been made by all with discrimination, and in a manner conformable to the rules of the Church, if two or three oppose from pure love of contradiction, it will be carried by the majority."

I. The fourth and fifth canons had determined the rights of provincial councils and of ordinary metropolitans; the sixth canon is taken up with the recognition and regulation of an institution of a higher order of the hierarchy. It is most clear from the words of the canon, that the Synod had no intention of introducing anything new. It desires that the ancient tradition should be preserved, by which the Bishop of Alexandria had jurisdiction over Egypt (in the narrower sense of the word), Libya, and Pentapolis.

It is very evident that it is an exceptional position that had been already given to the Bishop of Alexandria, which is recognised and ratified by the Council. The Bishop of Alexandria had not alone under his jurisdiction one civil province, like the other metropolitans, of whom the fourth canon has already treated: he had several provinces depending upon him,—Egypt (properly so called), and to the west two other provinces, Libya (Libya sicca vel inferior) and Pentapolis, or Cyrenia (situated to the west of Libya, which separates it from Egypt properly so called). There is, of necessity, attached to these provinces the Thebaïs, or Upper Egypt, which at the time of the Council of Nicæa was certainly under the jurisdiction of the Bishop of Alexandria. Our canon does not specially name it, because it includes it in Egypt, whose limits are not, as may be seen, very exactly determined by the Fathers of Nicæa. The four provinces here named formed, at the time of the Synod, the diocese (political division) of Egypt, or Egypt taken in its largest signification; some time after the diocese was divided into six provinces—Pentapolis (Libya superior), Libya inferior, Thebaïs, Egypt, Augustamnica (the eastern part of Egypt), and Arcadia or Eptanomis (Middle Egypt).

These explanations prove that the sense of the first words of the canon is as follows: "This ancient right is assigned to the Bishop of Alexandria, which places under his jurisdiction the whole diocese of Egypt." It is without any reason, then, that the French Protestant Salmasius (Saumaise), the Anglican Beveridge, and the Gallican Launoy, try to show that the Council of Nicæa granted to the Bishop of Alexandria only the rights of ordinary metropolitans.

But since it is evident that an exceptional position is appointed for him, we must now ask in what this position consisted. Two cases here present themselves:—

a. The four civil provinces, Egypt; Libya, Pentapolis, and Thebaïs, might be united into a single ecclesiastical province, of which the Bishop of Alexandria would be declared the sole metropolitan. This supposition has been · adopted by Van Espen.

b. Or else each one of these civil provinces might form an ecclesiastical province, and have its metropolitan, whilst the Archbishop of Alexandria (who was metropolitan of the province of Egypt, taken in its narrower signification) had a certain ecclesiastical supremacy over the civil diocese, so that the other metropolitans (that is to say, those of Pentapolis, of Thebaïs, and of Libya) would be under his jurisdiction. At the time of the Council of Nicæa there was no particular title to describe the chief metropolitan, who was usually called at a later period Patriarch or Exarch.

It seems to me beyond a doubt, that in this canon there is a question about that which was afterwards called the patriarchate of the Bishop of Alexandria; that is to say, that he had a certain recognised ecclesiastical authority, not only over several civil provinces, but also over several ecclesiastical provinces (which had their own metropolitan): it is in this sense that Valesius in earlier times, and in our days Phillips and Maassen, have interpreted the sixth canon of Nicæa. The reasons for this explanation are:—

(α.) The general rule, confirmed by the fourth canon of the Council of Nicæa, determined that each civil province should be an ecclesiastical province as well, and that it should have its metropolitan. Now nothing proves that Libya, Pentapolis, and Thebaïs were an exception to this general rule, and had no metropolitans of their own.

(β.) According to S. Epiphanius, Meletius was ἀρχιεπίσκοπος of the province of Thebaïs; and according to the same author, he had the first place after the Archbishop of Alexandria, over all the bishops of Egypt. Although the title of ἀρχιεπίσκοπος was not in use in the time of Meletius, Epiphanius does not hesitate to make use of it in accordance with the usage of his own time, and to show by it that he considers Meletius as the metropolitan of the Thebaïs; but as, in his account of the history of the Meletian schism, S. Epiphanius has made serious mistakes, we do not, as we have shown elsewhere, attach much importance to his testimony.

(γ.) We find a letter of Synesius to Theophilus Archbishop of Alexandria, in which he says, "that S. Athanasius having discovered in Siderius, formerly Bishop of Palæbisca and

Hydrax, a capacity for higher functions, had translated him to Ptolemais in Pentapolis, to govern the metropolitan church there." As this Synesius was Bishop of Ptolemais at the beginning of the fifth century, his assertion, which bears witness to the fact that this city was at the time of S. Athanasius, and consequently at the time of the Council of Nicæa, an ecclesiastical metropolis, is of the greatest value.

(δ.) Other passages of this letter of Synesius, in particular the following passage, show that Ptolemais was in reality formerly an ecclesiastical metropolis: "He was reproached with not having sufficiently guarded the maternal rights of his city (τὰ μητρῷα τῆς πόλεως δίκαια), that is to say, the rights of his metropolitan church, against the Bishop of Alexandria."

(ε.) Synesius acted also repeatedly as metropolitan of Pentapolis. He brought together the other bishops of the province, and gave his consent to the choice of a new bishop; thus making use of a right that the fourth canon of Nicæa accorded to a metropolitan.

(ζ.) Finally, we may appeal to the Emperor Theodosius II., who, in a letter dated March 30, 449, gave orders to Dioscurus Bishop of Alexandria to present himself at Ephesus for the great Synod (that which was known later as the Latrocinium Ephesinum), with the ten metropolitans who belonged to his diocese.

It is, then, incontestable that the civil provinces of Egypt, Libya, Pentapolis, and Thebaïs, which were all in subjection to the Bishop of Alexandria, were also ecclesiastical provinces with their own metropolitans; and consequently it is not the ordinary rights of metropolitans that the sixth canon of Nicæa confirms to the Bishop of Alexandria, but the rights of a superior metropolitan, that is, of a patriarch. We are able to define in what these rights consisted:—

a. The Bishop of Alexandria ordained not only the metropolitans who were subject to him, but also their suffragans; while the ordinary rule was, that the suffragans should be ordained by their own metropolitans.

b. But the Bishop of Alexandria could only (as patriarch) ordain those whose election had the consent of the immediate metropolitan, that is, of the metropolitan in whose province he found himself. The letter of Synesius again proves this, in which he requests Theophilus Patriarch of Alexandria to consecrate the new Bishop of Olbia in Pentapolis. After making the request, Synesius adds this phrase: "I moreover give my vote for this man" (Φέρω κἀγὼ τὴν ἐμαυτοῦ ψῆφον ἐπὶ τὸν ἄνδρα).

Finally, we shall see a little further on that this sixth canon also decreed measures to prevent the rights of simple metropolitans being completely absorbed in the privileges of the patriarchs.

II. The sixth canon of Nicæa acknowledged for the Bishop of Antioch the rights which it had acknowledged for the Bishop of Alexandria; that is, as it would be expressed at a later period, the rights attached to a patriarchate. The second canon of the Council of Constantinople, held in 381, proves that the patriarchate of the Bishop of Antioch was identical with the civil diocese of Oriens. This diocese of Oriens contained, according to the Notitia dignitatum, fifteen civil provinces: Palæstina, Fœnice, Syria, Cilicia, Cyprus, Arabia, Isauria Palæstina salutaris, Palæstina (ii.), Fœnice Lybani, Eufratensis, Syria salutaris, Osrhoëna, Cilicia (ii.).

Whatever might be the number of civil provinces that the diocese of Oriens contained at the time of the Council of Nicæa, it is not less certain that, in the canon before us, a supremacy was acknowledged for the Bishop of Antioch, extending to several provinces which had their own metropolitans. Thus, for example, Palestine acknowledged as its metropolitan the Bishop of Cæsarea, as we shall see in the seventh canon of the Council of Nicæa; but the metropolitan of Cæsarea, in his turn, was under the jurisdiction of the Bishop of Antioch, as his superior metropolitan (patriarch). S. Jerome says expressly that these rights of the Church of Antioch proceeded from the sixth canon of Nicæa, "in which it was ruled that Antioch should be the general metropolis of all Oriens, and Cæsarea the particular metropolis of the province of Palestine (which belonged to Oriens)." Pope Innocent I. wrote to Alexander Bishop of Antioch: "The Council of Nicæa has not established the Church of Antioch over a province, but over a diocese. As, then, in virtue of his exclusive authority, the Bishop of Antioch ordains metropolitans, it is not allowed that other bishops should hold ordinations without his knowledge and consent."

These passages show us in what the rights of the metropolitan of Antioch consisted: (α) He ordained the metropolitans immediately: (β) The other bishops, on the contrary, were ordained by their metropolitan, yet by his permission; whilst, as we have seen further back, the patriarchs of Alexandria ordained immediately the suffragan bishops also.

III. For the support of its rule, the Council of Nicæa points out that the Bishop of Rome has also rights analogous to those which it acknowledges for the Bishop of Alexandria (and for the Bishop of Antioch). It is evident that the Council has not in view here the primacy of the Bishop of Rome over the whole Church, but simply his power as a patriarch; for only in relation to this could any analogy be established between Rome and Alexandria or Antioch. This subject will be considered more in detail further on.

IV. After having confirmed the claim of the three great metropolitan cities of Rome, Alexandria, and Antioch to patriarchal rights, our canon adds: "The rights (πρεσβεῖα) of the Churches in the other eparchies must also be preserved." The question is, What is here understood by the words, "the Churches of the other eparchies?" Salmasius and others think that the question in point here is about ordinary ecclesiastical provinces and their metropolitan cities; but Valesius, Dupin, Maassen and others have maintained that this passage relates to the three superior eparchies (sensu eminenti) of Pontus, proconsular Asia, and Thrace, which possessed similar rights to those of the patriarchal Churches of Rome, Alexandria, and Antioch, and which later were usually called exarchates. The metropolitan cities of these three eparchies, sensu eminenti, were Ephesus for proconsular Asia, Cæsarea in Cappadocia for Pontus, and Heraclea (afterwards Constantinople) for Thrace. The Council of Constantinople, held in 381, speaks of these three exceptional metropolitan cities; and for my own part, I see no difficulty in believing that the Council of Nicæa also speaks of them in this sentence: "The rights of the Churches must also be preserved in the other eparchies;" for (α) our canon does not speak of ordinary eparchies (that is to say, of simple metropolitan cities), but of those which have particular rights (πρεσβεῖα).

(β.) The word ὁμοίως shows that the Synod places these eparchies in the same rank as the sees of Alexandria and Antioch.

(γ.) It is very true that the sixth canon does not determine these other eparchies sensu eminenti; but as the second canon of the Council of Constantinople (381) groups these three sees of the eparchies of Pontus, Asia, and Thrace just in the same way as the Council of Nicæa had grouped the Churches of Rome, Antioch, and Alexandria, there can be no doubt that the Council of Nicæa had also in view these three eparchies sensu eminenti.

(δ.) This passage, taken from a letter of Theodoret to Pope Flavian, may also be quoted: "The Fathers of Constantinople had (by this second canon) followed the example of the Fathers of the Council of Nicæa, and separated the dioceses the one from the other." It follows from this, according to Theodoret, that the Synod of Nicæa had acknowledged as ecclesiastical provinces, distinct and governed by a superior metropolitan, the dioceses of Pontus, Asia, and Thrace (as it had done with regard to the dioceses of Rome, Alexandria, and Antioch); for, as the Council of Constantinople desired to separate the dioceses the one from the other, it is evidently necessary that the limits of these dioceses should be known, and that the three, patriarchates of Rome, Alexandria, and Antioch should not be the only ones distinct.

V. The sixth canon proceeds: "It is plain enough, that if any one has become a bishop without the approval of the metropolitan, the great Synod (of Nicæa) does not allow him to remain bishop." By metropolitan, Valesius understands patriarch, and explains the passage in this manner: "Without the consent of the patriarch, a bishop should never be instituted." Dupin and Maassen think, on the contrary, that the question is here that of an ordinary metropolitan, and explain the sentence in this manner: "In those ecclesiastical provinces which form part of a patriarchate, care must be taken to preserve the rights of the simple metropolitan, and for that reason no person can be made a bishop without the consent of his immediate metropolitan; that is to say, the patriarch himself cannot ordain any one without the consent of the metropolitan of the future bishop."

This explanation shows why the Synod of Nicæa repeats in its sixth canon this sentence already inserted in the fourth: "No one can be made a bishop without the consent of his metropolitan."

VI. According to what has been said, the end of the sixth canon, "When, from a mere spirit of contradiction, two or three oppose an election which has been made by all, and which is at the same time reasonable and in accordance with the rules of the Church, the majority must prevail," should be explained in this manner: "When any one has been elected bishop by the majority of the clergy and of the bishops of the province, and with the consent of the metropolitan and of the patriarch, then," etc.

VII. This sixth canon was possibly the result of the Meletian schism; for, as it is a fact that these schismatics slighted the rights of the Bishop of Alexandria, this confusion probably decided the Synod of Nicæa to define clearly the rights of that bishop.

VIII. It may now be seen how clear and intelligible the sense of this sixth canon is, and yet it has been the object of the most wide-spread controversies.

1. The first question is, What is the value of the canon before us with respect to the Catholic doctrine of the Papacy? And while some have desired to see in it a confirmation of the doctrine of the Roman primacy, others have adduced it as a weapon against the primacy of the Holy See. Phillips remarks with justice, in speaking of this canon: "It is evident that this canon cannot be used to demonstrate the primacy of the Pope; for the Council of Nicæa did not speak of the primacy, which had no need of being established or confirmed by the Council of Nicæa."

It must not be forgotten that the Pope unites in himself several ecclesiastical dignities: he is bishop, metropolitan, patriarch, and lastly, primate of the whole Church. Each one of these dignities may be regarded separately, and that is what the canon has done: it does not consider the Pope as primate of the universal Church, nor as simple Bishop of Rome; but it treats him as one of the great metropolitans, who had not merely one province, but several, under their jurisdiction.

2. There has also been a question as to what extent was
given to this metropolitan diocese of Rome by the Council
of Nicæa; but the very text of the canon shows that the
Council of Nicæa decided nothing on this point: it is
content to ratify and confirm the order of existing things.
There has been a great conflict of opinions to explain in
what this order of things consisted. The translation of this
canon by Rufinus has been especially an apple of discord.
Et ut apud Alexandriam et in urbe Roma vetusta
consuetudo servetur, ut vel ille Ægypti vel hic
suburbicariarum ecclesiarum sollicitudinem gerat. In the
seventeenth century this sentence of Rufinus gave rise to a
very lively discussion between the celebrated jurist Jacob
Gothfried (Gothofredus) and his friend Salmasius on one
side, and the Jesuit Sirmond on the other. The great
prefecture of Italy, which contained about a third of the
whole Roman Empire, was divided into four vicariates,
among which the vicariate of Rome was the first. At its
head were two officers, the præfectus urbi and the vicarius
urbis. The præfectus urbi exercised authority over the city
of Rome, and further in a suburban circle as far as the
hundredth milestone. The boundary of the vicarius urbis
comprised ten provinces—Campania, Tuscia with Ombria,
Picenum, Valeria, Samnium, Apulia with Calabria, Lucania,
and Brutii, Sicily, Sardinia and Corsica. Gothfried and
Salmasius maintained, that by the regiones suburbicariæ the
little territory of the præfectus urbi must be understood;
whilst, according to Sirmond, these words designate the
whole territory of the vicarius urbis. In our time Dr.
Maassen has proved. in his book, already quoted several
times, that Gothfried and Salmasius were right in
maintaining that, by the regiones suburbicariæ, the little

territory of the præfectus urbi must be alone understood. But, on the other hand, according to Maassen, it is a complete mistake to suppose the patriarchal power of the Bishop of Rome restricted to this little territory.

The sixth canon of Nicæa proves that it was not so; for, on comparing the situation of the two Churches of Alexandria and of Rome, it evidently supposes that the patriarchate of Rome extended over several provinces. In fact, the ten provinces composing the territory of the vicarius urbis, and which were hundreds of times larger than the regio suburbicaria, did not contain all the territory over which the authority of the Pope as patriarch extended; for, in our days, Phillips has proved, by reference to the work of Benetti (Privilegia S. Petri), that the Bishop of Rome had the right of ordaining bishops, and consequently the rights of a patriarch, over other countries than those which are contained in the ten provinces of the vicarius urbis. If the question is put in this way, it must be said, either that Rufinus does not identify the ecclesiæ suburbicariæ with the regiones suburbicariæ, or that he is mistaken if he has done so. Phillips thinks that Rufinus has not really fallen into this error. Having remarked that the provinciæ suburbicariæ (that is to say, the ten provinces enumerated above) took their name from the vicarius urbis, he considered that the ecclesiæ suburbicariæ also took theirs from the episcopus urbis; and he has comprised under this name of ecclesiæ suburbicariæ all the churches which form part of the Roman patriarchate.

For my part, I willingly believe that the expression of Rufinus is inaccurate; for the Prisca (an old Latin translation of the canons) translates the passage of our

canon in question as follows: Antiqui moris est, ut urbis
Romæ episcopus habeat principatum, ut suburbicaria loca
ET OMNEM PROVINCIAM SUAM sollicitudine
gubernet; (a) understanding by suburbicaria loca the little
territory of the præfectus urbi, but (b) not restricting the
authority of the Pope as patriarch within the limits of this
territory; and therefore it adds, et omnem provinciam suam.

But what was in fact the extent of this patriarchate of the
Church of Rome?

The Greek commentators Zonaras and Balsamon (of the
twelfth century) say very explicitly, in their explanation of
the canons of Nicæa, that this sixth canon confirms the
rights of the Bishop of Rome as patriarch over the whole
West. We see, then, that even the Greek schismatics of
former times admitted that the Roman patriarchate
embraced the entire West, as the following testimonies and
considerations prove:—

a. Mention is made a hundred times by the ancients, of the
patriarchates into which the Churches of the East were
divided (Alexandria, Antioch, etc.); but no one has ever
hinted at the existence of a second patriarchate of the West.
On the contrary, it may be seen that in all the West there
was only one patriarchate.

b. S. Augustine shows that the Bishop of Rome was looked
upon as this Patriarch of all the West, for he gives to Pope
Innocent I. the title of "President of the Church of the
West."

c. S. Jerome gives the same testimony. He writes to the
presbyter Mark, "that he was accused of heresy on account

of his clinging to the homoousios, and that this charge had been carried to the West and into Egypt; that is to say, to Damasus Bishop of Rome, and to Peter (Bishop of Alexandria)." It may be seen that, as the Bishop of Alexandria is here regarded as Patriarch of Egypt, so the Bishop of Rome is considered the Patriarch of the West.

d. The Synod of Arles, held in 314, speaks in the same way. In a letter to Pope Sylvester, it says to him: Qui majores diœceses tenes. It considers, then, that the Bishop of Rome has under his jurisdiction several (civil) dioceses, while the other patriarchs had, as we have seen, only one.

e. We may finally appeal to the authority of the Emperor Justinian, who in his 119th Novel, speaking of the ecclesiastical division of the whole world, numbers five patriarchates: those of Rome, of Constantinople, of Alexandria, of Antioch, and of Jerusalem. Now, as these four last patriarchates contain only the Church of the East, it is evident that the patriarchate of Rome contains in itself alone all the West.

The Roman patriarchate contained, then, eight dioceses, which at the beginning of the sixteenth century were divided into sixty-eight provinces; and although, at the accession of Theodosius the Great—that is to say, in 378—Eastern Illyricum ceased to form part of the Empire of the West, and was joined to that of the East, yet the provinces of this prefecture continued to be joined to Rome for ecclesiastical purposes, and a special papal vicar was charged with the ecclesiastical government of these dioceses. The first of these vicars was Bishop Ascholius of Thessalonica, appointed by Pope Damasus.

It must not, lastly, be overlooked that the Bishop of Rome did not exercise in an equal degree, over the whole West, the full rights of patriarch; for in several provinces simple bishops were ordained without his consent. On the other hand, the Pope exercised his patriarchal right in convoking at different renewals the general and private synods of the Western Church (synodos occidentales)—for example, the Synod of Arles in 314—and in making himself the judge of the metropolitans of the West, either directly or indirectly, as in Illyricum by his vicar.

In some ancient Latin translations, this canon begins with the words, Ecclesia Romana semper habuit primatum; and this variation is also found in the Prisca. So the Emperor Valentinian III., in his edict of 445 on the subject of Hilary of Arles, issued also in the name of his Eastern colleague Theodosius II., maintained that the holy Synod had confirmed the primacy of the Apostolic See. The Emperor Valentinian evidently makes allusion to the sixth canon of Nicæa; for at that time the second canon of the Council of Constantinople, held in 381, which speaks in the same sense, was not yet known at Rome.

It must be added that, at the time of the sixteenth session of the fourth Œcumenical Council at Chalcedon, the Roman legate Paschasinus read the sixth canon of Nicæa in the following manner: Quod Ecclesia Romana semper habuit primatum; teneat autem et Ægyptus, ut episcopus Alexandriæ omnium habeat potestatem, quoniam et Romano episcopo hæc est consuetudo.

The actual text of the acts of the Council of Chalcedon proves that the translation given by Paschasinus was placed over against the Greek text of the sixth canon of Nicæa. An attempt has been made to see in this juxtaposition a protest of the Synod against the Roman translation; but even if it is admitted that the portion of the acts which gives these two texts is perfectly authentic, it is very evident that the legate Paschasinus had no intention, in quoting the sixth canon of Nicæa, to demonstrate the primacy of the Holy See: he only desires to prove that the Bishop of Constantinople ought not to take precedence of those of Antioch and Alexandria, because that would be a violation of the canon of Nicæa. It was not the words of the translation of Paschasinus with reference to the see of Rome which engaged the attention of the Council; it was those which referred to the sees of Antioch and Alexandria, and those were very faithfully translated from the Greek. On the other hand, the Ballerini have shown in a nearly conclusive way, in their edition of the Works of S. Leo the Great, that the acts of Chalcedon have been interpolated, that the Greek text of the sixth canon of Nicæa must have been introduced by some later copyist, and that the text of Paschasinus was the only one which was read in the Synod. We shall return to this question in the history of the Council of Chalcedon.

It seems to us that Dr. Maassen goes too far, when he says that the Council of Chalcedon expressly confirmed the Roman interpretation of the sixth canon of Nicæa, and consequently its recognition of the Roman primacy. It is true that, after the reading of the Latin version of the canon in question, followed by the reading of the first, second, and third canons of Constantinople (of 381), the imperial commissioners who were present at the Synod made this declaration: "After what has been cited on both sides, we

acknowledge that the most ancient right of all (πρὸ πάντων
τὰ πρωτεῖα), and the pre-eminence (καὶ τὴν ἐξαίρετον
τιμὴν), belong to the Archbishop of old Rome; but that the
same pre-eminence of honour (τὰ πρεσβεῖα τῆς τιμῆς)
ought to be given to the Archbishop of new Rome."
Maassen has considered that, after these words of the
imperial commissioners, it may be concluded that the sixth
canon of the Council of Nicæa had already recognised, in
fact, the right of the Pope to take precedence of all other
bishops; but it was not so. The commissioners said: On
both sides, that is to say, in what the papal legate has read,
and in what has been read by the consistorial secretary
Constantine as well, the precedence of Rome is recognised.
This is the same as saying: This precedence, which we do
not in the least contest (there is no question, in fact, of
that), is set forth (a) in the Latin version of the sixth canon
of Nicæa, read by Paschasinus, and is contained (b) in the
canons of Constantinople read by Constantine. But the
imperial commissioners of the Synod go no further in their
declarations; and in particular, they have not declared that
the original text of the sixth canon of Nicæa—a text which
had not been read—contains affirmatively a recognition or
a confirmation of the primacy of the Pope.

But it will be said, How could the ancient translators of
these canons, as well as the legates of the Pope and
Emperors, suppose that the sixth canon of Nicæa included
a confirmation of the primacy of Rome? In answer to this
question, Dr. Maassen has put forward a theory, which we
produce simply as a theory: "The Fathers (of Nicæa)
confirmed the rights of each see (of Alexandria, of Antioch,
etc.). Why did they take as an example in their decree the

constitution of the Roman patriarchate? Why were they not content simply to give their sanction to those patriarchal rights without adducing this analogy? We cannot imagine a more striking proof of the deep respect that the Fathers of Nicæa had for the visible head of the Church; for no one will suppose that the simple confirmation by the Council of the rights of superior metropolitans would not be perfectly sufficient.... But that which was sufficient for mere law did not satisfy the Fathers of Nicæa: their own sentiments on the utility of the institution of patriarchates did not appear sufficient to influence their decree: they did not wish to present to the approbation of the Pope those decrees simply confirming the privileges of superior metropolitans. They preferred to refer to the fact that 'the Bishop of Rome already enjoyed the same position:' it was to show that at Rome an institution existed analogous to that which they wished to confirm. In reserving to himself a certain number of provinces which he might deal with in a peculiar manner, did not the Pope most clearly recognise it as necessary that the same should be the case with other Churches; and that a portion of the power which belonged exclusively to him in his position as chief pastor of the universal Church, should be committed to other bishops? The Bishop of Rome was then, strictly speaking, the founder of the institution of patriarchates (that is to say, he gave to certain patriarchs a portion of that power over the universal Church which belonged to him). He had himself given the type, that is, the motive, upon which the Fathers of Nicæa founded their canon. Can we wonder, then, that the most remote antiquity found in this canon, to use the expression of Pope Gelasius I., 'an unique and irrefragable testimony' in support of the primacy?"

The sixth canon of Nicæa has been inserted in the Corpus juris canonici, but there it has been divided into three smaller canons.

CAN. 7

Ἐπειδὴ συνήθεια κεκράτηκε καὶ παράδοσις ἀρχαῖα, ὥστε τὸν ἐν Αἰλίᾳ ἐπίσκοπον τιμᾶσθαι, ἐχέτω τὴν ἀκολουθίαν τῆς τιμῆς τῇ μητροπόλει σωζομένου τοῦ οἰκείου ἀξιώματος.

"As custom and ancient tradition show that the Bishop of Ælia ought to be honoured (in a special manner), he should have precedence; without prejudice, however, to the dignity which belongs to the metropolis."

Short as this canon is, its explanation presents great difficulties. One thing is certain: it is, that the Council desires to confirm an ancient right of the Bishop of Ælia, that is to say, of Jerusalem, to enjoy certain honours; but in what they consisted, and what must be understood by the words ἀκολουθία τῆς τιμῆς, we cannot easily determine.

If the city of Jerusalem had not been taken and destroyed by Titus, August 31st, in the seventieth year after Christ, it would certainly have had, in the organization and economy of the Church, a very distinguished place as the ancient Mother-Church of Christendom; but of old Jerusalem there remained only three towers and a portion of the city wall: all the rest was levelled with the ground, and the plough had passed over the ruins.

A short time after the year 70, certain Jewish and Christian colonists settled in the midst of these ruins, and built huts there, and even a little Christian church in the place, in which the first believers were in the habit of meeting after the ascension of Christ to celebrate the eucharistic feast. A short time after the commencement of the second century, the Emperor Hadrian had a new city built upon the ruins of Jerusalem, with a temple to Jupiter Capitolinus. He also gave the new city the name of Ælia Capitolina, in remembrance of this temple and of his own family. He peopled it with fresh colonists, after the entire exclusion of the Jews.

We find in this new city a large community of Christians, converts from heathenism, who had at their head the Bishop Marcus; but for two hundred years the name of Jerusalem appears no more in history. The new city was treated as though it had nothing in common with the old; there was even considerable difficulty in knowing and distinguishing the differences which existed between the one and the other. Thus it happened that the city of Hadrian had not the ecclesiastical rank which belonged by right to old Jerusalem. After Jerusalem had been destroyed by Titus, Cæsarea (Turris Stratonis), which had formerly been only the second city in the country, became the civil and ecclesiastical metropolis, and the, Bishop of Ælia was only a simple suffragan of the metropolitan of Cæsarea. But it might be foreseen that the reverence of all Christians for the holy places, sanctified by the life, sufferings, and death of our Lord, would contribute little by little to raise the importance of the old city, and consequently that of its Church and bishop; and thus it came to pass that the metropolitan of Cæsarea was gradually equalled, if not surpassed, by the dignity of the Holy City κατ' ἐξοχὴν,— without, however, the subordinate ecclesiastiaal position of the latter being altered. Towards the end of the second century the gradation was already so sensible, that at a Synod of Palestine the Bishop of Ælia occupied the presidency conjointly with the metropolitan of Cæsarea (secundo loco, it is true); as Eusebius, who was himself afterwards metropolitan of Cæsarea, plainly tells us in the fifth book and twenty-third chapter of his History: "At a Synod held on the subject of the Easter controversy in the time of Pope Victor, Theophilus of Cæsarea and Narcissus of Jerusalem were presidents." The same Eusebius shows us, in his fifth book and twenty-fifth chapter, how near in honour the Bishops of Jerusalem and Cæsarea were to each other; for, when writing a list of the bishops, he places Narcissus of Jerusalem before the metropolitan Theophilus of Cæsarea. It is true that in the twenty-second chapter he does the contrary. The synodal letter of the bishops assembled at Antioch in 269 on the subject of the errors of Paul of Samosata is very remarkable on this point. It is signed first by Helenus Bishop of Tarsus, immediately afterwards by Hymenæus Bishop of Jerusalem, whilst Theotecnus Bishop of Cæsarea signs only quarto loco. It must not, however, be hastily concluded from this that the Bishop of Jerusalem had already at this time priority of the metropolitan of Cæsarea; but it cannot be doubted that the entirely exceptional position in which he found himself would of necessity raise difficulties between himself and his metropolitan. It is this which probably induced the Synod of Nicæa to pass its seventh canon. The eminent De Marca, as well as other historians, have supposed that by this canon the Synod wished to grant the first place to the Bishop of Jerusalem, immediately after the three great Patriarchs of Rome, Alexandria, and Antioch, without altogether raising him to the rank of Patriarch, and leaving him subject to the jurisdiction of the metropolitan of Cæsarea. Marca explains in this way the words ἐχέτω τὴν ἀκολουθίαν τῆς τιμῆς: 1. He should have the honour (respectu honoris) of following immediately after the metropolitans of Rome, Alexandria, and Antioch; 2. The last words of the canon signify that the dignity which belongs to the metropolitan must not, however, be infringed. Marca appeals in support of his theory to an old translation by Dionysius the Less, and to another yet older translation which was composed for the Synod of Carthage held in 419. But not one of these translations supports Marca, for not one of them gives any explanation of the words ἀκολουθία τῆς τιμῆς. Beveridge has especially taken it upon himself to refute Marca. A patriarch placed under the jurisdiction of a metropolitan is, according to him, an impossibility. He considers that, by the words ἐχέτω τὴν ἀκολουθίαν, the Council of Nicæa has simply desired to confirm to the Bishop of Jerusalem the first place after the metropolitan of Cæsarea, just as in the Anglican hierarchy the Bishop of London comes immediately after the Archbishop of Canterbury. Beveridge remarks on this, that it may be answered, that in this same Synod of Nicæa, where the bishops signed by provinces, Macarius Bishop of Jerusalem nevertheless signed before Eusebius the metropolitan of Cæsarea. Beveridge acknowledges the accuracy of this reply; but he adds that two other bishops of Palestine also signed before Eusebius, and yet no one will maintain that they were not under the jurisdiction of the metropolitan of Cæsarea. The signatures at the Council of Nicæa are not, then, conclusive. It might be added that, in these same signatures of the Council, the metropolitan of the province of Isauria is found signing in the fifth place, that is to say, after four of his suffragans; and even the metropolitan of Ephesus did not sign first among the bishops of Asia Minor (although Ephesus was one of the largest metropolitan cities of the Church): his name comes after that of the Bishop of Cyzicus.

A more remarkable incident is, that almost immediately after the Council of Nicæa, the Bishop of Jerusalem, Maximus, convoked, without any reference to the Bishop of Cæsarea, a Synod of Palestine, which pronounced in favour of S. Athanasius, and proceeded further to the consecration of bishops. Socrates, who records this fact, adds, it is true, that he was reprimanded for having so acted. But this fact shows that the Bishop of Jerusalem was endeavouring to make himself independent of the Bishop of Cæsarea. It may also be seen by the signatures of the second Œcumenical Synod, that Cyril Bishop of Jerusalem wrote his name before that of Thalassius Bishop of Cæsarea. And, on the other side, it is not less certain that in 395 John metropolitan of Cæsarea nominated Porphyrius, a priest of Jerusalem, Bishop of Gaza; and that the Synod of Diospolis, held in 415, was presided over by Eulogius metropolitan of Cæsarea, although John Bishop of Jerusalem was present at the Synod. These different researches show us that the question of precedence between the Bishops of Cæsarea and Jerusalem cannot be determined; for sometimes it is the Bishop of Cæsarea who is first, sometimes the Bishop of Jerusalem. This state of things lasted on to the time of the third Œcumenical Council held at Ephesus in 431. Juvenal Bishop of Jerusalem took a very prominent place, and signed immediately after Cyril of Alexandria (it is true the Bishop of Cæsarea in Palestine was not present). But this same Cyril was at this Synod a declared opponent of Juvenal; and when the latter wished by the help of false documents to have his ecclesiastical primacy over Palestine acknowledged by the Council, Cyril appealed on the subject to the authority of the Roman See. This same Juvenal Bishop of Jerusalem had attempted, after a long contest with Maximus Bishop of Antioch, to make himself a patriarch; and the Bishop of Antioch, weary of the controversy, determined that the three provinces of Palestine should be under the patriarchate of Jerusalem, whilst Phœnicia and Arabia should remain attached to the see of Antioch. The fourth Œcumenical Council held at Chalcedon ratified this division in its seventh session, without, as it appears, the least opposition being offered.

The last words of the seventh canon, τῇ μητροπόλει, κ.τ.λ., have also been explained in different ways. Most writers— and we share their opinion—think that these words designate the metropolis of Cæsarea; others have supposed that the question is about the metropolis of Antioch; but Fuchs has supposed that the reference is wholly to Jerusalem. According to him, the Council simply wished to show the reason of the existence of certain honours granted to this Church, because this metropolis (as an original Church) had a special dignity. This last theory clearly cannot be sustained: if the canon had this meaning, it would certainly have had a very different form. This seventh canon has been inserted in the Corpus juris canonici.

CAN. 8

Περὶ τῶν ὀνομαζόντων μὲν ἑαυτοὺς Καθαροὺς ποτε,
προσερχομένων δὲ τῇ καθολικῇ καὶ ἀποστολικῇ Ἐκκλησίᾳ,
ἔδοξε τῇ ἁγίᾳ καὶ μεγάλῃ συνόδῳ, ὥστε χειροθετουμένους
αὐτοὺς μένειν οὕτως ἐν τῷ κλήρῳ πρὸ πάντων δὲ τοῦτο
ὁμολογῆσαι αὐτοὺς ἐγγράφως προσήκει, ὅτι συνθήσονται καὶ
ἀκολουθήσουσι τοῖς τῆς καθολικῆς καὶ ἀποστολικῆς
Ἐκκλησίας δόγμασι• τοῦτ᾽ ἔστι καὶ διγάμοις κοινωνεῖν καὶ
τοῖς ἐν τῷ διωγμῷ παραπεπτωκόσιν• ἐφ᾽ ὧν καὶ χρόνος
τέτακται, καὶ καιρὸς ὥρισται• ὥστι αὐτοὺς ἀκολουθεῖν ἐν
πᾶσι τοῖς δόγμασι τῆς καθολικῆς Ἐκκλησίας• ἔνθα μὲν οὖν
πάντες, εἴτε ἐν κώμαις, εἴτε ἐν πόλεσιν αὐτοὶ μόνοι
εὑρίσκοιντο χειροτονηθέντες, οἱ εὑρισκόμενοι ἐν τῷ κλήρῳ
ἔσονται ἐν τῷ αὐτῷ σχήματι• εἰ δὲ τοῦ τῆς καθολικῆς
Ἐκκλησίας ἐπισκόπου ἢ πρεσβυτέρου ὄντος προσέρχονταί
τινες, πρόδηλον, ὡς ὁ μὲν ἐπίσκοπος τῆς Ἐκκλησίας ἕξει τὸ
ἀξίωμα τοῦ ἐπισκόπου, ὁ δὲ ὀνομαζόμενος παρὰ τοῖς
λεγομένοις Καθαροῖς ἐπίσκοπος τὴν τοῦ πρεσβυτέρου τιμὴν
ἕξει• πλὴν εἰ μὴ ἄρα δοκοίη τῷ ἐπισκόπῳ, τῆς τιμῆς τοῦ
ὀνόματος αὐτὸν μετέχειν• εἰ δὲ τοῦτο αὐτῷ μὴ ἀρέκοι,
ἐπινοήσει τόπον ἢ χωρεπισκόπου ἢ πρεσβυτέρου, ὑπὲρ τοῦ
ἐν τῷ κλήρῳ ὅλως δοκεῖν εἶναι, ἵνα μὴ ἐν τῇ πόλει δύο
ἐπίσκοποι ὧσιν.

"With regard to those who call themselves Cathari, the holy
and great Synod decides, that if they wish to enter the
Catholic and Apostolic Church, they must submit to
imposition of hands, and they may then remain among the
clergy: they must, above all, promise in writing to conform
to and follow the doctrines of the Catholic and Apostolic
Church; that is to say, they must communicate with those
who have married a second time, and with those who have

lapsed under persecution, but who have done penance for their faults. They must then follow in every respect the doctrines of the Catholic Church. Consequently, when in villages or in cities there are found only clergy of their own sect, the oldest of these clerics shall remain among the clergy, and in their position; but if a Catholic priest or bishop be found among them, it is evident that the bishop of the Catholic Church should preserve the episcopal dignity, whilst any one who has received the title of bishop from the so-called Cathari would only have a right to the honours accorded to priests, unless the bishop thinks it right to let him enjoy the honour of the (episcopal) title. If he does not desire to do so, let him give him the place of rural bishop (chorepiscopus) or priest, in order that he may appear to be altogether a part of the clergy, and that there may not be two bishops in one city."

The Cathari who are here under discussion are no other than the Novatians (and not the Montanists, as is maintained in the Göttinger gelehrten Anzeigen, 1780, St. 105), who from a spirit of severity wished to exclude for ever from the Church those who had shown weakness during persecution. They arose at the time of the Decian persecution, towards the middle of the third century, and had for their founder the Roman priest Novatian, who accused his Bishop Cecilian of showing too much lenity towards the lapsi. These schismatics were called Novatians from the name of their leader; but from a spirit of pride they gave themselves the name of Cathari (Puritans), κατ᾽ ἐξοχὴν, because their communion alone was in their eyes the pure bride of Christ, whilst the Catholic Church had been contaminated by the readmission of the lapsi. Their fundamental principle of the perpetual exclusion of the lapsi was in a manner the concrete form of the general principle, brought forward two generations before, that whoever after baptism once fell into mortal sin, should never be received back into the Church. The Catholic Church was herself in those times very much inclined to severity: she granted permission to perform penance only once; whoever fell a second time was for ever excluded. But the Montanists and Novatians exceeded this severity, and professed the most merciless rigour. A portion of the Novatians—those of Phrygia—followed the Montanists in a second kind of rigourism, in declaring that any one of the faithful who married again after the death of his consort committed adultery. What we have said shows that the Novatians were in truth schismatics, but not heretics; and this explains the mild manner in which the Council of Nicæa treated the Novatian priests (for it is of them only that this canon speaks). The Council treats them as it had treated the Meletians. It decides, in fact, 1st, ὥστε χειροθετουμένους, κ.τ.λ., that is to say, "they must receive imposition of hands." The meaning of these words has been a matter of dispute. Dionysius the Less translates them in this way: ut impositionem manus accipientes, sic in clero permaneant. The Prisca gives a similar translation; and then it may be said that the eighth canon, according to the two authors, would be entirely in accordance with the decision given by the Council of Nicæa on the subject of the Meletians. That decision ordered that the Meletian clergy should not indeed be ordained anew by a Catholic bishop, but that they ought nevertheless to receive from him imposition of hands. They were treated as those who had received baptism at the hands of heretics. Beveridge and Van Espen have explained this canon in another manner, resting upon Rufinus, and the two Greek commentators of the middle ages, Zonaras and Balsamon. According to them, the χειροθετουμένους does not signify the imposition of hands which was to be received on their returning to the Catholic Church: it simply refers to the priesthood received in the community of the Novatians; and consequently the sense of the canon of the Council of Nicæa is as follows: "Whoever has been ordained when amongst the Novatians, must remain among the clergy." It seems to me that the Greek text is more favourable to the first opinion than to the second, as the article is wanting before χειροθετουμένους, and αὐτοὺς is added; but this first opinion itself supposes that the reference is to those who were already clerics when they were in Novatianism, so that the meaning and fundamental idea is nearly the same in the one interpretation as in the other: for even supposing that Beveridge and Van Espen are in the right, it does not follow that the Novatian clerics were admitted among the orthodox clergy without any condition, particularly without some imposition of hands; on the contrary, it is clear that they were not treated with more consideration than the Meletian clergy. Gratian appears to us to be in opposition to what our text tells us, and to the practice of the ancient Church, as well as to the analogy of the case of the Novatians with that of the Meletians, in supposing that the eighth canon of Nicæa prescribes a re-ordination.

The Synod decided, besides, that the Novatians who came over should promise in writing a full submission to the doctrines of the Catholic Church. By these doctrines the canon does not seem to mean the doctrines of the faith in the special sense of the words: it seems rather to have reference to the admission of the lapsi, and those who contracted second marriages. To quiet the Novatians on the subject of the lapsi, care is taken to add that they must have submitted to a prescribed penance; that is to say, that the lapsi should, before being readmitted into the Church, undergo a long and severe penance.

After having established these two rules of discipline, the Synod adds the general condition, that Novatians (that is to say, the Novatian clergy) who desire restoration to the Church shall submit in general to all the doctrines of the Catholic Church.

The Council adds also the following directions:—

(α.) If in any city or village there exist only Novatian clergy, they are to retain their offices; so that, for example, the Novatian bishop of an entirely Novatian district may remain as a regular bishop when he re-enters the Catholic Church.

(β.) But if there be found somewhere (perhaps it is necessary to read εἰ δέ που instead of εἰ δὲ ποῦ) a Catholic bishop or priest along with Novatians, the Catholic bishop is to preserve his office; and the Novatian bishop must take the position of a simple priest, unless the Catholic bishop thinks it well to allow him the honour of the episcopal title (but without any jurisdiction). The Council does not say what is to be done with the Novatian priests; but we may infer that, in places which possess but one priest, the cure should return to a Catholic priest, and the Novatian priest should retain only the title. The Synod did not provide for the case of a conflict between several priests, but the rules made on the subject of the Meletians enable us to supply this omission. Converts are allowed to remain in the office and rank of the priesthood, but they are to take their place after the other priests, and they are to be excluded from elections.

(γ.) Lastly, in a case where a Catholic bishop would not leave the Novatian bishop the continuance of the episcopal title, he should give him the post of a chorepiscopus or priest, and this that the Novatian might continue to be visibly one of the clergy, and yet there might not be two bishops in the same city.

This mildness of the Synod of Nicæa in the case of the Novatians had no more effect in extinguishing this schism than in the case of the Meletians; for Novatianism continued until the fifth century.

Amongst the Novatian bishops who took part in the Synod, we must especially mention Acesius, bishop of this sect at Constantinople, whom the Emperor Constantine held in great esteem on account of the austerity of his life, and had in consequence invited him to the Synod. Constantine asked him if he were willing to subscribe the Creed and the rule on the feast of Easter. "Yes," replied Acesius, "for there is here, O Emperor, nothing new introduced by the Council; for it has been so believed since the time of the apostles, and thus has Easter been kept." And when the Emperor further asked, "Why, then, do you separate from the communion of the Church?" Acesius replied by quoting different acts which had been passed under the Emperor Decius, and by declaring that no one who had committed mortal sin should be admitted again to the holy mysteries. He might be exhorted to repentance, but the priest had not the right to pronounce him really absolved, but the penitent must look for pardon from God alone. Upon this the Emperor replied, "Acesius, take a ladder, and climb up to heaven alone." Sozomen has suggested that Acesius was of very great use to his party, and it is generally believed that this canon was made so mild towards the Novatians out of respect for him.

CAN. 9

Εἴ τινες ἀνεξετάστως προσήχθησαν πρεσβύτεροι, ἢ ἀνακρινόμενοι ὡμολόγησαν τὰ ἡμαρτημένα αὐτοῖς, καὶ ὁμολογησάντων αὐτῶν, παρὰ κανόνα κινούμενοι ἄνθρωποι τοῖς τοιούτοις χεῖρα ἐπιτεθείκασι· τούτους ὁ κανὼν οὐ προσίεται· τὸ γὰρ ἀνεπίληπτον ἐκδικεῖ ἡ καθολικὴ Ἐκκλησία.

"If any persons have been admitted to the priesthood without inquiry, or if upon inquiry they have confessed their crimes, and the imposition of hands has nevertheless been conferred upon them in opposition to the canon, such ordination is declared invalid; for the Catholic Church requires men who are blameless."

The crimes in question are those which were a bar to the priesthood, such as blasphemy, (successive) bigamy, heresy, idolatry, magic, etc., as the Arabic paraphrase of Joseph explains. It is clear that these faults are punishable in the bishop no less than in the priest, and that consequently our canon refers to the bishops as well as to the πρεσβύτεροι in the more restricted sense. These words of the Greek text,

"In the case in which any one might be induced, in opposition to the canon, to ordain such persons," allude to the ninth canon of the Synod of Neocæsarea. It was necessary to pass such ordinances; for even in the fifth century, as the twenty-second letter of Pope Innocent the First testifies, some held that as baptism effaces all former sins, so it takes away all the impedimenta ordinationis which are the result of those sins.

The ninth canon of Nicæa occurs twice in the Corpus juris canonici.

The following canon has a considerable resemblance to the one which we have just considered.

CAN. 10

Ὅσοι προεχειρίσθησαν τῶν παραπεπτωκότων κατὰ ἄγνοιαν, ἢ καὶ προειδότων τῶν προχειρισαμένων, τοῦτο οὐ προκρίνει τῷ κανόνι τῷ ἐκκλησιαστικῷ· γνωσθέντες γὰρ καθαιροῦνται.

"The lapsi who have been ordained in ignorance of their fall, or in spite of the knowledge which the ordainer had of it, are no exception to the law of the Church, for they are excluded as soon as their unworthiness is known."

The tenth canon differs from the ninth, inasmuch as it concerns only the lapsi and their elevation, not only to the priesthood, but to any other ecclesiastical preferment as well, and requires their deposition. The punishment of a bishop who should consciously perform such an ordination is not mentioned; but it is incontestable that the lapsi could not be ordained, even after having performed penance: for, as the preceding canon states, the Church requires those who were faultless. It is to be observed that the word προχειρίζειν is evidently employed here in the sense of "ordain," and is used without any distinction from χειρίζειν; whilst in the synodal letter of the Council of Nicæa on the subject of the Meletians, there is a distinction between these two words, and προχειρίζειν is used to signify eligere.

This canon is found several times in the Corpus juris canonici.

CAN. 11

Περὶ τῶν παραβάντων χωρὶς ἀνάγκης ἢ χωρὶς ἀφαιρέσεως ὑπαρχόντων ἢ χωρὶς κινδύνου ἢ τινος τοιούτου, ὃ γέγονεν ἐπὶ τῆς τυραννίδος Λικινίου· ἔδοξε τῇ συνόδῳ, κἂν ἀνάξιοι ἦσαν φιλανθρωπίας, ὅμως χρηστεύσασθαι εἰς αὐτούς· ὅσοι οὖν γνησίως μεταμέλονται, τρία ἔτη ἐν ἀκροωμένοις ποιήσουσιν οἱ πιστοί, καὶ ἑπτὰ ἔτη ὑποπεσοῦνται· δύο δὲ ἔτη χωρὶς προσφορᾶς κοινωνήσουσι τῷ λαῷ τῶν προσευχῶν.

"As to those who lapsed during the tyranny of Licinius, without being driven to it by necessity, or by the confiscation of their goods, or by any danger whatever, the Synod decides that they ought to be treated with gentleness, although in truth they have shown themselves unworthy of it. Those among them who are truly penitent, and who before their fall were believers, must do penance for three years among the audientes, and seven years among the substrati. For two years following they can take part with the people at divine service, but without themselves participating in the oblation."

The persecution of Licinius had come to an end only a few years before the meeting of the Council of Nicæa, and at the downfall of that Emperor. The cruelty with which they were persecuted led a large number into apostasy. Thus the Council had to take notice in several of its canons of the lapsi; and as there were different classes to be made among these lapsi—that is to say, as some among them had yielded at the first threat, whilst others had undergone long tortures before their fall—the Synod wished to take account of the extenuating as well as of the aggravating circumstances, and to proportion the punishment to the degree of the fault. This canon does not say how the least guilty are to be treated; but it decides that those who are the most guilty, and the least excusable, should pass three years in the second degree of penitence, seven years in the third, and two years in the fourth or lowest class.

The canon supposes that those who are to receive this treatment were before their fall fideles, i.e. members of the Church, and not simple catechumens. We shall see in the fourteenth canon what the Synod decides with respect to catechumens who showed themselves weak.

CAN. 12

Οἱ δὲ προσκληθέντες μὲν ὑπὸ τῆς χάριτος, καὶ τὴν πρώτην ὁρμὴν ἐνδειξάμενοι, καὶ ἀποθέμενοι τὰς ζώνας, μετὰ δὲ ταῦτα ἐπὶ τὸν οἰκεῖον ἔμετον ἀναδραμόντες ὡς κύνες, ὡς τινὰς καὶ ἀργύρια προέσθαι, καὶ βενεφικίοις κατορθῶσαι τὸ ἀναστρατεύσασθαι· οὗτοι δέκα ἔτη ὑποπιπτέτωσαν μετὰ τὸν τῆς τριετοῦς ἀκροάσεως χρόνον. ἐφ᾽ ἅπασι δὲ τούτοις προσήκει ἐξετάζειν τὴν προαίρεσιν, καὶ τὸ εἶδος τῆς μετανοίας. ὅσοι μὲν γὰρ καὶ φόβῳ καὶ δάκρυσι καὶ ὑπομονῇ

καὶ ἀγαθοεργίαις τὴν ἐπιστροφὴν ἔργῳ καὶ οὐ σχήματι
ἐπιδείκνυνται, οὗτοι πληρώσαντες τὸν χρόνον τὸν ὡρισμένον
τῆς ἀκροάσεως, εἰκότως τῶν εὐχῶν κοινωνήσουσι, μετὰ τοῦ
ἐξεῖναι τῷ ἐπισκόπῳ, καὶ φιλανθρωπότερόν τι περὶ αὐτῶν
βουλεύσασθαι. ὅσοι δὲ ἀδιαφόρως ἤνεγκαν, καὶ τὸ σχῆμα
τοῦ [μὴ] εἰσιέναι εἰς τὴν Ἐκκλησίαν ἀρκεῖν αὐτοῖς ἡγήσαντο
πρὸς τὴν ἐπιστροφήν, ἐξάπαντος πληρούτωσαν τὸν χρόνον.

"Those who, called by grace, have shown the first zeal, and
have laid aside their belts, but afterwards have returned like
dogs to their vomit, and have gone so far as to give money
and presents to be readmitted into military service, shall
remain three years among the audientes, and ten years
among the substrati. But in the case of these penitents, their
intention and the character of their repentance must be
tried. In fact, those among them who, by fear and with
tears, together with patience and good works, show by
deeds that their conversion is real, and not merely in
appearance, after having finished the time of their penance
among the audientes, may perhaps take part among those
who pray; and it is in the power of the bishop to treat them
with yet greater lenity. As to those who bear with
indifference (their exclusion from the Church), and who
think that this exclusion is sufficient to expiate their faults,
they will be bound to perform the whole period prescribed
by the law."

In his last contests with Constantine, Licinius had made
himself the representative of heathenism; so that the final
issue of the war would not be the mere triumph of one of
the two competitors, but the triumph or fall of Christianity
or heathenism. Accordingly, a Christian who had in this war

supported the cause of Licinius and of heathenism might be considered as a lapsus, even if he did not formally fall away. With much more reason might those Christians be treated as lapsi, who, having conscientiously given up military service (this is meant by the soldier's belt), afterwards retracted their resolution, and went so far as to give money and presents for the sake of readmission, on account of the numerous advantages which military service then afforded. It must not be forgotten that Licinius, as Zonaras and Eusebius relate, required from his soldiers a formal apostasy; compelled them, for example, to take part in the heathen sacrifices which were held in the camps, and dismissed from his service those who would not apostatize. It must not be supposed, then, that the Council forbade military service generally, as the writer has shown in the Tübinger Theol. Quartalschrift for 1841 (S. 386). But equally untenable is the opinion of Aubespine. He supposes that the canon speaks of those who promised to perform a lifelong penance, and to retain the accustomed penitential dress, but who afterwards broke their vow, and took part in secular matters, and tried to make their way to posts of honour. The cingulum which the canon mentions is evidently the cingulum militiæ. It is in this sense too that Pope Innocent the First has used it in his letter to Victricius of Rouen. He says to that bishop, making, it is true, a mistake upon another point: Constituit Nicæna synodus, si quis post remissionem peccatorum cingulum militiæ secularis habuerit, ad clericatum admitti omnino non debet.

The Council punishes with three years in the second degree of penance, and with ten years in the third, those of the faithful who had taken the side of Licinius in his struggle against Christianity. It was, however, lawful for the bishop to promote the better disposed penitents of the second rank (ἀκρόασις) to the fourth, in which they could be present at the whole of divine service (εὐχή). It is not stated how long they should remain in this fourth rank; but from what the eleventh canon says, it may be supposed that they remained in it two years. As to those who underwent their penance with more indifference, and who were content to pray outside the Church, without taking any active part in divine service, they were required to fulfil the whole time of their penance. It is by considering the negation μὴ which comes before εἰσιέναι as an interpolation, as Gelasius of Cyzicus, the Prisca, Dionysius the Less, the pseudo-Isidore, Zonaras, and others have done, that the interpretation given above may be obtained. When inserting this canon in the de Pœnitentia, Gratian gives it the same meaning that we do. If it is desired at any cost to retain the negation, the last clause will be explained as follows: "They consider it as sufficient obedience to the Church not to go beyond what is allowed to them as penitents, and not to attend without permission the missa fidelium."

CAN. 13

Περὶ δὲ τῶν ἐξοδευόντων ὁ παλαιὸς καὶ κανονικὸς νόμος φυλαχθήσεται καὶ νῦν, ὥστε, εἴ τις ἐξοδεύοι, τοῦ τελευταίου καὶ ἀναγκαιοτάτου ἐφοδίου μὴ ἀποστερεῖσθαι· εἰ δὲ ἀπογνωσθεὶς καὶ κοινωνίας πάλιν τυχὼν, πάλιν ἐν τοῖς ζῶσιν ἐξετασθῇ, μετὰ τῶν κοινωνούντων τῆς εὐχῆς μόνης ἔστω· καθόλου δὲ καὶ περὶ παντὸς οὑτινοσοῦν ἐξοδεύοντος, αἰτοῦντος τοῦ μετασχεῖν Εὐχαριστίας, ὁ ἐπίσκοπος μετὰ δοκιμασίας ἐπιδότω.

"With respect to the dying, the old rule of the Church should continue to be observed, which forbids that any one who is on the point of death should be deprived of the last and most necessary viaticum. If he does not die after having been absolved and admitted to communion, he must be placed amongst those who take part only in prayer. The bishop should, however, administer the Eucharist, after necessary inquiry, to any one who on his deathbed asks to receive it."

The Synod of Nicæa provides for the case of a lapsus being in danger of death before he has fulfilled the period of his penance, and decides that, in conformity with the old custom and with old rules—for example, the sixth canon of the Council of Ancyra—the holy Eucharist (ἐφόδιον) should be administered to the dying person, although he has not fulfilled all his penance. Van Espen and Tillemont have proved, against Aubespine, that the word ἐφόδιον here signifies the communion, and not merely absolution without communion. The opinion of those two authors is also that of the two old Greek commentators Zonaras and Balsamon, and of the Arabian paraphrast Joseph. If the sick person should recover his health, he should take his place in the highest rank of penitents. The Council does not state the period he should pass in it, but it is clear, and the ancient collector of canons, John of Antioch, adds, "that such an one should remain in that class the whole time of penance prescribed in canons 11 or 12."

The Synod ends this canon more generally. In the beginning it treats only of the lapsi, but at the end it considers all those who are excommunicated, and orders that the bishop, after having made personal inquiry into the state of matters, may administer the communion to every man on his deathbed, whatever his offence may have been.

This thirteenth canon has been inserted in the Corpus juris can.

CAN. 14

Περὶ τῶν κατηχουμένων καὶ παραπεσόντων ἔδοξε τῇ ἁγίᾳ καὶ μεγάλῃ συνόδῳ, ὥστε τριῶν ἐτῶν αὐτοὺς ἀκροωμένους μόνον, μετὰ ταῦτα εὔχεσθαι μετὰ τῶν κατηχουμένων.

"The holy and great Synod orders that catechumens who have lapsed be audientes for three years; they can afterwards join in prayer with the other catechumens."

The catechumens are not, strictly speaking, members of the Church: their lapse, therefore, in time of persecution, may be considered as less serious than actual apostasy. But it was also natural to prolong their time of probation, when, after persecution, they asked again to be admitted among the catechumens; and it is this of which the fourteenth canon treats. These catechumens should, it says, remain three years among the audientes, that is to say, among the catechumens, who only take part at the didactic part of worship, at sermons, and at reading. If they showed during this time of penance zeal and marks of improvement, they might be admitted to prayer with the catechumens; that is to say, they might form part of the higher class of those who made up the catechumeni sensu strictiori. These could be present at the general prayers which were offered at the end of the sermon; and they received, but kneeling, the bishop's blessing.

In the same way as Origen and several other writers, more especially several Greek historians of the Church, so the Council of Nicæa speaks only, as we have seen, of two classes of catechumens. Some Latin writers, amongst whom Isidore of Seville may be quoted, speak only of these two grades of catechumens; and it may be said, without any doubt, that the primitive Church knew of no others. Bingham and Neander have maintained, and the opinion is generally held, that in the fourth century there was formed a third class of catechumens, composed of those who should receive baptism immediately; and also that the meaning of the ceremonies for the reception of this sacrament was explained to them. They were called φωτιζόμενοι and competentes; but we notice that S. Isidore makes competentes synonymous with γονυκλίνοντες. Beveridge endeavours to prove that S. Ambrose also spoke of this third class of catechumens; but the words of this Father, Sequenti die erat dominica; post lectiones atque tractatum, dimissis catechumenis, symbolum aliquibus competentibus in baptisteriis tradebam basilicæ, show us that by catechumenis he understands the first and second classes, and that the competentes belonged to the third class.

The fourteenth canon of Nicæa has not been inserted in the Corpus juris canonici, probably because the old system of catechumens had ceased to exist at the time of Gratian.

CAN. 15

Διὰ τὸν πολὺν τάραχον καὶ τὰς στάσεις τὰς γινομένας ἔδοξε παντάπασι περιαιρεθῆναι τὴν συνήθειαν, τὴν παρὰ τὸν κανόνα εὑρεθεῖσαν ἔν τισι μέρεσιν, ὥστε ἀπὸ πόλεως εἰς πόλιν μὴ

μεταβαίνειν μήτε ἐπίσκοπον μήτε πρεσβύτερον μήτε
διάκονον. εἰ δέ τις μετὰ τὸν τῆς ἁγίας καὶ μεγάλης συνόδου
ὅρον τοιούτῳ τινὶ ἐπιχειρήσειεν, ἢ ἐπιδοίη ἑαυτὸν πράγματι
τοιούτῳ, ἀκυρωθήσεται ἐξάπαντος τὸ κατασκεύασμα, καὶ
ἀποκατασταθήσεται τῇ ἐκκλησίᾳ, ᾗ ὁ ἐπίσκοπος ἢ ὁ
πρεσβύτερος ἐχειροτονήθη.

"On account of the numerous troubles and divisions which
have taken place, it has been thought good that the custom
which has been established in some countries in opposition
to the canon should be abolished; namely, that no bishop,
priest, or deacon should remove from one city to another.
If any one should venture, even after this ordinance of the
holy and great Synod, to act contrary to this present rule,
and should follow the old custom, the translation shall be
null, and he shall return to the church to which he had been
ordained bishop or priest."

The translation of a bishop, priest, or deacon from one
church to another, had already been forbidden in the
primitive Church. Nevertheless several translations had
taken place, and even at the Council of Nicæa several
eminent men were present who had left their first
bishoprics to take others: thus Eusebius Bishop of
Nicomedia had been before Bishop of Berytus; Eustathius
Bishop of Antioch had been before Bishop of Berrhœa in
Syria. The Council of Nicæa thought it necessary to forbid
in future these translations, and to declare them invalid.
The chief reason of this prohibition was found in the
irregularities and disputes occasioned by such change of
sees; but even if such practical difficulties had not arisen,
the whole doctrinal idea, so to speak, of the relationship

between a cleric and the church to which he had been ordained, namely, the contracting of a mystical marriage between them, would be opposed to any translation or change.

In 341the Synod of Antioch renewed, in its twenty-first canon, the prohibition passed by the Council of Nicæa; but the interest of the Church often rendered it necessary to make exceptions, as happened in the case of S. Chrysostom. These exceptional cases increased almost immediately after the holding of the Council of Nicæa, so that in 382 S. Gregory of Nazianzus considered this law among those which had long been abrogated by custom. It was more strictly observed in the Latin Church; and even Gregory's contemporary, Pope Damasus, declared himself decidedly in favour of the rule of Nicæa. It has been inserted in the Corpus juris canonici.

CAN. 16

Ὅσοι ῥιψοκινδύνως μήτε τὸν φόβον τοῦ Θεοῦ πρὸ ὀφθαλμῶν ἔχοντες, μήτε τὸν ἐκκλησιαστικὸν κανόνα εἰδότες, ἀναχωρήσουσι τῆς ἐκκλησίας, πρεσβύτεροι ἢ διάκονοι ἢ ὅλως ἐν τῷ κανόνι ἐξεταζόμενοι· οὗτοι οὐδαμῶς δεκτοὶ ὀφείλουσιν εἶναι ἐν ἑτέρᾳ ἐκκλησίᾳ, ἀλλὰ πᾶσαν αὐτοῖς ἀνάγκην ἐπάγεσθαι χρὴ, ἀναστρέφειν εἰς τὰς ἑαυτῶν παροικίας, ἢ ἐπιμένοντας ἀκοινωνήτους εἶναι προσήκει. εἰ δὲ καὶ τολμήσειέ τις ὑφαρπάσαι τὸν τῷ ἑτέρῳ διαφέροντα, καὶ χειροτονῆσαι ἐν τῇ αὐτοῦ ἐκκλησίᾳ, μὴ συγκατατιθεμένου τοῦ ἰδίου ἐπισκόπου, οὗ ἀνεχώρησεν ὁ ἐν τῷ κανόνι ἐξεταζόμενος, ἄκυρος ἔσται ἡ χειροτονία.

"Priests, deacons, and clerics in general, who have with levity, and without having the fear of God before their eyes, left their church in the face of the ecclesiastical laws, must not on any account be received into another: they must be compelled in all ways to return to their dioceses; and if they refuse to do so, they must be excommunicated. If any one should dare to steal, as it were, a person who belongs to another (bishop), and to ordain him for his own church, without the permission of the bishop from whom he was withdrawn, the ordination is null."

This sixteenth canon has a good deal of connection with the preceding. It contains two general principles: a. It threatens with excommunication all clerics, of whatever degree, if they will not return to their first church (according to Balsamon, exclusion from communio clericalis.); b. It forbids any bishop to ordain for his own diocese a person belonging to another diocese. It may be supposed that the Council of Nicæa has here again in view the Meletian schism; but it must not be forgotten that Meletius did not ordain strangers to his diocese, and retain them afterwards, but the reverse—he ordained clergymen for other dioceses.

We notice also, that in this canon the expression ἐν τῷ κανόνι ἐξεταζόμενος occurs twice to designate a cleric; it means literally, any one who belongs to the service of the Church, who lives under its rule (κανὼν), or whose name is inscribed in its list (κανὼν).

Gratian has inserted this canon, and divided it into two.

CAN. 17

Charles Joseph Hefele, D.D.

Ἐπειδὴ πολλοὶ ἐν τῷ κανόνι ἐξεταζόμενοι τὴν πλεονεξίαν καὶ τὴν αἰσχροκέρδειαν διώκοντες ἐπελάθοντο τοῦ θείου γράμματος λέγοντος· Τὸ ἀργύριον αὐτοῦ οὐκ ἔδωκεν ἐπὶ τόκῳ· καὶ δανείζοντες ἑκατοστὰς ἀπαιτοῦσιν· ἐδικαίωσεν ἡ ἁγία καὶ μεγάλη σύνοδος, ὡς, εἴ τις εὑρεθείη μετὰ τὸν ὅρον τοῦτον τόκους λαμβάνων ἐκ μεταχειρίσεως ἢ ἄλλως μετερχόμενος τὸ πρᾶγμα ἢ ἡμιολίας ἀπαιτῶν ἢ ὅλως ἕτερόν τι ἐπινοῶν αἰσχροῦ κέρδους ἕνεκα, καθαιρεθήσεται τοῦ κλήρου καὶ ἀλλότριος τοῦ κανόνος ἔσται.

"As many clerics, filled with avarice and with the spirit of usury, forget the sacred words, 'He that hath not given his money upon usury,' and demand usuriously (that is, every month) a rate of interest, the great and holy Synod declares that if any one, after the publication of this law, takes interest, no matter on what grounds, or carries on the business (of usurer), no matter in what way, or if he require half as much again, or if he give himself up to any other sort of scandalous gain, he must be turned out of the clergy, and his name struck off the list."

Several of the oldest Fathers of the Church considered that the Old Testament forbade interest to be received: thus, in the fourth book of his controversial work against Marcion, Tertullian wishes to prove to this Gnostic the harmony which exists between the Old and the New Testament, by taking as an example the teaching given about a loan at interest. According to Ezekiel, says Tertullian, he is declared just who does not lend his money upon usury, and who does not take what comes to him from it, that is to say, the interest. By these words of the prophet, God had prepared for the perfection of the New Testament. In the

Old, men had been taught that they should not make gain by lending money, and in the New that they should even bear the loss of what they had lent.

Clement of Alexandria expresses himself in the same way: "The law forbids to take usury from a brother, and not only from a brother by nature, but also from one who is of the same religion as ourselves, or who is one of the same nation as ourselves, and it looks upon lending money at interest as unjust: unfortunate persons should rather be assisted with open hand and open heart."

In taking account of the prohibitions declared by the Jewish law against lending at interest, the customs of that time must have filled the Christian mind with horror of this quæstus. As in the Jewish language there is only one word to express usury and lending at interest, so with the Romans the word fœnus was also ominous in its double meaning. During the last period of the republic and under the emperors, the legal and mildest interest was twelve per cent., or, as the Romans called it, interest by month, or usura centesima; but sometimes it increased to twenty-four per cent., binæ centesimæ, and even to forty-eight per cent., quaternæ centesimæ. Horace speaks even of a certain Fufidius, who demanded sixty per cent.; and what is remarkable is, that he speaks of this Fufidius when on the subject of apothecaries. As this exorbitant interest was generally paid at the beginning of the month, the reason why Ovid speaks of the celeres, and Horace of the tristes Kalendas, is explained.

The early Christians knew this loan at interest but little; they also kept themselves from it conscientiously, so long as that brotherly love prevailed from which had come a community of goods. But unhappily other Christians became apt scholars of the heathen in this matter. It was most blameworthy in the clergy, whose savings, according to canon law, belonged to the poor and to the Church, and least of all ought to be abused to usurious gain through the oppression of the poor. Therefore the forty-fourth (or forty-third) apostolical canon gave this order: "A bishop, priest, or deacon who receives interest for money lent, must cease from this traffic under pain of deposition;" and the Council of Arles, held in 314, says in the twelfth canon: De ministris, qui fœnerant, placuit, eos juxta formam divinitus datam a communione abstinere. The seventeenth canon of Nicæa also forbids all the clergy to lend money on interest; we say to all the clergy, because in the preceding canon we have shown that by the words ἐν τῷ κανόνι ἐξεταζόμενοι the clergy must be understood. The Synod, fearing lest the clergy should in future practise usury in a hidden and underhand manner, was careful at the end of the canon to define the different sorts of usury which are forbidden.

The seventeenth canon of Nicæa is found twice in the Corpus juris canonici.

CAN. 18

Ἦλθεν εἰς τὴν ἁγίαν καὶ μεγάλην σύνοδον, ὅτι ἔν τισι τόποις καὶ πόλεσι τοῖς πρεσβυτέροις τὴν Εὐχαριστίαν οἱ διάκονοι διδόασιν, ὅπερ οὔτε ὁ κανὼν οὔτε ἡ συνήθεια παρέδωκε, τοὺς ἐξουσίαν μὴ ἔχοντας προσφέρειν τοῖς προσφέρουσι διδόναι τὸ σῶμα τοῦ Χριστοῦ. κἀκεῖνο δὲ ἐγνωρίσθη, ὅτι ἤδη τινὲς τῶν διακόνων καὶ πρὸ τῶν ἐπισκόπων τῆς Εὐχαριστίας ἅπτονται. Ταῦτα μὲν οὖν ἄπαντα περιῃρήσθω·

καὶ ἐμμενέτωσαν οἱ διάκονοι τοῖς ἰδίοις μέτροις, εἰδότες ὅτι
τοῦ μὲν ἐπισκόπου ὑπηρέται εἰσί, τῶν δὲ πρεσβυτέρων
ἐλάττους τυγχάνουσι· λαμβανέτωσαν δὲ κατὰ τὴν τάξιν τὴν
Εὐχαριστίαν μετὰ τοὺς πρεσβυτέρους, ἢ τοῦ ἐπισκόπου
διδόντος αὐτοῖς ἢ τοῦ πρεσβυτέρου. ἀλλὰ μηδὲ καθῆσθαι ἐν
μέσῳ τῶν πρεσβυτέρων ἐξέστω τοῖς διακόνοις· παρὰ κανόνα
γὰρ καὶ παρὰ τάξιν ἐστὶ τὸ γινόμενον. Εἰ δέ τις μὴ θέλοι
πειθαρχεῖν καὶ μετὰ τούτους τοὺς ὅρους, πεπαύσθω τῆς
διακονίας.

"It has come to the knowledge of the holy and great Synod,
that in certain places and cities deacons administer the
Eucharist to priests, although it is contrary to the canons
and to custom to have the body of Christ distributed to
those who offer the sacrifice by those who cannot offer it.
The Synod has also learned that some deacons receive the
Eucharist even before the bishops. This must all now cease:
the deacons should remain within the limits of their
functions, and remember that they are the assistants of the
bishops, and only come after the priests. They must receive
the Eucharist in accordance with rule, after the priests—a
bishop or a priest administering it to them. The deacons
ought no longer to sit among the priests, for this is against
rule and order. If any one refuses to obey after these rules
have been promulgated, let him lose his diaconate."

Justin Martyr declares that in the primitive Church the
deacons were in the habit of administering to each one of
those present the consecrated bread and the holy chalice.
Later it was the bishop or the celebrating priest who
administered the holy bread, and the deacon administered
only the chalice: this is what the Apostolical Constitutions

order. We see that this was still the custom in the time of S. Cyprian, by this sentence taken from his work de Lapsis: Solemnibus adimpletis calicem diaconus offerre præsentibus cœpit. It is evident that the word offerre cannot signify here to celebrate the holy sacrifice, but merely to administer; the expression solemnibus adimpletis shows that the divine service was already finished, and consequently there is no question here of celebrating, but merely of administering the chalice for communion. In other analogous passages this meaning of offerre is not so clearly indicated, and thence has arisen the mistake that the deacons could also offer the holy sacrifice. It must not be forgotten, however, that certain deacons did in fact venture to offer the holy sacrifice; for the first Council of Arles says in its fifteenth canon: De diaconibus quos cognovimus multis locis offerre, placuit minimè fieri debere. It is not unlikely that during the persecution of Diocletian, when very many bishops and priests had been driven away or put to death, some deacon allowed himself to celebrate the eucharistic sacrifice; but such an act was altogether opposed to the spirit and rules of the primitive Church. The Apostolical Constitutions show very plainly that it is forbidden for deacons to pronounce the blessing and to offer the holy sacrifice (benedicere et offerre). They could only fulfil the duties indicated by their name διάκονος. But it very probably happened that in some places the deacon had overstepped the limit of his powers, and for that reason had rendered necessary the prohibition of the Council of Arles. I know, indeed, that Binterim has wished to explain this canon of the Council of Arles in another way. He supposes that the rebuke is not annexed to the word offerre, but merely the words multis locis, and he explains the canon as follows: "In future, the deacon must no longer celebrate and administer the holy Eucharist to other congregations besides his own." I cannot believe in the accuracy of this explanation, and Binterim has certainly done violence to the text of the Council of Arles.

But besides, this canon of Nicæa says nothing directly of this pretension of the deacon to wish to consecrate: it has rather in view certain other abuses; and we know from another source, that in Christian antiquity there was often complaint of the pride of deacons. The deacons of the city of Rome have especially been reproached on account of pride, and the Council of Arles says on this subject in its eighteenth canon: De diaconibus urbicis, ut non sibi tantum præsumant, sed honorem presbyteris reservent, ut sine conscientia ipsorum nihil tale faciant. It has been supposed that these presumptuous deacons of the city of Rome had given occasion for the passing of this canon, and that it was decreed on the motion of the two Roman priests who represented the Pope at the Council of Nicæa.

In the primitive Church, the holy liturgy was usually celebrated by a single person, more frequently by the bishop, or by a priest when the bishop was hindered from being present; but the other priests were not merely present at the holy sacrifice, as is the custom now: they were besides consacrificantes; they did what newly ordained priests do now, when they celebrate together with the bishop the mass at their ordination. These consacrificing priests ought to have received the communion from the hands of the celebrant; but in some places the deacons had taken upon themselves the right of administering the holy communion to priests as well as to the people, and this is

the first abuse which the canon condemns. The second
abuse of which they were guilty was, that they τῆς
Εὐχαριστίας ἅπτονται before the bishop. It is doubtful what
these words mean. The pseudo-Isidore, Zonaras, and
Balsamon give the meaning which most naturally presents
itself: "They go so far as to take the Eucharist before the
bishop." The Prisca, as well as Dionysius the Less and
others, translate ἅπτονται by contingant, that is to say,
touch; and Van Espen interprets the canon in this way:
"The deacons touch (but do not partake of) the holy
Eucharist before the bishop." But the word ἅπτονται
includes the idea of partaking as well, as the subsequent
words in the canon prove, which settle the order to be
followed in the reception of the Eucharist, and show us
consequently that these words τῆς Εὐχαριστίας ἅπτονται
signify Eucharistiam sumere. It may be asked how it could
happen that the deacon could communicate before the
bishop. When the bishop himself celebrated, this was
clearly impossible; but it very often happened that the
bishop caused one of his priests to celebrate, and contented
himself with being present at the holy sacrifice. The same
thing would happen if one bishop visited another, and was
present at divine service. In both cases the bishop would
receive the communion immediately after the celebrant, and
before the priests. But if a deacon undertook to administer
the communion to the priests, and to the bishop as well, it
would happen that the bishop would not receive the
communion until after the deacon, for he would always
begin by communicating himself before administering the
communion to others; and this is the abuse which the
Council found it necessary to forbid.

The third encroachment of which the deacons were guilty had reference to their places in church. Several among them had placed themselves among the priests. The Synod condemns this abuse, and finishes with this threat: "Whoever shall not obey, after the publication of these rules, shall be removed from his diaconate." Unhappily they were not strictly observed; for even after the Council of Nicæa complaints continued to be made of the pride of the deacons, and S. Jerome says that "he saw at Rome a deacon who took his place among the priests, and who at table gave his blessing to the priests."

Van Espen remarks with truth that this canon of discipline proves the belief of the Council of Nicæa in three great dogmatic truths: (1.) The Council of Nicæa saw in the Eucharist the body of Christ; (2.) It called the eucharistic service a sacrifice (προσφέρειν); and (3.) It concedes to bishops and priests alone the power of consecrating.

This canon is found in the Corpus juris canonici.

CAN. 19

Περὶ τῶν Παυλιανισάντων, εἶτα προσφυγόντων τῇ καθολικῇ Ἐκκλησίᾳ, ὅρος ἐκτέθειται, ἀναβαπτίζωσθαι αὐτοὺς ἐξάπαντος· εἰ δέ τινες ἐν τῷ παρεληλυθότι χρόνῳ ἐν τῷ κλήρῳ ἐξητάσθησαν, εἰ μὲν ἄμεμπτοι καὶ ἀνεπίληπτοι φανεῖεν, ἀναβαπτισθέντες, χειροτονείσθωσαν ὑπὸ τοῦ τῆς καθολικῆς Ἐκκλησίας ἐπισκόπου· εἰ δὲ ἡ ἀνάκρισις ἀνεπιτηδείους αὐτοὺς εὑρίσκοι, καθαιρεῖσθαι αὐτοὺς προσήκει. Ὡσαύτως· δὲ καὶ περὶ τῶν διακονισσῶν, καὶ ὅλως περὶ τῶν ἐν τῷ κακόνι ἐξεταζομένων ὁ αὐτὸς τύπος παραφυλαχθήσεται. Ἐμνήσθημεν δὲ διακονισσῶν τῶν ἐν τῷ σχήματι ἐξετασθεισῶν, ἐπεὶ μηδὲ χειροθεσίαν τινὰ ἔχουσιν, ὥστε ἐξάπαντος ἐν τοῖς λαϊκοῖς αὐτὰς ἐξετάζεσθαι.

"With respect to the Paulianists, who wish to return to the Catholic Church, the rule which orders them to be re-baptized must be observed. If some among them were formerly (as Paulianists) members of the clergy, they must be re-ordained by the bishop of the Catholic Church after they have been re-baptized, if they have been blameless and not condemned. If, on inquiry, they are found to be unworthy, they must be deposed. The same will be done with respect to the deaconesses; and in general, the present rule will be observed for all those who are on the list of the Church. We remind those deaconesses who are in this position, that as they have not been ordained, they must be classed merely among the laity."

By Paulianists must be understood the followers of Paul of Samosata, the anti-Trinitarian who, about the year 260, had been made Bishop of Antioch, but had been deposed by a great Synod in 269. As Paul of Samosata was heretical in his teaching on the Holy Trinity, the Synod of Nicæa applied here the decree passed by the Council of Arles in its eighth canon: Si ad Ecclesiam aliquis de hæresi venerit, interrogent eum symbolum; et si perviderint, eum in Patre et Filio et Spiritu Sancto esse baptizatum, manus ei tantum imponatur ut accipiat Spiritum sanctum. Quod, si interrogatus non responderit hanc Trinitatem, baptizetur.

The Samosatans, according to S. Athanasius, named the Father, Son, and Holy Spirit in administering baptism; but as they gave a false meaning to the baptismal formula, and did not use the words Son and Holy Spirit in the usual sense, the Council of Nicæa, like S. Athanasius himself, considered their baptism as invalid. Pope Innocent the First said of them in his twenty-second epistle, "They do not baptize in the name of the Father, and of the Son, and of the Spirit," wishing above all to make it understood by that, that they gave to these names an altogether false signification.

The Synod of Nicæa, regarding the baptism of the Paulianists as invalid, would logically affirm that their ordinations were also without value; for he who is not really baptized can clearly neither give nor receive holy orders. Accordingly the Synod orders that the Paulianist clergy should be baptized; but by a wise condescension they permit those among these clergy who have received Catholic baptism, and who have given proofs of ability and of good conduct, to be ordained as clergy of the Catholic Church. Those who have not these conditions are to be excluded.

The rest of the text presents insurmountable difficulties, if the reading of the Greek manuscripts be adopted, ὡσαύτως καὶ περὶ τῶν διακονισσῶν. In this case, in fact, the canon would order: The deaconesses of the Paulianists can, if they are of irreproachable manners, retain their charge, and be ordained afresh. But this sentence would be in direct contradiction to the end of the canon, which declares that the deaconesses have received no ordination, and ought to be considered as simply laity. The difficulty disappears, if in the first sentence we read with Gelasius, διακόνων instead of διακονισσῶν. The Prisca, with Theilo and Thearistus, who in 419 translated the canons of Nicæa for the bishops of Africa, have adopted the same reading as Gelasius. The pseudo-Isidore and Gratian have done the same; whilst Rufinus has not translated this passage, and Dionysius the Less has read διακονισσῶν.

Van Espen has tried to assign an intelligible meaning to this canon, without accepting the variation adopted by so great a number of authors. According to him, the Synod meant to say this in the last sentence: "We have mentioned above in particular the deaconesses, because it would not have been otherwise possible to grant them the conditions which have been made for the Paulianist clergy, and because they would have been looked upon as simple lay-persons, seeing that they have not been ordained." It is easy to see that Van Espen here inserts a meaning which is foreign to the text. Aubespine has attempted another explanation, which has been in later times adopted by Neander. He supposes that the deaconesses of the Paulianists were of two kinds: those who were really ordained, and those widows who had never received ordination, and who had only by an abuse the name of deaconesses. The canon would continue the first in their charge, and place the second among the laity. But the text itself does not make the least allusion to these two kinds of deaconesses; and what Neander alleges against the opinion of those who read διακόνων instead of διακονισσῶν has no weight. According to him, it would have been superfluous to speak again specially of the deacons in this passage, since the clergy in general had already been spoken of in that which precedes. It may be answered, that if the Synod wished to make it understood that the present rules extended to all degrees of the clergy, there is an explanation of its reason for making express mention of the deacons and inferior clergy.

The words of the canon, ἐπεὶ μηδὲ χειροθεσίαν τινὰ
ἔχουσιν, still make the meaning of the sense difficult, and
appear opposed to the variation we have adopted. It cannot
be denied that the Apostolical Constitutions really speak of
the ordination of deaconesses by the imposition of hands,
and the Council of Chalcedon speaks of it still more clearly
in its fifteenth canon. According to this canon, on the
contrary, the deaconesses would not have received any
imposition of hands. Valesius and Van Espen have sought
to solve this difficulty by saying that, at the time of the
Council of Nicæa, the custom had not yet been introduced
of laying hands on deaconesses. But the Apostolical
Constitutions testify to the contrary. Aubespine has put
forward another explanation, which proceeds from his
theory analysed above: he maintains that the deaconesses of
the Catholic Church were truly ordained by the imposition
of hands, but that among the Paulianists there were two
classes of deaconesses, an ordained and an unordained. It
seems to us that a third solution of this difficulty might be
found, put forward by Baronius, and adopted by Justell. In
supposing that at the time of the Council of Nicæa the
deaconesses received imposition of hands, it must,
however, be remembered that this act was essentially
different from clerical ordination properly so called: it was a
mere benediction, not an ordination. In describing, then,
clerical ordination by χειροθεσία sensu strictiori, it might be
said that the deaconesses had received no χειροθεσία. The
decree against the Meletians, and the eighth canon of Nicæa
against the Novatians, prove that the Fathers of Nicæa took
the word χειροθεσία as synonymous with mere benediction.

CAN. 20

Charles Joseph Hefele, D.D.

Ἐπειδή τινές εἰσιν ἐν τῇ κυριακῇ γόνυ κλίνοντες καὶ ἐν ταῖς τῆς πεντεκοστῆς ἡμέραις· ὑπὲρ τοῦ πάντα ἐν πάσῃ παροικίᾳ φυλάττεσθαι, ἑστῶτας ἔδοξε τῇ ἁγίᾳ συνόδῳ τὰς εὐχὰς ἀποδιδόναι τῷ Θεῷ.

"As some kneel on the Lord's day and on the days of Pentecost, the holy Synod has decided that, for the observance of a general rule, all shall offer their prayers to God standing."

Tertullian says in the third chapter of his book de Corona, that Christians considered it wrong to pray kneeling on Sundays. This liberty of remaining standing, he adds, is granted us from Easter to Pentecost. By the word πεντηκοστὴ the single day of Pentecost must not be understood, but rather the whole time between Easter and Pentecost. It is thus, for example, that S. Basil the Great speaks of the seven weeks of the τῆς ἱερᾶς Πενηκοστῆς. Instead, then, of praying kneeling, as they did on other days, Christians prayed standing on Sundays and during Eastertide. They were moved in that by a symbolical motive: they celebrated during these days the remembrance of the resurrection of Christ, and consequently our own deliverance through His resurrection. All the Churches did not, however, adopt this practice; for we see in the Acts of the Apostles that S. Paul prayed kneeling during the time between Easter and Pentecost. The Council of Nicæa wished to make the usual practice the universal law; and the later Fathers of the Church, e.g. Ambrose and Basil, show that this custom spread more and more. The Catholic Church has preserved to our days the principal direction of this canon, and it has been inserted in the Corpus juris canonici.

SEC. 43. Paphnutius and the projected Law of Celibacy

Socrates, Sozomen, and Gelasius affirm that the Synod of Nicæa, as well as that of Elvira (can. 33), desired to pass a law respecting celibacy. This law was to forbid all bishops, priests, and deacons (Sozomen adds subdeacons), who were married at the time of their ordination, to continue to live with their wives. But, say these historians, the law was opposed openly and decidedly by Paphnutius, bishop of a city of the Upper Thebaïs in Egypt, a man of a high reputation, who had lost an eye during the persecution under Maximian. He was also celebrated for his miracles, and was held in so great respect by the Emperor, that the latter often kissed the empty socket of the lost eye. Paphnutius declared with a loud voice, "that too heavy a yoke ought not to be laid upon the clergy; that marriage and married intercourse are of themselves honourable and undefiled; that the Church ought not to be injured by an extreme severity, for all could not live in absolute continency: in this way (by not prohibiting married intercourse) the virtue of the wife would be much more certainly preserved (viz. the wife of a clergyman, because she might find injury elsewhere, if her husband withdrew from her married intercourse). The intercourse of a man with his lawful wife may also be a chaste intercourse. It would therefore be sufficient, according to the ancient tradition of the Church, if those who had taken holy orders without being married were prohibited from marrying afterwards; but those clergy who had been married only once, as laymen, were not to be separated from their wives

(Gelasius adds, or being only a reader or cantor). This discourse of Paphnutius made so much the more impression, because he had never lived in matrimony himself, and had had no conjugal intercourse. Paphnutius, indeed, had been brought up in a monastery, and his great purity of manners had rendered him especially celebrated. Therefore the Council took the serious words of the Egyptian bishop into consideration, stopped all discussion upon the law, and left to each cleric the responsibility of deciding the point as he would.

If this account be true, we must conclude that a law was proposed to the Council of Nicæa the same as one which had been carried twenty years previously at Elvira, in Spain: this coincidence would lead us to believe that it was the Spaniard Hosius who proposed the law respecting celibacy at Nicæa. The discourse ascribed to Paphnutius, and the consequent decision of the Synod, agree very well with the text of the Apostolic Constitutions, and with the whole practice of the Greek Church in respect to celibacy. The Greek Church as well as the Latin accepted the principle, that whoever had taken holy orders before marriage, ought not to be married afterwards. In the Latin Church, bishops, priests, deacons, and even subdeacons, were considered to be subject to this law, because the latter were at a very early period reckoned among the higher servants of the Church, which was not the case in the Greek Church. The Greek Church went so far as to allow deacons to marry after their ordination, if previously to it they had expressly obtained from their bishop permission to do so. The Council of Ancyra affirms this (c. 10). We see that the Greek Church wished to leave the bishops free to decide the matter; but in reference to priests, it also prohibited them from marrying after their ordination.

Therefore, whilst the Latin Church exacted of those presenting themselves for ordination, even as subdeacons, that they should not continue to live with their wives if they were married, the Greek Church gave no such prohibition; but if the wife of an ordained clergyman died, the Greek Church allowed no second marriage. The Apostolic Constitutions decided this point in the same way. To leave their wives from a pretext of piety was also forbidden to Greek priests; and the Synod of Gangra (c. 4) took up the defence of married priests against the Eustathians. Eustathius, however, was not alone among the Greeks in opposing the marriage of all clerics, and in desiring to introduce into the Greek Church the Latin discipline on this point. S. Epiphanius also inclined towards this side. The Greek Church did not, however, adopt this rigour in reference to priests, deacons, and subdeacons; but by degrees it came to be required of bishops, and of the higher order of clergy in general, that they should live in celibacy. Yet this was not until after the compilation of the Apostolic Canons (c. 5) and of the Constitutions (l.c.); for in those documents mention is made of bishops living in wedlock, and Church history shows that there were married bishops, for instance Synesius, in the fifth century. But it is fair to remark, even as to Synesius, that he made it an express condition of his acceptation, on his election to the episcopate, that he might continue to live the married life. Thomassin believes that Synesius did not seriously require this condition, and only spoke thus for the sake of escaping the episcopal office; which would seem to imply that in his time Greek bishops had already begun to live in celibacy. At the Trullan Synod (c. 13) the Greek Church finally settled the question of the marriage of priests. Baronius, Valesius, and other historians, have considered the account of the part taken by Paphnutius to be apocryphal. Baronius says, that as the Council of Nicæa in its third canon gave a law upon celibacy, it is quite impossible to admit that it would alter such a law on account of Paphnutius. But Baronius is mistaken in seeing a law upon celibacy in that third canon: he thought it to be so, because, when mentioning the women who might live in the clergyman's house—his mother, sister, etc.—the canon does not say a word about the wife. It had no occasion to mention her; it was referring to the συνεισάκτοι, whilst these συνεισάκτοι and married women have nothing in common. Natalis Alexander gives this anecdote about Paphnutius in full: he desired to refute Bellarmin, who considered it to be untrue, and an invention of Socrates to please the Novatians. Natalis Alexander often maintains erroneous opinions, and on the present question he deserves no confidence. If, as S. Epiphanius relates, the Novatians maintained that the clergy might be married exactly like the laity, it cannot be said that Socrates shared that opinion, since he says, or rather makes Paphnutius say, that, according to ancient tradition, those not married at the time of ordination should not be so subsequently. Moreover, if it may be said that Socrates had a partial sympathy with the Novatians, he certainly cannot be considered as belonging to them, still less can he be accused of falsifying history in their favour. He may sometimes have propounded erroneous opinions, but there is a great difference between that and the invention of a whole story. Valesius especially makes use of the argument ex silentio against Socrates, (a.) Rufinus, he says, gives many particulars about Paphnutius in his History of the Church: he mentions his martyrdom, his miracles, and the Emperor's reverence for him, but not a single word of the business about celibacy. (b.) The name of Paphnutius is wanting in the list of Egyptian bishops present at the Synod. These two arguments of Valesius are very weak; the second has the authority of Rufinus himself against it, who expressly says that Bishop Paphnutius was present at the Council of Nicæa. If Valesius means by lists only the signatures at the end of the acts of the Council, this proves nothing; for these lists are very imperfect, and it is well known that many bishops whose names are not among these signatures were present at Nicæa. This argument ex silentio is evidently insufficient to prove that the anecdote about Paphnutius must be rejected as false, seeing that it is in perfect harmony with the practice of the ancient Church, and especially of the Greek Church, on the subject of clerical marriages. On the other hand, Thomassin pretends that there was no such practice, and endeavours to prove by quotations from S. Epiphanius, S. Jerome, Eusebius, and S. John Chrysostom, that even in the East priests who were married at the time of their ordination were prohibited from continuing to live with their wives. The texts quoted by Thomassin prove only that the Greeks gave especial honour to priests living in perfect continency, but they do not prove that this continence was a duty incumbent upon all priests; and so much the less, as the fifth and twenty-fifth apostolic canons, the fourth canon of Gangra, and the thirteenth of the Trullan Synod, demonstrate clearly enough what was the universal custom of the Greek Church on this point. Lupus and Phillips explain the words of Paphnutius in another sense. According to them, the Egyptian bishop was not speaking in a general way: he simply desired that the contemplated law should not include the subdeacons. But this explanation does not agree with the extracts quoted from Socrates, Sozomen, and Gelasius, who believe Paphnutius intended deacons and priests as well.

SEC. 44. Conclusion: Spurious Documents

It was probably at the conclusion of its business that the Council of Nicæa sent to the bishops of Egypt and Libya the official letter containing its decisions relative to the three great questions which it had to decide, viz. concerning Arianism, the Meletian schism, and the celebration of Easter.

When the Synod had completed its business, the Emperor Constantine celebrated his vicennalia, that is, the twentieth anniversary of his accession to the empire. Consequently this festival shows the terminus ad quem of the Council. Constantine was declared Emperor during the summer of 306; his vicennalia must therefore have taken place during the summer or autumn of 325. In order to testify his peculiar respect for the Fathers of Nicæa, i.e. for the Synod itself, the Emperor invited all the bishops to a splendid repast in the imperial palace. A hedge was formed of a multitude of soldiers with drawn swords; and Eusebius can find no words to describe the beauty of the scene—to tell how the men of God passed through the imperial apartments without any fear, through the midst of all these swords. At the conclusion of the banquet, each bishop received rich presents from the Emperor. Some days afterwards, Constantine commanded another session to be held, at which he appeared in person, to exhort the bishops to use every endeavour for the maintenance of peace; he then asked them to remember him in their prayers, and finally gave them all permission to return home. They hastened to do so; and filled with joy at the great work of pacification just concluded by the Emperor and the Council, they made known its resolutions in their own countries.

On his part the Emperor also sent many letters, either in a general way to all the Churches, or to the bishops who had not been present at the Council; and in these letters he declared that the decrees of the Council were to be considered laws of the empire. Eusebius, Socrates, and Gelasius have preserved three of these imperial edicts: in the first, Constantine expresses his conviction that the Nicene decrees were inspired by the Holy Spirit; which shows the great authority and esteem in which the decisions of Nicæa were held from the very beginning. S. Athanasius gives similar testimony. He says, in the letter which he sent to the African bishops, in the name of ninety bishops assembled in synod: "It (the Synod of Nicæa) has been received by the whole world (πᾶσα ἡ οἰκουμένη); and as several synods are just now being assembled, it has been acknowledged by the faithful in Dalmatia, Dardania, Macedonia, Epirus, Crete, the other islands, Sicily, Cyprus, Pamphilia, Lycia, Isauria, all Egypt, Libya, and the greater part of Arabia." S. Athanasius expresses himself in like manner in his letter to the Emperor Jovian in 363: he often calls the Synod of Nicæa an œcumenical synod, adding that a universal synod had been convoked, that provincial councils, which might easily fall into error, might not have to decide on so important a subject as Arianism. Finally, he calls the Council of Nicæa "a true pillar, and a monument of the victory obtained over every heresy." Other Fathers of the Church, living in the fourth or fifth centuries, speak of the Council of Nicæa in the same terms as S. Athanasius, showing the greatest respect for its decisions. We may mention Ambrose, Chrysostom, and especially Pope Leo the Great, who wrote as follows: Sancti illi et venerabiles patres, qui in urbe Nicæna, sacrilego Ario cum sua impietate damnato, mansuras usque in finem mundi leges ecelesiasticorum canonum condiderunt, et apud nos et in toto orbe terrarum in suis constitutionibus vivunt; et si quid usquam aliter, quam illi statuere, præsumitur, sine cunctatione cassatur: ut quæ ad perpetuam utilitatem generaliter instituta sunt, nulla commutatione varientur. Pope Leo therefore considered the authority of the Nicene canons to be everlasting; and he says in the same epistle (ch. 2), that they were inspired by the Holy Ghost, and that no subsequent council, however great, could be compared to it, still less preferred to it. (Leo here especially alludes to the fourth Œcumenical Council.) Eastern Christians had so much reverence for the Council of Nicæa, that the Greeks, Syrians, and Egyptians even established a festival for the purpose of perpetuating the remembrance of this assemblage of 318 bishops at Nicæa. The Greeks kept this festival on the Sunday before Pentecost, the Syrians in the month of July, the Egyptians in November. Tillemont says truly: "If one wished to collect all the existing proofs of the great veneration in which the Council of Nicæa was held, the enumeration would never end. In all ages, with the exception of a few heretics, this sacred assembly at Nicæa has never been spoken of but with the greatest respect."

The words of Pope Leo which we have quoted especially show the high esteem in which Rome and the Popes held the Council of Nicæa. The acts of the Synod were first signed, as before said, by the representatives of the Holy See; and it is perfectly certain that Pope Silvester afterwards sanctioned what his legates had done. The only question is, whether the Council of Nicæa asked for a formal approbation, and whether it was granted in answer to their request. Some writers have answered this question in the affirmative; but in order to establish their opinion, have relied upon a set of spurious documents. These are: 1st, A pretended letter from Hosius, Macarius of Jerusalem, and the two Roman priests Victor and Vincentius, addressed to Pope Silvester, in the name of the whole Synod. The letter says, "that the Pope ought to convoke a Roman synod, in order to confirm the decisions of the Council of Nicæa." 2d, The answer of Pope Silvester, and his decree of confirmation. 3d, Another letter from Pope Silvester, of similar contents. 4th, The acts of this pretended third Roman Council, convoked to confirm the decisions of the Council of Nicæa: this Council, composed of 275 bishops, must have made some additions to the Nicene decrees. To these documents must be added, 5th, the Constitutio Silvestri, proceeding from the pretended second Roman Council. This Council does not indeed speak of giving approval to the Nicene decrees; but with this exception, it is almost identical in its decisions and acts with those of the third Roman Council. These five documents have been preserved in several MSS., at Rome, Köln, or elsewhere: they have been reproduced in almost all the collections of the Councils; but now all are unanimous in considering them to be spurious, as they evidently are. They betray a period, a way of thinking, and circumstances, later than those of the fourth century. The barbarous, almost unintelligible Latin of these documents, particularly points to a later century, and to a decay in the Latin language, which had not taken place at the time of the Nicene Synod.

We may further observe on the subject of these documents:

1. Concerning the first: (α.) Macarius of Jerusalem, in this document, appears as the principal representative of the Synod of Nicæa; and he is, in fact, made to take precedence of the Patriarchs of Alexandria and of Antioch, who are not even named. Now, at the period of the Council of Nicæa, the see of Jerusalem had no peculiar place of eminence. (β.) In the superscription, instead of "the Synod of Nicæa," etc., the document has the words, "the 318," etc., an expression which was not in use at the time of the Council of Nicæa. (γ.) This document is dated viii. Cal. Julias: we should therefore be led to conclude, if we trusted to that date, that the Council asked the Holy See for approval of its work a few days after its commencement.

2. Coustant and others prove the spuriousness of the second document—namely, Silvester's supposed confirmation of the Synod—on the following grounds:—

(α.) There is in the document a reference to the (false) Easter canon of Victorinus (or Victorius) of Aquitania. Now Victorinus did not flourish until 125 years later, about the middle of the fifth century. It is true that Döllinger has recently offered a different opinion respecting this Victorinus, suggesting that it is not Victorius of Aquitania who is referred to, but a Roman heretic (a Patripassian) of that name, who lived at the beginning of the third century.

This Victorius was a contemporary of Pope Callistus and of the priest (afterwards antipope) Hippolytus, and subsequently resisted the Easter canon drawn up by the latter, which afterwards came into use, and even the Church doctrine of the Trinity. In favour of this theory is the fact, that in the fifth of these forged documents Victorius is mentioned along with Callistus and Hippolytus, and an anathema is pronounced upon all the three. If Döllinger is right, as we cannot doubt, the argument of Coustant must fall away; but the spuriousness of the document is still entirely beyond doubt, and has been recognised by Döllinger.

(β.) At the end of the document an entirely false chronological date is given, Constantine VII. et Constantio Cæsare IV. consulibus. When Constantine became consul for the seventh time (A.D. 326), his son Constantius was invested with that dignity for the first time, and not for the fourth. Such a chronological error would certainly not have been committed in a wilting so important in the Roman archives.

3. The spuriousness of the third document betrays itself chiefly in the fact that it contains the anathema pronounced upon Photinus of Sirmium, which was not put forth until the year 351, at the first Synod of Sirmium.

4. The fourth document is rendered doubtful by the consideration, that it is impossible for all the writers of ancient times to have been silent on the subject of a Roman synod so important, and at which 275 bishops were present. Athanasius and Hilary speak ex professo of the synods of that period; but neither of them says a word of

this great Roman Synod, nor gives the slightest intimation of it. Besides, if we give credence to the superscription of this document, the Synod must have been held in the presence of Constantine the Great, whereas the Emperor was not once in Rome during the whole of the year 325. But even if, as Binius has suggested, the words præsento Constantine have been erroneously removed from the place where they were followed by apud Nicænum, and placed in the title of this, it cannot, however, be denied: (α.) That the decree passed by this alleged Roman Synod, which orders that Easter shall be celebrated between the 14th and 21st of Nisan, is nonsensical and anti-Nicene. (β.) Equally incompatible with the Nicene period is the rule that clerics are not to be brought before a secular tribunal. This privilegium fori was at that time unknown. (γ.) Equally absurd is the ordinance respecting the degrees in advancing to the episcopate or the presbyterate, which directs that one must be an Ostiarius for a year, twenty years a Lector, ten years an Exorcist, five years an Acolyte, five years a Subdeacon, and five years a Deacon; that is to say, altogether forty-six years in the ministry, before he could become a priest. Such an absurdity was certainly never promulgated by a Roman council.

5. We have no need to give a particular account of the supposed acts of an alleged second Roman Council in 324, which form the fifth document, as they say nothing of a confirmation of the Nicene Synod. As, however, this document seems to have proceeded from the same pen as the other four, we may, by way of showing how little knowledge the forger had of that period, simply point out that this second Roman Council was professedly held

during the Nicene Synod, as is expressly stated in the Epilogue, and that it came to an end on the 30th of May 324, that is to say, a whole year before the beginning of that of Nicæa.

Coustant suggests that all these documents must have been forged in the sixth century. He has treated particularly of the fifth of these spurious documents, and in his preface he suggests that it was composed soon after the time of Pope Symmachus. Symmachus had been unjustly accused of several crimes, but was acquitted by a Synod which met in 501 or 503; and at the same time the principle was asserted, that the Pope could not be judged by other bishops. In order to establish this principle and that of the forum privilegiatum, which is closely connected with it, Coustant says they fabricated several documents, and among others this fifth: the bad Latin in which it is written, and the fact that it was discovered in a Lombard MS., have caused it to be thought that it was composed by a Lombard residing at Rome. A principal argument employed by Coustant to show that this piece dated from the sixth century, the period during which Victorinus of Aquitania lived, has been overthrown by Döllinger's hypothesis, to which we have referred.

All these documents are therefore without doubt apocryphal; but though they are apocryphal, we must not conclude from this that all their contents are false, that is to say, that the Council of Nicæa never asked Pope Silvester to give his approval to their decrees. Baronius thinks that this request was really made, and on our part we think we can add to his arguments the following observations:

(a.) We know that the fourth Œcumenical Council, held at
Chalcedon, sent to Pope Leo their acts to be approved by
him. Anatolius Patriarch of Constantinople wrote in the
following manner to Leo: Gestorum vis omnis et
confirmatio auctoritati vestræ Beatitudinis fuerit reservata.
The Council speaks in the same way as Anatolius in the
letter which they wrote to the Pope: Omnem vobis
gestorum vim insinuavimus, ad comprobationem nostræ
sinceritatis, et ad eorum, quæ a nobis gesta sunt, firmitatem
et consonantiam. The Emperor Marcian also regarded this
approval of the Pope as necessary for the decrees passed at
Chalcedon; and he asked repeatedly and earnestly for this
approval, with the suggestion that it should be given in a
special writing; and he directed that it should also be read
everywhere in his Greek dominions, that there might be no
doubt of the validity of the Council of Chalcedon. The
Emperor says he is astonished that the Pope had not sent
these letters of approval: Quas videlicet in sanctissimis
ecclesiis perlectas in omnium oportebat notitiam venire.
This omission, he goes on, nonnullorum animis
ambiguitatem multam injecit, utrum tua Beatitudo, quæ in
sancta synodo decreta sunt, confirmaverat. Et ob eam rem
tua pietas literas mittere dignabitur, per quas omnibus
ecclesiis et populis manifestum fiat, in sancta synodo
peracta a tua Beatitudine rata haberi.

(b.) These texts, explicit as they are, authorize us in
believing, not quite without doubt, but nevertheless with a
certain degree of probability, that the principles which
guided the fourth Council were not strange to the first; and
this probability is greatly increased by the fact that a Synod
composed of more than forty bishops, assembled from all

parts of Italy, very explicitly and confidently declared, and
that in opposition to the Greeks, that the 318 bishops at
Nicæa confirmationem rerum, atque auctoritatem sanctæ
Romanæ ecclesiæ detulerunt.

(c.) Socrates tells us that Pope Julius asserted: Canon
ecclesiasticus vetat, ne decreta absque sententia episcopi
Romani ecclesiis sanciantur. Pope Julius then clearly
declared not only that œcumenical councils ought to be
approved by the Bishop of Rome, but also that a rule of
ecclesiastical discipline (canon ecclesiasticus) demanded
this. We must not regard these words as an allusion to this
or that particular canon. But as Pope Julius filled the Holy
See only eleven years after the Council of Nicæa, we are
forced to believe that such a rule must have existed at the
time of the Nicene Synod.

(d.) The Collectio Dionysii exigui proves that, about the
year 500, it was the general persuasion at Rome that the
acts of the Council of Nicæa had been approved by the
Pope. Dionysius in fact added to the collection of the
Nicene acts: Et placuit, ut hæc omnia mitterentur ad
episcopum Romæ Silvestrum. It is this general persuasion
which probably made people think of fabricating the false
documents of which we have spoken, and gave the forger
the hope of passing his wares as genuine.

APPENDIX

THE SO-CALLED APOSTOLIC CANONS

ABOUT the year 500 A.D., Dionysius the Less, who was
an abbot in a monastery at Rome, translated a collection of
canons from Greek into Latin, for Bishop Stephen of
Salona, at the head of which he placed fifty canons, which,
according to him, proceeded from the apostles, and had
been arranged and collected by their disciple Clement of
Rome. Dionysius placed after them the canons of Nicæa, of
Ancyra, of Constantinople, of Chalcedon, etc. We are still
in possession not only of this collection, but even of its
Præfatio, which was addressed to Bishop Stephen: it is to
be found in every good collection of the Councils. The
words of this preface, Canones, qui dicuntur apostolorum,
show that Dionysius had some doubt as to the apostolic
origin of these canons, which is made more evident when
he adds; quibus plurimi consensum non præbucre facilem.
Dr. von Drey, who is the author of the best work upon
these apostolic canons, and also upon the Apostolic
Constitutions, thinks that by plurimi we must here
understand only the Greeks, for the translation by
Dionysius is the first Latin translation of these canons. This
last statement is true; but we must not conclude from it that
the Greek text of these canons was not known in the West,
and especially in Italy, where at this period so many spoke
Greek. We must not conclude, however, that this sentence
of Dionysius, Quamvis postea quædam constituta
pontificum ex ipsis canonibus assumpta esse videantur,
referred to the Popes: the word pontifices rather signifies
the bishops, and especially the Greek bishops, who made

use of the so-called apostolic canons in their Synod, in the arrangement of their own canons.

About fifty years after Dionysius the Less, Joannes Scholasticus of Antioch, who was made Patriarch of Constantinople in 565, published a Greek collection of canons, σύνταγμα κανόνων, which also contained the apostolic canons; but instead of numbering fifty, they here amounted to eighty-five. This collection is still in existence, and was printed in the second volume in folio of the Bibliotheca juris canonici, by Voellus and Justellus (Paris 1661). The arrangement of the apostolic canons is here also attributed to Clement of Rome, and Joannes Scholasticus implies that the most ancient Greek collections of canons also contain the eighty-five apostolic canons.

It is undeniable that the Greek copy which Dionysius had before him belonged to a different family of collections of Councils from that used by Joannes Scholasticus, for they differ frequently, if not essentially, both in text and in the way of numbering the canons; and hence it is explained how Dionysius the Less knew only of fifty apostolic canons. It is supposed that at first there were indeed only fifty in circulation, and that the thirty-five others were added subsequently. However that may be, it is quite certain that, if Dionysius the Less did omit these thirty-five canons, it was not out of consideration for Rome, as was suggested by De Marca; for none of these canons was so much calculated to shock the Roman Church as was the forty-sixth of the first series, which, in contradiction of the Roman practice, declared all baptism by heretics to be invalid.

When Joannes Scholasticus became Patriarch of Constantinople, he brought his collection, and consequently also the eighty-five apostolic canons contained in it, into ecclesiastical use; and in 792, in its second canon, the Trullan Synod declared not only that the eighty-five apostolic canons had the force of laws, but besides this, that they must be considered as of apostolic origin, whilst they rejected the Apostolic Constitutions. It is quite true, it says, that the apostolic canons recommend the observance of the Constitutions; but as the latter were soon falsified, the Synod could not accept them. It did not, however, doubt their apostolic origin.

The Synod in Trullo being, as is well known, regarded as œcumenical by the Greek Church, the authenticity of the eighty-five canons was decided in the East for all future time. It was otherwise in the West. At the same period that Dionysius the Less translated the collection in question for Bishop Stephen, Pope Gelasius promulgated his celebrated decree, de libris non recipiendis. Drey mentions it, but in a way which requires correction. Following in this the usual opinion, he says that the Synod at Rome in which Gelasius published this decree was held in 494; but we shall see hereafter that this Synod was held in 496. Also Drey considers himself obliged to adopt another erroneous opinion, according to which Gelasius declared in the same decree the apostolic canons to be apocryphal. This opinion is to be maintained only so long as the usual text of this decree is consulted, as the original text as it is given in the ancient manuscripts does not contain the passage which mentions the apostolic canons. This passage was certainly added subsequently, with many others, probably by Pope

Hormisdas (514–543), when he made a new edition of the decree of Gelasius. As Dionysius the Less published his collection in all probability subsequently to the publication of the decree of Gelasius, properly so called, in 496, we can understand why this decree did not mention the apostolical canons. Dionysius the Less did not go to Rome while Gelasius was living, and did not know him personally, as he himself says plainly in the Præfatio of his collection of the papal decrees. It is hence also plain how it was that in another collection of canons subsequently made by Dionysius, of which the preface still remains to us, he does not insert the apostolic canons, but has simply this remark: Quos non admisit universalitas, ego quoque in hoc opere prætermisi. Dionysius the Less, in fact, compiled this new collection at a time when Pope Hormisdas had already explicitly declared the apostolic canons to be apocryphal. Notwithstanding this, these canons, and particularly the fifty mentioned by Dionysius the Less, did not entirely fall into discredit in the West; but rather they came to be received, because the first collection of Dionysius was considered of great authority. They also passed into other collections, and particularly into that of the pseudo-Isidore; and in 1054, Humbert, legate of Pope Leo IX., made the following declaration: Clementis liber, id est itincrarium Petri apostoli et canones apostolorum numerantur inter apocrypha, EXCEPTIS CAPITULIS QUINQUAGINTA, quæ decreverunt regulis orthodoxis adjungenda. Gratian also, in his decree, borrowed from the fifty apostolic canons, and they gradually obtained the force of laws. But many writers, especially Hincmar of Rheims, like Dionysius the Less, raised doubts upon the apostolical origin of these canons. From the sixteenth century the opinion has been universal that these documents are not authentic; with the exception, however, of the French Jesuit Turrianus, who endeavoured to defend their genuineness, as well as the authenticity of the pseudo-Isidorian decrees. According to the Centuriators of Magdeburg, it was especially Gabriel d'Aubespine Bishop of Orleans, the celebrated Archbishop Peter de Marca, and the Anglican Beveridge, who proved that they were not really compiled by the apostles, but were made partly in the second and chiefly in the third century. Beveridge considered this collection to be a repertory of ancient canons given by Synods in the second and third centuries. In opposition to them, the Calvinist Dallæus (Daillé) regarded it as the work of a forger who lived in the fifth and sixth centuries; but Beveridge refuted him so convincingly, that from that time his opinion, with some few modifications, has been that of all the learned. Beveridge begins with the principle, that the Church in the very earliest times must have had a collection of canons; and he demonstrates that from the commencement of the fourth century, bishops, synods, and other authorities often quote, as documents in common use, the κανὼν ἀποστολικός, or ἐκκλησιαστικὸς, or ἀρχαῖος; as was done, for instance, at the Council of Nicæa, by Alexander Bishop of Alexandria, and by the Emperor Constantine, etc. According to Beveridge, these quotations make allusion to the apostolic canons, and prove that they were already in use before the fourth century.

Dr. v. Drey's work, undertaken with equal learning and critical acuteness, has produced new results. He has proved, 1st, that in the primitive Church there was no special codex canonum in use; 2d, that the expression κανὼν ἀποστολικὸς does not at all prove the existence of our apostolic canons, but rather refers to such commands of the apostles as are to be found in Holy Scripture (for instance, to what they say about the rights and duties of bishops), or else it simply signifies this: "Upon this point there is a rule and a practice which can be traced back to apostolic times;" but not exactly a written law. As a summary of Drey's conclusions, the following points may be noted:—Several of the pretended apostolic canons are in reality very ancient, and may be assigned to apostolic times; but they have been arranged at a much more recent period, and there are only a few which, having been borrowed from the Apostolic Constitutions, are really more ancient than the Council of Nicæa. Most of them were composed in the fourth or even in the fifth century, and are hardly more than repetitions and variations of the decrees of the Synods of that period, particularly of the Synod of Antioch in 341. Some few are even more recent than the fourth Œcumenical Council held at Chalcedon, from the canons of which they have been derived. Two collections of the apostolic canons have been made: the first after the middle of the fifth century; the second, containing thirty-five more than the other, at the commencement of the sixth century. From these conclusions Drey draws up the following table:—

The apostolic canons are taken,—

1. C. 1, 2, 7, 8, 17, 18, 20, 27, 34, 46, 47, 49, 51, 52, 53, 60, 64, and 65, from the six first books of the Apostolic Constitutions, which originated in the East, and particularly in Syria, in the second half of the third century.

2. C. 79, from the eighth book of the Apostolic Constitutions, considerably more recent than the six first, but which, together with the seventh, was united to the six first books before 325.

3. C. 21–24 and 80, from the Council of Nicæa.

4. C. 9–16 inclusive, c. 29, 32–41 inclusive, and 76, from the Council of Antioch held in 341.

5. C. 45, 64, 70, and 71, from the Synod of Laodicea.

6. C. 75, from the sixth canon of the Council of Constantinople, held in 381.

7. C. 28, from the Synod of Constantinople, held in 394.

8. C. 30, 67, 74, 81, 83, from the fourth Œcumenical Council.

9. C. 19 is an imitation of the second canon of Neocæsarea.

10. C. 25 and 26 are from Basil the Great.

11. C. 69 and 70 from the pretended letter of S. Ignatius to the Philippians.

12. Rather less than a third of the apostolic canons are of unknown origin.

Bickell, in his History of Ecclesiastical Law, while he adopts for the most part Drey's conclusions, has shown that he brought down the origin of our canons to a period somewhat too recent. When, for instance, Drey supposes that the thirtieth apostolic canon is taken from the second canon of the fourth Œcumenical Council held at

Chalcedon, that the eighty-first apostolic canon is taken from the third canon, and the eighty-third apostolic canon from the seventh canon of the same Council, Bickell remarks that the three canons of Chalcedon, of which we are speaking, certainly bear some analogy to the apostolic canons; but this analogy, he says, is far from being striking, and certainly does not prove that the composer of these canons extracted them from those of the Council. Besides, it must not be forgotten, that in giving directions as to what is to be done when a bishop is formally disobedient (that he should be cited three times), the Council of Chalcedon, nay, even that of Ephesus (431) and that of Constantinople (448), quote canons which they call ecclesiastical and divine. Now these canons are nothing else but the seventy-fourth apostolic canon, which alone gives directions as to what is to be done in such a case. Bickell further quotes a passage from the acts of the seventh session of the Synod of Ephesus held in 431, in which Rheginus Archbishop of Cyprus, in a memorandum of which we have now only the Latin translation, appeals to the canones apostolici, and to the definitiones Nicænæ Synodi, to prove his Church to be independent of that of Antioch. If, as we doubt not, Rheginus intends here to speak of the apostolic canons, and especially of the thirty-sixth (according to Dionysius), it is evident that these canons were then in use. This may be further proved from the Synod of Constantinople held in 394, which, in the words καθὼς οἱ ἀποστολικοὶ κανόνες διωρίσαντο, seems to allude to the apostolic canons.

It is true that Drey endeavours to explain κανόνες ἀποστολικοὶ in the sense pointed out above; but it is probable that we must here think of canons formulated and written, and not only of an ancient ecclesiastical practice. In fact, (α) there is no ancient ecclesiastical custom which ordains that a disobedient bishop should be summoned three times. (β) At such a recent period, when there were already collections of canons, it was more natural to quote these canons than a simple ecclesiastical tradition, (γ) The definitiones Nicænæ Synodi and the canones apostolici would not have been placed on an equal footing if these canones had not been positively reduced to form. (δ) Since these ancient Synods themselves quoted canons which they called apostolic, and which, as we have seen, were then in use, it must be concluded that it was not the apostolic canons which were framed according to the canons of these Councils, but that the contrary was the case. Drey, as we have already remarked, supposes that a great number of the apostolic canons were taken from those of the Council of Antioch held in 341, and Bickell agrees with him on this point. It cannot be denied that Drey's opinion has much to be said for it: it does not, however, appear to us quite unassailable; and perhaps it may still be possible to prove that the canons of this Council of Antioch were rather taken from the apostolic canons. It may also be the same with the Synod of Nicæa, which, in its first, second, fifth, and fifteenth canons, alludes to ancient canons in use in the Church. Perhaps the Council placed the canons referred to among the apostolic canons which may have circulated in the Church before being inserted in our present collection. This hypothesis is in a certain way confirmed by a document to which Galland has drawn attention, but which Drey and Bickell have overlooked. We have mentioned in the present volume, that in 1738 Scipio Maffei published three ancient documents, the first of which was a Latin translation of a letter written on the subject of Meletius by the Egyptian bishops Hesychius, Phileas, etc. This letter was written during the persecution of Diocletian, that is, between 303 and 305: it is addressed to Meletius himself, and especially accuses him of having ordained priests in other dioceses. This conduct, they tell him, is contrary to all ecclesiastical rule (aliena a more divino et REGULA ECCLESIASTICA), and Meletius himself knows very well that it is a lex patrum et propatrum ... in alienis parœciis non licere alicui episcoporum ordinationes celebrare. Maffei himself supposes that the Egyptian bishops were here referring to the thirty-fifth canon (the thirty-sixth according to the enumeration of Dionysius), and this opinion can hardly be controverted.

The Greek text of the apostolic canons exists in many ancient manuscripts, as well in those which contain the Apostolic Constitutions (and then they are placed at the end in a chapter by themselves), as in the manuscripts of ancient collections of canons. In the ancient collections they generally number eighty-five, corresponding to the number found in the copies employed by Dionysius the Less and Joannes Scholasticus. On the other hand, when they are collected in the manuscripts of the Apostolic Constitutions, they are divided into seventy-six canons. For it must not be forgotten that in ancient times the number of canons, and the way in which they were divided, varied greatly.

The fifty apostolic canons in the translation by Dionysius the Less appeared for the first time in the collection of the Councils by Merlin, published in 1523, and they are found in the more recent collections of Hardouin and Mansi. The

Greek text was edited for the first time by Gregory Haloander in 1531. In 1561, Gentianus Hervetus published a superior edition of them. These two latter authors divide the canons into eighty-four, and Hervetus' division has been adopted by Hardouin, Mansi, and Bruns. In our edition we also have adopted the number of eighty-five, at the same time accepting for the fifty-first the division established by Dionysius the Less. For the sake of perspicuity, we have besides placed the two methods of enumeration side by side: first that of Dionysius the Less, then that of Hervetus, Hardouin, Mansi, and Bruns; so much the more, as all our quotations up to this time have been made according to the second enumeration. We shall also borrow their Greek text from those authors, which here and there differs from the text placed at the end of the Constitutions. The Latin translation of the first fifty canons is by Dionysius the Less; that of the last thirty-five is by Cotelerius.

ΚΑΝΟΝΕΣ

ΤΩΝ ΑΓΙΩΝ ΚΑΙ ΠΑΝΣΕΠΤΩΝ ΑΠΟΣΤΟΑΩΝ

Regulæ ecclesiasticæ sanctorum apostolorum prolatæ per Clementem Ecclesiæ Romanæ pontificem

CAN. 1

Ἐπίσκοπος χειροτονείσθω ὑπὸ ἐπισκύπων δύο ἢ τριῶν.

Episcopus a duobus aut tribus episcopis ordinetur.

According to Drey, this canon is among those whose apostolic origin cannot indeed be proved, but which dates back to a very remote antiquity, that is, to the first three centuries of the Christian era. Its sources are certainly the Apostolic Constitutions.

CAN. 2

Πρεσβύτερος ὑφ᾽ ἑνὸς ἐπισκόπου χειροτονείσθω, καὶ διάκονος καὶ οἱ λοιποὶ κληρικοί.

Presbyter ab uno episcopo ordinetur, et diaconus et reliqui clerici.

The same remarks are applicable as to the first canon.

CAN. 3

Εἴ τις ἐπίσκοπος ἢ πρεσβύτερος παρὰ τὴν τοῦ Κυρίου διάταξιν, τὴν ἐπὶ τῇ θυσίᾳ, προσενέγκῃ ἕτερά τινα ἐπὶ τὸ θυσιαστήριον, ἢ μέλι ἢ γάλα ἢ ἀντὶ οἴνου σίκερα ἢ ἐπιτηδευτὰ ἢ ὄρνεις ἢ ζῷά τινα ἢ ὄσπρια, ὡς παρὰ τὴν διάταξιν Κυρίου ποιῶν, καθαιρείσθω, πλὴν νέων χίδρων ἢ σταφυλῆς, τῷ καιρῷ τῷ δέοντι.

Si quis episcopus et presbyter præter ordinationem Domini alia quædam in sacrificio offerat super altare, id est aut mel, aut lac, aut pro vino siceram, aut confecta quædam, aut volatilia, aut animalia aliqua, aut legumina, contra constitutionem Domini faciens, congruo tempore, deponatur.

The Latin text by Dionysius the Less, and the Greek text as it is to be found in the collections of the Councils, here present variations on several points. Thus, (a) the Greek text unites into one single canon what Dionysius divides into Nos. 3 and 4; so that in the collections of the Councils the numbers of the Greek text no longer coincide with those of the translation by Dionysius. We have preserved the enumeration of Dionysius, and have accordingly divided the Greek canon into two. (b) We have not, however, thus produced complete harmony between the two texts; for, according to the Greek text, the words præter novas spicas et uvas belong to the third canon, whilst according to Dionysius they form part of the fourth. These words are evidently a translation of the Greek phrase, πλὴν νέων χίδρων ἢ σταφυλῆς. (c) Bearing in mind these transpositions, the words congruo tempore in the third canon may be explained as follows: "Except fresh ears of corn and grapes when it is the right time for them." (d) If the words præter novas spicas et uvas are not placed in the third canon, but in the fourth, we must also place the words congruo tempore in the fourth, and then the meaning is the same as before. As to the antiquity of canons 3–5, we will make the following remarks:—All three speak of what ought or ought not to be offered upon the altar. The substance of these rules is ancient: one might even perhaps say that it is partly ordained by our Lord Himself; and it is to this that the first words of the third canon refer. The details contained in this same third canon seem to have been inserted in order to combat the customs of the ancient heretics. The fourth and fifth canons are hardly more than explanations and commentaries on the third, and thus betray a more recent origin.

CAN. 4 (3)

Μὴ ἐξὸν δὲ ἔστω προσάγεσθαί τι ἕτερον εἰς τὸ θυσιαστήριον, ἢ ἔλαιον εἰς τὴν λυχνίαν καὶ θυμίαμα τῷ καιρῷ τῆς ἁγίας προσφορᾶς.

Offerri non licet aliquid ad altare præter novas spicas et uvas, et oleum ad luminaria, et thymiama id est incensum, tempore quo sancta celebratur oblatio.

CAN. 5 (4)

Ἡ ἄλλη πᾶσα ὀπώρα εἰς οἶκον ἀποστελλέσθω, ἀπαρχὴ τῷ ἐπισκόπῳ καὶ τοῖς πρεσβυτέροις, ἀλλὰ μὴ πρὸς τὸ θυσιαστήριον• δῆλον δέ, ὡς ὁ ἐπίσκοπος καὶ οἱ πρεσβύτεροι ἐπιμερίζουσι τοῖς διακόνοις καὶ τοῖς λοιποῖς κληρικοῖς.

Reliqua poma omnia ad domum, primitiæ episcopo et presbyteris, dirigantur, nec offerantur in altari. Certum est autem, quod episcopus et presbyteri dividant et diaconis et reliquis clericis.

For these two, see the remarks on the third canon.

CAN. 6 (5)

Ἐπίσκοπος ἢ πρεσβύτερος ἢ διάκονος τὴν ἑαυτοῦ γυναῖκα μὴ ἐκβαλλέτω προφάσει εὐλαβείας• ἐὰν δὲ ἐκβάλλῃ, ἀφοριζέσθω• ἐπιμένων δέ, καθαιρείσθω.

Episcopus aut presbyter uxorem propriam sub obtentu religionis nequaquam abjiciat; si vero ejecerit, excommunicetur; et si perseveraverit, dejiciatur.

Drey supposes that Eustathius of Sebaste gave occasion for this canon towards the middle of the fourth century. Compare canons 1 and 4 of the Synod of Gangra. According to the Greek text, it would be necessary to place the words et diaconus after the word presbyter in the Latin translation.

CAN. 7 (6)

Ἐπίσκοπος ἢ πρεσβύτερος ἢ διάκονος κοσμικὰς φροντίδας μὴ ἀναλαμβανέτω• εἰ δὲ μὴ, καθαιρείσθω.

Episcopus aut presbyter aut diaconus nequaquam seculares curas assumat; sin aliter, dejiciatur.

This belongs to the most ancient canons, which contain rules perhaps proceeding from the apostles and their disciples; but it must have been arranged more recently (in the third century). The Apostolic Constitutions contain a similar rule.

CAN. 8 (7)

Εἴ τις ἐπίσκοπος ἢ πρεσβύτερος ἢ διάκονος τὴν ἁγίαν τοῦ Πάσχα ἡμέραν πρὸ τῆς ἐαρινῆς ἰσημερίας μετὰ. Ἰουδαίων ἐπιτελέσει, καθαιρείσθω.

Si quis episcopus aut presbyter aut diaconus sanctum Paschæ diem ante vernale æquinoctium cum Judæis celebraverit, abjiciatur.

We have seen in the present volume that a fresh difficulty arose during the third century, added to those already existing, for determining the time for celebrating the Easter festival. After having discussed whether it ought to be fixed according to the day of the week or the day of the month, and after having inquired at what time the fast should end, it was besides questioned, during the third century, whether Easter ought always to be celebrated after the vernal equinox. The Council of Nicæa answered this question in the affirmative—if not expressly, at least implicitly. The

Synod of Antioch, held in 341, gave a similar decision, and Bickell considers that this canon was taken from the first canon of Antioch. Drey, on the contrary, believes that the canon of Antioch was derived from the Apostolic Constitutions.

CAN. 9 (8)

Εἴ τις ἐπίσκοπος ἢ πρεσβύτερος ἢ διάκονος ἢ ἐκ τοῦ καταλόγου τοῦ ἱερατικοῦ προσφορᾶς γενομένης μὴ μεταλάβοι, τὴν αἰτίαν εἰπάτω· καὶ ἐὰν εὔλογος ᾖ, συγγνώμης τυγχανέτε· εἰ δὲ μὴ λέγει, ἀφοριζέσθε, ὡς αἴτιος βλάβης γενόμενος τῷ λαῷ καὶ ὑπόνοιαν ποιήσας κατὰ τοῦ προσενέγκαντος.

Si quis episcopus aut presbyter aut diaconus vel quilibet ex sacerdotali catalogo facta oblatione non communicaverit, aut causam dicat, ut si rationabilis fuerit, veniam consequatur, aut si non dixerit, communione privetur, tanquam qui populo causa læsionis extiterit, dans suspicionem de eo, qui sacrificavit, quod recte non obtulerit.

The Latin text of Dionysius the Less seems to imply that these words ought to have been added at the end of the Greek text, ὡς μὴ ὑγιῶο ἀνενεγκόντος (as if he had not regularly offered); and these words are to be found in some Greek manuscripts. As to the antiquity of this canon, see the note on the one following.

CAN. 10 (9)

Πάντας τοὺς εἰσιόντας πιστοὺς καὶ τῶν γραφῶν ἀκούοντας, μὴ παραμένοντας δὲ τῇ προσευχῇ καὶ τῇ ἁγίᾳ μεταλήψει, ὡς ἀταξίαν ἐμποιοῦντας τῇ ἐκκλησίᾳ, ἀφορίζεσθαι χρή.

Omnes fideles, qui ingrediuntur ecclesiam et scripturas audiunt, non autem perseverant in oratione, nec sanctam communionem percipiunt, velut inquietudines ecclesiæ commoventes, convenit communione privare.

This tenth canon is evidently connected with the ninth. Drey believed that in substance they were both very ancient, and arose from those times of persecution, during which some Christians abstained from receiving the holy communion from remorse of conscience. Drey is evidently in the wrong when he maintains that this tenth apostolic canon was copied word for word from the second canon of the Council of Antioch held in 341. The reverse of this is more probable. See our introductory remarks on these canons.

CAN. 11 (10)

Εἴ τις ἀκοινωνήτῳ κἂν ἐν οἴκῳ συνεύξηται, οὗτος ἀφοριζέσθω.

Si quis cum excommunicato, etiam domi, simul oraverit, et ipse communione privetur.

This canon must be considered, as to its contents, as among the most ancient of the apostolic canons, which stretch back to apostolic times. As to its present form, Drey supposes that it was taken from the second canon of the Council of Antioch; but see what is said at the end of the note on the preceding canon.

CAN. 12 (11)

Εἴ τις καθηρημένῳ κληρικὸς ὢν ὡς κληρικῷ συνεύξηται, καθαιρείσθω καὶ αὐτός.

Si quis cum damnato clerico, veluti cum clerico, simul oraverit, et ipse damnetur.

On the antiquity of this canon the same observations may be offered as those upon the tenth and eleventh. According to Drey, this canon must have been formed from the second canon of the Council of Antioch.

CAN. 13 (12)

Εἴ τις κληρικὸς ἢ λαικὸς ἀφωρισμένος ἤτοι ἄδεκτος, ἀπελθὼν ἐν ἑτέρᾳ πόλει, δεχθῇ ἄνευ γραμμάτων συστατικῶν, ἀφοριζέσθω καὶ ὁ δεξάμενος καὶ ὁ δεχθείς· εἰ δὲ ἀφωρισμένος εἴη, ἐπιτεινέσθω αὐτῷ ὁ ἀφορισμός, ὡς ψευσαμένῳ καὶ ἀπατήσαντι τὴν Ἐκκλησίαν τοῦ Θεοῦ.

Si quis clericus aut laicus a communione suspensus vel communicans, ad aliam properet civitatem, et suscipiatur praeter commendaticias literas, et qui susceperunt et qui susceptus est, communione priventur. Excommunicato vero proteletur ipsa correptio, tanquam qui mentitus sit et Ecclesiam Dei seduxerit.

The Greek text has ἤτοι ἄδεκτος, that is, sive excommunicatus. It is supposed that we should rather read ἤτοι δεκτός, because in the latter part of the canon two sorts of penalties are appointed: (α) When one who is not excommunicated is elsewhere received, without having letters of recommendation from his bishop, he is to be excommunicated, and also he who received them; (β) If one who is excommunicated succeeds in being received elsewhere, the period of his excommunication shall be prolonged. The contents of this canon are certainly ante-Nicene. Drey supposes the form to be derived from the sixth canon of the Council of Antioch. See the note on the tenth canon.

CAN. 14 (13)

Ἐπίσκοπον μὴ ἐξεῖναι καταλείψαντα τὴν ἑαυτοῦ παροικίαν ἑτέρᾳ ἐπιπηδᾶν, κἂν ὑπὸ πλειόνων ἀναγκάζηται, εἰ μή τις εὔλογος αἰτία ᾖ τοῦτο βιαζομένη αὐτὸν ποιεῖν, ὡς πλέον τι κέρδος φυναμένου αὐτοῦ τοῖς ἐκεῖσε λόγῳ εὐσεβείας συμβάλλεσθαι· καὶ τοῦτο δὲ οὐκ ἀφ' ἑαυτοῦ, ἀλλὰ κρίσει πολλῶν ἐπισκόπων καὶ παρακλήσει μεγίστῃ.

Episcopo non licere alienam parochiam, propria relicta, pervadere, licet cogatur a plurimis, nisi forte quia eum rationabilis causa compellat, tanquam qui possit ibidem constitutis plus lucri conferre, et in causa religionis aliquid profectus prospicere; et hoc non a semetipso pertentet, sed multorum episcoporum judicio et maxima supplicatione perficiat.

The prohibition to leave one church for another is very ancient. It had been before set forth by the Council of Arles in 314, and by the Council of Nicæa in its fifteenth canon, as well as by the Synod of Antioch in 341, and it was renewed by that of Sardica. This fifteenth canon is therefore, as to its substance, very ancient; but its present form, Drey supposes, is post-Nicene, as may be inferred, he thinks, from the lightening of the penalty, which could not have been decreed by the ancient canons. Drey therefore concludes that this canon was framed after the eighteenth and twenty-first canons of Antioch. But see the note on the tenth canon.

CAN. 15 (14)

Εἴ τις πρεσβύτερος ἢ διάκονος ἢ ὅλως τοῦ καταλόγου τῶν κληρικῶν ἀπολείψας τὴν ἑαυτοῦ παροικίαν εἰς ἑτέραν ἀπέλθῃ, καὶ παντελῶς μεταστὰς διατρίβῃ ἐν ἄλλῃ παροικίᾳ παρὰ γνώμην τοῦ ἰδίου ἐπισκόπου· τοῦτον κελεύομεν μηκέτι λειτουργεῖν, τοῦ ἰδίου ἐπισκόπου· τοῦτον κελεύομεν μηκέτι λειτουργεῖν, μάλιστα εἰ προσκαλουμένου αὐτὸν τοῦ ἐπισκόπου αὐτοῦ ἐπανελθεῖν οὐχ ὑπήκουσεν ἐπιμένων τῇ ἀταξίᾳ· ὡς λαϊκὸς μέντοι ἐκεῖσε κοινωνείτω.

Si quis presbyter aut diaconus aut quilibet de numero clericorum relinquens propriam parochiam pergat ad alienam, et omnino demigrans præter episcopi sui conscientiam in aliena parochia commoretur, hunc alterius ministrare non patimur, præcipue si vocatus ab episcopo redire contempserit, in sua inquietudine perseverans; verum tamen tanquam laicus ibi communicet.

The same remark is applicable as to the fourteenth canon. According to Drey, this fifteenth, as well as the following canon, must have been formed from the third canon of the Council of Antioch, held in 341. See the note on the tenth canon.

CAN. 16 (15)

Εἰ δὲ ὁ ἐπίσκοπος, παρ' ᾧ τυγχάνουσι, παρ' οὐδὲν λογισάμενος τὴν κατ' αὐτῶν ὁρισθεῖσαν ἀργίαν, δέξεται αὐτοὺς ὡς κληρικοὺς, ἀφοριζέσθω ὡς διδάσκαλος ἀταξίας.

Episcopus vero, apud quem moratos esse constiterit, si contra eos decretam cessationem pro nihilo reputans, tanquam clericos forte susceperit, velut magister inquietudinis communione privetur.

The same remark is applicable as to the fourteenth canon.

CAN. 17 (16)

Ὁ δυσὶ γάμοις συμπλακεὶς μετὰ τὸ βάπτισμα ἢ παλλακὴν κτησάμενος οὐ δύναται εἶναι ἐπίσκοπος ἢ πρεσβύτερος ἢ πρεσβύτερος ἢ ὅλως τοῦ καταλόγου τοῦ ἱερατικοῦ.

Si quis post baptisma secundis fuerit nuptiis copulatus aut concubinam habuerit, non potest esse episcopus aut presbyter aut diaconus, aut prorsus ex numero eorum, qui ministerio sacro deserviunt.

It is certain that this canon in its substance is an apostolic ordinance. The form, however, is taken from the Apostolic Constitutions, consequently about the third century.

CAN. 18 (17)

Ὁ χήραν λαβὼν ἢ ἐκβεβλημένην ἢ ἑταίραν ἢ οἰκέτλν ἢ τῶν ἐπὶ σκηνῆς οὐ δύναται εἶναι ἐπίσκοπος ἢ πρεσβύτερος ἢ διάκονος ἢ ὅλως τοῦ καταλόγου τοῦ ἱερατικοῦ.

Si quis viduam aut ejectam acceperit, aut meretricem aut ancillam, vel aliquam de his qui publicis spectaculis mancipantur, non potest esse episcopus aut presbyter aut diaconus aut ex eorum numero qui ministerio sacro deserviunt.

A similar remark applies to this as to the seventeenth canon. See Lev. 21:14, where we have a similar ordinance for the Jewish priests.

CAN. 19 (18)

Ὁ δύο ἀδελφὰς ἀγαγόμενος ἢ ἀδελφιδῆν οὐ δύναται εἶναι κληρικός.

Qui duas in conjugium sorores acceperit, vel filiam fratris, clericus esse non poterit.

This canon, like the preceding, renews a command contained in the Old Testament. The Synods of Elvira and of Neocæsarea enforced it also. This nineteenth canon may therefore be considered to be contemporary with those synods, especially to be an imitation of the second canon of Neocæsarea.

CAN. 20 (19)

Κληρικὸς ἐγγύας διδοὺς καθαιρείσθω.

Clericus fidejussionibus inserviens abjiciatur.

We have seen in sec. 4, that from the third century it was decidedly forbidden that priests should be tutors or guardians; in a word, that they should meddle with the settlement of worldly business. A similar prohibition is given in the present canon, which in the main is very ancient, and was taken from the Apostolic Constitutions.

CAN. 21 (20)

Εὐνοῦχος εἰ μὲν ἐξ ἐπηρείας ἀνθρώπων ἔγενετό τις, ἢ ἐν διωγμῷ ἀφῃρέθη τὰ ἀνδρῶν, ἢ οὕτως ἔφυ, καὶ ἔστιν ἄξιος, γινέσθω.

Eunuchus si per insidias hominum factus est, vel si in persecutione ejus sunt amputata virilia, vel si ita natus est, et est dignus, efficiatur episcopus.

The Œcumenical Synod of Nicæa, in its first canon, gave a similar command to that contained in this and the two following canons. In enforcing it, the Synod professed to be conforming to ancient canons, by which it intended the twenty-first, also the twenty-second and twenty-third apostolic canons. Drey, on the contrary, considers that this apostolic canon was framed from those of Nicæa; perhaps it may have been the Valesians who gave occasion for these rules.

CAN. 22 (21)

Ὁ ἀκρωτηριάσας ἑαυτὸν μὴ γινέσθω κληρικός· αὐτοφονευτὴς γάρ ἐστιν ἑαυτοῦ καὶ τῆς τοῦ Θεοῦ δημιουργίας ἐχθρός.

Si quis absciderit semetipsum, id est, si quis sibi amputavit virilia, non fiat clericus, quia suus homicida est, et Dei conditionibus inimicus.

See the note on the preceding canon.

CAN. 23 (22)

Εἴ τις κληρικὸς ὢν ἑαυτὸν ἀκρωτηριάσει, καθαιρείσθω, φονευτὴς γάρ ἐστιν ἑαυτοῦ.

Si quis, cum clericus fuerit, absciderit semetipsum, omnino damnetur, quia suus est homicida.

The same remark as on the twenty-first canon.

CAN. 24 (23)

Λαϊκὸς ἑαυτὸν ἀκρωτηριάσας ἀφοριζέσθω ἔτη τρία· ἐπίβουλος γάρ ἐστι τῆς ἑαυτοῦ ζωῆς.

Laicus semetipsum abscindens annis tribus communione privetur, quia suæ vitæ insidiator exstitit.

The first canon of Nicæa, which is also on the subject of voluntary mutilation, has reference only to the clergy, and does not appoint any penalty for the laity who mutilate themselves. This might incline us to the opinion that the present canon was given to complete those of the Council of Nicæa, and consequently that it is more recent than that Council. But there is no doubt that the Council of Nicæa had this canon before it, and spoke of self-mutilation only as an impedimentum ordinis. Athanasius, in his Historia Arianorum ad monachos, shows that voluntary mutilation was also severely punished in the laity, and that they were excluded from communio laicalis. Drey is of opinion that these canons are more recent than those of Nicæa, and that they were formed from the latter.

CAN. 25 (24)

Ἐπίσκοπος ἢ πρεσβύτερος ἢ διάκονος ἐπὶ πορνείᾳ ἢ ἐπιορκίᾳ ἢ κλοπῇ ἁλοὺς καθαιρείσθω, καὶ μὴ ἀφοριζέσθω· λέγει γὰρ ἡ γραφή· Οὐκ ἐκδικήσεις δὶς ἐπὶ τὸ αὐτό· ὁμοίως δὲ οἱ λοιποὶ κληρικοὶ τῇ αὐτῇ αἱρέσει ὑποκείσθωσαν.

Episcopus aut presbyter aut diaconus, qui in fornicatione aut perjurio aut furto captus est, deponatur, non tamen communione privetur; dicit enim Scriptura: Non vindicabit Dominus bis in idipsum.

This canon alludes to a passage in the prophet Nahum. It certainly belongs in the main to the most ancient canons; for S. Basil the Great says in his letter to Amphilochus (c. 3), that, according to an ancient rule (ἀρχαῖον κανόνα), thieves, etc., were to be deprived of their ecclesiastical offices. Leo the Great, however, calls this an apostolic tradition. Drey supposes that this sentence of S. Basil's gave rise to the canon.

CAN. 26

Similiter et reliqui clerici huic conditioni subjaceant.

In the Greek this canon is not separately counted; it forms only the last sentence of the one preceding. As for its antiquity, see the remarks on the twenty-fifth canon.

CAN. 27 (25)

Τῶν εἰς κλῆρον προσελθόντων ἀγάμων κελεύομεν βουλομένους γαμεῖν ἀναγνώστας καὶ ψάλτας μόνους.

Innuptis autem, qui ad clerum provecti sunt; præcipimus, ut si voluerint uxores accipiant, sed lectores cantoresque tantummodo.

Paphnutius had declared in the Council of Nicæa in favour of an ancient law, which decided that, whoever had taken holy orders when unmarried, could not be married afterwards. The Synod of Ancyra, held in 314, also recognised this law, and for that reason, in its tenth canon, established an exception in favour of deacons. The Council of Elvira went still further. These approaches prove that the present canon is more ancient than the Council of Nicæa, and that it is a faithful interpreter of the ancient practice of the Church. Even Drey says that this canon is taken from the Apostolic Constitutions (vi. 17), and consequently is ante-Nicene.

CAN. 28 (26)

Ἐπίσκοπον ἢ πρεσβύτερον ἢ διάκονον τύπτοντα πιστοὺς ἁμαρτάνοντας ἢ ἀπίστους ἀδικήσαντας, τὸν διὰ τοιούτων φοβεῖν θέλοντα, καθαιρεῖσθαι προστάττομεν· οὐδαμοῦ γὰρ ὁ Κύριος τοῦτο ἡμᾶς ἐδίδαξε· τοὐναντίον δὲ αὐτὸς τυπτόμενος οὐκ ἀντέτυπτε, λοιδορούμενος οὐκ ἀντελοιδόρει, πάσχων οὐκ ἠπείλει.

Episcopum aut presbyterum aut diaconum percutientem fideles delinquentes, aut infideles inique agentes, et per hujusmodi volentem timeri, dejici ab officio suo præcipimus, quia nusquam nos hoc Dominus docuit; e contrario vero ipse, cum percuteretur non repercutiebat, cum malediceretur non remaledicebat, cum pateretur non comminabatur.

Drey believes this canon to be one of the most recent of the apostolic canons, for no ancient synod ever thought it necessary to put forth such decisions. The Synod of Constantinople, held A.D. 394, was the first to forbid the clergy to strike the faithful, and this apostolic canon is only an imitation of that.

CAN. 29 (27)

Charles Joseph Hefele, D.D.

Εἴ τις ἐπίσκοπος ἢ πρεσβύτερος ἢ διάκονος καθαιρεθεὶς δικαίως ἐπὶ ἐγκλήμασι φανεροῖς τολμήσειεν ἅψασθαι τῆς ποτε ἐγχειρισθείσης αὐτῷ λειτουργίας, οὗτος παντάπασιν ἐκκοπτέσθω τῆς Ἐκκλησίας.

Si quis episcopus aut presbyter aut diaconus, depositus juste super certis criminibus, ausus fuerit attrectare ministerium dudum sibi commissum, hic ab Ecclesia penitus abscindatur.

This canon is similar to the fourth of the Council of Antioch, held in 341. Drey believes this apostolic canon to be more recent than that of Antioch, and intended to correct it; for the latter refers only to the case of a bishop who is regularly deposed, and that for acknowledged sins. But it may be, on the contrary, that our canon is more ancient than that of Antioch. The Fathers of Antioch perhaps only applied to S. Athanasius the orders of a rule before known. See the comments upon the tenth canon.

CAN. 30 (28)

Εἴ τις ἐπίσκοπος διὰ χρημάτων τῆς ἀξίας ταύτης ἐγκρατὴς γένηται, ἢ πρεσβύτερος ἢ διάκονος, καθαιρείσθω καὶ αὐτὸς καὶ ὁ χειροτονήσας, καὶ ἐκκοπτέσθω τῆς κοινωνίας παντάπασιν, ὡς Σίμων ὁ μάγος ἀπὸ ἐμοῦ Πέτρου.

Si quis episcopus aut presbyter aut diaconus per pecunias hanc obtinuerit dignitatem, dejiciatur et ipse et ordinator ejus, et a communione omnibus modis abscindatur, sicut Simon magus a Petro.

We have seen in the comments upon the canons of the Synod of Elvira, that this Council in its forty-eighth canon forbade all fees for the administration of baptism as simoniacal. The Council, however, did not use the word simony; but at the time when the thirtieth apostolic canon was formed, the word simony seems to have been used as a technical term. This observation would go to prove that this apostolic canon has a later origin: it is hardly probable, indeed, that in times of persecution it should have been attempted to buy bishoprics for money. But the Synod of Sardica shows from its second canon that it was then aware of such cases. Abuses of the same kind also drew S. Basil's attention. Drey thinks that this thirtieth apostolic canon is only an extract from the second canon of the Council of Chalcedon. See the remarks above.

CAN. 31 (29)

Εἴ τις ἐπίσκοπος κοσμικοῖς ἄρχουσι χρησάμενος δι' αὐτῶν ἐγκρατὴς γένηται ἐκκλησίας, καθαιρείσθω καὶ ἀφοριζέσθω, καὶ οἱ κοινωνοῦντες αὐτῷ πάντες.

Si quis episcopus secularibus potestatibus usus ecclesiam per ipsos obtineat, deponatur, et segregentur omnes, qui illi communicant.

The object of this canon is to oppose the intervention of Christian Emperors in the choice of bishops: it is not probable that it was decreed by an ancient council; rather it must have been composed by whoever collected the apostolic constitutions and canons. Drey strongly doubts whether any ancient council would have dared to offer such explicit and declared opposition to the Emperors.

CAN. 32 (30)

Charles Joseph Hefele, D.D.

Εἴ τις πρεσβύτερος καταφρονήσας τοῦ ἰδίου ἐπισκόπου χωρὶς συναγωγὴν καὶ θυσιαστήριον πήξει, μηδὲν κατεγνωκὼς τοῦ ἐπισκόπου ἐν εὐσεβείᾳ καὶ δικαιοσύνῃ, καθαιρείσθω ὡς φίλαρχος· τύραννος γάρ ἐστιν· ὡσαύτως δὲ καὶ οἱ λοιποὶ κληρικοὶ καὶ ὅσοι ἐν αὐτῷ προσθῶνται· οἱ δὲ λαϊκοὶ ἀφοριζέσθωσαν· ταῦτα δὲ μετὰ μίαν καὶ δευτέραν καὶ τρίτην παράκλησιν τοῦ ἐπισκόπου γινέσθω.

Si quis presbyter contemnens episcopum suum seorsum collegerit et altare aliud erexerit, nihil habens quo reprehendat episcopum in causa pietatis et justitiæ, deponatur, quasi principals amator existens, est enim tyrannus; et cæteri clerici, quicumque tali consentiunt, deponantur, laici vero segregentur. Hæc autem post unam et secundam et tertiam episcopi obtestationem fieri conveniat.

It happened, even in the primitive Church, that priests caused schisms: this was the case, for instance, in the Novatian schism. But as the synods of the fourth century, and particularly that of Antioch, held in 341, treat of the same subject as the thirty-second apostolic canon, Drey considers that this canon was formed after the fifth of Antioch. But we will here once more recall what we said on the tenth canon.

CAN. 33 (31)

Εἴ τις πρεσβύτερος ἢ διάκονος ἀπὸ ἐπισκόπου γένηται ἀφωρισμένος, τοῦτον μὴ ἐξεῖναι παρ' ἑτέρου δέχεσθαι, ἀλλ' ἢ παρὰ τοῦ ἀφορίσαντος αὐτὸν, εἰ μὴ ἂν κατὰ συγκυρίαν τελευτήσῃ ὁ ἀφορίσας αὐτὸν ἐπίσκοπος.

Si quis presbyter aut diaconus ab episcopo suo segregetur, hunc non licere ab alio recipi, sed ab ipso, qui eum sequestraverat, nisi forsitan obierit episcopus ipse, qui eum segregasse cognoscitur.

We have several times had occasion to remark that the ancient councils gave similar rules to those of the thirty-third apostolic canon. Drey believes this canon to be in substance of very high antiquity, but in its form taken from the sixth canon of Antioch.

CAN. 34 (32)

Μηδένα τῶν ξένων ἐπισκόπων ἢ πρεσβυτέρων ἢ διακόνων ἄνευ συστατικῶν προσδέχεσθαι· καὶ ἐπιφερομένων αὐτῶν ἀνακρινέσθωσαν· καὶ εἰ μὲν ὦσι κήρυκες τῆς εὐσεβείας, προσδεχέσθωσαν, εἰ δὲ μήγε, τὴν χρείαν αὐτοῖς ἐπιχορηγήσαντες εἰς κοινωνίαν αὐτοὺς μὴ προσδέξησθε· πολλὰ γὰρ κατὰ συναρπαγὴν γίνεται.

Nullus episcoporum peregrinorum aut presbyterorum aut diaconorum sine commendaticiis recipiatur epistolis; et cum scripta detulerint, discutiantur attentius, et ita suscipiantur, si prædicatores pietatis exstiterint; sin minus, hæc quæ sunt necessaria subministrentur eis, et ad communionem nullatenus admittantur, quia per subreptionem multa proveniunt.

The thirteenth canon contains a similar rule. In the primitive Church, Christians who travelled could not in fact be received into a foreign church without letters of recommendation—litteris commendaticiis. Thus, for instance, about the middle of the second century, Marcion was not received at Rome, because he had no letters with him from his father the Bishop of Sinope. There is also mention of these letters of recommendation in the twenty-fifth canon of the Synod of Elvira, and in the ninth of that of Arles. According to Drey, this canon in the main belongs to the most ancient apostolic canons; but according to the same author, it must have been arranged after the Apostolic Constitutions, and after the seventh and eighth canons of Antioch.

CAN. 35 (33)

Τοὺς ἐπισκόπους ἑκάστου ἔθνους εἰδέναι χρὴ τὸν ἐν αὐτοῖς πρῶτον, καὶ ἡγεῖσθαι αὐτὸν ὡς κεφαλὴν, καὶ μηδέν τι πράττειν περιττὸν ἄνευ τῆς ἐκείνου γνώμης· ἐκεῖνα δὲ μόνα πράττειν ἕκαστον, ὅσα τῇ αὐτοῦ παροικίᾳ ἐπιβάλλει καὶ ταῖς ὑπ' αὐτὴν χώραις. ἀλλὰ μηδὲ ἐκεῖνος ἄνευ τῆς πάντων γυώμης ποιείτω τι· οὕτω γὰρ ὁμόνοια ἔσται καὶ δοξασθήσεται ὁ Θεὸς διὰ Κυρίου ἐν ἁγίῳ Πνεύματι.

Episcopos gentium singularum scire convenit, quis inter eos primus habeatur, quem velut caput existiment, et nihil amplius præter ejus conscientiam gerant quam illa sola singuli, quæ parochiæ propriæ et villis, quæ sub ea sunt, competunt. Sed nec ille præter omnium conscientiam faciat aliquid. Sic enim unanimitas erit, et glorificabitur Deus per Christum in Spiritu sancto.

According to Drey's researches, this canon is either an abridgment of the ninth canon of the Council of Antioch, held in 341, which treats of the same subject, or else this canon of Antioch is an amplification of the apostolic canon. Drey finally adopts the former opinion.

CAN. 36 (34)

Ἐπίσκοπον μὴ τολμᾶν ἔξω τῶν ἑαυτοῦ ὅρων χειροτονίας
ποιεῖσθαι εἰς τὰς μὴ ὑποκειμένας αὐτῷ πόλεις καὶ χώρας· εἰ
δὲ ἐλεγχθείη τοῦτο πεποιηκὼς παρὰ τὴν τῶν κατεχόντων τὰς
πόλεις ἐκείνας ἢ τὰς χώρας γνώμην, καθαιρείσθω καὶ αὐτὸς
καὶ οὓς ἐχειροτόνησεν.

Episcopum non audere extra terminos proprios
ordinationes facere in civitatibus et villis, quæ ipsi nullo jure
subjectæ sunt. Si vero convictus fuerit hoc fecisse præter
eorum conscientiam, qui civitates illas et villas detinent, et
ipse deponatur, et qui ab eo sunt ordinati.

A similar rule was adopted by the Synod of Elvira, by that
of Nicæa, and by that of Antioch. Drey acknowledges (S.
271 and 406) that the rule here expressed has been
observed from the first times of the Church; he also makes
no difficulty in classing this canon, in the main, among the
most ancient apostolic canons. He thinks, besides, that it
was taken from the Synod of Antioch held in 341.

CAN. 37 (35)

Εἴ τις χειροτονηθεὶς ἐπίσκοπος μὴ καταδέχοιτο τὴν
λειτουργίαν· καὶ τὴν φροντίδα τοῦ λαοῦ τὴν ἐγχειρισθεῖσαν
αὐτῷ, τοῦτον ἀφωρισμένον τυγχάνειν, ἕως ἂν καταδέξηται·
ὡσαύτως καὶ πρεσβύτερος ἢ διάκονος. Εἰ καὶ μὴ δεχθείη, οὐ
παρὰ τὴν ἑαυτοῦ γνώμην, ἀλλὰ παρὰ τὴν τοῦ λαοῦ
μοχθηρίαν, αὐτὸς μενέτω ἐπίσκοπος, ὁ δὲ κλῆρος τῆς
πόλεως ἀφοριζέσθω, ὅτι τοιούτου λαοῦ ἀνυποτάκτου
παιδευταὶ οὐκ ἐγένοντο.

Si quis episcopus non susceperit officium et curam populi sibi commissam, hic communione privetur, quoadusque consentiat obedientiam commodans, similiter autem et presbyter et diaconus. Si vero perrexerit, nec receptus fuerit non pro sua sententia, sed pro populi malitia, ipse quidem maneat episcopus, clerici vero civitatis communione priventur, eo quod eruditores inobedientis populi non fuerint.

This rule was made partly by the Synod of Ancyra and partly by that of Antioch. Drey holds this canon to be an imitation of the two canons of Antioch; but perhaps the contrary is really the truth. See the note on canon 10.

CAN. 38 (36)

Δεύτερον τοῦ ἔτους σύνοδος γινέσθω τῶν ἐπισκόπων, καὶ ἀνακρινέτωσαν ἀλλήλους τὰ δόγματα τῆς εὐσεβείας καὶ τὰς ἐμπιπτούσας ἐκκλησιαστικὰς ἀντιλογίας διαλυέτωσαν· ἅπαξ μὲν τῇ τετάρτῃ ἑβδομάδι τῆς πεντηκοστῆς, δεύτερον δὲ ὑπερβερεταίου δωδεκάτῃ.

Bis in anno episcoporum concilia celebrentur, ut inter se invicem dogmata pietatis explorent, et emergentes ecclesiasticas contentiones amoveant; semel quidem quarta septimana pentecostes, secundo vero duodecima die mensis Hyperberetæi (id est juxta Romanos quarto idus Octobris).

The Synods of Nicæa and of Antioch also gave rules about provincial synods. According to Drey, this canon must be more recent than these two Synods, and especially must have been taken from the canon of Antioch.

CAN. 39 (37)

Πάντων τῶν ἐκκλησιαστικῶν πραγμάτων ὁ ἐπίσκοπος ἐχέτω
τὴν φροντίδα καὶ διοικείτω αὐτά, ὡς Θεοῦ ἐφορῶντος• μὴ
ἐξεῖναι δὲ αὐτῷ σφετερίζεσθαί τι ἐξ αὐτῶν ἢ συγγενέσιν ἰδίοις
τὰ τοῦ Θεοῦ χαρίζεσθαι• εἰ δὲ πένητες εἶεν, ἐπιχορηγείτω ὡς
πένησιν, ἀλλὰ μὴ προφάσει τούτων τὰ τῆς Ἐκκλησίας
ἀπεμπολείτω.

Omnium negotiorum ecclesiasticorum curam episcopus
habeat, et ea velut Deo contemplante dispenset; nec ei liceat
ex his aliquid omnino contingere, aut parentibus propriis
quæ Dei sunt condonare. Quod si pauperes sunt, tanquam
pauperibus subministret, nec eorum occasione Ecclesiæ
negotia deprædetur.

This canon and the two following are in a measure similar
to the twenty-fourth and twenty-fifth canons of Antioch; so
that Drey considers them more recent, and derived from
those two canons. But see what was said about the tenth
canon.

CAN. 40 (38)

Οἱ πρεσβύτεροι καὶ οἱ διάκονοι ἄνευ γνώμης τοῦ ἐπισκόπου
μηδὲν ἐπιτελείτωσαν• αὐτὸς γάρ ἐστιν ὁ πεπιστευμένος τὸν
λαὸν τοῦ Κυρίου, καὶ τὸν ὑπὲρ τῶν ψυχῶν αὐτῶν λόγον
ἀπαιτηθησόμενος.

CAN. (39)

Ἔστω φανερὰ τὰ ἴδια τοῦ ἐπισκόπου πράγματα, εἴγε καὶ ἴδια
ἔχει, καὶ φανερὰ τὰ κυριακά, ἵνα ἐξουσίαν ἔχῃ τῶν ἰδίων
τελευτῶν ὁ ἐπίσκοπος, οἷς βούλεται καὶ ὡς βούλεται
καταλεῖψαι, καὶ μὴ προφάσει τῶν ἐκκλησιαστικῶν πραγμάτων

Charles Joseph Hefele, D.D.

διαπίπτειν τὰ τοῦ ἐπισκόπου, ἐσθ' ὅτε γυναῖκα καὶ παῖδας κεκτημένου ἢ συγγενεῖς ἢ οἰκέτας· δίκαιον γὰρ τοῦτο παρὰ Θεῷ καὶ ἀνθρώποις τὸ μήτε τὴν Ἐκκλησίαν ζημίαν τινὰ ὑπομένειν ἀγνοίᾳ τῶν τοῦ ἐπισκόπου πραγμάτων, μήτε τὸν ἐπίσκοπον ἢ τοὺς αὐτοῦ συγγενεῖς προφάσει τῆς Ἐκκλησίας πημαίνεσθαι, ἢ καὶ εἰς πράγματα ἐμπίπτεν τοὺς αὐτῷ διαφέροντας, καὶ τὸν αὐτοῦ θάνατον δυσφημίαις περιβάλλεσθαι.

Presbyteri et diaconi præter episcopum nihil agere pertentent, nam Domini populus ipsi commissus est, et pro animabus eorum hic redditurus est rationem. Sint autem manifestæ res propriæ episcopi (si tamen habet proprias) et manifestæ dominicæ, ut potestatem habeat de propriis moriens episcopus, sicut voluerit et quibus voluerit relinquere, nec sub occasione ecclesiasticarum rerum, quæ episcopi sunt, intercidant, fortassis enim aut uxorem habet, aut filios aut propinquos aut servos. Et justum est hoc apud Deum et homines, ut nec Ecclesia detrimentum patiatur ignoratione rerum pontificis, nec episcopus vel ejus propinqui sub obtentu Ecclesiæ proscribantur, et in causas incidant qui ad eum pertinent, morsque ejus injuriis malæ famæ subjaceat.

See our remarks on the thirty-ninth canon.

CAN. 41 (40)

Προστάττομεν ἐπίσκοπον ἐξουσίαν ἔχειν τῶν τῆς Ἐκκλησίας πραγμάτων· εἰ γὰρ τὰς τιμίας τῶν ἀνθρώπων ψυχὰς αὐτῷ πιστευτέον, πολλῷ ἂν μᾶλλον δέοι ἐπὶ τῶν χρημάτων ἐντέλλεσθαι, ὥστε κατὰ τὴν αὐτοῦ ἐξουσίαν πάντα διοικεῖσθαι, καὶ τοῖς δεομένοις διὰ τῶν πρεσβυτέρων καὶ διακόνων ἐπιχωρηγεῖσθαι μετὰ φόβου τοῦ Θεοῦ καὶ πάσης εὐλαβείας· μεταλαμβάνειν δὲ καὶ αὐτὸν τῶν δεόντων (εἴγε δέοιτο) εἰς τὰς ἀναγκαίας αὐτῷ χρείας καὶ τῶν ἐπιξενουμένων ἀδελφῶν, ὡς κατὰ μηδένα τρόπον αὐτοὺς ὑστερεῖσθαι· ὁ γὰρ νόμος τοῦ Θεοῦ διετάξατο, τοὺς τῷ θυσιαστηρίῳ ὑπηρετοῦντας ἐκ τοῦ θυσιαστηρίου τρέφεσθαι· ἐπείπερ οὐδὲ στρατιῶταί ποτε ἰδίοις ὀψωνίοις ὅπλα κατὰ πολεμίων ἐπιφέρονται.

Præcipimus, ut in potestate sua episcopus Ecclesiæ res habeat. Si enim animæ hominum pretiosæ illi sunt creditæ, multo magis oportet eum curam pecuniarum gerere, ita ut potestate ejus indigentibus omnia dispensentur per presbyteros et diaconos, et cum timore omnique sollicitudine ministrentur, ex his autem quibus indiget, si tamen indiget, ad suas necessitates et ad peregrinorum fratrum usus et ipse percipiat, ut nihil omnino possit ei deesse. Lex enim Dei præcipit, ut qui altari deserviunt, de altari pascantur; quia nec miles stipendiis propriis contra hostes arma sustulit.

See our remarks on the thirty-ninth canon.

CAN. 42 (41)

Ἐπίσκοπος ἢ πρεσβύτερος ἢ διάκονος κύβοις σχολάζων καὶ μέθαις ἢ παυσάσθω ἢ καθαιρείσθω.

Episcopus aut presbyter aut diaconus aleæ atque ebrietati deserviens, aut desinat, aut certe damnetur.

The Council of Elvira, in its seventy-ninth canon, has a similar prohibition of the game of thimbles. As to the different kinds of usury of which the forty-fourth apostolic canon speaks, they were all prohibited by the twentieth canon of Elvira, the twelfth of Arles, and the seventeenth of Nicæa. This and the two following canons should be included in the number of the most ancient so-called apostolic canons. Their origin is unknown.

CAN. 43 (42)

Ὑποδιάκονος ἢ ψάλτης ἢ ἀναγνώστης τὰ ὅμοια ποιῶν ἢ παυσάσθω ἢ ἀφοριζέσθω, ὡσαύτως καὶ οἱ λαϊκοί.

Subdiaconus, lector aut cantor similia faciens, aut desinat, aut communione privetur. Similiter etiam laicus.

Compare the remarks on the forty-second canon.

CAN. 44 (43)

Ἐπίσκοπος ἢ πρεσβύτερος ἢ διάκονος τόκους ἀπαιτῶν τοὺς δανειζομένους ἢ παυσάσθω ἢ καθαιρείσθω.

Episcopus aut presbyter aut diaconus usuras a debitoribus exigens, aut desinat, aut certe damnetur.

Compare the remarks on the forty-second canon.

CAN. 45 (44)

Ἐπίσκοπος ἢ πρεσβύτερος ἢ διάκονος αἱρετικοῖς συνευξάμενος μόνον, ἀφοριζέσθω• εἰ δὲ καὶ ἐπέτρεψεν αὐτοῖς ὡς κληρικοῖς ἐνεργῆσαί τι, καθαιρείσθω.

Episcopus, presbyter et diaconus, qui cum hæreticis oraverit tantummodo, communione privetur; si vero tanquam clericus hortatus eos fuerit agere vel orare, damnetur.

This canon is merely an application to a particular case of general rules given by the apostles, and this application must have been made from the first centuries: therefore this canon must in its substance be very ancient. Yet Drey believes that it was derived from the ninth, thirty-third, and thirty-fourth canons of the Council of Laodicea.

CAN. 46 (45)

Ἐπίσκοπον ἢ πρεσβύτερον αἱρετικῶν δεξάμενον βάπτισμα ἢ θυσίαν καθαιρεῖσθαι προστάττομεν· Τίς γὰρ συμφώνησις τοῦ Χριστοῦ πρὸς τὸν Βελίαλ; ἢ τίς μερὶς πιστοῦ μετὰ ἀπίστου;

Episcopum aut presbyterum hæreticorum suscipientem baptisma damnari præcipimus. Quæ enim conventio Christi ad Belial, aut quæ pars fideli cum infideli?

Drey holds this canon and the one following to be very ancient. Döllinger, on the contrary, as we have said, considers it to be more recent. This opinion had before been enunciated by Peter de Marca, who argued justly, that if this canon had been in existence at the period of the discussion upon baptism administered by heretics, that is, about the year 255, S. Cyprian and Firmilian would not have failed to quote it. This canon and the following are taken from the Apostolic Constitutions.

CAN. 47 (46)

Ἐπίσκοπος ἢ πρεσβύτερος τὸν κατ᾿ ἀλήθειαν ἔχοντα βάπτισμα ἐὰν ἄνωθεν βαπτίσῃ, ἢ τὸν μεμολυσμένον παρὰ τῶν ἀσεβῶν ἐὰν μὴ βαπτίσῃ, καθαιρείσθω, ὡς γελῶν τὸν σταυρὸν καὶ τὸν τοῦ Κυρίου θάνατον καὶ μὴ διακρίνων ἱερέας τῶν ψευδιερέων.

Episcopus aut presbyter, si eum qui secundum veritatem habuerit baptisma, denuo baptizaverit, aut si pollutum ab impiis non baptizaverit, deponatur tanquam deridens crucem et mortem Domini, nec sacerdotes a falsis sacerdotibus jure discernens.

See the remarks on the preceding canon.

CAN. 48 (47)

Εἴ τις λαϊκὸς τὴν ἑαυτοῦ γυναῖκα ἐκβάλλων ἑτέραν λάβῃ ἢ παρ' ἄλλου ἀπολελυμένην, ἀφοριζέσθω.

Si quis laicus uxorem propriam pellens, alteram vel ab alio dimissam duxerit, communione privetur.

The same rule was given by the eighth and tenth canons of Elvira, and by the tenth of Arles. Drey reckons this canon among the most ancient. Its source is unknown.

CAN. 49 (48)

Εἴ τις ἐπίσκοπος ἢ πρεσβύτερος κατὰ τὴν τοῦ Κυρίου διάταξιν μὴ βαπτίσῃ εἰς Πατέρα καὶ Υἱὸν καὶ ἅγιον Πνεῦμα, ἀλλ' εἰς τρεῖς ἀνάρχους ἢ τρεῖς υἱοὺς ἢ τρεῖς παρακλήτους, καθαιρείσθω.

Si quis episcopus aut presbyter juxta præceptum Domini non baptizaverit in nomine Patris et Filii et Spiritus sancti, sed in tribus sine initio principiis, aut in tribus filiis, aut in tribus paracletis, abjiciatur.

This canon must be reckoned among the most ancient canons, and is taken from the Apostolic Constitutions.

CAN. 50 (49)

Εἴ τις ἐπίσκοπος ἢ πρεσβύτερος μὴ τρία βαπτίσματα μιᾶς μυήσεως ἐπιτελέσῃ, ἀλλ' ἓν βάπτισμα εἰς τὸν θάνατον τοῦ Κυρίου διδόμενον, καθαιρείσθω· οὐ γὰρ εἶπεν ὁ Κύριος· Εἰς τὸν θάνατόν μου βαπτίσατε, ἀλλά· Πορευθέντες μαθητεύσατε πάντα τὰ ἔθνη, βαπτίζοντες αὐτοὺς εἰς τὸ ὄνομα τοῦ Πατρὸς καὶ τοῦ Υἱοῦ καὶ τοῦ ἁγίου Πνεύματος.

Si quis episcopus aut presbyter non trinam mersionem unius mysterii celebret, sed semel mergat in baptismate, quod dari videtur in Domini morte, deponatur. Non enim dixit nobis Dominus: In morte mea baptizate; sed: Euntes docete omnes gentes, baptizantes eos in nomine Patris et Filii et Spiritus sancti.

This canon is among the most recent of the collection. It is not known from what source it was derived.

Here the Latin translation made by Dionysius the Less ends. From the fifty-first canon we give the translation by Cotelerius.

CAN. 51 (50)

Εἴ τις ἐπίσκοπος ἢ πρεσβύτερος ἢ διάκονος ἢ ὅλως τοῦ καταλόγου τοῦ ἱερατικοῦ γάμων καὶ κρεῶν καὶ οἴνου οὐ δι' ἄσκησιν ἀλλὰ διὰ βδελυρίαν ἀπέχεται, ἐπιλαθόμενος ὅτι πάντα καλὰ λίαν, καὶ ὅτι ἄρσεν καὶ θῆλυ ἐποίησεν ὁ Θεὸς τὸν ἄνθρωπον, ἀλλὰ βλασφημῶν διαβάλλει τὴν δημιουργίαν, ἢ διορθούσθω ἢ καθαιρείσθω καὶ τῆς Ἐκκλησίας ἀποβαλλέσθω· ὡσαύτως καὶ λαϊκός.

Si quis episcopus aut presbyter aut diaconus, aut omnino ex numero clericorum, a nuptiis et carne et vino non propter exercitationem, verum propter detestationem abstinuerit, oblitus quod omnia sunt valde bona, et quod masculum et feminam Deus fecit hominem, sed blasphemans accusaverit creationem, vel corrigatur, vel deponatur, atque ex Ecclesia ejiciatur. Itidem et laicus.

This canon is evidently directed against the Gnostics and Manichæans, who, in accordance with their dualistic theory, declare matter to be satanic. Therefore it may be said to be very ancient, that is, from the second or third century: it is very similar to the ordinances in the Apostolic Constitutions.

CAN. 52 (51)

Εἴ τις ἐπίσκοπος ἢ πρεσβύτερος τὸν ἐπιστρέφοντα ἀπὸ ἁμαρτίας οὐ προσδέχεται, ἀλλ᾽ ἀποβάλλεται, καθαιρείσθω, ὅτι λυπεῖ Χριστὸν τὸν εἰπόντα· Χαρὰ γίνεται ἐν οὐρανῷ ἐπὶ ἑνὶ ἁμαρτωλῷ μετανοοῦντι.

Si quis episcopus aut presbyter eum, qui se convertit a peccato, non receperit sed ejecerit, deponatur, quia contristat Christum dicentem: Gaudium oritur in cœlo super uno peccatore pœnitentiam agente.

This canon in substance belongs to a period before the end of the third century, and is directed against the severity of the Montanists and Novatians. It is taken from the Apostolic Constitutions.

CAN. 53 (52)

Εἴ τις ἐπίσκοπος ἢ πρεσβύτερος ἢ διάκονος ἐν ταῖς ἡμέραις τῶν ἑορτῶν οὐ μεταλαμβάνει κρεῶν καὶ οἴνου, βδελυσσόμενος καὶ οὐ δι' ἄσκησιν, καθαιρείσθω ὡς κεκαυτηριασμένος τὴν ἰδίαν συνείδησιν, καὶ αἴτιος σκανδάλου πολλοῖς γινόμενος.

Si quis episcopus aut presbyter aut diaconus in diebus festis non sumit carnem aut vinum, deponatur, ut qui cauteriatam habet suam conscientiam, multisque sit causa scandali.

This canon, like the fifty-first, is aimed against the Gnostic and Manichæan errors, and probably is of the same antiquity. It was also taken from the Apostolic Constitutions.

CAN. 54 (53)

Εἴ τις κληρικὸς ἐν καπηλείῳ φωραθείη ἐσθίων, ἀφοριζέσθω, παρὲξ τοῦ ἐν πανδοχείῳ ἐν ὁδῷ δι' ἀνάγκην καταλύσαντος.

Si quis clericus in caupona comedens deprehensus fuerit, segregetur, præterquam si ex necessitate de via divertat ad hospitium.

This canon is very ancient, and of unknown origin.

CAN. 55 (54)

Εἴ τις κληρικὸς ὑβρίζει τὸν ἐπίσκοπον, καθαιρείσθω· Ἄρχοντα γὰρ τοῦ λαοῦ σου οὐκ ἐρεῖς κακῶς.

Si quis clericus episcopum contumelia affecerit injuste, deponatur; ait enim Scriptura: Principi populi tui non maledices.

Drey supposes that this canon and the one following are not ancient: 1st, because in the primitive Church the clergy would not have behaved so outrageously against a bishop; and 2d, because the lower clergy, whom the fifty-sixth canon mentions, were not known in the primitive Church,—bishops, priests, and deacons not being distinguished. The source of the canon is unknown.

CAN. 56 (55)

Εἴ τις κληρικὸς ὑβρίζει πρεσβύτερον ἢ διάκονον, ἀφοριζέσθω.

Si quis clericus presbyterum vel diaconum injuria affecerit, segregetur.

See the remarks on the preceding canon.

CAN. 57 (56)

Εἴ τις [κληρικὸς] χωλὼν ἢ κωφὸν ἢ τυφλὸν ἢ τὰς βάσεις πεπληγμένον χλευάζει, ἀφοριζέσθω· ὡσαύτως καὶ λαϊκός.

Si quis clericus mutilatum, vel surdum aut mutum, vel cæcum aut pedibus debilem irriserit, segregetur. Item et laicus.

The coarseness alluded to in this canon, as also in the fifty-fifth, proves that it was formed at a recent period.

CAN. 58 (57)

Ἐπίσκοπος ἢ πρεσβύτερος ἀμελῶν τοῦ κλήρου ἢ τοῦ λαοῦ καὶ μὴ παιδεύων αὐτοὺς τὴν εὐσέβειαν, ἀφοριζέσθω, ἐπιμένων δὲ τῇ ῥαθυμίᾳ καθαιρείσθω.

Episcopus aut presbyter clerum vel populum negligens, nec eos docens pietatem, segregetur; si autem in socordia perseveret, deponatur.

This canon seems to have been formed towards the middle of the fourth century, at a time when the clergy, and especially the bishops, often left their churches, and betook themselves frequently to the city where the Emperor resided.

CAN. 59 (58)

Εἴ τις ἐπίσκοπος ἢ πρεσβύτερός τινος τῶν κληρικῶν ἐνδεοῦς ὄντος μὴ ἐπιχορηγεῖ τὰ δέοντα, ἀφοριζέσθω· ἐπιμένων δὲ καθαιρείσθω, ὡς φονεύσας τὸν ἀδελφὸν αὐτοῦ.

Si quis episcopus aut presbyter, cum aliquis clericorum inopia laborat, ei non suppeditet necessaria, segregetur; quod si perseveret, deponatur, ut occidens fratrem suum.

We may repeat here what was said about the canons 39–41, to which the present canon is related. Drey considers it to be more recent than the somewhat similar twenty-fifth canon of the Synod of Antioch of the year 341.

CAN. 60 (59)

Εἴ τις τὰ ψευδεπίγραφα τῶν ἀσεβῶν βιβλία ὡς ἅγια ἐπὶ τῆς Ἐκκλησίας δημοσιεύει ἐπὶ λύμῃ τοῦ λαοῦ καὶ τοῦ κλήρου, καθαιρείσθω.

Si quis falso inscriptos impiorum libros, tanquam sacros in Ecclesia divulgarit, ad perniciem populi et cleri, deponatur.

This canon belongs in substance to the second century of the Christian era. It bears a certain similarity to the Apostolic Constitutions; but, according to Drey, it must have been composed much later, as he concludes from the expressions "to spread in the Church," and "people and clergy," which entered into ecclesiastical language at a later period.

CAN. 61 (60)

Εἴ τις κατηγορία γένηται κατὰ πιστοῦ πορνείας ἢ μοιχείας ἢ ἄλλης τινὸς ἀπηγορευμένης πράξεως καὶ ἐλεγχθείη, εἰς κλῆρον μὴ ἀγέσθω.

Si qua fiat accusatio contra fidelem, fornicationis vel adulterii, vel alterius cujusdam facti prohibiti, et convictus fuerit, is non provehatur ad clerum.

This canon belongs to the third century. A similar rule was made in the thirtieth and seventy-sixth canons of Elvira, in the ninth of Neocæsarea, and in the ninth and tenth of Nicæa. The source of this canon is unknown.

CAN. 62 (61)

Εἴ τις κληρικὸς διὰ φόβον ἀνθρώπινον Ἰουδαίου ἢ Ἕλληνος ἢ αἱρετικοῦ ἀρνήσηται, εἰ μὲν ὄνομα Χριστοῦ, ἀποβαλλέσθω, εἰ δὲ καὶ τὸ ὄνομα τοῦ κληρικοῦ, καθαιρείσθω• μετανοήσας δὲ ὡς λαϊκὸς δεχθήτω.

Si quis clericus propter metum humanum Judæi vel gentilis vel hæretici negaverit, siquidem nomen Christi, segregetur; si vero nomen clerici, deponatur; si autem pœnitentiam egerit, ut laicus recipiatur.

Drey thinks that the persecutions of the Christians at the commencement of the fourth century, under the Emperors Diocletian, Galerius, Maximin, and Licinius, gave occasion for this canon, which is from an unknown source.

CAN. 63 (62)

Εἴ τις ἐπίσκοπος ἢ πρεσβύτερος ἢ διάκονος ἢ ὅλως τοῦ καταλόγου τοῦ ἱερατικοῦ φάγῃ κρέα ἐν αἵματι ψυχῆς αὐτοῦ ἢ θηριάλωτον ἢ θνησιμαῖον, καθαιρείσθω τοῦτο γὰρ ὁ νόμος ἀπεῖπεν. Εἰ δὲ λαϊκὸς εἴη, ἀφοριζέσθω.

Si quis episcopus aut presbyter aut diaconus, aut omnino ex catalogo clericorum, manducaverit carnem in sanguine animæ ejus, vel captum a bestia, vel morticinium, deponatur; id enim lex quoque interdixit. Quod si laicus sit, segregetur.

This canon must be classed among the most ancient of the collection.

CAN. 64 (63)

Εἴ τις κληρικὸς ἢ λαϊκὸς εἰσέλθῃ εἰς συναγωγὴν Ἰουδαίων ἢ αἱρετικῶν συνεύξασθαι, καθαιρείσθω καὶ ἀφοριζέσθω.

Si quis clericus vel laicus ingressus fuerit synagogam Judæorum vel hæreticorum ad orandum, ille deponatur, hic segregetur.

The same remark applies to this as to the sixty-third canon. This canon was formed from the Apostolic Constitutions.

CAN. 65 (64)

εἴ τις κληρικὸς ἐν μάχῃ τινὰ κρούσας καὶ ἀπὸ τοῦ ἑνὸς κρούσματος ἀποκτείνει, καθαιρείσθω διὰ τὴν προπέτειαν αὐτοῦ εἰ δὲ λαϊκὸς εἴη, ἀφοριζέσθω.

Si quis clericus in contentione aliquem ferierit, atque ex ictu occiderit, deponatur ob suam præcipitantiam; laicus vero segregetur.

It was not thought necessary to make such a law as this during the ancient Church: it was only subsequently, in the midst of the contentions excited by Arianism, that it became indispensable that such acts of brutality should be condemned. The origin of this canon is unknown. We must remark, further, that according to the order followed in the apostolic canons, where they are placed after the Apostolic Constitutions (as in Cotelerius, Galland, Drey), the present canon follows the sixty-sixth, so that they change places. We prefer to follow the order which is observed in the ancient collections of canons and of councils.

CAN. 66 (65)

Εἴ τις κληρικὸς εὑρεθῇ τὴν κυριακὴν ἡμέραν νηστεύων ἢ τὸ σάββατον πλὴν τοῦ ἑνὸς μόνου, καθαιρείσθω εἰ δὲ λαϊκὸς, ἀφοριζέσθω.

Si quis clericus inventus fuerit die dominica vel sabbato, præter unum solum, jejunans, deponatur; si fuerit laicus, segregetur.

In some countries—for instance in Rome, and also in Spain—Saturday was a fast-day; but in other countries this fast was not observed, and this difference is very ancient. The custom of fasting on Sunday is to be met with only among those sects who professed a sort of Gnostic dualism,—for instance, the Marcionites. It may therefore be said that this canon belongs to the most ancient of the collection, and that it is formed from the Apostolic Constitutions.

CAN. 67 (66)

Εἴ τις παρθένον ἀμνήστευτον βιασάμενος ἔχει, ἀφοριζέσθω μὴ ἐξεῖναι δὲ αὐτῷ ἑτέραν λαμβάνειν ἀλλ᾽ ἐκείνην, ἥν ἠρετίσατο, κἂν πενιχρὰ τυγχάνῃ.

Si quis virginem non desponsatam vi illata teneat, segregetur, nec aliam ducat, sed hanc, quam sic elegit, retineat, etiamsi paupercula fuerit.

The eleventh canon of Ancyra had before condemned the rape of girls, but it concerned only those girls who were betrothed, as also did S. Basil the Great, in the twenty-second chapter of his second canonical letter to Amphilochius. As, in point of severity, this canon holds the middle course between the ancient ordinances of Ancyra and of S. Basil, and the more recent rules of the Council of Chalcedon, Drey concludes that its origin must be referred to the period between these Councils of Ancyra and Chalcedon, and it must therefore be considered as among the most recent of the collection. He goes so far as to think that we should not be wrong in regarding it as an imitation of the twenty-second canon of Chalcedon.

CAN. 68 (67)

Εἴ τις ἐπίσκοπος ἢ πρεσβύτερος ἢ διάκονος δευτέραν χειροτονίαν δέξεται παρά τινος, καθαιρείσθω καὶ αὐτὸς καὶ ὁ χειροτονήσας, εἴ μήγε ἄρα συσταίη, ὅτι παρὰ αἱρετικῶν ἔχει τὴν χειροτονίαν τοὺς γὰρ παρὰ τῶν τοιούτων βαπτισθέντας ἤ χειροτονηθέντας οὔτε πιστοὺς οὔτε κληρικοὺς εἶναι δυνατόν.

Si quis episcopus vel presbyter aut diaconus secundam ordinationem acceperit ab aliquo, deponatur et ipse, et qui eum ordinavit, nisi ostendat ab hæreticis ordinationem se habere; a talibus enim baptizati et ordinati neque fideles neque clerici esse possunt.

The same remark applies to this as to the forty-sixth canon. Its origin is not known.

CAN. 69 (68)

Εἴ τις ἐπίσκοπος ἤ πρεσβύτερος ἤ διάκονος ἤ ἀναγνώστης ἤ ψάλτης τὴν ἁγίαν τεσσαρακοστὴν τοῦ πάσχα ἤ τετράδα ἤ παρασκευὴν οὐ νηστεύοι, καθαιρείσθω, ἐκτὸς εἰ μὴ δι᾿ ἀσθένειαν σωματικὴν ἐμποδίζοιτο εἰ δὲ λαϊκὸς εἴη, ἀφοριζέσθω.

Si quis episcopus aut presbyter aut diaconus aut lector aut cantor sanctam Quadragesimam non jejunat, aut quartam sex-tamque feriam, deponatur, nisi infirmitate corporis impediatur; laicus vero segregetur.

The custom of fasting before Easter, during Lent, is very ancient. S. Irenæus even believes that it proceeded from the apostles. Therefore Drey considers this Canon to be one of the most ancient, and that it may be traced back to about the third century. In another passage, Drey gives it as his opinion that this canon and the one following were taken from the spurious Epistle of S. Ignatius to the Philippians.

CAN. 70 (69)

Εἴ τις ἐπίσκοπς ἢ πρεσβύτερος ἢ διάκονος ἢ ὅλως τοῦ καταλόγου τῶν κληρικῶν νηστεύοι μετὰ τῶν Ἰουδαίων ἢ συνεορτάζοι μεί αὐτῶν ἢ δέχοιτο παρ' αὐτῶν τὰ τῆς ἑορτῆς ξένια, οἷον ἄζυμα ἢ τι τοιοῦτον, καθαιρείσθω· εἰ δὲ λαϊκὸς, ἀφοριζέσθω.

Si quis episcopus aut alius clericus cum Judæis jejunet, vel dies festos agat, aut festorum munera ab ipsis accipiat, veluti azyma hisque similia, deponatur; si laicus hæc fecerit, segregetur.

According to Drey, this canon and the one following date from the end of the third or the middle of the fourth century. The Synod of Elvira had before recommended, in its forty-ninth and fiftieth canons, that too intimate connections with Jews should be avoided. Drey is, however, of opinion that this canon and the one following were derived from the thirty-seventh, thirty-eighth, and thirty-ninth canons of Laodicea.

CAN. 71 (70)

Εἴ τις Χριστιανὸς ἔλαον ἀπενέγκη εἰς ἱερὰ ὠθνῶν ἢ εἰς συναγωγὴν Ἰουδαίων ἐν ταῖς ἑορταῖς αὐτῶν, ἢ λύχνους ἅπτει, ἀφοριζέσθω.

Si quis christianus ad templa Gentilium aut ad synagogas Judæorum oleum deferat, vel in istorum festis lucernas accendat, segregetur.

See the comments on the preceding canon. The Council of Elvira had before made several rules for preventing Christians from communicating in sacris with pagans.

CAN. 72 (71)

Εἴ τις κληρικὸς ἢ λαϊκὸς ἀπὸ τῆς ἁγίας ἐκκλησίας ἀφέληται κηρὸν ἢ ἔλαιον, ἀφοριζέσθω [καὶ τὸ ἐπίπεμπτον προστιθέτω μεθ᾽ οὗ ἔλαβεν].

Clericus aut laicus ceram aut oleum e sancta ecclesia auferens, segregetur, ultraque ablatum quintam partem restituat.

The robbery here spoken of shows that this canon was formed in corrupt times: it must therefore be reckoned among the least ancient, and is of unknown origin.

CAN. 73 (72)

Σκεῦος χρυσοῦν καὶ ἀργυροῦν ἁγιασθὲν ἢ ὀθόνην μηδεὶς ἔτι εἰς οἰκείαν χρῆσιν σφετεριζέσθω· παράνομον γάρ. Εἰ δέ τις φωραθείη, ἐπιτιμάσθω ἀφορισμῷ.

Vasa argentea aureave, necnon linteamina Deo consecrata nemo deinceps in proprios usus vertat, nefas enim est. Deprehensus in eo segregatione multetur.

What this canon says is entirely in harmony with the views and customs of the ancient Church. It supposes, indeed, an opulence which the churches hardly possessed in the first ages: it is proved, however, that from the third century several churches were in possession of a considerable number of vessels of gold and silver. We may therefore trace this seventy-third canon back as far as the second half of the third century. Drey, however, holds it to be more recent; it is of unknown origin.

CAN. 74 (73)

Ἐπίσκοπον κατηγορηθέντα ἐπί τινι παρὰ ἀξιοπίστων ἀνθρώπων, καλεῖσθαι αὐτὸν ἀναγκαῖον ὑπὸ τῶν ἐπισκόπων· κἂν μὲν ἀπαντήσῃ καὶ ὁμολογήσῃ ἢ ἐλεγχθείη, ὁρίζεσθαι τὸ ἐπιτίμιον· εἰ δὲ καλούμενος μὴ ὑπακούσοι, καλείσθω καὶ δεύτερον, ἀποστελλομένων ἐπ᾽ αὐτὸν δύο ἐπισκόπων· ἐὰν δὲ καὶ οὕτω καταφρονήσας μὴ ἀπαντήσῃ, ἡ σύνοδος ἀποφαινέσθω κατ᾽ αὐτοῦ τὰ δοκοῦντα, ὅπως μὴ δόξῃ κερδαίνειν φυγοδικῶν.

Episcopum ab hominibus christianis et fide dignis de crimine accusatum in jus vocent episcopi. Si vocationi paruerit responderitque, fueritque convictus, pœna decernatur; si vero vocatus haud paruerit, missis ad eum duobus episcopis iterum vocetur; si ne sic quidem paruerit, duo rursus ad eum missi tertio vocent episcopi Si hanc quoque missionem aspernatus non venerit, pronunciet contra eum synodus quæ videbuntur, ne ex judicii detrectatione lucrum facere videatur.

This canon and the one following are certainly ancient in some parts; but they are undoubtedly subsequent to the Council of Nicæa. Drey supposes that this canon was formed in compliance with what the Synod of Chalcedon decreed against Dioscurus. See our remarks at the commencement of the Appendix.

CAN. 75 (74)

Εἰς μαρτυρίαν τὴν κατ᾽ ἐπισκόπου αἱρετικὸν μὴ προσδέχεσθαι, ἀλλὰ μηδὲ πιστῶν ἕνα μόνον· ἐπὶ στόματος γὰρ δύο ἢ τριῶν μαρτύρων σταθήσεται πᾶν ῥῆμα.

Ad testimonium contra episcopum dicendum nec hæreticum hominem admittite, nec etiam fidelem unicum; ait enim lex: In ore duorum vel trium testium stabit omne verbum.

See the comments on the preceding canon.

CAN. 76 (75)

Οτι οὐ χρὴ ἐπίσκοπον τῷ ἀδελφῷ ἢ υἱῷ ἢ ἑτέρῳ συγγενεῖ χαρίζεσθαι πάθει ἀνθρωπίνῳ· οὐ γὰρ τὴν τοῦ Θεοῦ Ἐκκλησίαν ὑπὸ κληρονόμους ὀφείλει τιθέναι· εἰ δέ τις τοῦτο ποιήσει, ἄκυρος μενέτω ἡ χειροτονία, αὐτὸς δὲ ἐπιτιμάσθω ἀφορισμῷ.

Episcopum fratri suo, aut filio vel alteri propinquo episcopatum largiri, et quos ipse vult, ordinare non decet; æquum enim non est, ut Dei dona humano affectu divendantur, et Ecclesia Christi, episcopatusque hæreditatum jura sequatur. Si quis ita fecerit, ejus quidem ordinatio sit irrita, ipse vero segregationis ferat pœnam.

The twenty-third canon of the Synod of Antioch, in 341, makes a rule almost similar to this in the main. Therefore Drey believes that the apostolic canon was formed from that of Antioch.

CAN. 77 (76)

Εἴ τις ἀνάπηρος ἢ τὸν ὀφθαλμὸν ἢ τὸ σκέλος πεπληγμένος, ἄξιος δὲ ἐστιν, ἐπίσκοπος γινέσθω· οὐ γὰρ λώβη σώατος αὐτὸν μιαίνει, ἀλλὰ ψυχῆς μολυσμός.

Si quis fuerit vel oculo læsus vel crure debilis, cæteroquin dignus, qui fiat episcopus, fiat; non enim vitium corporis polluit, sed animi.

The canons 77–79 inclusive belong to the first three centuries of the Church. Their origin is unknown.

CAN. 78 (77)

Κωφὸς δὲ ὢν καὶ τυφλὸς μὴ γινέσθω ἐπίσκοπος· οὐχ ὡς βεβλαμμένος, ἀλλ᾽ ἵνα μὴ τὰ ἐκκλησιαστικὰ παρεμποδίζοιτο.

Surdus vero, mutus aut cæcus ne fiat episcopus, non quod pollutus sit, sed ne impediantur ecclesiastica.

CAN. 79 (78)

Ἐάν τις δαίμονα ἔχῃ, κληρικὸς μὴ γινέσθω, ἰλλὰ μηδὲ τοῖς πιστοῖς συνευχέσθω· καθαρισθεὶς δὲ προσδεσχέσθε καὶ, ἐὰν ᾖ ἄξιος, γινέσθω.

Dæmonem qui habet, clericus non sit, nec etiam cum fidelibus oret. Emundatus autem recipiatur, et si dignus habeatur, clericus existat.

This canon may have been formed from the Apostolic Constitutions.

CAN. 80 (79)

Τὸν ἐξ ἐθνικοῦ βίου προσελθόντα καὶ βαπτισθέντα ἢ ἐκ φαύλης διαγωγῆς οὐ δίκαιόν ἐστι παραυτίκα προχειρίζεσθαι ἐπίσκπον· ἄδικον γὰρ τὸν μηδὲ πρόειραν ἐπιδειξάμενον ἑτέρων εἶναι διδάσκαλον· εἰ μήπου κατὰ θείαν χάριν τοῦτο γίνεται.

Qui ex gentibus, aut post vitam non laudabiliter actam per baptismum ad ecclesiam accessit, hunc non decet mox prove-here ad episcopatum; iniquum enim est, aliorum existere doctorem, qui probationem non dederit, nisi forte divino id munere contingat.

S. Paul gives a similar rule. Cf. Drey, who considers it to be an imitation of the second canon of Nicæa.

CAN. 81 (80)

Εἴπομεν, ὅτι οὐ χρὴ ἐπίσκοπον ἢ πρεσβύτερον καθιέναι ἑαυτὸν εἰς δημοσίας διοικήσεις, ἀλλὰ προσευκαιρεῖν ταῖς ἐκκλησιαστικαῖς χρείαις· ἢ πειθέσθω οὖν τοῦτο μὴ ποιεῖν ἢ καθαιρείσθω· οὐδεὶς γὰρ δύναται δυσὶ κυρίοις δουλεύειν, κατὰ τὴν κυριακὴν παρακέλευσιν.

Diximus non oportere, ut episcopus in publicas administrationes sese demittat, sed Ecclesiæ utilitatibus vacet. Aut igitur persuadeatur hoc non facere, aut deponatur. Nemo enim potest duobus dominis servire, juxta Domini admonitionem.

So long as heathenism predominated, it was exceedingly dangerous for Christians to accept public offices, because they obliged those who filled them to communicate often in sacris with pagans. See (sec. 12) the canons of Elvira, and the comments accompanying them. At this period, however, it was only the laity who competed for public offices: among the bishops, Paul of Samosata was the first known example of this kind. Such cases increased when, under Constantine the Great and his successors, Christianity gained more and more the upper hand; and it became important to forbid bishops to accept civil employment by a special ordinance. Drey considers this canon as an abridgment of the third canon of Chalcedon.

CAN. 82 (81)

Οἰκέτας εἰς κλῆρον προχειρίζεσθαι ἄνευ τῆς τῶν δεσποτῶν γνώμης, ἀνατροπὴν τὸ τοιοῦτο ἐργάζεται· εἰ δέ ποτε καὶ ἄξιος φανείη ὁ οἰκέτης πρὸς χειροτονίαν βαθμοῦ, οἷος καὶ ὁ ἡμέτερος Ὀνήσιμος ἐφάνη, καὶ συγχωρήσουσιν οἱ δεσπόται καὶ ἐλενθερώσουσι καὶ τοῦ οἴκου ἑαυτῶν ἐξαποστελοῦσι, γινέσθω.

Servos invitis dominis ad clerum promoveri non permittimus, ne molestia possessoribus flat, hoc namque domos evertit. Si quando vero servus dignus videtur, ut ad ordinationem ascendat, quemadmodum visus est Onesimus noster, et consentit dominus ac manumittit, suique juris facit, fiat clericus.

We are not in a position to fix the antiquity and origin of this canon.

CAN. 83 (82)

Ἐπίσκοπος ἢ πρεσβύτερος ἢ διάκονος στρατείᾳ σχολάζων καὶ βουλόμενος ἀμφότερα κατέχειν, Ῥωμαϊκὴν ἀρχὴν καὶ ἱερατικὴν διοίκησιν, καθαιρείσθω· τὰ γὰρ τοῦ Καίσαρος Καίσαρι καὶ τὰ τοῦ Θεοῦ τῷ θεῷ.

Episcopus vel presbyter vel diaconus militiæ dans operam, et utraque volens retinere, Romanum magistratum et sacerdotalem administrationem, deponatur. Quæ enim sunt Cæsaris Cæsari, et quæ sunt Dei Deo.

Drey considers this canon to have been formed from the seventh of the fourth Œcumenical Council, and consequently that it is one of the most recent of the collection. See, in opposition to his opinion, our remarks at the beginning of this Appendix.

CAN. 84 (83)

Ὅστις ὑβρίζει βασιλέα ἢ ἄρχοντα, τιμωρίαν τιννύτω• καὶ εἰ μὲν κληρικὸς, καθαιρείσθω, εἰ δὲ λαϊκὸς, ἀφοριζέσθω.

Quicunque commiserit aliquid contra jus adversus Cæsarem aut magistratum, puniatur; et quidem si clericus fuerit, deponatur; si laicus, segregetur.

It might be thought that this canon was formed in a time of persecution, when it could be more easily understood that Christians should despise the Emperors; but nevertheless it was not so. This canon fits in much better to the time of the Arian struggle, when such offences against the Emperors were much more abundant. The origin of the canon is unknown.

CAN. 85 (84)

Ἔστω πᾶσιν ὑμῖν κληρικοῖς καὶ λαϊκοῖς βιβλία σεβάσμια καὶ ἅγια, τῆς μὲν παλαιᾶς διαθήκης Μωυσέως πέντε, Γένεσις, Ἔξοδος, Λευϊτικὸν, Ἀριθμοὶ, Δευτερονόμιον• Ἰησοῦ υἱοῦ Ναυῆ ἓν, Ῥοὺθ ἓν, Βασιλειῶν τέσσαρα, Παραλειπομένων τοῦ

βιβλίου τῶν ἡμερῶν δύο, Ἐσθὴρ ἓν, Μαχαβαϊκῶν τρία, Ἰὼβ
ἓν, ψαλτήριον ἓν, Σολομῶντος τρία, Παροιμίαι,
Ἐκκλησιαστὴς, Ἆσμα ἀσμάτων· Προφητῶν δεκαδύο ἓν,
Ἡσαΐου ἓν, Ἰερεμίου ἓν, Ἰεζεκιὴλ ἓν, Δανιὴλ ἕν· ἔξωθεν δὲ
προσιστορείσθω ὑμῖν, μανθάνειν ὑμῶν τοὺς νέους τὴν σοφίαν
τοῦ πολυμαθοῦς Σειράχ. Ἡμέτερα δὲ, τοῦτ' ἔστι τῆς καινῆς
διαθήκης, Εὐαγγέλια τέσσαρα, Ματθαίου, Μάρκου, Λουκᾶ,
Ἰωάννου· Παύλου ἐπιστολαὶ δεκατέσσαρες, Πέτρου
ἐπιστολαὶ δύο, Ἰωάννου τρεῖς, Ἰακώβου μία Ἰούδα μία,
Κλήμεντος ἐπιστολαὶ δύο καὶ αἱ διαταγαὶ ὑμῖν τοῖς
ἐπισκόποις δι' ἐμοῦ Κλήμεντος ἐν ὀκτὼ βιβλίοις
προσπεφωνημέναι, ἃς οὐ δεῖ δημοσιεύειν ἐπὶ πάντων διὰ τὰ
ἐν αὐταῖς μυστικὰ, καὶ αἱ Πράξεις ἡμῶν τῶν ἀποστόλων.

Sint autem vobis omnibus, cum clericis tum laicis, libri
venerabiles et sancti: veteris quidem testamenti, Moysis
quinque,—Genesis, Exodus, Leviticus, Numeri,
Deuteronomium; Jesu filii Navæ unus; Judicum unus, Ruth
unus; Regnorum quatuor, Paralipomenon libri dierum duo;
Esdræ duo; Esther unus; Judith unus; Machabæorum tres;
Hiobi unus; Psalmi centum quinquaginta; Salomonis libri
tres, Proverbia, Ecclesiastes, Canticum canticorum;
Propheæ sexdecim; præter hos nominetur vobis etiam
Sapientia multiscii Sirachi, quam adolescentes vestri discant.
Nostri autem, id est libri novi testamenti: Evangelia
quatuor, Matthæi, Marci, Lucæ, Joannis; Pauli epistolæ
quatuordecim; Petri duæ; Joannis tres; Jacobi una; Judæ
una; Clementis epistolæ duæ;. et Constitutiones vobis
episcopis per me Clementem octo libris nuncupatæ, quas
non oportet inter omnes divulgare, ob mystica quæ in eis
sunt, et Acta nostra apostolorum.

This is probably the least ancient canon in the whole collection. In most of the Greek manuscripts the apostolic canons are followed by a short epilogue, containing an exhortation addressed to the bishops, recommending them to observe these canons. It ends with a prayer, which was printed with the apostolic canons in Cotelerius, Galland, Mansi, Ueltzen, and also in Latin in Drey.

Made in the USA
Middletown, DE
25 September 2023

39269515R00335